MW01148412

FERRITTO

AN
ASSASSIN
SCORNED

SUSAN DESANTIS-FERRITTO

Copyright © 2012 by Susan deSantis-Ferritto

Published by:
Ragpaper Press
Erie, Pennsylvania

All Rights Reserved

No part of this book may be reproduced, stored in a retrieval system, or transmitted in any form, by any means, including mechanical, electronic, photocopying, recording or otherwise, without the prior written permission of the publisher, except by reviewer who wishes to quote brief passages in connection with a review written for inclusion in a magazine, newspaper or broadcast. Some names have been changed to protect the privacy of certain individuals.

Cover and text design: Jonathan Gullery

ISBN: 978-0-578-10829-2

Printed in the United States of America

FERRITTO

CHAPTER 1

———————◦———————

"Little Italy" was located on the west side of Erie, Pennsylvania and it was like any other Italian neighborhood in larger cities. Everyone knew everyone else, and you always had more relatives than you could count. Most families were very happy and content to raise their children there and rarely ventured outside the perimeter of their tightly guarded sector.

During the 1930's,there stood at least a dozen corner grocery stores, gin stops, five and dimes, movie theaters, furniture stores, pool parlors, print shops, clubs & social halls. There was also St. Georges Funeral Parlor, Christopher Columbus

School and two Roman Catholic Churches: St. Michael's and St. Paul's. They were held deep within this tiny but encapsulated world, protected by Jesus Christ, the Virgin Mary... and the Mob.

The streets bustled constantly with activity. Kids played on the sidewalks, and ran through sprays of water from open hydrants to cool themselves off from the sweltering heat. If you were lucky, your mother let you go to Columbus Park, adjacent to the school ground where the older kids were splashing around in the public swimming pool. Of course the boys often played kickball, stickball, baseball and football with their makeshift sports equipment, or simply hung out on their front porches and stoops.

The older Italian guys patronized the corner bars and pool halls or they relaxed on their porch sharing their homemade wine, playing skin games or shooting craps. The women could be seen tending their gardens or hanging their hand washed laundry on clothes lines strung firmly between the buildings or garages. The old widows clasping their rosary beads and dressed in black from head to toe would walk along the curbside on their way to church to pray for their dead husbands.

An elderly German farmer who was referred to as, "the ragman" would clomp through the narrow streets, with his old worn out horse and open wagon, shouting out loud with his thick accent... "rrrrags ...rrrrags...rrrrags." He'd tug ever so gently, slowly directing the old nag around the corners, looking for anyone who would donate their old and tattered clothing to his cause or perhaps purchase his baskets of fruits and vegetables.

The ice man was seen delivering his huge blocks of ice to homes in the neighborhood, while constantly stopping kids from clambering onto the back of his truck – to sneak a ride. At the central marketplace, fruits went for fifty cents a bushel from the farmers peddling their goods and cigarettes were two for a penny.

Mostly, the immigrants struggled to feed their families, working hard at the factories that lined across Twelfth Street, which was the northern border of Little Italy. They usually walked to work, as cars in those days were not affordable. Some of these men would stop at the Monte Club, D'Aurora's Café, Sliver's Tavern or Cannavino's Bar in the mornings to fill their thermoses with a little liquor to get them through the day and others would stop after their shifts for a shot and a beer. At the end of the day you couldn't recognize who they were, as their sweaty faces and clothes were solid black from the factory's soot.

Nonetheless, they were proud, honest working people, who happened to live in flats and tenements throughout most of their lives. If you worked hard enough, your family might have been lucky to afford a small, decent single family home with a colorful, flourishing garden.

In spite of all the suffering from the Great Depression, the local kids felt like rulers of their own turf. If they weren't indulging in sports or mischievous antics, you could find them competing in rough housing, playing petty pranks or seeing who could urinate the furthest.

This was a neighborhood where the wise guys felt safe and racketeers were treated like heroes. Gambling was prominent, and it certainly wasn't beneath some housewives, storeowners or even the beat cops to be taking the daily bets for the older racketeers. The local gangsters ordered hench- men to collect their take from the bookies that seemed to be everywhere, and made sure that "The Black Hand" wasn't getting cheated or perhaps they were just sizing up the young broads, "trying to score."

The old mafia bosses that ran the neighborhood were referred to as, "the Mustache Pete's." They watched their ter- ritories like hawks and always made their presence known. During the 1940's they offered asylum to their constituents on the lam and Erie became the country's number one hide- out for mobsters running from the law.

Within certain circles it became known as "Little Chicago". At one time there had been at least twenty of the nations most wanted mob figures taking refuge, and being treated like royalty at the Richford Hotel on State Street. Most poli- ticians were on the payroll then, assuring their silence and providing protection from the federal authorities. It was a standing joke that no one would ever find them because Erie wasn't even on the map yet.

CHAPTER 2

MOBSTERS FELT SAFE THERE AND THE YOUNGSTERS LOOKED up to these wise guys, having a fascination with emulating them. It seemed like the only people with a pile of cash, well dressed and with fancy cars back then were definitely hoodlums. The kids thought of them as their heroes, imitating them constantly.

Raymond W. Ferritto was one of those kids. Like some others, he had hopes of becoming one of them. His ultimate desire was to have the same respect that they seem to regard so highly.

Raymond's birth certificate reads "Remo Ferretti", born

on April 8, 1929. But, because of some family squabble, his family changed the spelling of their last name to Ferritto. As the custom was back then, one of his teachers had also Americanized his first name to Raymond when he began attending school. Back at St. Paul's was another story. Monsignor Marino, a tough old immigrant himself, didn't appreciate the school district interfering with the neighborhood customs and demanded that all his parishioners, including the children use their Italian birth names while in his presence. No one would dare disrespect the monsignor and were more than happy to abide by his wishes. Besides which, the Italian language was mandatory in most homes at that time or communication with your parents, grandparents or half of the older generation would have been impossible.

Ray's parents were tough but honest hard working people who ruled their brood of five with an iron fist. His dad's passion and pride was their lush vegetable garden, which helped them put food on the table for their family. His mother was blessed with a talent for making divine wines that could please even the most delicate of palates. Their daily nourishment was usually accompanied by a small glass of their mom's homemade wine, before the elders finished off their jugs. Today, you'd get "pinched" – charged with contributing to minors – if you supplied your kids with booze at the supper table.

This was the era of silence and considered normal standards in most households. Children were expected to be seen and not heard. You only spoke when an adult spoke to you and the most important of all rules was that you never show

your emotions publicly. If you did, God forbid, that would be
a sign of weakness and shame.

Ray watched his parents work hard and struggle to provide
for their family while the hoodlums lounged about enjoying
the finer things in life. In his mind, this wasn't fair and presented a problem for him. He too, wanted the finer things
and was not going to settle for anything less. His only way out
was to rebel.

He always thought there was something different about
himself, but he could never quite put a finger on it. He was
popular and athletic and very competitive. His buddies called
him "Knuckles" because he liked to have a fistful of coins
when he fought the neighborhood kids. He always liked the
extra weight behind his punch. But the nickname never really
stuck.

Ray was forever into some kind of mischief and became
profoundly defiant of authority. He was intelligent but hated
school. He'd rather skip classes, trying to make a buck or
two around the pool halls. Ray saw this as his opportunity
to learn the ropes from the older racketeers while hanging
out and shining their classy wheels. He knew it was forbidden to repeat anything he overheard in regard to their future
plans or plots for an upcoming scam and enjoyed being their
errand boy.

Ray was fascinated by the gangsters' toughness. He felt
their pride and dignity when he was around them. All the
while he dreamed that the day would come for him to be able
to share that same power and freewheeling lifestyle.

Unfortunately,not before he was caught skipping school.

One afternoon the truant officer paid a visit Ray's parents. He took a good beating from his dad, and returned to school as ordered to prevent his family from paying the fine.

By the time he entered Roosevelt Junior High School, he joined forces with classmates, Armond "Peeps" Farranti and Tommy LaCastro. The trio quickly became fast friends and inseparable. All three boys shared a love of sports. They were also very good at competing with the older pranksters, too. They'd sneak out at night, rifle through the neighbor's gardens, steal vegetables or fruit and smoke discarded cigarette butts that they found along the curbs.

Ray and Peeps found their first employment with the local grocer on 18th and Cherry Streets, Mr. Pedano. They each earned a quarter a day by killing chickens, but soon realized this menial work wasn't their dream job. The storekeeper had them stationed in the basement where the chickens were awaiting their fate, squawking all day.

Customers would point to the chubby fowl of their choice and the boys scrambled to catch them, chopping off their heads and handing them over the small wooden counter. This is where Ray first learned the art of killing for pay…"by eliminating" chickens. It wasn't too long before the boys realized they could generate more profit by cutting out the middleman. They would steal the chickens through an unlocked basement window and peddle them off themselves. Ray was in the middle of selling a few dead birds to a local hoodlum when the joker made a crack about his knickers that the boys wore back in the day. Embarrassed, Ray went directly home to beg his mother for some extra cash to buy a pair of real dress pants like the older guys were wearing.

He insisted that he was too old to be wearing knickers, but she sternly refused him saying they didn't have money for such a purchase. So Ray planned his first heist at the neighborhood clothier's, just a few doors down from Pedano's grocery store. That weekend, Ray, Peeps and Tommy were proudly sporting their finely pressed threads. That was until his father found out. However, Ray had felt his fathers' wrath before and the beatings were no longer fazing him.

Making a last ditch effort to save his son's immortal soul, the old man finally put Ray to work at the farm of an old friend, out of temptations way. Unbeknownst to his parents, this cruelty was going to affect him far worse than taking a good old fashioned beating. He was made to sleep in a dilapidated cold barn with only a tattered nasty blanket that the farmer's wife gave him for warmth. He could barely eat his breakfast at 4 a.m. from the stench of the barn animals that he had slept alongside. After his breakfast and only meal of the day he was forced to work in the fields until he was exhausted. When he would stop for a break the farmer would poke him with a stick to get him going again. Finally the old man went too far and cracked him across the face because he asked for food one evening.

The rage in his gut was just beginning and the young kid only lasted a week under such terrible slavery conditions. After that hit to his self-esteem, he waited until dark and managed to escape, hitchhiking his way back into town.

There he found Peeps and convinced him that they should run away to Ohio.

The boys had the good fortune to make it as far as Ashtabula, Ohio – about an hour away from home – before it dawned on them they had no money between them for food and they were starving. It was dark, and the gas station they'd come across was now closed and nothing but an open invitation to these two hungry and desperate little renegades.

They broke in, ransacking the counter area and jimmied open the cash drawer where they found just barely enough money to grab a bite. The boys were still rank amateurs, and it only took the state cops a few hours to bust them at a small diner down the road from the crime scene.

Laughing, the officers told the boys that they fit the description of the "infamous gas station robbers," and they had to be brought in. But, as they were still mere juveniles, they were remanded to their parents and forced to wait in custody until their angry mothers arrived by bus to pick them up the following day. They took their little hoodlums home to face the music and of course Ray took a few more lashings from his disgusted father.

His wounds weren't healed yet when temptation again reared its ugly head. Tommy and Peeps were tapping quietly trying to get Ray's attention through his bedroom window. It was only about eleven o'clock and everyone in the house was fast asleep so he snuck away with his partners just to have a little fun. Who would be the wiser?

The three wandered aimlessly over to Columbus Park where they laughed, joked and roughhoused a little, too. They never expected to run into the neighborhood bad girls and were quick to have their first sexual encounters that night. This meant they were men now, at least in their own minds, and no one was going to tell them what to do anymore. In fact, Ray's father soon came to the realization that his son was lost to him. The more he beat him for his teenage pranks, the tougher and more rebellious Ray would be.

CHAPTER 3

---◦---

B Y THE TIME RAY WAS FOURTEEN, HE WAS TALLER AND
appeared much older than his counterparts. Beside
himself with disgust over the way his son's life was
going, Ray's father reluctantly approved of the kid getting a
job at Urick Foundry on Cherry Street. He lied on the application and told the foreman that he was indeed sixteen and
of legal age to work.

Almost a month had passed and Ray was pulling his own
weight at the foundry. He worked right alongside the older
men around the enormous pots of hot smelted iron and
helped them pour the blasting hot liquids into the molds for

cooling. The temperatures were off the charts with steaming heat and the black soot clung to their sweaty bodies until you couldn't recognize who they were.

A jitney driver unaware that Ray was too close, accidentally, slammed the lift down, smashing it on Ray's unprotected foot. He had not been wearing the steel-toed boots necessary for factory employees.

Hollering from the excruciating pain, his co-workers rushed him to the emergency room at St. Vincent Hospital where the medical team discovered the mangled toes. The doctors immediately performed surgery to reconstruct each smashed toe and luckily for Ray, they were successful.

Ray's uncles convinced his parents to sue the foundry for his injuries, but the pending lawsuit was squashed when the foundry owners threatened to counter-sue the parents and force the sale of their family home because their son lied about his age on the application. Using his best, broken English, Ray's father, scared of losing his home, settled for the total sum of fifty dollars.

Ray, Tommy and Peeps never stopped spreading their wings, becoming almost unstoppable in their penchant for crime. They were quite popular around the neighborhood and began recruiting other neighborhood hoodlums and heading up their own gang, called "The Wasps". This small group hit coin-operated vending machines at gas stations, movie theaters and snack bars. Their two-year long looting spree ended after they robbed Dee's Cigar Store on 17th & State Streets. They had stepped over that fine line by stealing from Dee

Auditori, who happened to be one of the neighborhoods top crime figures.

This was when Ray was introduced to his first probation officer. The four boys stood nervously in front of the judges' bench, waiting to hear the pronouncement of their fate, while their parents anxiously looked on. Raymond Ferritto, Armond Farranti, Peter Carlo and Armond DeSantis had put the ultimate shame on their families' heads. They didn't know who or what to fear the most, Dee Auditori, their parents or the judge's harsh sentencing. Saint Paul's parish priest, Father Gabamonte also stood before the court, pleading for the boy's freedom. He begged the Honorable Judge Miles Kiley to release them into his custody, explaining the boys were basically good kids...probably while crossing his fingers behind his back.

The good father swore that the boys would learn under his tutelage to walk the straight and narrow, stating that he knew the parents well and depended on the boys to help him around the church. He added that if they were indeed released to his custody, he'd see to it that they received a fitting punishment.

The judge was reluctant to do so, but then permitted them to be under the watchful eye of the good priest but, they would have to follow up with a new probation officer. The blessed father had just saved the boys from doing a stint at George Junior Republic, a boy's reformatory, some seventy-five miles away from home. But as the boys left the courthouse snickering about their good luck, Father Gabamonte's temper flared.

"So...you think you got away with this, do you? I got up

there and lied through my teeth for you hoodlums. Now for the rest of the summer...you belong to me! Do we understand each other? I'll straighten you four out if it's the last thing I do!" he stammered while storming away. It's doubtful that the boys were all that impressed. By no means was Father Gabamonte going to change their perceptions of what they were going to become. Dee Auditori, however, let them slide with a harsh warning that he'd have their fingers cut off if they ever even thought about burglarizing him again.

CHAPTER 4

B Y THE TIME RAY TURNED SIXTEEN, HIS JUVENILE RECORD
read as long as his arm and he had gained the reputation for being a "hot-headed" tough guy. It wasn't
hard for him to prove himself in this department and he was
always quick to "cold cock" whomever got in his way.

One of the Braebender boys, who were the neighborhood's up and coming wrestling champs, insulted Ray at the
park one afternoon, and he immediately rose to the challenge. It was a typical afternoon with a bunch of kids playing
baseball when a German kid from the dead end side of Little
Italy got smart. Benny "The Brat" Braebender made the sad

mistake of loudly spewing disparaging remarks about Italians during the game.

True to form Ray hurled his fist into Benny's face. Benny scrambled to his feet and proudly screamed, "When I get done kicking your ass, my brother is gonna finish you off!" Enraged, Ray ordered the kid to go home and get his fucking brother and he'd take both on at the same time.

Benny returned quickly with his sibling in tow and tempers flared. A crowd of their teammates cheered them on. Ray was one mean Italian bastard when provoked. By the time the dust settled, Ray had beaten both twins senseless. From that day forward the neighborhood knew that he was a force to be reckoned with.

Ray and his gang usually hung around the pool halls, betting on a few racks, hustling someone or casing downtown stores for their next score. They were good, fast on their feet and had already gotten away with a rash of small burglaries.

A beat cop spotted Ray late one night in a back alley, attempting to crack open a lock on the back door of a jewelry store and pulled his firearm on him yelling, "halt...on your knees or I'll shoot!" Ray became infuriated and "cocky" when the officer began questioning him. The cop raised his nightstick, shoving it into Ray's chest and ordered him to remove his shoes and lie face down on the ground.

With Ray lying face down, the officer began wildly beating the soles of his feet with the Billy club until Ray screamed from the pain. The cop laughed as he walked away. "That'll teach you to stay off my beat, you fuckin' Italian hoodlum."

Curled up in a ball and groaning with pain, Ray was left

there holding his bruised and bloodied feet. The incident was
only fueling the rage that was growing inside him. Somehow,
someway…he was going to get even.

Ray was barely able to walk for a week or so and it took a
few months for his feet to completely heal during which time
he plotted revenge. The need for vengeance consumed him,
but he was smart enough to know that he had to wait until
the time was right to remove suspicion from himself.

So, as months passed and his timing felt right, Ray stood
in a back alley in the dark of night patiently waiting for the
unsuspecting cop to make his usual rounds.

As the cop strolled by, Ray leaped from behind, a large
old dumpster wearing brass knuckles, a hooded mask and
screaming, "Hey, you cock sucker!" Ray used his brute
strength, and began pummeling the officer's face and head
until the cop dropped to the ground, bloodied and wailing
from Ray's vicious blows. After the cop fell, Ray kicked him
mercilessly. The officer didn't know who or what had hit him.
When Ray was finished, he gave one last kick to the head and
spat down on his face for good measure. He felt as though
he could have killed him with his bare hands with the rage
that fueled within. But he was satisfied knowing this man
was in for a long and excruciatingly painful recovery. That
officer wouldn't be seen walking his beat for several months
afterwards.

Through the grapevine, this incident made one of Erie's
then top crime bosses take notice of Ray's capabilities. Serafino Romeo a tough immigrant from Calabria, Italy, reputed
to be a member of the "Black Hand" and stepfather to Ray's

cousin, Fredo Ferritto. Serafino owned and operated "Serafino's Amusement". His company was in the business of
placing their slot machines that included cigarettes, pinball
machines and juke- boxes into pool halls, bars restaurants
and other venues.

Ray and Fredo occasionally worked together on weekends
when the old man needed an extra hand delivering or picking up his machines. Ray would never refuse Serafino out of
respect for his position as a boss.

In fact it had been rumored for years, Serafino had fallen
in love with little Fredo's mother, who at the time was married to Ray's paternal uncle. Serafino had brazenly taken the
life of Fredo's father by tying his body to the railroad tracks
after brutally beating him. He then took the beautiful widow
for his wife. Serafino always took what he wanted and no
one dared to challenge him. Un-like Ray, cousin Fredo wasn't
mob material and his stepfather knew it. Serafino had been
highly impressed with Ray's sense of vigilante justice after he
taken his vengeance out on the cop in that dark alley. Now,
Serafino was secretly taking Ray under his wing and putting
him to work as muscle for Serafino Amusements.

This newfound status pleased Ray and he decided it was
time to legally abandon his formal education. Feeling as
though the public school system was interfering with his
criminal endeavors, he quit. This didn't surprise his parents.
However, the subject of Serafino's sins would be forbidden
within the Ferritto household.

Ray received a draft notice shortly after starting work for
Serafino. Uncle Sam had called and Ray now found himself

taking orders from officers in the United States Marine Corps. He was stationed at Parris Island, South Carolina. A few weeks into his training, the daily grueling exercise caused his foot to painfully swell from the factory injury he received when he was a kid. The constant pain and swelling were enough to earn him an honorable discharge.

It was as though he never left and Serafino was thrilled to have his muscle back. Sometimes, all it would take for Ray to keep a customer in line was to pull up in front of their establishment with a cold dark stare. Other times his harsh methods of persuasion left his victims bloodied and broken. Either way, it delighted Serafino to see that Ray's intimidating tactics and ability to inflict terror at moment's notice were keeping his business flourishing.

CHAPTER 5

A T A SECRET MONTHLY MEETING AT THE HOME OF SERAFINO, several mafia heads from surrounding cities were present to settle a dispute. They were deciding which family's soldiers were going to carry out the execution of mobsters who were cheating them.

"This kid's got balls," Serafino laughed as he twirled the fork in his plate of spaghetti and meatballs. "Since all of us have an interest in solving this problem I motion that we send in some fresh blood and someone who is familiar with the area. Besides, my young protege', needs seasoning."

Russ Buffalino protested the use of the inexperienced

young gangster, and some others agreed. "I have a bigger piece of the pie at stake here," said Russ, "and I want my pound of flesh."

"Not to worry, my friend", answered Serafino. "I wouldn't send him if I thought he couldn't deliver. You just worry about your men."

In the grand scheme of things, Serafino was indeed molding Ray for a spot in the organization. He later sat Ray down and gave him his orders. "If you do this for me...my friend, you'll always have an ace in your pocket, but you must do it for yourself as well. Due diligence is your key...and never forget that. So next Friday you'll go for your "lost weekend" and do your work. Make me proud."

Ray not only made the old man proud, but he also entered the realm of no return and intended to take this particular disturbing scenario to his grave.

However, the gut wrenching task took its toll and left him with a severe ulcer that plagued him throughout his younger years. Despite his youth, he was quickly moving up within the criminal circuit and he had "felt the excitement of being respected" by his peers. He continued to pay his dues and it would shape his character throughout his career.

Another young and upcoming gangster in the neighborhood was also gaining attention. The only difference was that they were traveling in separate circles when they met at the pool parlor on West 18th Street. His name was Anthony "Cy" Sciotti. Cy was more arrogant and a bit cockier than Ray. His looks resembled that of Michael Corleone from the "Godfather", but his temperament seemed more in tune with

Corleone's brother's character, Sonny...sort of a hotheaded, "in your face" type of guy. Aside from the differences in their personalities, Ray and Cy were both chasing the same dreams and that made for the perfect crew.

After several successful small burglaries that year, the ambitious thieves decided to opt for more lucrative scores and hone their amateur safecracking skills.

Back then, security systems weren't as sophisticated as they are now and most times they simply presented ordinary "locks" to a skilled burglar. However, in one incident, Ray wasn't able to crack the combination. This infuriated him to no end and he wasn't about to walk away from the challenge. Unfortunately, time was not on their side so Ray ordered the crew to cart the heavy valuable container to the getaway car and drive to their hideout, which happened to be above Serafino's Amusement Company. There they would be able to take their sweet time "cracking" the safe.

It would have made a great comedic slapstick routine, had anyone been watching these guys. The weight of the safe was a little more than they could handle and they struggled at first, but not before a few tempers flared and they got on each other's last nerve. The ride to Serafino's warehouse was hilarious. They managed to get to the car with few cuts and bruises but the safe took a few good falls with no luck of breaking open. It took all four of them to plunge the safe into the trunk, which had to be left open. They were forced to drive over side streets with the weight of the damned safe overworking the car's engine and in plain view. Arriving at their destination, Tommy hopped out and grabbed a dolly to help hoist the monster upstairs.

After hours of beating, prying, poking and cursing, they still had not opened it. Ray and Cy finally decided to get a blowtorch to retrieve its valuables. They divided up the loot, and dreaded having to remove the safe from the premises, but it had to be done before the sun came up, which meant they only had one hour left.

The fastest and easiest way to get rid of the wreckage was to dump it in Lake Erie…its final resting place.

Even though the content was more fruitful than they had hoped, the whole fiasco and the lengths in which it took them to open it disappointed Ray. The failure drove Ray to learn his craft with such diligence that there wasn't a safe in existence he couldn't crack.

He read what was available on all types of security locks carefully examining the mechanics of alarms and safes. What he couldn't learn from studying, he picked up from older experts in the field.

Ray was never lazy. He may have been a criminal, but he was industrious. Crime was simply more lucrative and productive than an ordinary blue-collar job.

There was temptation around every corner and not all robberies were planned events. One afternoon while driving past Robert Hall's, a high-end men's clothing store on Glenwood Park Avenue, Ray and Cy spotted the clothier having a brand new alarm system installed. They pulled over and curiously watched as several workers wired the front door and large framed glass display window in the front and stayed long enough to see them carrying the conduit around the rear entrance to secure the huge metal double doors. As they pulled away, Ray grinned at Cy saying, "If you got any dates tonight...cancel them. We're going shopping for some new suits."

Returning that night, the pair backed up a large rented truck alongside of the commercial cement block building that housed their next score. With just their regular burglar tools and a couple of sledgehammers, they broke through by hammering past the huge blocks of stone completely bypassing both entry doors and the brand new alarm system.

Once they cleared the way, they carted several dozen racks of suits to the getaway truck and on to Pittsburgh for delivery where the goods would be fenced. Ray later said he would have given anything to see the expression on the owner's face upon opening his newly secured business the following morning.

CHAPTER 6

---•---

BARELY INTO HIS TWENTIES RAY UNEXPECTEDLY FOUND himself a father-to-be. Half-heartedly, his father handed him a hundred dollars, which was quite a few bucks for the family back then, and told him to "do the right thing and marry the girl."

With his blessings, his mentor Serafino thought this would be a good time for Ray to step up in the business. Serafino permitted him to organize and operate his own vending and numbers racket as long as the powers that be got their usual piece of the action.

This was a huge move for Ray and he took in his close

friend Tommy LoCastro as his partner. As T&R Vending entered the picture, so did "James "Westfield Jimmy" Salamone, a lieutenant for the Maggedino family from New York. Erie was growing and things were changing with the mob leadership, now under the rule of families from Buffalo and Pittsburgh. There was enough business to go around, and although there was underlying resentment amongst the capos, they all agreed to get along.

T&R Vending was thriving, but Ray would stop at nothing to rise up in the ranks himself. Whether it was extortion, arson, safecracking, hijacking or shaking someone down his focus always remained on the reward of leadership one day.

Several years later, his family had grown to three beautiful children with his wife Roz. But Roz, a quiet, simple Russian girl hadn't bargained for this type of lifestyle. She tried hard to provide stability for her family, but it was harder to tame Ray than she thought. Separation was eminent and they eventually divorced in 1956.

Only a year later at the age of twenty-eight, Ray met the second love of his life and married "Della." She was an Italian beauty and much tougher than the first. Della was much more in tune with his lifestyle and blissfully enjoyed the fruits of his labor as well as the festive social engagements and friends. But before too long, the nightlife caught up with her and she began abusing alcohol. Ray wasn't about to put up with her drinking and they fought constantly. She thought getting pregnant would save the marriage but after their child was born things only got worse.

The marriage had been rocky from the start and there

were often knockdown, drag out fights over Della's embarrassing drunken squabbles. She would infuriate him to no end and wasn't afraid of his bad temper. He'd backhand her for the explosive insults while dining in the company of their friends and she'd get right back in his face for more. She couldn't stop herself after a few drinks and would start rambling about his philandering and abrupt disappearances. More than once Cy and his wife Carmen had to pry Ray's hands from her throat, fearful that he was going to kill her.

The crew's luck ran out one night when Ray, Cy, Johnnie Lupo, Victor Minedeo and Blackie Paradise were burglarizing Gus Angelo's Gas Station. The cops had the place surrounded and forced them out at gunpoint. They were all charged, convicted and sentenced up to three years in Rockview Pennitentiary. In the back of his mind, Ray always thought that it was Della who had dropped the dime on them.

As bitter as he was, he thought it was to his good fortune that while doing his time, he met some very tough and influential wise guys from Philadelphia and the Warren-Youngstown areas. These racketeers were under the heads of Cleveland and East coast families and Ray knew there would be a lot to gain through their friendships.

In particular, it was Frank "Skinny" Velotta, Ronnie "The Crab" Carabbia, Allie Calabrese, Pasquale "Butchie" Cisternino and Eugene "The Animal" Ciasullo, all professional burglars, loan sharks and vicious killers that took such a liking to Ray that they offered him induction into their private loop. They all had a lot in common and extended that close friendship beyond the prison walls.

Ray was released in 1960. By the age of thirty-one he had arranged to meet up with his old inmates in Cleveland's Little Italy, their home turf. It was through these men that he had the pleasure of rubbing elbows with Cleveland's Mafia bosses, James "Jack White" Licavoli and John Scalish. Jack White also took a liking to Ray and said he liked his confidence and the way he carried himself. White was definitely interested in using Ray as a soldier after he had him checked out.

After a phone conversation between Buffalino and White, Ray came into the picture highly recommended, but not before his tenacity would be put to the test.

Ray, Allie Calabrese, Tony Delsanter, Ronnie the Crab, Skinny Vellotta, Julius Petros and Bob Walsh (an ex-cop turned gangster) became better known as "The infamous Cleveland crew." They all carried their own weight when it came to jewelry store heists, supermarket safes and on occasion cracking a few heads to keep someone in line for the bosses.

But now, the crew had been summoned by White to collect a debt from a barbut player by the name of Bones who made the mistake of skipping out on his $75,000 payment. Bones had declared he was cheated and wasn't paying up.

It was difficult getting to the old man as evidence that paranoia and safety for him and his religious wife had set in when they barricaded themselves in their sizeable fortress. However, being all too familiar with staunch Catholics, Ray seized the opportunity by appealing to the wife's vulnerability of her faith to gain entry. When he appeared at the entrance gate disguised as a priest, she was delighted to "buzz" him through.

He drove slowly up the grand entrance, with Julius Petro crouched down in the back seat of the Cadillac. He exited the car and approached the doorway, concealing his weapon under his vestment and he was welcomed with open arms. The old woman couldn't have been more thrilled to offer her hospitality to a man of the cloth.

Her glowing smile quickly turned to a horrified look as the "clergyman" pulled his weapon. With a calm gentlemanly tone, he told her to be quiet and that he was not going to harm her as he gestured to his partner to come in. For a moment, he felt sympathetic for the aging woman who reminded him of his own mother. But he was there to do a job and instantly willed himself to look past the similarity.

Julius held the wife at bay while Ray went room to room, searching for the old man, until finally he came across him in the library quietly watching a football game on television. The unsuspecting victim, shocked at the sight of Ray point-ing a gun at him, became enraged at the invasion. He quickly tried his best reverse psychology on Ray, showing no fear and demanding that he have a face to face with Scalish to recon-cile the problem.

Unfortunately, Ray's reputation was on the line with this one and he wasn't going to blow it. "There is one of two people that are going to pay this debt...you or your fucking widow!" The old man bolted sideways as if he was reaching for a weapon and Ray fired twice. It was first to the chest, then again to the temple.

The panic-stricken wife was shaking and begging for her life. Ray, using the same slow talking low tone of voice as before, reassured her that he was not going to harm her. "Just behave and show us where the money is. No one is going to hurt you...I promise," he said calmly. The widow stayed quiet and nervously led them to the bedroom safe where she rambled off the combination. Juli tied her to a chair which gave the duo time to escape. All Ray could think of on the ride back to town was that he was now in the good graces of Licavoli and Scalish.

CHAPTER 7

HEREVER HIS TRAVELS TOOK HIM, ERIE ALWAYS
remained Ray's sanctuary. When he returned it
was as though he had never left and he would
pick up with the old Erie crew when opportunity arose.

Blackie Paradise, one of Ray's co-conspirators on the Gus
Angelo burglary back in the late fifties had also met some
new friends after serving his time in the joint. His new friend
and partner, Eli "Whitney" Rosenswager was a retired treasury engraver, who just happened to be in the market for a
select crew for a counterfeiting scheme. The three of them
set up shop in Blackie's basement where they went to work

engraving the new plates for twenties and one hundred dollar bills. They decided that since Ray had the connections, it would be his job to get rid of the cash.

Appealing to their greed, Ray organized a meeting with Kansas City and Chicago mob associates who controlled most of Las Vegas. A deal was cut for ten cents on the dollar and the counterfeit loot was successfully filtered through dozens of casinos and businesses. As long as it didn't pass through the Tropicana, the Lady Luck and the Nevada Club...everything else was game.

This two-year long run of easy cash lined the pockets of some very influential mobsters that appreciated his loyalty and generosity and would move Ray's name up the chain of command.

Unfortunately, his luck ran out when Whitney fell asleep and crashed his car while running another load of cash to his Baltimore network. Whitney ended up with minor injuries, but the authorities discovered the trunk full of loot and their two-year spree came to a grinding halt. Ray knew the party was over and it was time to make the plates disappear. A final deal was struck for the counterfeit engraving materials and they were shipped out of the country by courier to Venezualan connections.

Whitney however, was convicted and sentenced to three years in the penitentiary. Never once, did Whitney implicate his co-conspirators, Ray or Blackie through his impending legal maneuvers or trials.

In the meantime, the Cleveland crew had been wreaking

havoc robbing stores throughout the greater Los Angeles area. Skinny Vellotta invited Ray out for some of their action.

During an eighteen-month streak of burglarizing and safe-cracking, this accomplished team of thieves made so much money that they actually invested in a luxury apartment complex near Universal Studios. Life was good, women were everywhere, money was plentiful and they lived like kings.

Still separated from his wife, Della, he kept in contact with her while she remained in Erie with his youngest son. She managed to convince him that she had changed and they should be together in California and try to make a new start. For his son's sake, he made a last ditch attempt to salvage an otherwise doomed marriage.

Around that time, a member of the Chicago family was in the process of purchasing an old warehouse from a coin dealer. He offered Ray half the proceeds if he could confiscate the contents of the building before the owner had the chance to move his inventory out at closing. Of course, to Ray, it sounded like a real winner.

The warehouse was loaded with old wooden military ammunition boxes filled with hundreds of thousands of coins. But not all jobs are so fruitful and often times don't go without "slapstick comedy routines," coming at the expense of the would-be burglars.

Ray, Skinny and Butchie easily picked the giant lock on the warehouse door to gain entry...only to discover that the goods were located on the second floor and not the first as they were told. Well, that was no problem; there was an elevator to help them cart the heavy boxes down to the first floor.

Surely, this wouldn't take them that much extra time, they figured.

But the elevator turned out to be broken. As a result it took them four extra hours to cart the boxed up coins to the crew's rental truck parked against the loading dock. Then it turned out that they had over-packed the vehicle so much that the enormous weight of the coins literally lifted the front end of the truck off the ground. They had no choice other than to remove some of the boxes, to finally make their get-away.

Skinny and Butchie weren't happy to realize they would only be getting twenty cents on the dollar for their merchandise and decided they could do better at a coin show, leaving Ray to relax at the motel.

Unbeknownst to them, they had approached a coin dealer at the show who just happened to be the son of the warehouse owner. Recognizing the old ammunition boxes, he was smart enough to lure the two thieves into a deal after the coin show was over. When the crew returned for their exchange; the feds were waiting. The two were charged with burglary, receiving and trying to sell stolen property. Although Ray didn't make any money on that one…he got away clean. Disappointed by this turn of events, all he could say was "The bastards should've taken the first deal. They always get too fucking greedy."

CHAPTER 8

NOW, ON HIS DEATHBED, SERAFINO ROMEO SUMMONED
Ray to his side. Ray knew the old man's time had
come and was sad for him. He thought about when
Serafino had taken him under his wing and what the old man
had done for him.

Ray guessed it was time for repayment. He was right. As he
stood at the bedside of his frail and vulnerable mentor, Serafino spoke Italian to him. "You were the one who was going to
succeed. I saw it in your heart when you were a boy. You made
me proud Remo. Now I need you to look after your cousin
Fredo, when I'm gone. Fredo gets too emotional. He needs

your help to survive in the business I'm handing down to him". Ray politely promised the old man he would do whatever he could for his cousin and never to worry.

Ray felt burdened by the request, but knowing he owed this much to the dying man, he felt bound to his word. From that day forward, Ray made it a point to keep an eye on Fredo and the business, even if it was from afar.

Things were getting a little out of hand back in California. The crew was getting sloppy with some jobs and soon they found the feds parked down the street watching their comings and goings. His gut told him it was time to get out of there and take his wife and son back to Erie.

Back in Erie, he opened a legitimate business, called "Della's Smoke Shop on West 12th Street. Della ran the storefront shop while Ray on the other hand ran his illegal number racket out of the back door. By nature, Ray was a gambler and always hustled to make a buck. Things weren't about to change.

When baseball season was over he jumped right into football. He was known for being an honorable man paying daily winners and never stiffed anyone. Even, if it meant he would go broke on the pay-off.

He was taking in bigger bets by the week and it all seemed too good to be true. But, while he succeeded in increasing his client list, other bookies were losing theirs. As hard feelings mounted over the losses, a competitor who often stiffed his clientele, decided to drop a dime on Ray and put him out of business.

The Pennsylvania State Police busted Ray and his

employees in an afternoon raid at Della's Smoke Shop, destroying everything in their path until they found the betting slips.

Once again in custody, the diehard Ferritto shrugged it off by willing himself to think positive. He would shake himself off and start all over again like he had done a dozen times before.

Upon his release from that stint behind bars, Ray's marriage was in ruin and he left Della behind. Della blamed him for all of their hardships, especially with the law. She would never admit that she was ever at fault for either.

Ray soon found himself crisscrossing the country with Skinny Velotta and Bob Walsh for what seemed to be the hundredth time. Their most recent slew of burglaries was robbing wealthy Jewish businessmen of their exquisite jewels. Occasionally, they'd even hit a few supermarkets in their path. It was as though they had a license to steal as they made their way back to Los Angeles.

The F.B.I. had been alerted that this band of thieves were living in L.A and put several agents on the detail. Once the crew realized that they were being tailed, they all went into a stop mode. They often mocked the lame agents that sat parked down the street watching their every move. They all took turns offering them coffee and donuts to let the agents know their presence didn't go unnoticed.

Consequently, the other investigative agents behind the scene, is whom they should have been worrying about. They were the ones interrogating witnesses from the supermarkets that were robbed. A young female cashier recognized their

FERRITTO

mug shots and wasn't shy about pointing to Ray's saying, "I remember that one in particular, because I thought he was so good looking...he just caught my eye." Even though she fingered them in the courtroom during the trial, they out-maneuvered the prosecution on the basis of insufficient evidence that would have placed them at the scene of the crime.

Longtime childhood friend Gino D'Marco flew in from Erie for the defense team and declared that on the evening of the alleged burglary, Ray was celebrating his birthday with family and friends back home, some three-thousand miles away and there was no way could he have been in two places at once.

The Cleveland crew managed to skip on that one but they weren't out of the woods just yet. The trio faced yet another impending trial linking them to a half dozen other super-market hold ups. Before the feds were done with them, implications in similar burglaries, known crime associates and past convictions would be enough to hang them on "con-spiracy to commit burglary." They were all incarcerated at the Chino Penitentiary in California.

CHAPTER 9

A ll of these wise guys knew the drill with the down-
side of getting caught. They didn't see each other
during the initial weeks of being processed through
the system but once they reached population status they
enjoyed being out in the yard as much as they could.

They also knew all too well that the prison was being run
by mobsters inside and looked forward to meeting them.

Jimmy "The Weasel" Fratianno, an up and coming Mob boss
from San Franciso was one of the first ones they met. Jimmy,
a small guy about fifteen years older than Ray came up in the
ranks by gambling, dealing in extortion via pornography and

approximately fifteen murders were attributed to his career as an enforcer. He was best known in the criminal community for his bad temper, tenacity and iron fists…as well as being reputed to be under boss for the West Coast Mob. He and Ray would learn they ran with some of the same crowd.

Jimmy was a real name dropper going way back in time and reminisced often with the guys about his personal dealings with Sam Giancano, Johnny Roselli, Paulie Castellano, Carlo and Joseph Gambino, Johnny Battaglia, Tony Accardo, Dope Desanter, Dominic Brooklier, Tom Louie, Jack Dragna, Blackie Licavoli, and John Scalish. That was just to name a few and all of which were made bosses across the country.

Ray understood Jimmy's need to be the center of attention but was often leery of his openness amongst the wise guys in the prison. It's was nice to converse and have a few laughs about old times, but certain things weren't meant to be repeated…even amongst friends.

As close as they became, Ray always kept his darkest secrets close to the vest. He'd worked too hard to get to the level he was at and of course distrusting of most.

Later in life, he'd thank himself for trusting that instinct. He always believed that the greatest arsenal he could ever build for protecting himself wasn't only having guns, but the leverage of his secret sins. Used wisely, it would put him in a position where the enemy couldn't attack. This was a philosophy that Serafino had taught him well.

Jimmy's web of mob hierarchy was a little more impressive than Ray's list of associates but nevertheless they had a lot in common. "Look Ray, I took a likin to ya when we first met. How's about working with me on the outside? We can help each other and make some good money at the same time. Between your friends and mine we got nowhere to go but up. Whad ya say kid? Are we partners?"

Ray and Jimmy shook hands and they sealed their new partnership inside the joint.

Needless to say they had more in common than they originally thought and plenty of "juice with the warden". They dined well, had their golf clubs shipped to them and their L.A. cronies brought in hookers every month for a weekend conjugal visit where they had their privacy in one of the trailers parked within the prison gates, and within view of the guards walking prison's walls.

Not bad for being punished, but the best was yet to come. Jimmy's favorable recommendation to the warden on Ray's expert safecracking skills landed him a job as Chino's top locksmith. The inseparable duo even had the guards supplying them with enough pot, vino and valium to forget where they were. Calming their nerves and amusing themselves, by referring to the joint, as their "Private Country Club" was the standing joke around the huge stone gray confines.

When they were released, Ray offered Jimmy some peace and quiet at his apartment building in Van Nuys where they could keep a low profile until he got back on his feet. Ray owned the apartment building jointly with Skinny and Bob Walsh and that was going to be their headquarters for a while.

You could always find a bunch of mobsters hanging out there, planning their next score, while Ray was stirring his famous spaghetti sauce over the stove and frying his meatballs. Jimmy was always laying on the sofa with one foot on the floor, usually watching sports on TV.

One evening after they were settled, Ray, Juli, Skinny and Bob sat over their dinners sipping red wine, and mapped out their plan of action for the next heist at Sears Department Store in Glendale California.

On the day of the score, Bob Walsh sat on the couch cleaning off any old prints from their burglary tools and packed them carefully into duffle bags while Juli stood at the window scanning the neighborhood for any sign of the feds who might be keeping an eye on the crew. Jimmy was currently out on bond pending an appeal for his latest conviction so he wasn't going to be in on this particular heist. Ray sputtered for Walsh to throw in a few sticks of dynamite, "just in case."

The job went down as planned. You would have thought they owned the building the way they stormed their way through to the second floor. It was exactly 1:05 am and Ray was standing in front of the huge safe cracking the combination as if he had personally written the codes. The successful job had netted the thieves almost two hundred thousand dollars after everything was said and done.

CHAPTER 10

R ay hoped he'd never see the day that he would have to kill someone close to him. Consequently, that was their world. They justified this as a "legitimate hit." The definition of a legitimate hit was killing a person that was only involved with the mob. They thought nothing of this and treated it just as it was..."a job."

Unfortunately, that day arrived when in 1969 when Ray received a phone call from the biggest sports bookmaker in Los Angeles, John "Sparky" Monica. "Ray... this is Sparky, I'd like to discuss a business venture if you've got the time. Can you meet me at the Gardens tonight?" "Sure, Sparky," Ray replied. "I'll be there at eight."

After some initial pleasantries over a drink, Sparky had no hesitation about getting right to the point. "Look Ray, that cocksucker Juli Petro used to be my muscle and now the fucker is shakin me down. I'm not coughin up a thing to this bastard. I gave him a fuckin break when he was broke, now he's turned on me. I'd rather give it to you for takin him out. What do ya think," Sparky questioned.

"Well, not so fast Sparky?" Ray replied. "What exactly is my end?"

"I got twenty grand and a piece of my action for you if you get rid of my headache" Sparky declared. "Make it twenty grand and fifty percent for your new partner and it's a deal," Ray said firmly.

They shook hands on the deal just that quickly and Ray was on his way home to plan his hit. It shouldn't be too difficult as Juli was still staying at the apartment with Ray. He knew his every move.

When Ray arrived back at the apartment, Jimmy was dozing on the sofa and Juli was playing cards with Bob Walsh. Ray made a pot of coffee and sat in deep thought of what method he was going to use to kill his roommate. Ray knew certain mobsters considered Juli a crazy bastard from Collinwood, a part of Cleveland Ohio"s east side. He had been frequently stepping on the wrong toes and there had been a sneaking, unsubstantiated rumor that he was going to turn informant. So with this in mind, Ray rejected any bad feelings of having to take him out. It was just a matter of when and where the dirty deed was to be done.

Knowing full well that Juli hated to walk anywhere Ray suggested to Juli and Bob Walsh that the three of them take a walk down to the corner donut store. As he had hoped, Juli passed on the offer and Ray was in the clear to discuss the hit with Bob as they strolled down the block. For a piece of the action…Bob was in. The plan was to car bomb Juli outside of a restaurant a few blocks away. They knew he'd be there precisely at 10:0'clock for breakfast the following morning.

It was about 4: a.m. when Ray & Bob quietly snuck out to the parking lot. While Bob was the lookout, Ray was wiring the explosives in Juli's car when he accidentally crossed the wrong wire and a spark crackled in the dark of the night. He instantly knew he was in trouble and swiftly turned to duck. Covering his face as he heard the roar of the explosion, he felt the heat fuming over his body.

Bob immediately rushed to his aid and managed to drag Ray away from the burning car and out of sight. Lady luck was with him that night as he only sustained some minor burns on the back of his legs and a torn shoulder.

Jimmy and Juli were awakened by the sound of the explosion and panicked, but felt helpless to go outside and investigate. Not knowing what was happening they feared the worst and waited inside the safety of the building to figure out what the noise was.

Bob was helping Ray, disheveled and bleeding back into that very same apartment. "What the fuck is going on out there, Jimmy screamed.

The quick thinking thug Bob Walsh fired off to Juli. "You better get the fuck out of town. Someone's trying to kill you!" In the commotion, Bob managed to convince Juli that they had been standing near his car smoking a joint while waiting for some broads to arrive, when a Cadillac drove slowly past them in the dark and the next thing they saw was Juli's car exploding. Shaken, but relieved he was still alive Ray angrily pulled out a .22 and pointed it at Juli. "You almost got me killed...I oughtta whack you myself, you cocksucker!"

Jimmy jumped between the two and trying to make sense of it all. "Ray...you calm down," then pointing his finger to a ruffled Juli, Jimmy said, "and if you got somebody gunnin for you, take it somewhere else. I don't need this fuckin bullshit and more fuckin heat than I already got! Understand!"

Sirens in the distance were closing in. Sure enough, the authorities were positive that the crew that lived there had something to do with this. While Ray and Bob were able to flee the scene before the police arrived, Jimmy and Juli stayed behind and of course were interrogated for hours. But they too were just as baffled as the authorities. They argued that obviously someone else had it out for one of them and possibly were sending "a message." Otherwise, having no concrete evidence to link them to the incident they were released but their investigation would remain ongoing.

A few days later, Ray talked Juli into staying low and going back east for a while until they figured who had a "hard on" for Juli. He agreed. On the ruse that Bob and Ray would safely accompany him to the airport for his flight out, they made their move.

Juli drove his rental car while Bob sat next to him on the passenger side. Ray directed him to take a short cut around the airport. As they approached the landing area, Ray sputtered. "We're a little early kid. Why don't you pull over and we'll smoke a joint.".

Juli a seasoned killer himself never had a clue what was coming. He made a joke about grabbing a stewardess for a "blow job" and laughed as they watched one of the jets begin its takeoff from the runway. Ray pulled out his .22 and fired into the back of Juli's head as the mighty roar of the aircraft muffled the sound of the shot. As he slumped over the steering wheel, Ray and Bob jumped from the car making their way inside the airport. Bob headed for the main entrance to hail a cab while Ray boldly walked over to the counter area and purchased a one-way ticket to Erie.

Anxiously waiting over a drink in the airport lounge he heard his flight announcement and reached in his pocket to leave a tip. Not having any small bills he automatically threw a hundred dollar bill down on the bar and headed for the gate when a male voice rang out.

"Hey...sir!" Ray froze for a moment thinking it was the cops. He instinctively reached behind his back for his weapon and jolted around to see a pleased bus boy holding up the one hundred dollar bill saying, "Sir...thanks for the big tip." That kid never realized how close he came to getting a bullet in his chest before Ray made his exit. There was one last quick stop to the men's room where he disposed of the gun and then boarded his flight home.

CHAPTER 11

By early 1970 Ray hadn't collected his twenty grand from Sparky for the contract on Julius Petro. The authorities in California were still baffled as to who was behind this murder and a frustrated Weasel remained in the realm of suspicion.

Ray had waited long enough and decided it was time to take the bull by its horns. He called Sparky in California. He was ready to get into sports booking with his new partner in L.A., Sparky Monica. "Sparky, this is Ray Ferritto callin' from back east…how's it goin?" A surprised Sparky answered. "Hey man, ah…where ya been?" "I'm planning on flying into L.A.

this weekend to pick my money up and thought we'd discuss "our" books, Ray said in a friendly tone. "Uh, well, you need to call Tony Plate in Miami. He'll settle up with you on this one," Sparky replied. The response infuriated Ray. He knew what Sparky meant...he wasn't going to pay up.

"Listen you cocksucker! We made a fuckin deal and Tony's got nothing to do with it! Don't make me fuck you up Sparky," Ray barked.

"Just give me a few days Ray and I'll take care of it...we shouldn't have a headache over this. Take it easy and I'll get back to you," he said cautiously.

Unbeknownst to Ray, Sparky had gone under in the sports business and Tony Plate, a Gambino soldier from New York was now operating under Miami underboss, Aniello Della-croce and bankrolling Sparky's action in Los Angeles.

Ray wasn't going to be stalled any longer. He had no other choice than to put a call through to Tony Plate. "Listen Tony, this is Ray Ferritto. I understand there were some changes over the L.A. books. I made a deal and all I want is my end. Is that going to be a problem?" Ferritto asked. "I really don't want to see something happen out there."

Ray knew there was no way Tony was going to jeopardize losing his sports connections in L.A. over a lousy twenty grand. "Look Ray, this is just a misunderstanding. I'll get you your twenty grand, but I can't give you half the book. What d'ya say I just owe you a favor my friend...you know I'm a man of my word."

Ray was a pissed that he was duped on the sports book but

took his losses and decided to make it up with a few scores in L.A.

The Cleveland gang was hatching a plan to heist a private vault company in LA that warehoused millions in cash, jewelry and other valuables. This was going to be the motherload of all heists. So the idea of calling in another master burglar seemed necessary to pull it off.

Phil Christopher, another professional thief from Cleveland was elated at the invitation and immediately flew to California to meet with his counterparts. He met with Ray, Skinny, Al and Bob Walsh to discuss the details of the grand heist and did their homework.

There would be no one at the company from the close of business on Friday until opening Monday morning. They couldn't believe they'd have the whole entire weekend to safe crack this magnificent wall of iron. The men planned carefully, but the Frattianno declined.

He had a dinner engagement with Johnny Carson, the famous tonight show host and a few of his celebrity friends. Jimmy wasn't one to turn down an invitation like that. He enjoyed rubbing elbows with celebrities and it made him feel important amongst his cronies.

Armed with walkie-talkies, precision tools and a pre-made duplicate key for the front door, all five of them entered as if they owned the joint. Phil and Al were supposed to clip the alarms, Ray and Bob were prepping the tools and Skinny was the lookout who was going to have the getaway truck ready and waiting for them.

Something went terribly wrong almost immediately.

There was a huge glaring bright light shining over top of the building. Skinny laid on his horn and screeched into his walkie-talkie that it wasn't a "go".

Ray yelled. "Get out! The fuckin alarm was triggered! I thought this cock sucker (referring to Phil) knew what he was doing!" The crew made their exit. There weren't any cruisers in sight but they heard sirens blaring from a distance.

Ray and Skinny were able to jump into the truck while everyone scattered for cover from the police helicopter circling above. They made a quick once around but the others couldn't be found. Skinny and Ray drove away from the glaring lights and just had to sit tight hoping the others would make it by foot to the spot they'd be waiting.

The two waited as long as they could before returning back to the apartment without the rest of their crew. Ray was livid with rage and blamed Phil for the mess. "You people better quit inviting fuckin amateurs on these scores or I'm out! We just blew the biggest score of our lives. We would've been on easy street for a long fuckin time! God damn it!" He slammed his fist on the counter, pacing rapidly around the room, lost in anger and spewing threats of killing Phil Christopher for the botched attempt.

"Relax Ray: there'll be more. Take it easy man!" Skinny barked. Skinny was all too familiar with Ray's hair trigger temper and did his best to settle him down.

Just returning home from his dinner engagement, Jimmy walked right into Ray's fit of rage. Skinny was pacing back and forth hoping Ray wouldn't shoot Christopher in the head when he got there.

Jimmy was quick to ask if everyone got out okay and warned Ray..."You can't just go off half-cocked whacking people Ray. If, that's the case, we'd all be shootin each other all the time. Get a grip...things will work out. Let me talk to this bastard and see what happened."

CHAPTER 12

---◆---

The cooling off period was tense for all involved in the failed private vault scheme, but the entire crew came away undaunted. Old habits die hard. It was only a matter of picking themselves up, dusting themselves off and on to the next scheme.

Youngstown, Ohio mobster Frankie Gallatti was mounting plans on a big heist of his own, compliments of his girlfriend and her insider knowledge. Maria Lanza, niece of a wealthy New York politician provided her boyfriend Frankie with a rough draft, design and exact location of a safe at her uncle's mansion in the ritzy area of Albany, New York. All she wanted was a piece of the action and a promise that her uncle wouldn't be harmed.

Gallatti systematically organized what he thought was the best crew in the business to take this one down. Ray Ferritto, Phil Christopher, Bob Walsh, Ronnie Carabbia and the Don Dinisio all flew in to Albany and met Gallatti at the airport where they were taken to a hotel and received instructions on the score.

After studying the location of the mansion and the floor plans, they equally agreed that Ray and Bob's job would be to divert attention away from the target area by setting off a large amount of explosives approximately a mile away where Electric Company employees were on strike. Phil Christopher and Ronnie Carabbia would trip the alarm system at the home while Gallatti, Walsh and Dinisio stormed the residence in pursuit of their fortune.

At the strike, of midnight the nitro was triggered causing huge fiery explosions creating a chaos that drew dozens of police and firemen to put out the blaze. Ray and Bob had done their part and now had to scour the neighborhood making sure that the other guys made it into the mansion without incident.

The commotion at the Electric Company certainly grabbed the attention of the fire departments and half the police force, but the usual beat cop that performed nightly checks on the politician's home was a little premature.

Now their second position being the lookout men, Ray and Bob slowly cruised past the mansion spotting the uniformed officer checking out the front of the huge estate. From their view they could see shadows of three crewmembers, exiting a side entrance with visibly overstuffed duffle bags.

Ray radioed the crew to get the hell out of there as he watched the officer approaching the same side of the home. The cop must have heard the voices from the walkie-talkies. The startled officer drew his weapon and sprang into action yelling, "Stop…or I'll shoot," and darted towards the intruders.

At that point, it was every man for his self and each of them took off in different directions. Ray and Bob circled around the area one last time attempting contact them by radio before pushing their luck and to no avail could find any of the crew.

Frustrated at the disappearance of the other men in the wooded area surrounding the home, they had no other choice than to return to their motel room. A few hours and a pot of coffee later they again went in search of their counterparts.

By this time the cops were crawling all over the grounds and the rest of the crew was nowhere to be found. They assumed that if the cops were still searching that there was a good chance they had all escaped and took cover somewhere with the goods. Their second unsuccessful attempt at finding anyone once again would land them back at the motel in wonder.

Unbeknownst to Ray and Bob, the lost crew narrowly escaped by following the edge of the highway for miles, crawling and ducking passing motorists and police cars with their walkie-talkies off until it was safe enough to stop and get their bearings.

What seemed to be a long weary night, Ray and Bob decided one last try at finding the lost crew. It was almost dawn as they drove along the highway in anticipation of locating any of men until finally a familiar and welcomed voice sounded from the hand held radio.

Distressed, Ronnie's plea for assistance was loud and clear. He tried to give Ray and Bob the approximate area where they were hiding under some thick shrubbery along the road. In an effort to pinpoint the location all they could do was retrace the road back and forth. Exhausted, but happy to see their car Ronnie leaped out in the path of their getaway vehicle. As Ray slammed on the brakes, the weary ravaged burglars relieved to have been found took no time stuffing the duffle bags in the trunk, squeezing themselves in the car speeding off.

In transit back to the safety of their motel, the drained crew laughed and joked as they shared their harrowing escape tactics and close calls.

Excited with the huge successful score, no one could sleep before equally dividing up the mountain of jewelry, cash and bonds that they boldly spread out on the motel room floor and celebrated their victory with a shot of scotch.

CHAPTER 13

---◦---

Ray was on easy street for a while and turned his attention back to Erie. This time opening up the sports books again with his longtime associates Cy and Frank "Bolo" Dovishaw.

But thoughts of Serafino's last wishes hung over Ray's head like a swirl of smoke after he was home. His indebtedness to the old man prompted him to first stop at Serafino's Amusements where he felt the need to check on his cousin Fredo and make sure things were going as they should.

After the initial greetings and some small talk, Ray inquired about the status of the accounts and Fredo uneasily explained that business wasn't too good. "You know Cuz, you haven't been around and things aren't like they used to be. There's more competition moving in and we've got five different families out there fighting for the same action...it's been tough," Fredo squawked. "So push the cock suckers back," Ray fired. "I came home to relax and now I have to straighten this shit out!"

He was pissed but on the other hand most of the same vendors were Ray's potential sports betting customers, so he would kill all his birds with one stone.

Henchmen escorted Ray, Bolo and Cy to every single operation and joint that he thought Fredo should have been controlling. The sight of Ray angrily approaching the traitors was enough to scare them stiff. They apologetically resigned themselves, not only to rekindle Serafino's business relationships, but also to pick up Ray's. Of course, he did sternly add a promise there would be "swift consequences without warning" now that he was in control again.

Inside of a month, Ray took Fredo's business from forty-two customers to over a hundred and fifty, tripling the profits. However, one does not do this without stepping on a lot of toes.

By this time, Cy and Bolo had made their bones and earned their way up to Lieutenant positions, commissioned under the Stefano Maggadino family.

To decipher borders, an impromptu meeting was held with "Jimmy Westfield," Erie's Underboss for Russel Buffalino out of New York. For the most part, Jimmy Westfield, a handsome, dapper but vicious mobster was becoming somewhat lenient and turned a blind eye to some of the competition. Ray needed to rein in the majority of Erie gambling and offered Westfield a deal he couldn't refuse.

In the past Westfield and Serafino often argued about territories and their last confrontation came to blows when Serafino put a knife to Westfield's throat in broad daylight on 12th and State Streets. He threatened to kill him if he didn't back off and stay on his own turf. It had been Ray who managed to pull Serafino away from what would have started a war between the factions in Erie.

Westfield had been appreciative of that moment and was clear in Ray's capabilities of resolving dangerous situations and an incident he wouldn't forget. So it didn't take much persuasion on Ray's part to convince Westfield and Russ Bufalino to partner up in the city's gambling operations.

From this new partnership, The "City Squire Club" was born. It was located on Erie's lower Peach Street just a few blocks away from City Hall in which the police station was housed.

For the most part, this quiet establishment entertained gamblers from as far as Pittsburgh, Buffalo and Cleveland and included visiting mob associates from around the country. The daily stakes were high and the list of politicians on the payroll, were offered private games and sessions with local hookers in return for their protection from the law.

Ray, Cy, Bolo and their silent partners ran their business with an iron fist. Affluent businessmen, mobsters and politicians were rubbing elbows and they all managed to maintain a level of secrecy amongst themselves. The crew made a boatload of cash and their customers enjoyed the privacy and entertainment.

Nevertheless, all good things must come to an end. After two years of riding this wave of easy money, there came a sore loser that decided to throw a monkey wrench in the game.

That someone was Detective Lillis, who happened to be on a losing streak and accused the house of cheating him. Ray was always known for running a clean game and this infuriated him. Lillis was intoxicated and stepped over that invisible boundary line one too many times. Ray had warned Lillis's of his drunken rowdiness before and this was the last straw. Bolo and Cy tossed him out of the club and barred him from ever returning unless he wanted to go for a one- way ride.

A very pissed-off detective was going to get his revenge. He approached his superiors about the illegal activities of the City Squire and collectively they organized a pre-dawn raid on the establishment. Unbeknownst to Lillis, his captain was on the payroll and gave the crew the heads up on the date and time of the sting.

Although Lillis ended up with egg on his face, the word of the raid slowed down the business. Those who had patronized the club weren't quite sure that there wouldn't be a heads up the next time.

The crew wasn't going to let this lack of business deter their investment, so the next logical move was to scare up some "Italian lightening." They'd burn the joint, collect the insurance and reestablish themselves at another location.

CHAPTER 14

———⟡———

It was the mid-sixties and the passing of the City Squire Club led to the rebirth of "The Calabrese Club," located on 16ᵗʰ & Walnut Streets in the heart of Little Italy.

The old club once served as a private establishment for their immigrant fathers who quietly enjoyed the strict unity of brotherhood and small social events for members only. But the old place was slowly sinking into debt and the membership was happy to see it handed down to the next generation.

The crew bought out the charter and paid the board of directors and longtime members a mere fifty dollars each to assume leadership and the crew took no time jumping in to renovate the interior of the two story antiquated corner building.

Cy, Ray and the crew took this once solemn social gathering place, and elegantly transformed it into the popular Disco Scene, thus organizing the biggest party in town. The open space that once housed the bowling alley, now served as the main ballroom with a spacious open dance floor, boasting a huge oval bar as the center of attention and dining tables surrounded the place. The clubs legal seating capacity jumped to fifteen hundred people, but often times there was standing room only and on occasion the club would be cited for overcrowding.

The colorful rotating glass chandeliers cast rainbows of sparkling light that greeted the likes of entertainers from that era such as Frank Sinatra,Jr, Edie and Steve Gormet, Louie Prima, Buddy Rich, Maynard Ferguson, Woody Herman, Jerry Vale and local bands as well.

Aromas from heaven seeped through the large kitchen where Cy's wife and a few neighborhood women cooked fine Italian recipes and nipped on their homemade wines. A second, smaller bar room, adjacent to the main entrance, housed a juke box, cigarette machine and additional tables for those who wanted a little more privacy with their dinners. But, the second floor and most highly guarded was strictly "by invitation only" for the privacy and protection of gamblers.

For lack of a parking lot, the patron's cars would line the narrow streets, parked haphazardly for blocks surrounding the club. The majority of forefathers' generation hadn't owned any vehicles. They rarely needed one as everything was conveniently in walking distance within the neighborhood.

Directly across the street, St. Paul's Church had ample parking spaces, but the priest wasn't about to let the sanctity of his holy grounds be tainted by the "sinners" who patronized the establishment. Although Cy was born Catholic, like the rest, his father was an Atheist and it was obvious that it rubbed off on the kid.

Cy's blood ran cold when anyone spoke of religion, even if they made the slightest gesture of their respect for God. His temper would flare into vile rages, condemning the Lord and his prophets with vicious unspeakable curses that would make the average man cringe with horror. Those who knew him well intentionally kept their "sacred thoughts" to themselves. They never wanted to be in the line of fire when God struck him…including the wise guys.

The Calabrese Club was open four nights a week from midnight to seven a.m. and Cy protected it like a fortress with bodyguards everywhere. And, they had inside spies too. Danno Adolph, a local wise guy just recently released from Huntingdon inconspicuously, maneuvered the crowds and kept an eye out for the barmaids or bartenders trying to pocket extra money from customers or stealing from the registers.

Unlike Cy, Ray was more reserved in his mannerisms and less temperamental in public. As was his nature, Ray preferred to stay behind the scenes as a silent partner and only voiced himself when the need arose. Cy was a meticulous good looking gangster and prided himself for wearing flashy expensive tailored suits, sported the finest gold jewelry and favored Italian Dinobli cigars always clenched between his teeth. Cy was notorious for his reputation for entertaining people whether it was relatives, friends, wise guys, wealthy businessmen, local politicians, "in or out" of town mobsters and even the entertainers themselves.

The crew thought they had complete control over the joint...or so they thought. Ray received a surprise phone call from a longtime boyhood friend who had become an F.B.I. agent and now working in a west coast field office. "Grapes" was his code name and would occasionally call to warn him if his name popped up during any investigations or if there were undercover operatives targeting him.

The call was concerning the barbut games at the club and the feds were planning a bust. But, by the time Ray got the call the feds had already infiltrated the club befriending their way into the private loop.

Grape's description of the infiltrators fit two men that had been trying to get into the dice games and Ray had remembered questioning them about their roots and supposed mob connections out of Pittsburgh. The two agents cautiously played their covers as out-of-town salesmen that passed through Erie now and then looking for some gambling action. Ray and Cy were ready for them.

They immediately moved the game from the second floor to a safer temporary location and cleaned the entire club for any evidence of gambling and stolen merchandise that was waiting there to be fenced.

The following week, the two agents appeared for their

usual drinks and some conversation when Cy invited them over to his private dinner table and ordered a feast fit for a king and rounds of drinks on the house. They must have been ecstatic thinking they got this close to the Erie mobsters and how they were going to be in on this huge bust.

When the two agents thought everyone was comfortable enough to bring up the subject, they would appeal to Cy's greed and inform him that they had a large sum of cash and wanted to get in on a game.

Cy was more than happy to please and dropped them off at a competitor's barbut game on the other side of town.

Weeks later, several barbut games around the city had been raided by the feds and it was indeed the topic of conversation at the Calabrese club. Ray and Cy toasted, as they joked, "It would be a nice gesture to send the two feds a thank you card for putting our competition out of business!"

CHAPTER 15

The early seventies, Ray entertained the idea of taking his sports book to the next level. His insane passion to build the biggest gambling empire consumed his every thought. It wasn't so much the money but rather the respect and power he needed to feel that seemed to be driving him.

He met with Russ Buffalino for a private sit down at a small cottage just outside of Silver Lake in New York. A dozen or so chieftains were enjoying a little annual get together. It was meant to be a quiet dinner hashing over some new business and reminiscing over a few bottles of wine.

While Ray and Russ had always remained silent partners in the numbers rackets, Ray was not a boss, so it would be unusual for him or anyone else that was not of rank to be sitting at these events. Russ Buffalino saw the potential monetary gain that Ray could offer and had invited him to their meeting of the minds.

As Russ introduced Ray around the table, there were some that were skeptical and voiced their reluctance to his presence. "What in the hell is going on here, Russ! No outsiders. That's the policy!"

And Russ simply replied back, "You know Mike, you might want to listen to what this kid has to say. We made a lot of money from him and he's got some fresh ideas, which I think will be well worth your time. Besides he belongs here more than you do. What the fuck have your people been doing but twiddling their thumbs down there. I don't see you bringing anything to the table."

They shrugged their shoulders and grumbled a bit, but finally agreed to take a listen. Ray was polite, but anxiously put his cards on the table not wanting to waste precious time.

He detailed his new betting system and described how he could expand their number rackets and sport betting into a multi-million dollar "franchise"...so to speak, and said to them.... "I'll make you so rich that your great grandchildren will never have to work. But there is one more person that has to be included in this operation if it's going to be successful....Jimmy Hoffa." Some were on bad terms with Hoffa and wanted no part of him, but Ray persisted and the majority ruled in favor.

Rays lucky stars must have been in alignment that day as he managed to convince them that a consultation with Hoffa and calling in an old favor from Tony Plate was necessary to get the ball rolling.

Eventually, this secret underground operation that was born that day became known as "The Ameche 13". The name Ameche was derived from their generation's reference to the telephone and seemed to be a fitting code.

The bad news was that to become a private lifetime partner in this elite group there was going to be a one-time entrance fee of $200,000. The good news was they would stand to receive ongoing residuals for the life of the gambling empire and they were talking millions.

By and large it was anything but easy. Over the next year, Ray had tirelessly organized the expansion of the largest illegal gambling operations in twelve states. With Hoffa's teamsters in place they were able to move the large sums of cash around the country with no one the wiser.

Some deals were over the barrel of a gun while others were with a shake of the hands. There were a lot of people in the sports world that went on the payroll and happy to hop into bed with the mob.

But, while Ray had his mind on serious business, Cy was getting out of hand. He was banging just about every broad that came through the front doors of the club and when he wasn't entertaining out of town mobsters, he was getting into jams left and right and Ray was getting tired of having to put out the fires. The last straw was when he found out that Cy was trafficking cocaine through their Venezualan associates.

That was it for Ray. He was old school and any type of drug business was forbidden. They argued often, but Cy was too stubborn and Ray thought it was best to keep away from him for a while and not jeopardize the sports betting business. Ray went back to LA where he could concentrate on his west coast source of operations after Tony Plate sealed his end of their deal.

On the pretense that Ray was setting up a small sports betting crew, he also convinced Jimmy a decent payday was in order for helping him out a bit. In reality, Jimmy was never going to be a privileged member and to no degree was he going to reap any rewards, due to lack of the hefty membership fee.

Jimmy Fratianno was brilliant when it came to names, numbers and opening doors in the criminal world. Although, he did have his share of troubles and enemies, for the most part he was a high-ranking underboss with unlimited influence. Without the slightest bit of hesitation, he was on his way setting up and introducing Ray to the movers and shakers in the sports arena that Tony Plate couldn't.

Around that time, the Jimmy was also working on a potential jewelry heist in southern California. This particular job was personal for him. Maury Saltzman a high-end jeweler had not only cheated Jimmy on a deal but openly insulted him at a party that was being held at a Hollywood mansion. Belittling Jimmy, an up and coming mafia boss, in front of a few celebrities and friends was not kosher.

Jimmy decided to take a trade-off with Ray. In return for the payday he wanted Ray to take care of Maury. Jimmy hated

Maury so much that he "did not" want him dead. He would have rather seen the bastard suffer for the rest of his life. "You know the worst thing that could happen to a fucking Jew," he said. "Take his money and break his fucking legs."

But, just as Ray was contemplating Jimmy's revenge on Mr. Saltzman, the doorbell rang. To Ray's surprise, it was the marshals with a federal arrest warrant charging him with burglary for a slew of robberies that had taken place the last time he had been with the Cleveland crew in L.A.

It had taken the authorities almost two years to close in on the crew, and Ray had been the last to be charged. But he wasn't about to face the music. Immediately, upon being released on bail he went on the lam leaving the feds scratching their heads again.

But before he left, he put his old Erie partner, Bolo in full charge of the gaming operations. The next eighteen months he spent in seclusion, held up mainly in hotels around the Warren-Youngstown area where his mob cronies indulged him. He even had the audacity to slip in and out of Erie a few times to meet with Bolo over that period without the slightest fear of getting caught. As long as he stayed low-key he figured he would be safe from the law.

Up at the crack of dawn and showered as his usual routine, he'd wait for the guys to come over to pick him up for his coffee and donuts at the Italian club where they'd hang out, play cards and then eat again at lunchtime. Being on the lam was really more boring than anything else but his day was coming. Never did he realize that it was going to be so dramatic.

It was 6 a.m. and he had just turned on the morning news when he heard what he thought to be someone with a bull-horn, yelling out, "James Smalley...This is the FBI. We know you're in there...Come out with your hands in the air!"

"James Smalley," he thought to himself. Who in the hell was James Smalley? He quickly jolted towards the window, slowly pulling back the blinds. The entire parking lot surrounding the motel was being overrun with agents wielding high-powered weapons and donning riot gear. You would have thought they were trying to capture a mass murderer or something.

He was stunned and at the same time wondering, who James Smalley was. Could it be that there was another criminal hold-up in the same motel? If there was, he must have been in the room next door because all the firearms were pointing pretty damn close, if not directly at Ray's front door.

Ray stood there frozen. It wasn't his name they were calling out. The feds repeated their demand. The jig was up for a toss of the old coin. He decided to let them make their move first, just in case there was such a person in the opposite room.

There wasn't! They rushed Ray's room by storm. It seemed as though it happened almost in an instant before they had him cuffed and had dragged him in plain view of the parking lot.

"Smalley, you're under arrest for bank robbery," yelled the federal marshal. "Hey, wait a minute here...I'm not Smalley," Ray said. You got the wrong guy!"

It took some time convincing them he wasn't this Smalley

character but after they ran his prints they realized who they did have in their custody and charged him with "Unlawful flight to avoid prosecution."

CHAPTER 16

After Ray was extradited to Los Angeles, he was recharged, convicted and sentenced to three years in Chino. May of 1973, about half way through his stint, he considered his life on hold. That's the way he liked to refer to it. He convinced himself to cut the outside world off to keep his sanity and felt it was easier than communicating with friends and relatives about family events he was missing or problems that he had no control over. But the one constant soul he wouldn't shut out was his mother.

It was Wednesday evening, the usual one weekly call to speak with his mom back home, when his sister Gemma answered the phone. "Hey Gem, put ma on the phone." She immediately burst into tears and couldn't speak, handing the phone to her brother. "What's going on," Ray anxiously quizzed. "Didn't anyone tell you Ray?" His brother's voice cracked and had a deep sadness. "Tell me what," Ray answered. He held the tears back a moment and then blurted out, "She's gone. Ma passed away last week Ray...the priest out there was supposed to give you the message. We wondered why you didn't call us."

Ray's heart sank in his chest and he went numb. He couldn't believe what he had just heard. He spoke briefly to his brother on the details, but had to cut the call short. He returned to his cell devastated by the great loss of his beloved mother and angry that this man of the cloth didn't have the decency to deliver the news to him.

At the time of his mother's death, the family specifically spoke to the prison pastor in the hopes he would console Ray in his time of grief. They knew Ray wouldn't take the news well. He and his mom had always been so close. But the priest didn't have the time after he took the call as he was on his way out the door to start his vacation.

That was the explanation to Ray upon the priest's return. It stunned Ray for a moment, before he spoke. Infuriated by the lack of the priests' empathy and duty, Ray went right for the jugular and put him up against the wall. Spewing vile remarks, Ray spat in his face before the guards jumped him and dragged him off to the hole. That was the incident that led Ray to denounce his catholic religion. He swore to himself, never again would he ever step inside of any church.

The rest of his time came hard. He felt guilty for the shame and heartache he put her through over the years with his freewheeling criminal lifestyle. Nonetheless, when she was alive, the subject always went unspoken between the two. In her eye's Ray could never do any wrong.

After being released from Chino he went directly back to L.A. to pick up where he left off. The sports business had been thriving, even during his absence.

Jimmy began to realize that Ray's action was more than just a small lucrative sports operation. He was curious to know more. As a ruse to get the dirt, he appealed to Ray's dream of one day becoming a boss.

They discussed breaking off from under the Los Angles family where Jimmy was still barely holding onto the title of under boss. But the truth was that Ray didn't need Jimmy anymore.

In the fall of 1974, the death of Los Angeles boss Nick Licata led to the new leadership of Dominick Brooklier and his new sidekick, Sam Sciortino. The two would keep Jimmy's status in the outfit on hold.

But only a year into their reign, both men were charged with extortion and racketeering under the federal Racketeer Influenced and Corrupt Organizations Act, also known as RICO ACT. Both men plead guilty to the charges and jailed.

Jimmy and Brooklier had been close business partners since their loan sharking days back in the sixties. Brooklier thought it best to hand over the title of "acting boss" to Jimmy. Brooklier assumed he would still be in control through Jimmy while he was doing his time.

But, the hotheaded, Jimmy Frattianno, was becoming a loose cannon. He sidestepped Brooklier's orders and overstepped the boundaries. Jimmy's top position of leadership had gone to his head. While he was undermining Brooklier's authorities, Brooklier was putting a hit out on Jimmy.

When Jimmy learned of the contract, he was infuriated, but he wasn't about to let it faze him. His mindset at that point was that he was untouchable. He felt strong enough that he didn't need the blessings of the powers that be to defect and take control of a new extended command. But the Los Angeles, Chicago and Vegas chieftains weren't about to let Jimmy from under their stranglehold just yet.

They thought Jimmy was getting too dangerous and out of control making too many decisions on his own. At a small dinner meeting in Vegas, the chieftains, made it very clear that they were putting the squash on his Brooklier's "hit" and any future plans Jimmy may have had on anything. He was coming off the books as far as they were concerned. That was going to serve as his punishment for stepping on toes. However, Jimmy was free to continue earning his place in the outfit.

During the spring of 1976, it came to light that a southern California mob hit man Frank Bompensiero, was working with the F.B.I. on a secret investigation involving the production of porn flicks. He convinced Dominick Brooklier and his crew to extort exorbitant amounts of monthly payments. What they didn't know is that the F.B.I. had created the porn company specifically for their sting operation.

Once the leadership realized what was happening, Jimmy

surmised that Bompensiero was the culprit. On several different occasions during that year, Jimmy picked up on Bompensiero's weird behavior and suspected that something wasn't right with him. But, by that time it was too late for Brooklier who would later, once again be indicted for the extortion. Jimmy and Ray were going to make things right. They'd do the hit themselves, to get Jimmy back in the good graces of the powers that be.

However, in a last minute decision, the contract was given to Los Angeles hit man Tom Ricciardi, who carried out the slaying with a shotgun style while Bompensiero was on a call inside of a telephone booth.

CHAPTER 17

Clearly he needed some time away from the madness of Los Angeles. Ray decided to spend some time back in Erie where he could relax a little with his family, catch up with his business partners Bolo and Cy to regroup.

When he arrived home, he found the Calabrese club dying a slow death and Cy was nowhere to be found. He left his wife and the crew to manage the place while he ran off on a vacation to entertain some mob allies in Miami.

Ray was always in contact with Bolo, and steadily received his "end" of the sports business usually by courier. However, the Calabrese Club envelopes were lighter than usual that

past year, but Ray assumed there was some re-investing and
didn't question it. When he found the Calabrese Club going
to hell, his Italian temper went short.

Even though the club literally made millions in the seventies, it had gone down the tubes fast due to bad management.
Cy was an entertainer of sorts and knew how to draw a crowd
in, but when it came down to taking care of the books he
didn't have an iota of business sense and it showed.

Along with lavish spending habits he loved the horses
and had thrown a fortune away at the track. He was banging broads left and right, snorting coke and disappearing
for weeks at a time, not to mention he was facing burglary
charges from a large record heist.

The insane circle of greed and craziness was just never
ending.

Ray was pretty burned up when he realized what was happening with Cy. He would put up with a lot from Cy but the
one thing, he wouldn't tolerate was drugs. Ray was old school.
He wasn't beneath smoking a joint or two or even a valium to
calm his nerves when the occasion arose. However, dealing in
it was never up for conversation. Naturally, after a while Ray
had cooled off. He realized that Cy was just being Cy and he
was never going to change him.

By this time the Pennsylvania Crime Commission had
already openly pegged Cy as a soldier under the Maggadino
family and Ray was disappointed knowing his friend was
becoming such a loose cannon that he would never make it
up the chain any further.

So he pulled up his bootstraps and initiated a new haunt.

He chose a location on 26th & Brown Avenue, just up above the Italian neighborhood, but still within walking distance for the older wise guys that didn't drive. He and his crew went to work rejuvenating the old building and reestablishing "The City Squire." It was a smaller but bustling version of the Calabrese Club, headquarters for visiting mobsters, catering to gamblers, home to his sports betting operations, and the henchmen that guarded the kingdom. Life was good again and he was on top of his game.

Things could not have been better for Ray. There was a new love in his life named Rita with a two year old son. He bought a stylish upper class home for the three of them on Greengarden Boulevard, not far from the City Squire.

He spent a most of his time at the club, keeping things in line and privately catered to select patrons and underworld associates whether it was for business or pleasure. Their secret meetings influenced everything from local politicians, gambling, loan sharking and acts of violence to hate filled murders that were taking place in Cleveland.

It was May 1976 when he received word that Cleveland boss John Scalish had passed away during heart surgery. Scalish had been in the middle of implementing the demise of an Irish gangster and his thugs who had been trying to take over the reins of leadership.

That year had been horrifying for the city of Cleveland as the feud between the factions created constant bloody violent attacks on each other resulting in numerous car bombings and murders that sent the city into a tailspin.

Ray and his partner Bolo Dovishaw took the two, hour trip

to respectfully attend John Scalish's funeral and congratulate the next in line in the chain of command. James "Jack White" Licavoli also present at the services was stepping into power with the same vengeance against the Irishman and his band of thugs. This was Ray's opportunity to "step up to the plate."

Their conversation was brief. Ray knew the funeral was no place for business. He was also completely aware that Cleveland bosses were up to their necks in the destructiveness of ongoing wars and attempts to eliminate the Irishman and his crew.

Ray offered his services to the new Godfather, but Jack White was optimistic about the upcoming retaliations on the Irishman and simply told Ray he had enough internal manpower to take out Greene and his men. Jack White then expressed confidence, that in the end, he would seize sole control of the Cleveland underworld empire without any outside help and thanked Ray for the gesture.

After Scalish's funeral, "Big Ange" Lonardo, "Jack" White, John Calandra and Tony Liberatore, all current ranking bosses were then butting heads to terminate the Irishman. Jack White and Ray's longtime friend, Warren-Youngstown's under boss "Ronnie Carabbia's enforcer's had already made a total of eight unsuccessful attempts to kill Greene, but the luck of the Irish had always seemed to be with him. The Italians were beginning to look like idiots and incapable of handling their own problems.

"Danny "The Irishman" Greene had been muscling the Italian mob out of their gaming, prostitution and other enterprises for years and began to assert his own visions and power to take over Cleveland and drown out the Italians.

His career with racketeering began in the sixties as president of his local International Association of Longshoreman, but he was eventually ousted for extortion, attempted murder and numerous other illegal activities.

He came up hard on the streets of Cleveland and made a name for himself as a ruthless businessman, envisioning himself as a fearless Celtic warrior out to mutilate anyone who got in his way.

His underworld activities and list of associates was impressive to say the least. He managed to partner up with Teamster boss, John Nardi and together they organized a new gang to take over the reins of leadership.

Over a decade or so he pushed himself and his Irish cohorts deeper and deeper into mob territory, calling the Italian gangsters "maggots" that didn't deserve anyone's respect.

The arrogant Irishman certainly wasn't a novice at being a target either when he had previously been an enforcer for local numbers racketeer, Alex "Shondor" Birns. After a furious dispute over a debt that Greene wouldn't repay, Birn's had ordered a bomb planted in Greene's car.

The first attempt on the Irishman's life failed and thus initiated Greene's so called mythic, "luck of the Irish". After discovering the bomb, Greene said openly, "I'll return this to the old bastard," and mere weeks later Birns was blown away by a car bomb.

Although he was suspected of killing Birns', murdering under boss Leo "Lips" Moceri and wounding Eugene "The

Animal" Ciasullo with a bomb, the Feds were never able to pin anything directly on him.

The Italian gangster's recklessness and inability to "whack" the Irishman was now turning into a giant dose of humiliation and the pressure was mounting.

CHAPTER 18

Entrenched in anger and frustration, a meeting of the minds was held at a private club just outside the Cleveland area. The get-together included a dozen or so of the top mobsters and since Jimmy Fratianno was in town he was invited to join them.

Jack White initiated the conversation by spilling their ongoing troubles about Danny Greene. At their wits end and heated arguments blaming each other for the blunders, Jimmy put his "two cents" on the table.

"Jesus Christ you guys. Think about puttin' aside your pride for this one. You got Ray Ferritto right next door here.

He's our top enforcer out in L.A. for cryin' out loud. Matter of fact he's gotten rid of a few headaches for our east coast people. Trust me! If you really want this taken care of...give him a call."

"Ya know, I just saw him at Scalish's funeral and he did offer his services to us" Jack White replied. Jimmy peered around the table for a response to his suggestion and it was unanimous. Finally admitting they needed outside help. They gave the go ahead for Jimmy to set up the meeting with Ray.

Jimmy contacted Ray that evening and made arrangements to meet with him the following weekend so they could discuss "urgent business." However, the surprising news of Tony "Dope" Delsanter dying suddenly of a heart failure would bring them together in Warren, Ohio for another funeral.

During the wake Jimmy, Ray, Ronnie Carabba, Jack White and Butchie Cisternino briefly discussed the Greene murder contract. Ray didn't have to think twice about this opportunity. He knew how badly they wanted Greene iced and he would have a lot to gain by accepting the contract.

The following week at Cherry's Restaurant in Warren, Ray met with Fratianno, Jack White and the new Teamster President Jackie Presser who by the way inherited Hoffa's seat, passing along the task of providing the money shipments for the Ameche' 13. So, Presser too, also had a vested interest in getting rid of Greene and Nardi.

While Fratianno poured over the Cleveland bosses dilemma, Presser couldn't underemphasize the importance of this "hit." Ray was no fool – he digested every word before he spoke.

"I'm in," Ray replied. "But what's my end?" Jack White wasn't prepared to give him that answer just yet, but he told him he'd have an offer at the next meeting. Ray didn't push the payoff. He waited to see what they were going to put on the table first.

On the streets of Cleveland, the violence was escalating badly. Dozens mob killers were fighting to get in on the contracts for both Greene and Nardi. The gangsters that had already given Greene a shot were pissed off and wanted a second chance. The others just wanted "in." It was getting insane...even for the killers.

A few more months would pass before Ray heard anything from the Cleveland bosses. In the meantime, Ronnie Carabba would keep Ray updated on the situation. Until finally, all hell broke loose in Cleveland's Little Italy. They were out of control.

Ray's associates, Butchie Cisternino and Allie Calabrese, had taken some pot shots at Greene with high-powered rifles – but they both missed. A week later there was an unsuccessful drive-by shooter and he missed Greene too. One car bomb attempt left Greene with some partial hearing loss, but that was all. In retaliation Greene gave it right back to them and arranged for their murders.

Ray became enraged when he realized they were trying to steal his contract and gave Licavoli a call. He yelled into the phone. "How many fuckin guys do you need to kill one asshole? Either I have the contract or I don't...which is it?" Ray was sure Licavoli didn't appreciate his tone, but he was livid to think he was losing a top scale payday.

FERRITTO

To Ray this was going to be more than a simple pay off and the price just went up. Licavoli assured Ray that he still had the contract and they would meet soon to seal the deal. But, little did anyone know that the chieftains didn't care who killed the Irishman ...no one was going to be compensated for the "hit."

Greene, a killer himself went on thriving and mocking the Italians publicly. He had a type of disdainful attitude about dying which he thought would earn him respect from his adversaries. Whether it did, no one knows. He did tell his friends that he showed no fear – he he had a seat waiting for him in heaven when he died. Greene even boasted that he was their generations Robin Hood.

Nonetheless, he was proving to be almost immortal. No one could believe he wasn't dead with all the brazen attacks on his life. He indeed had a ton of enemies and at least three of those who failed to kill him died before they got another chance.

Several weeks later, a car bomb intended for Allie Calabrese had instead killed an innocent man that was just moving the car for him.

Allie, spent that weekend "in relief" at the City Squire in Erie, and he wasn't reminiscing about old times...he was ranting to his best friend Ray about helping clip yet even more gangsters in a mad retaliation. So, for Ray this Cleveland war indeed was getting a little more personal.

Nardi on the other hand was not going to be so lucky. Unlike the Irishman, Nardi was more predictable which made him an easier target. Meantime, Ray and Butchie schemed up

Nardi's death by a car bomb. They decide to rig up a "joe blow" car with explosives and park it next to his in the Teamsters parking lot. As Nardi returned to his vehicle, Butchie detonated the bomb by remote control and in one single violent explosion...Nardi was dead. It happened that fast and they were ready for Greene.

Shortly after Nardi's death, Greene was being interviewed by a local TV reporter Bill McGee, and asked if he felt he was an intended target for the Italian mob, too. "In the world of the streets, I happen to have a very enviable position to many people because I'm in between both worlds; the square world and the street world and I think I have trust on both sides. I have no axe to grind, but if these maggots in this so called, "Mafia" want to come after me...I'm here at the Celtic Club. I'm not hard to find."

Actually, he was being difficult to track down. He was dodging every chance he had while out in the public. He never did the same thing twice and all his personal appointments were top secret.

The statement incensed Licavoli as well as the rest of the Cleveland family. Did this bold bastard really believe he would never feel their wrath? Or did he subconsciously have a death wish?

Greene stated he knew contracts were out on him. "I've been lucky so far," he bragged. But he guessed that someday he wouldn't walk away.

The Italian capos finally met with Ray at Sabbatino's Restaurant and put their offer on the table. They were sure that twenty grand would seal the deal but that only made Ray angrier than he already was. He felt as though he was getting the shaft from the old mob bosses and told them so. "You think I don't know that some of your fuckin amateurs were trying to steal this contract? I want to get this over with," he demanded. "I want twenty five percent of the rackets in Warren and Youngstown and I want my own territory in Northwestern Pennsylvania and I'll hand all of them including Green to you on a platter!"

Ray new that was a lot for them to swallow, but he also knew they were running out of time. They balked at the hefty price he was asking and counter offered with handing over Tony Dope's old domain now that he was dead. But, Ray stood his ground. There was going to be no more bargaining. Reluctantly, they finally agreed to give him what he asked for.

He was tired of their screwed up routines and wanted action. "I need some recent photos of this asshole, a description of his cars and someone to show me around Greene's playground."

Trying to maintain a calm attitude, Licavoli reassured Ray the job was still his. He'd get the things Ray needed for the job and counted out five-thousand dollars to cover his initial expenses.

CHAPTER 19

Another month passed without any communication from Licavoli and he was slow to provide the necessary information. Ray felt sidelined and it was driving him into stark raving lunacy. A thousand questions ran through his head. He was antsy and overly anxious to see this thing through and he couldn't rest until it was over.

The aging mobsters continued to drag their feet with each passing day. Ray's anger mounted at how inept the old Cleveland forces were showing themselves to be. They were looking more like a bunch of fucking clowns than the killers they were supposed to be.

Bad news spread quickly and they became the laughing stalk of the entire organization. Now dubbed, "The Gang who couldn't shoot straight," they were indeed subject of joke and word on the street was "they were an embarrassment to La Cosa Nostra."

Ray was not happy about this. It was putting his reputation in a bad light and once again, he let them have it. He took the two-hour ride over to Cleveland for a surprise visit.

"What the fuck is going on here?" He questioned. He leaned across the table from Licavoli and just sternly blurted out, "I'm no fuckin slouch at makin a hit, but you guys are screwing me up here.

What exactly is the fuckin problem?" "You got idiots thinking this is the Wild West and takin pot shots at Greene. You've been stalling our meetings and I'm sittin in Erie like an asshole when I should be lining things up here!"

Old man Licavoli trying to hold his pride realized he couldn't hold Ray off any longer and caved in. "You won't have to worry about a thing Ray." Said Licavoli, spreading the old oil as slick as possible. "How's about we call up the crew and get this thing going before it kills all of us."

Within hours, Carabba, Calandra and Cisternino were in deep discussion, supplying Ray with whatever he needed to kill the Irishman. You could cut the air with a knife for all the tension that was in the room. Everyone was touchy and agitated over all the mishaps with Greene and all the unsuccessful attempts on his life. Ray was on edge and pushed them for more information on plate numbers, car descriptions, photos or anything that could get a finger on. He started the ball rolling the following day.

Licavoli never seemed satisfied and threw yet another wrench into the mix.

"Wait just one minute Ray," Licavoli said, as he gestured with his hand. "How about takin out Ritson and McTaggart, Greene's enforcers too, and we can end all of this. You'll be well takin care of for life and "we'll make you!" Well that was music to Ray's ears. He paused for a moment not wanting them to see the excitement in his eyes and responded, "You get the legwork done and my supplies and it's a deal!"

Ray set up shop at the Sheraton Inn and rented an apartment under an assumed name in the same building where the Irishman and his girlfriend lived. He alternated between the two places to stalk his prey. Over the following six-month period he kept glued to the Irishman's every move.

Ray had Carmen Marconi, the mob's wireman, supply him with the devices he needed to tap Greene's phone and listen to endless boring conversations. He memorized his daily habits, and pegged certain dates where Greene would be vulnerable. He tailed the Irishman and hunted him like a hawk. Being the outsider, made it all the more easier for Ray to prowl and stalk his victim.

Greene and his cohorts never knew he was there. Ironically, by September of 1977, Danny Greene was without a doubt very conscious of being the target on the street. Contrary to his public statement that he was not hard to find was proving to be false and exaggerated. He covered himself at every turn and never traveled without his henchmen.

In the meantime, things were increasingly becoming even more complicated, when out of nowhere, Greene popped up and wanted a truce with Licavoli. The organization immediately decided to use this opportunity to double-cross this so-called Celtic warrior.

Present at this meeting was Licavoli, Fratianno, several New York soldiers and Danny Greene. Greene had stolen almost a hundred thousand dollars from the Gambino family and was willing to pay it back in return for the mob calling off the contract on him. They looked dead in his face and agreed to let him live. All while thinking that after they got their money back he was dead meat anyway.

Greene walked away thinking he out foxed the old crew, but little did he know the game was only postponed. Assuming he was in the clear he became a little lax with the flow of things and got sloppy.

After all his beefed up security and secretiveness, the one thing he did not covet was going to be his downfall. And that was his telephone conversations that Ray had privy to.

The Cleveland faction had the inkling, that Greene was playing both sides of the fence and Ray would confirm their suspicions. The wiretaps consisted of numerous calls to and from the feds with Greene identifying himself using different aliases and Ray had deciphered the codes.

That was amusing to Ray. He sort of prided himself on his own limited conversations on phone for that very reason. You never know if the feds might be listening. Here he was inadvertently spying on the FBI, of all people and their secret relationship with Greene. There it was for all the mobsters to hear. Actual tapes nailing the Irishman for the rat that he was all the while he had been claiming to be so righteous in the criminal world.

They directed Ray to make his move on Greene immediately after this critical news was discovered. Ray contacted his crew to map out the hit. There had been so much time invested and at the same time wasted on this project that they decided to finalize the whole mess and just "do it."

Once Ray and Carabba constructed the bomb, Cisternino assisted Ray in planting it under the hedges by the front of the apartment building in the darkness of night. They would simply detonate it as he passed the following morning and no one would be the wiser. Ray had also enlisted two back-up snipers that were staged above another building across the street. They were instructed to fire their weapons if so much as a hair flinched on Greene's body after the smoke cleared.

Daylight arrived and everyone was in place. The crew was communicating via walkie-talkies and all they had to do was wait. Each minute seemed like an hour and the anxiety slowly began to unnerve the snipers. Ray was hyped with adrenaline rushing through his body while the tension from the waiting snipers poured through the hand held devices. He sensed their jitteriness and it threw him off kilter. In a fit of anger he ordered them to leave.

Keeping a steady eye on target, he noticed there were a few elderly people unusually stopped and politely socializing exactly where the bomb was planted.

Instinctively he cringed to think that he would harm innocent parties in his determination to destroy this rotten Irish bastard. But whatever molecule of conscience he did have, wasn't about to let him hurt any innocent bystanders either and immediately called for a "cease fire."

CHAPTER 20

———◦———

Ray called Licavoli within those few days informing him that there was going to be a meeting with some crucial information that he would have about Greene. The first week of October, Ray attended this gathering that was held on the back deck of a cabin cruiser at a boat yard on Mosquito Lake. Licavoli, Cisternino, Ange Lonardo and Ray then sailed a short way out where they felt safe to talk openly.

Ray was ready and informed the old crew he'd overheard Greene confirming a dental appointment on his phone tap. He knew exactly where he'd put the Irishman in the crosshairs.

As previously agreed, Allie Calabrese and Butchie

Cisternino had furnished Ray with a 1973 blue Plymouth and a Chevy Nova, the latter of which was to be used as the "Joe blow" car for the bombing and the other was the getaway car.

Ray's nephew, "Joey" perceived himself as an up and coming mobster and wanted to get his feet wet. As Ray remembered so long ago when Serafino had taken Ray under his wing, he would reluctantly do the same for his nephew.

It was a simple job for Joey. His only involvement was to apply for the Pennsylvania license plates for both cars and have the vehicles properly inspected for the anticipated trip to Cleveland.

The instructions were clear. The cars supplied by Licavoli's crew were to be specifically registered in Pennsylvania to deter any suspicion away from the Cleveland family. The plates and registration were applied for under the fictitious name of "Guy Mitchell" and sent to a friend's address in Erie.

It was rare that Ray would use any of his Erie associates as an accomplice to a hit, but he wasn't so trusting anymore of the Cleveland gang and decided to bring in his business partner "Bolo Dovishaw" as the sniper backup.

On October 5th, 1977 Ray and Bolo drove the vehicles to Cleveland and met with Butchie Cisternino who directed them to an apartment where they assembled the bomb along with a remote control switch. Cisternino altered the Nova by welding a thick metal box inside the car's door that would act as a blast director and they carefully went over the procedures of how and when it was to be detonated. The timing was crucial. There weren't going to be any second chances.

Ray and Bolo checked into the Holiday Inn and as

promised, on October 6th they were waiting in the dentist's parking lot as their intended victim drove up and parked his Green Lincoln. They watched as the Irishman scoped the area as he walked into the building.

Once Greene disappeared inside for his appointment, Bolo carrying a semi-automatic rifle took his position inside of a phone booth within the target's range while Ray and Carabba parked the "Joe Blow" Chevy Nova next to the Irishman's Lincoln town car.

Holding his breath, Ray took the bomb and carefully placed it into the steel bomb box flipping the receiver on and bolting down the pins.

They hopped into the parked getaway Plymouth by a nearby phone booth next to Bolo and the entrance to the parking lot.

When Greene was observed returning to his car Bolo waited for him to grab his door handle and slowly walked out of the phone booth ready to open fire. Carabba put the getaway car in gear and Ray finally detonated the remote control switch.

The entire parking lot rocked with the fiery explosion that sent Greene's body flying in several different directions. Within seconds the hit team was off and running. Carabba jumped into a waiting car as Bolo and Ray sped back to Erie, Pennsylvania in the Plymouth.

When the smoke cleared the Irishman was clearly dead. His body was a twisted mangled and bludgeoned mass of bone muscle and guts lying there. The smell of burnt human flesh permeated the air around his lifeless corpse and the dirty deed was over.

The fire department, police cruisers and news teams were quick on the scene trying to make some sense of what was happening while they sifted through the horror of it all.

It was first reported as a car fire and some thought a boiler blew, but when the cops stepped closer they knew this was no accident. Both cars were destroyed and then there was that smell. Greene had only been inches away from the bomb that ripped through his life and he never saw it coming.

Carabba was on his way into town when he heard the news on the radio, while Ray and Bolo sped off on the two-hour trip back to Erie.

Ray wouldn't know what happened until he reached Erie and got the phone call from Carabba.

It was true! The unshakable Greene was "Morte," "Dead," "Whacked!" Any way you put it, the teamsters and the Cleveland bosses were duly celebrating their victory. Ray on the other hand had to wait to celebrate this much long awaited payday. It was all he could think of over the next few days.

In the meantime, Cleveland was thrown into absolute chaos as the authorities organized a major strike force with local, state and federal police all arguing over jurisdiction. The city police were naturally saying it was their case because it was tied to ongoing wars while the Lyndhurst police vied with the FBI for the right to investigate the murder.

However, the Alcohol, Tobacco and Firearms Division, the United States Attorney General's Office, the United States Organized Crime Strike Force and the Cuyahoga County

Prosecutor's Office were also seeking to control the process of prosecution. The Crime Strike Force in itself was an elite group of lawyers and investigators with powers equal to the federal government. If they chose to investigate a crime, the crime becomes a vehicle for a broader look, into yet a further reaching criminal conspiracy.

The Greene murder definitely had "strike force material" written all over it. It was decided between the ranks that they would assemble all the major law enforcement players into a task force, with each group having a representative and establishing a working relationship within themselves.

Feds included, thought the murder of Danny "The Irishman" Greene was greatly overdue. A crime of tremendous proportions was in their laps: and they wondered who it was that finally succeeded in this crime.

While the authorities were trying to figure this out, Ray was planning his return trip to Cleveland where he had his date with destiny. Finally after all these years, his due diligence to the cause and brotherhood, he was going to be "made."

CHAPTER 21

"Gentlemen, we are here today with our family – and now you, Raymond Ferritto…you have entered into our most private and honorary society of "La Cosa Nostra", that which welcomes only men of great courage, conviction and loyalty. You come in alive and you go out dead," rattled Licavoli in sonorous and serious tones.

"These instruments that lay before you are that which you live by. La Cosa Nostra is your life and comes before anything else. If and when you are summoned, you will appear before us. There are rules you will obey, and never betray our secrets in La Cosa Nostra. You will never indulge in or become involved in narcotics. You will never violate the wife or children of another member. If you do violate any of our laws, the punishment is death – without warning."

Licavoli then directed the newly "made man" to raise his right hand and the old mob boss fumbled as he nicked Ray's index finger with sharp tip of a sword that lay before him ceremonially crossed over a gun. "This blood symbolizes your birth into our great family. We are as one until death," finalized the old mobster.

Fratianno was also there and the second to congratulate his friend for his newfound status. Ray marveled at the whole formality of it all. He proudly walked around the ornate table, shaking hands, accepting congratulations and receiving kisses on the cheeks, from the aging Mafiosi kingpins.

Licavoli, the important mafia boss was amused and boisterous at this symbolic ritual that he just performed. Sipping his homemade wine, he laughed and joked saying they needed to do this more often to keep up with the rest of the families and recruit more soldiers.

But only hours before Ray had arrived for this glorious event, Licavoli held a closed door, meeting and the topic was mainly "murder." He motioned that Ray Ferritto be eliminated and the rest followed suit in support of the proposal. Yes indeed…"The man of the hour" was up for dead before he got to the party.

It wasn't anything personal. The greedy gangsters had been silent between themselves and adamant from the "get go" that no one would receive compensation for Greene's murder, nor would they give up a piece of their territory to anyone…let alone "an outsider."

Unbeknownst to Ray, he and the sanctity of La Cosa Nostra were deliberately placed in the center of this "mock" celebration strictly designed to pacify the new kid on the block.

So, while Ray's thoughts were a million miles away on how he was going to incorporate his new turf with the old, the unappreciative brazen band of mobsters had their sights on killing him. It was just simpler to have Ray whacked.

Little did any of them know that Ray's lifelong "loyalty" to them, wasn't going to last. He would soon have the last laugh at the old crew and personally crucify every mobster sitting at that table.

They let Ray leave that night for non-other than their own self- preservation and unwanted heat with the death of another soldier so soon after Greene's demise. They'd wait until things cooled off.

Ray drove the two-hour trip back home categorizing thoughts in his head and organizing his future plans. He was on a natural high envisioning himself with his newfound status. He was even more anxious to extend this windfall to the Ameche 13.

The feds on the other hand were quickly coming up to speed with clues of their own for Greene's untimely death. Within moments, of the bombing, a couple claimed they were driving up on the aftermath and could identify the fleeing culprits.

Allegedly, they spotted the two thought it was strange seeing one man driving the car and the other sitting in the back instead of both sitting in the front. When they realized the men were speeding from the explosion site, they wondered...could this be coincidence?

The young couple was Craig and Evy Spother, daughter and son-in-law of Armen Tolpe, a Berea police detective. Evy just happened to be a police sketch artist and she immediately drew a picture of the driver and jotted down the license plate numbers.

After showing her father the sketch and the plate numbers, he quickly pulled out Ray's mug shot from his police files. He had recalled him from a different case in which he was currently working on.

The authorities were thrilled with this find. All they needed now was some corroboration that Ray was in Ohio on the same day that the Irishman was assassinated. The task force had already been in place for John Nardi's killing, investigating a slew of the mob murders and the most recent car bombing attacks...but Greene's case was about to take on a life of its own.

As the feds reconstructed the "Joe Blow" car, they were able to trace the inspection sticker back to the garage in Erie. Further investigation led them to the name "Guy Mitchell, thus linking this person as Ray's friend and his address in Erie.

They discovered that the Plymouth was originally registered in Ohio through the vehicle identification number and the Chevy Nova's charred license plate was in sequence with the former Ohio and Pennsylvania registrations. It tied them to the very car the Spother's supposedly witnessed fleeing from the crime.

There it was in black and white…the confirmation they needed for the search warrant. On the chilly fall morning, Ray happened to be out having breakfast with the guys when Police chief Arnold Smith and Lieutenant Ward Vegas from Lyndhurst served the warrant at his home in Erie. His girl-friend answered the door and let the authorities sift through the house and car that was left parked in the driveway. To their amazement and delight they found just enough evidence needed to issue an arrest warrant.

Danno Adolph had picked up Ray forty-five minutes prior to Smith and Vegas arriving at the home on Greengarden Boulevard. The unsuspecting mobster was having coffee with his crew at Nick Filia's restaurant on West 18th Street when the phone rang. Nick turned to Ray and said, "It's, for you." It was Cy on the other end calling from Pittsburgh. He was in there for a meeting that weekend when the call came in for a contract on Ray's head.

"Ray, this is bad. The feds are on their way to your house with a warrant and Cleveland has a contract out on you. It's an open contract man…you got to get the fuck out of there!"

"What!" Ray stammered. He was stunned and confused for a moment. "This ain't no fucking joke, Ray…You're friends in Cleveland *set you up* for this. You gotta go. Get a hold of me in a few days…I'll see what I can find out."

He knew he had to move fast. And, of all the days, he didn't have his car. Without alerting the crew that was there was trouble, he went to the end of the breakfast bar and called Bolo.

"Bolo, pick me up in fifteen minutes on 23rd and Chestnut. We got a problem...come alone!" Unnoticed, Ray left through the back door and fled on foot a few blocks and through the Erie cemetery where he dodged around headstones until he reached 23rd Street.

As Bolo slowly drove along the side street looking for his partner, Ray jumped out from behind the hedges that lined the graveyard and hopped into the car.

"What's all this cloak and dagger shit?" Bolo questioned. "Just go!"

Ray blurted. "The fuckin cops are on their way to my house and Cy called telling me Cleveland's gone crazy and I got hits out on me. Take me to the Western Motel and get me a fuckin room 'til I can figure out what the fuck is goin on."

Bolo drove to the motel on the outskirts of town where he registered a room for Ray under an assumed name. There they could try and make some sense out of what was happening.

Hold up in the motel room, Ray was fit to be tied. Everything was crashing down around him and there was nothing he could do but rely on Cy to get the skinny for him. Or so he thought.

After pacing a hole in the motel room floor he sat down and turned on the television for a distraction when the evening news came on.

There it was for the world to hear. Danny "The Irishman" Greene's killer, sought on the run. Rays old mug shot plastered all over the screen. He sat for a moment in disbelief. The anchor described the chaotic Cleveland mess as the authorities claimed their number one most wanted mob assassin Raymond W. Ferritto was armed and dangerous. Blindsided by the newscast, he almost fell out of his chair.

CHAPTER 22

———◦———

Inevitably, the moment every hit man, henchman or mob associate dreaded was here. Ray was clearly at the end of his rope. But the rage that consumed him wasn't going to let him go down without a fight. He had come too far in his life for it to end here. With the massive manhunt and mob-style witch-hunt underway, he'd drastically take them all on.

He snuck out of the room to a nearby telephone booth in the dark of the night and luckily caught Cy at the club.

"Ray, this is worse than we thought," barked Cy. "The whole fuckin world's looking for ya! Jesus Christ, Ray, your picture is in all the fuckin newspapers half way across the country!"

"What the fuck did you find out," Ray snapped back.

"It's true Ray. The way I got it is that these Cleveland pricks had this all planned all along. You were their fall guy. And, the fuckin feds say they got evidence from your house, man...I got that from our people on the inside. You know that broad that's working in the Pittsburgh field office. And your nephew Joey, fucked up Ray. I hate to tell you that. He never got rid of that car paperwork like he was supposed to."

By this time, Ray was one raw nerve. "Look man I'm not runnin...and if that's the case, I'm gonna hit those fuckin Cleveland pricks head on. I'm goin to shake some people up first and if for some reason, I don't come back, tell everybody to do what they gotta' do. Tell my family I'm okay right now."

One way to take the bull by its horns was going to be "Ferritto style." Even, if he got whacked doing it. At this point he took Bolo's car and headed south for a face to face with the crew from Pittsburgh before he turned himself in.

With his doom hovering in the wind, he prepared himself for anything when he boldly walked into the Italian club. Three familiar faces at the bar were dumbstruck at the sight of him slowly approaching bar.

He stopped dead in his tracks and coldly stared around the room to a familiar face. "Hey Benny...I need to see the boss." In response, the gangster looks at the other two and then looks back at Ray. "I'll see if he's in. Have a seat."

Still in a bit of shock at the nerve of his presence, all eyes remained on Ray until Benny returned. "Follow me," he said to Ray. And he led Ray into the back room.

"Hey Ray. Long time...no see. I hear you got yourself in some trouble lately." "They set me up, Sam...I'm getting fucked by those Cleveland pricks. I understand they got contracts out on me and I can't believe I made it this far without being caught by the fuckin feds. They got my picture out all over the place."

"Sam cracked a cock-eyed smile and grunted...well, I ain't gonna kill ya...those fuckers in Ohio don't like to pay. He jokingly laughed. Ray still on edge wasn't laughing and not yet relieved because he knew he'd never see it coming anyway. "You always did have balls kid...never saw 'em any bigger. Just figure a way to keep our action goin and I got your back!"

"That's just it Sam. I had to look in your eye myself and tell you no matter what happens, you and the rest don't have to worry about me. The Ameche 13 is still in operation and you were always good to me. I gotta return that. I only know what I heard on the street and if it's true...I'm gonna bury 'em Sam. I did them a big favor and if they want me dead...I gotta strike back."

"Appreciate the gesture Ray. I don't know about the others, but I'm not gonna let those sloppy fuckers kill our payday? But, it's your call. Good luck to ya." Feeling trapped between both worlds, he chose the lesser of the two evils and surrendered a day later to the FBI at their headquarters in Pittsburgh.

His submission to the authorities would serve several purposes. First it would save him from being shot on sight by the law, secondly it would save him from a mob hit temporarily and lastly it would give him time to get to the truth before any more real damage was done.

Ray absolutely floored the feds when he walked through their doors claiming "I'm Ray Ferritto...the man you're looking for." Agents sprung up from their chairs trying not to look surprised. "Frisk him," one agent ordered. Ray put his hands in the air and quietly said. "I'm not armed...I'd like to speak with your man in charge." They immediately shuffled him into an interrogation room, while another, phoned their chain of command in disbelief.

The outstanding warrant had to be dealt with and Ray waited for the drill. Special Agent Thomas Fitzgerald, the Pittsburgh office's man in charge of the arrest, walked in the room and introduced himself. He politely asked. "Ray what can you tell us about the Greene murder?"

"I don't know what you're talking about," Ray smoothly replied. "Okay, you do understand we're charging you with the bombing death of Daniel Greene," stated Fitzgerald. The formal process began when Ray's rights were rattled off to him. Bingo! Those were the words Ray was waiting to hear. It provided him a level of safety in their custody and legally prevented the feds to question him any further without his attorney being present.

This bought him time to get to the bottom of things while he planned his defense. The authorities were totally unprepared for Ray's first bout and it showed.

Several hours later he was being transported over to the Ohio Federal Bureau. Even so, during the long three-hour drive to FBI headquarters, Ray was baffled and a thousand questions raced through his mind wreaking havoc on his somewhat imperiled constitution. He was shocked that this was coming down so fast.

He had been in this business all his life and knew that the speed of this legal process and investigation was escalating far too rapidly. To him it meant that someone definitely, "dropped a dime."

But as the recent "made man" was put through weeks of constant interrogation, Agent Fitzgerald trying to befriend Ray had slipped his business card into his shirt pocket saying, "You're gonna need this when you come to your senses."

Ray held his ground and kept silent as he learned that a witness described him and another man leaving the scene. But in his mind it still didn't add up. He remained unbending as he tried putting the pieces of the puzzle in place.

CHAPTER 23

Confinement under heavy guard in the Cuyahoga County Jail highly exceeded even the most dangerous of prisoners. This spoke volumes to Ray about the degree in which they were "protecting him" rather than only incarcerating him. Completely isolated, he had no way of getting information other than what the feds were feeding him.

Finally, Fitzgerald decided to "open up" with Ray in an effort to strike a deal. But Ray still wasn't going for it. Fitzgerald looked him dead in the eye and unloaded. "Ray, they're going to kill you! The contract has been on the street since the day they "made you" and I think the time is right for you to help us out. We can protect you. We want you prepared for this."

When Fitzgerald reiterated there was a mob contract out, it infuriated Ray. He pushed it out of his head for a moment. He was all too familiar with how the feds use these tactics to pit everyone against each other. Up to that point he was certain his only problem was Evy Spother for fingering him.

A thinker above all else, he had to be sure in his mind. Even though Cy had told him so, he didn't want to believe it. He'd stayed silent up to that point: the mobsters had to know he would never give them up he thought to himself. He would at least take his punishment from the authorities and do his time like a man. Just, as he had done so many times before.

Short of torture, they couldn't break him. In a last ditch attempt to force Ray's hand at cutting cut a deal, a desperate Fitzgerald brought the whole scenario to a grinding halt for Ray, finally laying the pieces of the puzzle in front of him.

Fitzgerald produced the original registration cards that were found hidden underneath the stairwell carpeting in Ray's home. Worse, they informed Ray that they had his nephew Joey in custody.

He was a novice at the game and thought his uncle would have liked the registration cards as a souvenir from the contract killing. Joey wasn't as tough as his uncle was and couldn't stand up to the scrutiny from the feds. He folded under the pressure.

Ray wanted to kill his nephew for the stupidity, but then blamed himself for pulling Joey into the game. He resigned himself to the thought of making a deal for Joey's sake and thought he'd quietly take the fall and "do" the time in exchange for Joey's freedom.

However, the worst of it came last when the agents allowed Ray to sit in the interrogation room for hours on end listening to wire tapped phone conversations about the contracts on Greene, Nardi and the other co-conspirators from Cleveland. Ray heard Licavoli, Delsanter, Lonardo and union official Tony Liberatore, on several different tapes.

The voices were clear. Ray listened attentively and he understood Licavoli to say, "We want Ferritto executed after he's done with Nardi, Greene and the two henchmen, Ritson and McTaggert. We'll "make him" first to appease the bastard...then do what we gotta do."

But the final and most painful blow was when he heard Jimmy Fratianno, of all the people, suggesting that they only "set him up" to take the fall. "He's a standup guy...I guarantee he won't talk if you guys pave the way for him to get grabbed for this. He'll do the time...you boys get to keep your territory and you can throw his family a few bones while he's in the joint. He'll never know what happened." Ray cringed to know Jimmy sat there, most likely chewing on his cigar bargaining for Ray's life.

At one point in the tapes, Licavoli responds with "what the fuck, the guy is takin advantage of the situation...he's askin for too much. We had to promise him anything just to whack these guys. We can't lose all that action. Do you have any idea how much fuckin' money we'd be losing? We'll just clip him when it's all over. That's the safest way to go right now."

He heard it, "straight from the horse's mouth" so to speak. They had set him up completely, blatantly and intentionally. There was no more room to worry about Evy Spother either, as was thought earlier.

Was she part of the set up? Now, it seemed "strange" to Ray that this woman who coincidentally happened to be a sketch artist just happened to drive by at that moment and of all the cars on the thruway and with all the commotion from the blast that she would pick that particular time to glance at passing cars? Furthermore, take the time to remember the license plate? C'mon Ray, he thought to himself. For a moment his mind reverted to Joey. He realized that was his own error in judgments for getting his nephew involved too.

With his guts silently churning inside he continued to listen to them laughing while scheming his demise and plotting against other enemies. They all knew Ray was hungry for power and equally as greedy for more territory and the millions it would bring in. Then there was the night they silently "mocked" him getting made.

First and foremost the old men had underestimated him and then insulted his intelligence. This was the one thing that Ray was not going to tolerate. Fitzgerald then proceeded to tell Ray the feds were going for the death penalty in the state of Ohio and without a doubt that would be his game changer.

Shock gave way to vitriolic anger at the thought of his own supposed beloved mafia family inciting such treacherous acts towards him. Now it was nothing but a full blown, barbaric betrayal. Rage and hatred began permeating every fiber of his being. He'd take revenge…if, it was the last thing he ever did.

He wanted to kill each one of them with his bare hands... but such an opportunity wasn't afforded to him. There was no freedom, nor weapons at his disposal. He entertained thoughts of doing his time then killing them when he got out. But, without his testimony, there would be no escaping the electric chair at the other end.

Even if he did somehow elude the fate of the state's execution, for the length of time he was looking at, they all would have been or in nursing homes or already dead before he had the luxury of taking them out.

Embattled by the complicated situation before him, he decided to make the feds an offer they couldn't refuse. Ray, an assassin scorned, sat there stone faced and ready to hang every mob boss and underboss that conspired to clip him. Their highly orchestrated plan was backfiring.

Ray was always resourceful and did the next best thing and struck his deal. First he wanted his children protected from any mob retaliation. Secondly, he demanded freedom for his nephew Joey and Bolo. And lastly his own bit of freedom so that he could put his personal affairs in order before any of the trials commenced.

The feds were more than happy to oblige him with the exception of releasing him. In no way, shape or form was their golden goose going to get out from under their protection.

Not only did they fear he'd be killed within mere days, but perhaps he'd be crazy enough to take his revenge to the streets of Cleveland.

Bargaining with other people's fate was as easy as that. Everyone has their price and the feds were no different.

However, in lieu of the tradeoff for refusing a bit of freedom, Ray insisted that he be put on the phone with Licavoli. Only after that he would start skewering the Cleveland chieftains with his insider knowledge at trials. Cornered and seething with revolt, he let the mind games begin.

CHAPTER 24

———————◆———————

"Hey, Jack...this is Ray Ferritto." Without pausing, the incredibly slick Licavoli on the other end of the phone coolly answered. "What's up Ray? I heard you got a headache." In response, Ray's face grew beet red and in what started out as a low slow venomous tone, instantly turned ugly.

"You think I got a headache? After I did you the biggest favor of your fuckin' lives...and you cocksuckers wanna kill me! You think you had a fuckin' headache with Nardi and Greene? Wait 'til I get done with you ...you, cocksuckers...

I'll fuckin wipe you pricks off the map! Merry Christmas you fuckin prick! FUCK YOUR LA COSA NOSTRA!"

It's all he could get out before Fitztgerald blurted out, "Stop Ray...he's gone...he hung up. He got the gist of it."

Still fuming, he slammed down the receiver, as the feds prepared to whisk him away back into protective custody. On the long drive to the Chicago authorities for safekeeping, he focused on the Cleveland bastards rotting in hell. All of them! Then afterward, he relished the thought of knowing that they'd spend the rest of their lives being humiliated and haunted with daily reminders of his curse, powerless to retaliate and most importantly, stripped of their freedom. A quick painless death would have been too good for them. And with that, there came a sense of satisfaction. They had indeed betrayed the wrong man and they were going to pay dearly.

In his own retaliation against the old crew...Ray would show them what it really was, to be an assassin scorned!

Not one of them would be safe from Ferritto's terrible wrath; every mob boss, under boss, lieutenant and Teamster, and most of all, Jimmy Fratianno were all in for the ride of their lives.

Even though he was hell bent on this path of destruction Ray always liked to think of himself as a strategist of sorts and now was the time to use these skills wisely. He thought long and hard on how he was going to proceed with destroying the infamous "Gang who couldn't shoot straight," without disturbing the long line of those in his past that had always been reputable with him.

He knew his days were numbered. That's just how it was.

But, it mattered to him to separate the massive tangled web of mobsters and maintain some measure of honor amongst those whom he felt didn't deserve to be in the cross hairs. And, did he think he was intelligent enough to outsmart the feds?

He first had to come to grips with the tags, "flipping", "informer" and "government witness." He hated those words and what they stood for. He struggled to think he had gotten to this point and wondered if his actions were justified. Regardless... the crew had deceived him first and deserved everything that was coming their way.

If nothing else, he thought it would at least serve as an eye opener to the other families. At the risk of death and being labeled a turncoat, Ray was going to exploit them for what they really were to the rest of the organization. He was certain that the honorable families would condemn the Cleveland's chieftains for the "mob misfits" they really were.

In his mind the old band of gangsters were "dead"...or should be dead, to the order of their entire organization. Since when did they think, the right to abuse this "Sacred oath of Omerta" only belonged to them?

Accordingly, the self-admitted assassin plunged in head first revealing the largest scope of confidential dealings the feds had heard in over a century. Their golden boy produced a priceless, endless list of criminal acts ranging from petty larceny, jewelry heists, loan-sharking, gambling, extortion, bombings, drugs, to hate-filled murder plots and straight out assassinations at the hands of Licavoli and his associates.

Ray's confession became so complicated that even the

authorities were confused. It took weeks for transcripts to be typed out while the feds tried to decipher the slew of information and charge the staggering amount of characters that were involved. Oddly enough, through it all, Ray managed to confine his "line of fire" to the Cleveland crew, omitting or denying the secret sins of his old respected allies from days gone by.

He struck the first blow with his signature on the confession and started the ball rolling. Murder indictments rolled down the pike for Jimmy Fratianno, Jack "White Licavoli, Ron Carabba, Butchie Cisternino, Allie Calabrese, John Calandra Thomas Sinito, Tony Liberatore, Ange Lonardo, Carmen Marconi, Louis Atari, Vic Guiles, Kenneth Ciarcia and Thomas Lanci. And that was only the beginning of it.

As each one tried to save their own skin, they too would "flip" on yet other criminal conspirators. Jimmy Frattianno came in second to Ray when it came to "flipping" and gave up mob bosses that dated back almost fifty years.

The feds were practically dancing in the streets in celebration at one of the largest takedowns in mob history. One by one, and two by two, they were picking up bosses on everything from conspiracy to murder charges and dealing with corrupt organizations.

The press scrambled for the stories and the public was getting a "peek" into the heart of this nation's most elite criminal outfit. They couldn't get enough of the mob's downfall and desecration. Some Cleveland mobsters were caught on the run, while others were in disbelief and thought they were untouchable.

While Ray had concentrated solely on the Cleveland faction, Jimmy was targeting the New York and California crews. Jimmy alone had enough evidence to put the entire bunch of them behind bars, which kept that proverbial ball rolling until not one Mafioso, across the country could sleep. According to FBI records, Ray and Jimmy were the first "made men" ever to testify in open court against such a multitude of their fellow gangsters.

Mob bosses and their soldiers were turning on each other so much that it would literally prompted the authorities to reopen dozens of unsolved murders nationwide submerging themselves in cases that the paperwork would never even see the light of day. It was pure unstoppable madness and mayhem amongst the criminal underground and no one was safe.

CHAPTER 25

From the beginning, the brutal gang wars and the Danny Greene murder case had been entirely overwhelming to the feds, the prosecution, the defense and even the multiple juries. Each consisted of a dozen normal people and certainly not a judging committee of the defendant's peers. The twelve individuals must have been dumb struck after listening to what sounded to be more like a movie script, rather than the mundane lifestyles that they were leading.

Yet, they were forced to sit there, view ghastly photos of twisted and bloodied corpses, listen and make decisions about these horrendous killers, henchmen and mob bosses. Certainly, it was a lifestyle that they could really never comprehend.

At times, jurors seemed terrified to be in the same room with these mobsters even with the dozens of FBI agents and federal marshals guarding their golden geese.

That would sometimes serve as Ray's amusement when he became bored in the courtroom. It didn't really matter what the jurors thought of him as he already had his free pass. He was the star witness and not the one on trial. Consequently, he was still custody as he recalled it. They never kept him at the same safe house for long. They moved around him constantly between trials and the feds were the ones calling it the witness protection program.

Ray readied himself for the long haul. With pure vengeance in his heart, round after round, he would deliver his pointed confessions. With daggers in his eyes he'd rehash the same old maniacal wars stories until he felt a sense of absolute satisfaction pulse through his veins. Even though it was maddening at times, he took pleasure in watching them squirm helplessly.

The prosecutors were relentless and the attorneys battled to stay on top of game. Most of the time the defendants either sat stone faced or huddled with their counsel trying hard to defuse the multiple testimonies. Others appeared elusive as the long line of government witnesses revealed the private inner workings of the so-called elite group.

What Ray didn't reveal to the feds, Fratianno and the rest,

did. Their game was on and they were generating terror into the very heart of La Cosa Nostra.

Ray and Jimmy never crossed paths during the trials, but they were paraded in and out of the courtrooms, flanked by dozens of U.S. marshals with high-powered weapons, protected as if, they were Fort Knox.

Ray gave the feds exactly what they needed to put the bunch away and no more. As a matter of fact, on two separate occasions he tried to get his friend Carabba off the hook. But, there was too much evidence to the contrary and they caught him in some lies. They warned Ray, if he twisted his testimony that their deal was off. He knew "that in itself" was a lie. There was no way in hell they were letting the goose that laid the golden egg go anywhere.

Jimmy was a different story. If he couldn't remember the incidents he'd make one up. They couldn't shut him up to save their lives so they had to be careful with him. For the most part he stuck to his guns, determined to see everyone go down. He figured his life after this mess was going to be a safe haven of retirement in some balmy weather out west. He was looking forward to it.

The trials hadn't gone as well as the feds expected but they had managed to put away the Cleveland leadership for starters. And, the old saying goes...when you cut off the head the rest of the body shall die.

The complications surrounding the circumstances were at times and to say the least, working itself around the edges. The feds still had a few crooks to rein in and were organizing their last bout that had been coming up on year three.

Ray was now living "incognito" in Minnesota and calling himself, "Ray Marciano." A new identity, complete with a brand new social security number and driver's license was generously handed over to him. He refused it but it was part of the agreement from the onset. Ray wasn't free of them just yet. He was still at the helm and waiting for the last of the trials.

But just as he thought this nightmare was almost over, Fitzgerald informed him he'd have to continue testifying in other court actions against outside associates with no ties to the Cleveland faction. Ray balked at the thought and sternly refused. The trials weren't going as well as the feds had hoped towards the end and there were mobsters slipping through the cracks.

Ray was satisfied with the convictions and sentences of all who conspired against his life, so the feds reluctance to release him from further testimony became his winning argument. "I kept my end of our bargain and you have to release me. That was the deal!" Ray's attorney proved that the feds had broken their plea agreement by extending other unforeseen trials and Ray was legally pulling the plug. He was taking matters into his own hands and told the authorities he was walking away.

Fitzgerald yelled. "No one walks away from something like this Ray. Have you lost your mind! There is going to be a dozen Mafiosi gunning for you and they are going to kill you!"

Ray didn't care. "They want me? Let them come after me. I'm ready and as capable of handling myself as the person they're sending after me. You live by the sword...you die by the sword. I'd be foolish to think anything else...and for the record...I'm taking my birth name back."

CHAPTER 26

He was living on sheer determination and like any wise gambler Ray always had an ace up his sleeve. He braced himself for the worst when he boldly took his hometown community by surprise.

Both local and national media saturated the public with news of his three-year rampage throughout the Greene trials. And, the people of Erie were mortified when they learned he was back.

The self-admitted hit man was back on the streets, full of spit and polish and as his old crew would describe "with balls of steel." In spite of his tainted reputation as being dubbed a rat in the public's eye, he maintained a calm and circumspect presence upon his return.

He had definite plans for the future and wasn't going to let the rest of his mob associates deal him out just yet. During the Greene trials, Bolo served as Ray's right arm and acting partner for all gaming operations. "The Ameche crew had no qualms about Bolo taking charge as long as they continued to rake in their six-figure profits. In the name of greed every one of them turned a blind eye to Ray's dilemma with the Cleveland associates. They indeed made millions over the years and were still collecting just as Ray promised them.

Ray could never be certain that there wouldn't be any retaliation for what he had done. Or for that matter, worry that another wise guy would be gunning for him for the sake of making their bones with the outfit. But he was prepared for anything.

What he did do was step up to the plate again. He vied assurance for his life with those who were benefitting in the grand scheme of things. In a calm deliberate tone, he preceded to call each one of them to let them know he was back.

"This is Ray Ferritto and I'm calling about my life and our futures. Now, you can try and kill me for testifying against those Cleveland pricks that wanted me dead, or we can continue business as usual." He paused. "Frankly, I don't even want you to answer that right now. I'll give you two weeks to think about it and in the meantime the games are shut down effective immediately. I'll call you in fourteen days."

Bolo was panic-stricken with Ray's decision to stop the

action. Knowing full well how much money they'd stand to lose in those weeks or worse yet...their lives. But, Ray was a man with nothing to lose and it was the only way to get their attention. He wanted them to understand the power he held in the gaming arena.

In those short weeks, without access to the giant web of connections the members were floundering. They were still running their own local betting systems, but could never reach the pay scale that Ray had them at financially. That, along with the realization of the Cleveland capos infighting and dissension amongst the other families was all it took for Ray to once again respectfully regain control of his domain.

This was huge. It would be the first time ever that anyone was permitted to walk away from their own death sentence. With these sanctions, he was back in the loop again, and the enormity of his leverage spoke volumes to him and other high-ranking gangsters.

Never in his wildest dreams did he ever think anyone, let alone his self could go so far as to cripple an entire leadership and walk away totally unscathed. That was just unheard of in the La Cosa Nostra. Then again, everyone understood it was indeed always about "the money." You never threaten the mafia's income or bite the hand that feeds you.

Relieved and anxious to get the game up and running again, he and Bolo resumed all sports betting activities within a record two day time period.

The first week of January, only three weeks into the renewed venture, Ray and Cy had some last minute telephone calls from two coaches in the Los Angeles area, when it caused them to run late picking up Bolo at his home.

Arriving at Bolo's house on West 21st Street, Ray noticed his Cadillac wasn't parked in the driveway and the front door was mysteriously ajar. Both men instinctively knew something was very wrong. Bolo was always extremely mindful of safety measures, particularly when so much was at stake and this was something he would never do.

They entered the Cape Cod, style home and saw everything in disarray. Cautiously, they scoured their way through when they spotted the basement door wide open. With his pistol drawn, Ray lead the way down the old wooden steps to discover Bolo's corpse bound to a chair, with half of his head blown off and blood spattered brain matter everywhere.

"Jesus Christ...he's fuckin' dead," hollered Ray. The two mobsters took a moment to get their senses together. Their first impulse was to see if the sports book and the money had been stolen.

Fortunately the murderers didn't find either. The book was recovered from inside the wall of the stove and hundreds of thousands of dollars lined in a fake furnace vent still neatly arranged as Bolo and Ray left them. However, they couldn't find one of the safety deposit keys for the two separate drawers at a local bank. There was a few hundred thousand for petty cash split between each box. Bolo had one box and Ray kept the other.

Ray's mind was going in a thousand different directions. He was totally at a loss for this brutal execution. Who could have done this? Why? Was it meant for all of them or was

Bolo a single target? Was this an oncoming death threat to warn Ray of his future fate? Was it a contract for him gone wrong? Or was it one of the Ameche partners trying to take over?

Still recuperating from his highly publicized three year, long involvement with the Danny Greene murder case, he had trouble believing what was happening. It felt as though lighting was striking him twice.

Nevertheless, he was determined to have some control over the situation when the authorities were called in. He knew that he and Cy would be suspect because of their close relationship.

The two stashed the goods taken from Bolo's house and then called an old boyhood friend that was now a detective with the local police force. Within an hour, the crooked cop, better known as Detective Frank Rinaldi met with Ray and Cy to discuss how it should be handled and the detective would be the one to call it in.

But no matter what, they were in up to their eyeballs. The scene that swiftly followed was utter chaos. The coroner appeared, assisted by dozens of police and agents crawling all over the house and grounds.

The guys were taken to the station where they were both questioned long into the night. They were released early the next morning with no more knowledge about the slaying than they first detected on their initial find.

Once word hit the street about Bolo's unfortunate demise the rumors began to surface that there was a power struggle brewing between the local smalltime bookies. Since the beginning of time they've competed for a bigger chunk of the change. That was nothing new.

Ray however, had a hard time believing that one of the local racketeers would have had the balls go this far. But, in spite of who massacred Bolo, he knew it would once again throw him into the spotlight. The last place he wanted to be.

CHAPTER 27

S trangely enough, this is where I finally enter the picture. On Friday, January 7th, 1983, I was on my way to Orlando's Funeral Parlor on 22nd and Raspberry Street to pay my last respects to an old friend: Bolo Dovishaw.

The poor bastard, I thought to myself. He was only 46 years old, and nobody deserves to die like that. But, the tragedy was still a mystery to everyone, and like everyone else I only knew what I read in the newspapers.

To my knowledge, Bolo was just another neighborhood, numbers racketeer and it seemed that I had known him forever. It was a casual, relationship and he would often send a drink to my table when I saw him out socially. He was always considerate, quiet and mostly stayed to himself. In some circles, he was better known as "Ash Wednesday" for the strawberry birthmark in the center of his forehead. I shuddered to think how his last hours must have been.

As I pulled my car up in the front of the funeral parlor, I couldn't help but notice there wasn't a soul anywhere in sight. The undertaker wasn't even standing at his usual spot in the foyer and for a moment I thought I was at the wrong funeral parlor.

Curiously, I strolled through heading towards the main viewing room when I heard voices coming from a small social room adjacent to the large reception area.

Glancing in, I spotted Cy and another gentleman in conversation. Cy looked up and grinned at me with his infectious smile. "Susie…

C'mon in. Long time no see honey; how ya been?" he asked politely.

Relieved to see a familiar face, I blurted out, "Where in the hell is everybody?" Cy quickly responded, "Well, the fuckin feds are outside takin pictures of everybody coming in here. They're scarin people off!" He paused in disgust for a moment then shook it off with an invitation to join them. "C'mon in and talk to us for a while."

This was wrong on so many levels. Poor Bolo should have had a packed funeral parlor for all the neighborhood wise guys, associates and relatives he had known in his life. However up to that point there were just the three of us.

Indulging in light pleasantries, Cy noticed that the

conversation was mainly between him and I, and spoke up. "What'sa matter? You two guys mad at each other?"

I didn't know the gentleman sitting with him, but I certainly wanted to. There was an instant attraction between us and the feeling was definitely mutual. We could barely keep our eyes off of each other.

"No," I replied. "We've never been introduced." Looking a little puzzled by my answer, Cy said, "You're fucking kidding me! How can you two come from the same neighborhood and not know each other? Okay...now you're pullin my leg."

Ray grinned. "You're the girl who wouldn't dance with me at the Calabrese Club." "Oh, my lord", I said. "That was like ten years ago. How could you possibly remember something like that?"

He smiled back. "I never forget a face...especially, one like yours."

"And he's a sucker for a tall redhead," Cy chimed in. "Ray this is Nunzi's daughter." Ray's eyebrow's rose up slightly and he apologetically said, I'm sorry...I should have known that. Your dad and I have been friends since we were kids. I've been away from the neighborhood for a while and friends just seem to get away from each other." He stood up to shake my hand. "I'm Ray Ferritto...it's my pleasure." At that moment I realized who he was.

He had a quiet, reserved mannerism about him, which didn't at all match the description of the highly publicized ruthless mob enforcer that I had heard so much about.

The three of us reminisced a little about the neighborhood and mutual friendships. As it turned out, my dad had also been part of that neighborhood rat pack back in the day. But while Ray and Cy went off to make their bones in the criminal world, my father, Frank "Nunzi" DeSantis, became the sports editor for the Erie Times Newspaper.

Mourners were finally beginning to arrive and I decided to leave for my prior engagement. Ray politely walked me to the front entrance and turned to me. "Things are kind of crazy for me right now. But, I'd like to see you sometime. When all of this is over, do you think maybe we could get together for dinner?"

I pulled a pen from my purse and wrote my phone number in the palm of his hand. Sarcastically, I joked. "Sure kid, I can wait another two years till the feds clean this one up." But, instinctively, I knew this man was going to be a major part of my life.

The following afternoon, my phone rang. It was Ray with an invitation for coffee somewhere. "I don't think I can wait till the feds clean this one up" he joked. "I can't get you out of my head."

I was delighted and suggested my place. What he didn't tell me is that he was bringing a friend along.

His long-time friend "Peeps" was in town for Bolo's funeral and thought he'd tag along to "meet the tall redhead Ray was so crazy about."

The introductions were interesting. I learned that Peeps too had been in that very same rat pack and he indeed knew my family well. As a matter of fact it was my uncle, Armond DeSantis who had been arrested with them for robbing Dee Auditori's Cigar Store when they were kids.

The only difference between that crew and me was that we were a generation apart. And I wasn't about to let our age difference get in the way of a potential relationship.

They stayed for a few hours and over a pot of coffee as we discovered the numerous mutual acquaintances and relatives we shared before they had to return to the funeral parlor. It was if we had known each other for years. His parting words were music to my ears when he confirmed my initial thoughts as he invited me to have dinner with him after the funeral.

In the meantime, rumors of the trio and Bolo's gangland style murder were running rampant on the street and had everyone on edge...everyone, but me. Frankly, I found them and Ray, rather entertaining and now I was putting myself dead center.

CHAPTER 28

I'd be remiss if I didn't level the playing field here. Even though my generation had it slightly easier than Ray's, I was no stranger to the ongoing stigma of growing up in little Italy, too.

Before I was twelve, I thought everyone had racketeers in their family. As a child, I'd run to the corner grocer with my grandmothers list of daily numbers. She'd collect them from her friends and it was my job to deliver them. That was commonplace. I assumed that was how everyone supplemented their husband's meager paychecks from the foundries.

Contrary to its distinguishing reference I was dubbed, The

"Queen of 16ᵗʰ Street" …perhaps it was because I thought I owned the neighborhood. It wasn't my nickname, but more or less how my family had characterized me ever since I was a kid. I was the eldest of seven and perhaps a little spoiled to their standards.

By no means was I an angel. I learned at a young age that you had to hold your own. And, it showed.

My dreams were shaped around the glamorous screen stars and all that glittered. It was all I had to escape the reality of living below the tracks.

Much to my parent's shame and disgust, at the age of sixteen, I was labeled incorrigible and sent off to Waynesburg Correctional Facility for girls. When I returned home a year later I was worse off than when I went in. It had done more harm than good.

From there, my world was on a collision course. When the night life got out of control, there was a brief time when I thought settling down was in order. But, by the age of twenty-three, I was married only three years, raising two toddlers and signing my divorce papers.

Packing up the kids in my old station wagon, I set out for Las Vegas. My new freedom gave me a license to see how the other half lived. The men, the madness and the money were going to be my muse.

Sammy "Harpo" DeMonte, an old friend of the family took me under his wing. He opened doors for me that otherwise would have been out of my reach. He was a big shot Baccarat dealer at Caesar's Palace who had a lot of juice in Vegas.

Harpo made it easy for me to get calls to party with Alan

King, Frank Gorshen, singer Tom Jones and on occasion with a host of other celebrities. I dined with the likes of F. Lee Bailey, had the honor of meeting the gorgeous Elizabeth Taylor and my dear friend Joe "The Brown Bomber" Louis, the boxing legend who loved to sit with me over coffee and reminisce about his life.

I was living the life that the girls back home only fantasized about and I was good at it. Never ending wild parties, fabulous people and easy money were always just a phone call away.

One evening at Caesar's Palace, Jerry Wilson who had been eyeballing me from a distance, finally strolled over and invited me to a private party that was taking place upstairs in the Frank Sinatra suite. I couldn't refuse.

It was standing room only in this lavish suite. The music was blasting while the waitresses maneuvered their elegant silver trays through the crowd. They were loaded with enough pot and cocaine to kill an elephant. Jerry grabbed two glasses of champagne off of a tray then turned to introduce me his partners and hosts of the party, the Chagra brothers from El Paso, Texas.

Jerry was not shy in telling me that this powerful group of businessmen had brought in over 20,000 pounds of top Columbian weed in the past month. And, this grand party was in celebration of their future flight to Columbia for more. I just met the biggest drug smuggling kingpins this side of the Mexican border...better known as "The Dixie Mafia."

Jerry, a professional pilot for Jet Avia out of Las Vegas would often fly his partners around the globe for their ventures. Now, he was flying me to romantic dinners in L.A. and New York in his twin engine plane. How impressive was that. I had my own private pilot.

Our relationship blossomed rather quickly and Jerry divulged their secret missions to me to keep up the attraction.

I thought it was going to be just another leisurely flight for a quiet dinner somewhere, but Jerry couldn't seem to hold his excitement this particular day. He was eager to show me a surprise that he insisted would "make me flip."

As he slowly began descending, I had to ask him. "Where, in the hell are we?" It looked like pure open dried up desert as I scoured the desolate scenery below us.

He laughed, proudly stating, "We're in Ardmore, Oklahoma, baby and do I have a big beautiful bird to show you." We landed on what appeared to be an old abandoned airstrip next to a dusty humongous aging hangar in the middle of nowhere.

We deplaned, and he led me hand in hand over to the giant doors that housed his new pride and joy. I couldn't believe what I was looking at…but there it was…This giant, magnificent, DC-6 jetliner…in all its glory sitting there…empty. We climbed on board and he wanted me to sit in the cockpit for a minute and take it all in.

The rest of the jet had been stripped of its contents, passenger seats and all in preparation for its next adventure to Columbia. Jerry was so excited he could hardly contain himself as he spilled the details of the next mission.

The fact that I was really standing in the belly of that metal monster was absolutely mind-blowing.

I didn't quite understand the pilot lingo, but he tried his best to describe how they outlined their flight path across the border.

They planned on using a smaller aircraft flying directly below, to divert their radar signals and pass overhead piggyback style without notice. For a moment, I caught myself thinking how exciting all of this was. And in an instant I realized the insanity. But in the meantime, it was going to be another one of life's interesting adventure for me. I was never one to think about consequences and I wasn't about to start then.

As their plans were coming to fruition, Jerry decided that I should go back and lay low in Erie, until their mission was over and things cooled down.

He convinced me that after the haul, we'd have all the money we needed. He flew me to Erie the following week and as a parting gift, he handed me a duffle bag stuffed with cash. "This should keep you for a while and I'll call you every chance I get. Wish me luck."

As twisted as I was, I actually wished him luck before the morning of his take-off for Bogota.

Days had passed and I was concerned that I hadn't heard from him. To keep my mind off of things I turned on the television to hear the morning news.

I froze in my seat while I listened to the anchor describing a horrific plane crash somewhere in Columbia. He rambled off familiar names and something about drug trafficking. But my mind was in such shock I couldn't hear the entire scenario. My gut was telling me it was Jerry and the crew. What I did catch was that one of the pilots was killed in a fiery explosion. As mortified as I was there was nothing to do but wait.

Two weeks later the phone rang and it was Jerry on the other end. "Oh, my God, I screamed. "What the hell happened?" Are you okay? Is everyone else okay? Where are you?"

"Just listen. I'm okay but Alan's dead. It was horrible. We overloaded the plane and the jet couldn't take it. We had a hard time getting off the ground and then someone started firing at us. The next thing we heard was the explosion. God... there was fire everywhere and we started bailing out of the cockpit windows. Alan didn't make it and all I can remember is the smell of his burning flesh. It was awful.

The authorities corralled everyone up and we were in custody for a while waiting for an American Attorney to bail us out. You have enough money to keep you for a while so just stay put right where you're at until it blows over."

So, as I was slipping away from the Dixie Mafia, Ray was escaping the Cleveland Mafia. And oddly enough we found each other at Bolo's wake.

CHAPTER 29

As promised, Ray arrived precisely at eight o'clock to pick me up for dinner and drinks at the Buoy Restaurant on the water's edge.

His demeanor was totally out of character from the tough, cocky and vicious mafia killer the media had made him out to be. Their portrayal didn't even begin to sum up the multi-faceted, intriguing person he really was. We soon found that the more we talked, the more we had in common.

This quiet, soft-spoken and articulate gentleman having dinner with me couldn't have been further away from the wicked elements of the seedy underworld. And it was obvious he was thinking the same of me.

My life was complicated as well. I'm sure Cy had filled him in on my bad girl reputation around town and my stint in Vegas. After that, it was all in who he spoke to find out the other side of me. By day I was a mother and by night I was the dame about town.

However polite and socially sophisticated we appeared, we knew we weren't fooling each other.

In the middle of our dinner, there was no doubt he understood what I was all about and put it to me firmly. "Look Susan...let's not play games. I know your situation and you know mine. If you're uncomfortable being with me, I'll understand. But, I need you to know that you're the girl I've been looking for my whole life. And, if you think you can handle the pressure surrounding my world...I want you in it."

I was a little shocked at the swiftness of his intentions, but just as quickly I whispered back, "I'm a big girl Ferritto...If I thought for a minute I couldn't handle it...I wouldn't be here. Besides, how could I possibly refuse such a charming man?"

Our first date turned whirlwind romance overnight. The fact that we both were living the hard life, made our relationship seem more easy and natural to us.

I realized exactly what came with the territory when I hooked up with Ray. I even understood the danger with the possibility of death and never gave it a second thought.

He made it clear to me from the beginning that his attraction to me far outweighed any doubts he had about getting close to someone at this tumultuous time in his life and we were willing to take those risks.

Taking our relationship further meant being both lovers and friends, in addition to maintaining the freedom we both needed to survive. Whether it was the mob taking him out, the authorities taking him in, or other females taking him on, I knew I'd was in for the ride of my life. And if I got in the way…it would just be my bad luck.

We both had failed marriages behind us…Ray had adult children with their own families and my two were just turning into teenagers. Even though he was twenty-two years older than me, we shared the same identical traditional Italian background, with its accompanying friends, relatives, vino, and most often, our colorful turbulent lifestyles.

Almost a year had passed and our realities were far from any normalcy of ordinary individuals. We both lived the lives that most people only daydream about and could never comprehend.

In private, we were as much in love and affectionate as anyone else while in public we appeared to be the perfect couple. With his crew and associates, he was a tough skinned, outspoken capable racketeer and I maintained my pretentious, sophisticated but brassy image.

A year slipped by and I had become Bolo's silent replacement in the scheme of things and no one was the wiser. The police still hadn't charged anyone yet for Bolo's vicious murder and Cy was now on the lam. He didn't want to face the music on some pending burglary charges prior to Bolo's slaying and Hong Kong was the perfect hideout for him.

There was so much heat around Ray that we thought it was best I take the load off of him. After all... the cops were watching him...not me. We agreed that I would run all interference for him.

The feds were still scratching their heads wondering why Ray hadn't been killed yet out of retaliation for crucifying the Cleveland overlords. As much as they noticeably tailed him after he walked away from them and through Bolo's ongoing murder investigation, they never had a clue what was keeping him alive and thriving. This seemed to irritate them to no end.

Unaccustomed to watching anyone survive the mob in this manner, the feds would have never believed he had the remarkable luck or as Ray defined it; his leverage.

Of course, the authorities assumed Ray and Cy conspired to have Bolo iced. But that couldn't have been further from the truth. Bolo's death was a great loss to them and had definitely thrown a monkey wrench into their business ventures. They too had been baffled over his death and wanted someone to answer for this crime. No one was anywhere near closing in on the real culprits, let alone a motive.

Christmas finally arrived and it was the height of football season where the Ameche crew made the bulk of their fortunes every year. I was getting ready to make my usual phone calls to some football locker rooms in Los Angeles. I was preparing to pass on the detailed information for the upcoming games when I received a call with the news that my father had passed away.

He had been recuperating from some complications from

bypass surgery at St. Vincent's Hospital. I had visited him the night before and he said was feeling good and preparing to come home in a few days. So the news came as a devastating shock.

In a panic, I called several places to find Ray. I finally phoned Dominick's Restaurant where he was having coffee with the guys. It was a risky move on his part not knowing if the feds would be following him that day, but under these circumstances he had to cover for me on the phones.

It seemed like it took him forever to arrive but it was only a half an hour that had passed. I quickly filled him in on what calls still had to be made and flew to my father's hospital bed.

His death was not only a shock to our family but to the entire community as well. My father was the Sports Editor for quite a few years and a local celebrity of sorts in our hometown. He was an honorable man amongst his colleagues and greatly respected by anyone who knew him.

CHAPTER 30

The funeral was a very sad four-day long event in the middle of the worst snowstorm we had ever experienced. The undertaker even discussed possibly delaying the burial a day or two because the ground had been so frozen they thought it was going to be impossible to inter the coffin at his gravesite.

Those were the four longest days of my life as I stood there with my family and greeted literally hundreds of mourners. It was a sobering experience for me. I witnessed family, friends, professional, sports figures and top politicians including the mayor and the Governor armed with their security, file by the casket to pay their last respects.

My father's demise came hard to me along with a heavy burden of guilt that I had shamed him over the years. It was often times too much for me to bear and would distract me for days on end.

Here I was at the age of thirty-two, a bookmaker, a mobster's girlfriend, and yet the daughter of one of Erie's most beloved and humbled sportswriter.

My dad, nor my family, would ever understand my disturbing lifestyle. But, I was still my father's daughter and my shortcomings were never up for discussion and simply dismissed.

Back in the daily grind, I thought a change was in order. I wanted to buy a house on the upper east side of town and a closer distance to the school my kids were attending.

Even though there was always tons of cash on hand, I was smart enough to know I had to show legitimate income to support that household. Neither Ray nor I had a penchant for lavish spending habits because of that very reason.

I set up a meeting with the mayor and convinced him that I would delete his name from my little black book if he would be so kind as to hire me as an employee at city hall. The following Monday I was working as a clerk typist in the treasurer's office.

Working eight to four, dashing home to feed the kids after school, maneuvering my number rounds and making it back to an apartment we had rented to take the lay-offs before 6 p.m. was exhausting.

While my kids were spending the weekends with their father, my time was spent on the sports book and entertaining Ray's crew at my house. On rare occasions we attended a wedding or two or a private social event otherwise, it was me alone with the guys. Not a one of them had a significant other and besides Ray would never permit them to bring any other friends or females in to our home anyway. Those were the rules.

Like any other couple we had our usual ups and downs. I began to resent the fact that I was putting so much time into the sports book while Ray and his cronies spent their time hanging out. They were always at Dominick's Restaurant or in the back room of his cousins Amusement Company playing cards.

We turned a simple discussion into a full blown heated argument when I blasted him with threats of dumping the entire load into his lap. I suggested that he take up the slack and I threw him out.

His stubbornness kept him away for about three weeks when my boss and Ray's close friend Chip, the city treasurer, called me into his office one morning. Ray was comfortably sitting with his legs crossed on the sofa and Chip bowed out gracefully closing and locking the door behind him.

I stood there for about one second with my teeth clenched and finally blurted out, "I can't believe you ambushed me Ferritto!" Smiling, he raised himself from the sofa and pulled me towards him, firmly holding my face as he leaned in to kiss me. "I can't stay away from you any longer. When are you going to come back to your senses," he asked calmly.

I surrendered under his calming spell and we made love on the sofa in the treasurer's office, right down the hall from the police station. And, if that wasn't bad enough, Chip's large outside window faced the Federal Building directly across the street. Ray nodded his head at the reference and we laughed.

Ray didn't push me back into the business right away. He was going to allow me some time to myself and prove that I was there for him and not to just help run the operation.

Only a week later, we still weren't over our make-up sex yet when I saw him grab his chest. "Ray...what's wrong?" I asked. He wrenched in pain and ordered me to pull the car up. "Take me to the hospital. I think I'm having a heart attack." He blurted. I reached for the phone to call an ambulance and he insisted that I drive him. It was no time to argue and I managed to get him to St. Vincent's emergency room.

It turned out to be a mild heart attack but nevertheless it was concerning. Doctors told us he had to take it easy, cut out the sausage and try not to get stressed. Obviously, the doctor had no idea who he was talking to.

His current medical scare put everything in a different light and I didn't want to see him under any more pressure than necessary. I once again took over the books.

He was uncomfortable with the term boss, but the fact was that he indeed ran most of the territory at large now. On occasion he would have to show a hand of force and relied totally on me to be his back up.

As the mob rarely permitted women into their secret

affairs, I was about to become one of the privileged and one
with the new nickname of "Sophie" for the records.

Ray and I drove to the Mona Lisa Restaurant in Meadville,
Pennsylvania to meet the under bosses that were repre-
senting their shared interest in the secret inner loop of the
Ameche crew.

Here I sat amongst eight men over wine, a bottle of scotch
and dinner, listening to Ray sealing the deal for my role in
the business.

There were a few who tried to hide their reluctance and
the others amused themselves by making small jokes. But it
was no joke. He made sure that it was clear when he good-
humoredly and politely stated…"By the way fella's, if anyone
is crazy enough to take a shot at the Queen…you'd better
fuckin kill her cause I taught her everything she needs to
know."

Although, intricacies of mob politics, is a dangerous game
I had quietly slipped into their realm and now officially running the show to keep Ray out of the spotlight.

CHAPTER 31

B y 1986, I requested the mayor transfer me down to
the water department that was located at the foot of
Chestnut Street on the water's edge. It was an out of
the way antiquated building that housed the bureaus large
equipment. The second floor served as the main office where
the contractors applied for permits regarding new water lines
and gave us copies of their blueprints.

On the other hand, there were just a few of female clerks
and a handful of blue-collar guys that were often out in the
field, but also shared my office adjacent to the front customer

desk. Then there was our immediate boss who was terrified of Ray and stayed clear of me at all times.

In essence, I pretty much had the run of the office and my job had been away from any prying eyes at city hall. That gave me the freedom to bring my sports book to work with me. After all, no one would be tapping the water bureaus phones and the bagmen making drop-offs to me appeared to be contractors or customers seeking permission to break ground. It was the perfect front.

However, 1987 was going to be the year we'd hardly ever forget. It was April 10th, around mid-morning and I was sitting at my desk fooling around with some paperwork when the phone rang.

Out of the blue, the caller identified himself as Detective Dom DeBello and continued…"Susan, out of common courtesy, I'm asking you to turn yourself in to the Attorney General's office at 1p.m. this afternoon. We have an indictment against you and I didn't want to arrest you in front of your co-workers to cause any further embarrassment. Do you understand?"

Shocked by the statement, I fired back. ""Do I understand? What the hell is going on here Dom? What's this all about?"

"You'll find out when you get here," he answered sternly then hung up.

My first instincts were to gather my thoughts. I concluded that I was being pinched for the sports booking as I hadn't committed any other criminal acts. I immediately grabbed my betting slips and slid them in between some files at a nearby cabinet. All I could think was that "the jig was up!" And to boot, Ray was out of town attending a meeting of the minds somewhere in New Jersey and there was no way to reach him. He would never carry a cell phone.

At one o'clock sharp, I stood in front of a dozen F.B.I. agents, expecting to hear gambling and racketeering charges while DeBello rattled off a list of something entirely different. It was a laundry list of Burglary and Criminal Conspiracy charges. I was totally dumbfounded and confused but stayed calm and quiet only requesting an attorney.

Dismissing my request as though they never heard me, they escorted me to their vehicles in the parking lot then proceeded driving to the back entrance of city hall where the police department was located.

As I was booked and fingerprinted, I couldn't help but notice six other familiar neighborhood crooks, handcuffed and standing alongside a wall.

The self-centered detective gave the media the "heads up" on the bust so that he'd be the star attraction on the evening news.

You'd have thought someone had been murdered, by the hordes of reporters and cameramen that surrounded the parking lot. They herded us over to the County Court House for arraignment.

Unbeknownst to me, Bolo's five-year unsolved brutal slaying was finally coming on its way towards closure.

DeBello stood proud that he was responsible for the roundup as the rest of us lined the center of the courtroom in front of the judge's bench for the proceedings. The judge perused the paperwork on his desk in preparation for the hearings before him when he spotted my name at the top of the list. He looked directly at me and questioned why I was the only one that was not being represented by counsel. I spoke up and said, "Your honor, I requested an attorney and Detective DeBello dismissed it as if he didn't hear me."

The judge scolded DeBello for not allowing me my phone call then proceeded to inform me that I was being released on my own recognizance. Disturbed by the judge's ruling, the detective spoke out to his defense, claiming my charges were too serious to let me off the hook so easily. But the judge stood firm on his decision and ordered me to wait at the back of the courtroom.

I waited patiently while the judge handed out harsh bails to the rest of them, when out of nowhere, the judge's secretary Irene, tapped me on the shoulder and whispered into my ear. "Susan...the judge wants to see you in his chambers... follow me."

No one noticed that I had slipped out the door to meet the judge. "Bill, I said shamefully, this is all bogus. I'm not a crook and you know it!" "Don't worry about anything," he replied. "I'll get you through this honey. I know all about DeBello's games and it won't work with me...as long as my name doesn't appear on any of your books, Susan." "No Bill", I assured him. "Your indiscretions are safe with me and thanks for the pass."

Knowing that Ray was going to be furious about the situation when he returned in a few days, I think I paced a hole through the floor. But when the mayor called me that night I was a little relieved to know he had my back and suggested that I return to work on Monday as if nothing happened. He said the press had already called and questioned him on how he was going to handle a city employee being indicted for felony burglary charges. His statement in the morning news read that he wasn't doing anything. "She's innocent until proven otherwise and will remain an employee of the city."

I could only pray that Ray was going to be as sensitive to this news when he got home, but I knew better.

Forty-eight hours had passed and I was mentally exhausted. I started to doze off when I heard the phone ring for the umpteenth time. I was hesitant, but answered it thinking it might have been a family member. Totally enraged, Ray hollered from the other end. "What the fuck is going on up there?" "Well", I said angrily. "I wish I could give you a straight answer, but I'm in the dark here...so, where are you?" "I'm four hundred fuckin miles away and I gotta hear this news from some wise guys in another state." Totally pissed off at his obnoxious reply I shot back, "Then you better get off the fuckin phone Ferritto...it's probably bugged," then slammed down the receiver.

CHAPTER 32

Preoccupied with the charges hanging over my head, it was mind-boggling trying to comprehend the gravity things. Especially, with the long list of others who were being arrested as every day passed.

Erie's criminal world was taking on a life of its own. It was getting more complicated by the day and likened to "Indictment Hysteria" as one newspaper writer described it. Other reporters scrambled for information on the pending arrests and it was rumored to include prominent people, as well.

Ray was livid that I could be in the middle of what the papers were describing the numerous defendants as everything from home invaders, to bank robbers, to cocaine traffickers and topped off with murder contracts.

And, for God's sake then came the arrest of the detective that Cy and Ray had contacted at the time of Bolo's death back in 1983. He was arrested for trying to kill someone for a drug deal gone wrong. No one seemed to be safe in our little city and soon that would include Ray.

Only one month into the carnage and it was his turn. The authorities came down on him like a ton of bricks and charged him with criminal conspiracy, pool selling, bookmaking, and corrupt organizations.

Little did we know that way back during our three-week separation the feds were wiretapping one of the offices we had set up.

Unfortunately that was the house he chose to work out of when I dumped the books in his lap. His charges included an FBI report that stated the exact two-week dated wiretap conversations and they listened as he took in well over a million dollars just in those few weeks.

Even though we were in over our heads, I thanked my lucky stars that I had the brains enough to have Ray's top numbers man, Whitey cover the book after I was indicted. But now, he too was on shaky ground as he was becoming a person of interest in the great conspiracy.

Then, out of the blue came the news of Cy's arrest. He had managed to elude capture for almost five years. He was now in the custody of New York's Federal marshals.

Cy could never resist calling his associates to keep in the loop and somehow the FBI had managed to use one of their mob informants to lure him back to the states with a big money deal.

By August of that year Ray and I were at each other's throats and our tension was off the charts. It was bad enough that the two of us were currently under indictments, now we were being subpoenaed to appear before the grand jury in Allegheny County.

To exacerbate the situation that month, I discovered Ray's infidelities. I wanted to kill him. I felt so betrayed, blindsided and crushed that all I had done for him over the years and now this.

In my rage, I realized that I was angrier with myself. I should have known better. I know how men think. What in God's name would have made me think, Ray was any different from the rest. I learned at a young age that when men pull their pants down their brains fall out.

How could I have been that stupid to let my guard down? We fought like crazy. The more we argued, the more he drank until he finally had another heart attack and I tried to forgive him.

My preliminary hearing turned out to be nothing but a circus. The original seven of us that were charged for the robberies all sat lined in the front row with our attorneys. One of the culprits "Fat Sam" Esper was being currently guarded in the Federal Witness Protection Program. We watched as federal marshals escorted the prosecution's star witness "Fat Sam", through the tiny courtroom up to the witness chair.

They began by questioning him about my participation in these so- called burglaries that had taken place as far back

as the late seventies and early eighties. When the prosecutor
pointed to me... Fat Sam looked puzzled and said. "She's not
the girl...you have the wrong one." It was a blatant "set up"
engineered by the detective in charge of Bolo's investigation.
They had to let me go.

Now, the task force that was put in place for Bolo's unsolved
murder case had clearly done their due diligence over the
years. With every one of these busts they managed to wiretap,
pull and coerce information from this giant web of corrup-
tion and it finally came to a head after five long years.

A small time neighborhood bookie and storekeeper,
"Nigzy", was finally thrown into the spotlight as the one
accused of hiring Cazar Monteveccio, a known bank robber
to orchestrate the murders of both Bolo and Ray. Running
late the night of Bolo's murder was perhaps Ray's salvation.

The fact surfaced that Nigzy too, was trying to rise up in
the ranks. He convinced himself that Ray and Bolo's murders
would be blamed on Cleveland's long awaited retaliation for
crippling their regime. After which, Nigzy figured he'd freely
inheriting the numbers territory in Erie.

The neighborhood bookies never had a clue that Ray's
tentacles were part of a bigger conspiracy that dwarfed their
little hometown racket business.

Ray's legal woes were fixed before the Christmas season
arrived. All it took was some cold hard cash to nudge Judge
Foster into postponing and canceling Ray's motions for literally years. He would be on parole till 1993 but would never
serve a day behind bars for his charges.

I quit my so-called position at the water department. My

presence there brought too much attention and I didn't want to embarrass the Mayor any further. Besides, it was just time to move on. Small town people will never let you forget your past and love to believe the worst. Lord only knows how we tried to live up to their expectations.

But it was who we were and for the time being, it wasn't going to change. Ray and I were always into things for the "thrill of the game." Risk taking was just our nature and the reason why we were so crazy about each other.

In 1990, three short years later, I had the nerve to tell Ray that I was bored and needed a project to work on. Even though we were still maneuvering the numbers games and the sports book, I needed something to spike up the atmosphere.

As if our lives weren't busy enough running a vast numbers racket and trying to keep some powerful mobsters happy, I had some extra energy to get rid of...and, what a better way than building a brothel of sorts.

I was the legal owner and drew up the plans while Ray put the crew to work renovating an older building on Peach Street. In months, we turned it into a thriving massage parlor and christened it, The "Jockey Health Club."

It was open 24/7 and generated a boatload of cash. The politicians and do-gooders of the city would use the back entrance and the regular Joe's used the front. Again, I would keep Ray away from that action too. He didn't need the headaches of being seen there. So, the only time he made an appearance is when we had to entertain some out of town mobsters and bagmen who couriered for us across state lines.

All it took was one year in operations before the local town crier found out who owned it and had it splashed across the news. Kara Pella, an investigative reporter and her camera crew enjoyed publicly exploiting the establishment and all it was worth. It didn't matter to us, but was another public embarrassment to our families, so we did a quick sale for a hefty sum and moved on.

CHAPTER 33

In the early 1990's we did an about face and did our best to stay off the radar. We rarely went out and only entertained the crew and our families privately.

However, the entrepreneur in me would provoke a new venture and it would not be as immoral as the last. I opened a new home care business and called it Heart to Heart Home Healthcare.

It kept me and my small staff of about twenty certified nurse's aides very busy providing 24/7 private care to patients in their homes. Our registered nurse would oversee the patient's logs and follow up on their doctor's orders and monthly visits.

Despite the endless hours I was putting into the healthcare business, our sports book still came first. But times were changing and our local numbers rackets were dwindling. Even though we were paying out 600 to one on the daily numbers, the state lottery was just a safer way to go for our patrons in the long run. The older bookies no longer wanted to risk their freedom and we couldn't blame them. So, in the spring of 1992 Ray closed the books on the local dailies.

He broke the news to the crew at a lavish wedding reception we held for my daughter's wedding. There in the midst of about five hundred guests the entire crew was informed. Ray always liked to kill two birds with one stone and it made for the perfect meeting for all of them to go unnoticed in one place.

Consequently, as everything must come to an end, almost a year and a half later in the fall of 1993, the Ameche sports book had finally run its course, too. Four members had passed, two were in a nursing facility and one had Alzheimer's disease. The contacts in the football leagues were changing courses and Ray had lost some good coaches that had been on the payroll.

With our Cadillac packed with the last pay-off, we set out for the three day drive to California. There, we would meet up with the last of the "13".

We met at an out of the way restaurant for dinner and a few drinks before we finished our business. "Chin don, my friends" was the parting toast from the old crew. In English it meant, "May you live, a hundred years." With their henchmen watching over, the final pay-off took place in the parking lot behind the eatery. With the shake of hands and a pinch to my cheek, we were on our way home.

We were happy the grandfatherly men didn't give us the kiss of death. So happy afterwards, in fact we celebrated by tying the knot. No family. No friends. No fanfare. And, we decided to keep it secret for a while. Besides which, how in the hell would we explain that one?

Simply put, had the last twenty-five years become public at that time, Ray indeed being the power broker to the mob would have tossed the sports world on its ear, or worse.

Over the next years we hoped to quietly spend our time trying to enjoy our family, friends and what was left of our money.

Even though we always had an endless amount of cash on hand, that was never important to us. It was always about the power and the thrill of it all.

Most importantly was, our roots. We still had some family left in Little Italy and even though it was now becoming a slum area, we had hopes of trying to revive a part of it.

We had multiple properties over the years, but our favorite was Morabito's old storefront building on the corner of 16th & Cherry Streets. No one could understand why we would ever choose to live in what was now being referred to as Little Italy's ghetto. But we saw it differently and we were comfortable there.

My first memories of Morabito's went back to 1956 when I was five years old and the neighborhood's youngest bookie.

Mr. Morabito was the storekeeper that I had to deliver gram's numbers to.

Ray's memories often times, were picking those same numbers up when getting started in the number business. It's funny how things turn out and your life seems to come full circle.

I turned the storefront into a thriving hair and tanning salon and we lived in the large first floor apartment adjacent to the business.

Ray and the aging wise guys took pleasure in remodeling the three upstairs apartments. Often times you could see them sitting in the side parking lot taking a break in between repairing the leaky roof or sitting on lawn chairs trying to catch a few rays. Their ever present jugs of wine were never without a few laughs and some old memories.

Once in a while they'd slip inside the salon to get a peek at the young beauties coming in to tan. Peeps, was always the worst and most verbal at times. His sordid remarks got the best of me one day when he blurted out, "Oh, my God...I'd give her a shot!"

"Are you insane?" I blasted back. "You're old, you're bald, you're broke and you're no fucking Romeo. What in the hell makes you think she'd give you one?"

That was enough for me. It was time for them to find another hangout. There were more wise guys sitting on the damn dryer chairs than I had customers some days. Plus, the older Italian women were complaining about being gawked at while getting their hair done, too.

By the late 90's, my kitchen became the headquarters for

the old crew of crooks, bookies and elderly mobsters that Ray hung out with. While I was working ten hours a day in the salon, I'd have to come home to my husband and the bunch indulging themselves in his special homemade sauce and pasta. We had limited privacy and the daily meetings were starting to get old and boring.

Cy finally returned home from prison so Ray and I gave him a new start with a get together charging fifty dollars a head. The last of the little neighborhood Italian clubs, La Nuova Aurora was packed as they welcomed him back and toasted to his new freedom.

That evening, I had taken all the cash we made from the party and stuffed it into an old three-pound coffee can. As usual, Cy was there for coffee at 8 a.m. the following morning and we presented it to him at my breakfast table. It was always a standing joke with the mobsters that you hid your ill-gotten gains in coffee cans and buried them in your backyards. They laughed at the inference as Cy counted his boost.

I never ran roughshod over the crew, but occasionally they forced me to put my foot down. Unfortunately, several months later...I wasn't laughing anymore and whatever humor I had left was quickly going down the tubes. As if it wasn't bad enough over the last few years listening to their old war stories, hysterical blunders and current aging medical problems, Cy was now entertaining plans of the criminal kind and I blew.

"What the fuck is your problem?" I yelled. "Jesus Christ, Cy. You are seventy fucking years old. When are you going to give up trying to get in someone else's pockets? Take your lousy social security and enjoy your grandchildren for a change. Everybody is retired here. You're old and sick for God's sake...and yet you still want to look over your shoulders for the cops? Get over it!"

Well that went over like a lead balloon. Everyone walked out and left Ray sitting there stunned. Cy never got over the fact that Ray allowed me to interfere with their lifelong relationship and the other guys awkwardly, took it with a grain of salt.

Most of them never forgave me for breaking up the crew but it had been a long time coming. None of them were in good health and Ray didn't have the heart to confront them as his own health condition worsened. So, I had to be the bad guy.

It was all for the best then. I sold the last of our businesses and properties in 1998, and we relocated to Sarasota, Florida where Ray could enjoy his last few years basking under the sun.

He was happy then and content with living in anonymity. We had even renewed our most intimate relationship. A few of the wise guys also moved to be close to Ray in Sarasota. They'd often visit and take him out for an occasional ride or to a golf outing. He wasn't permitted to drive anymore after his health gave out to his weakening heart.

By 2003, multiple heart surgeries had taken its toll and he had become vulnerable and frail looking. Still trying to protect his dignity and Italian male pride, I discouraged any visitors except the immediate family that last year and of course his lifelong and closest friends, Peeps and Elso who were always there for him.

My daughter Shauna, our grandsons and my niece Michelle, whom I always considered a daughter selflessly moved to Sarasota to help take care of Ray after learning how difficult it was for me.

The doctors advised me to admit him to a nursing home... but that subject was never up for conversation. I couldn't nor wouldn't ever do that to him.

His last pleasures were looking at old westerns on television and watching our two little grandsons splashing around in the pool or playing with them in bed until he was too tired and had to rest. In the end, seeing the little ones was the only thing that put a smile on his face and he would sing Italian songs to them.

CHAPTER 34

———————◆———————

It was Sunday, May 9ᵗʰ of 2004. Ray and I were babysitting the two little ones while Shauna and Michelle went to work that day.

Normally, we'd only watch them for a few hours in the afternoons. But this particular day my daughter received an unexpected request from her boss. He needed her to cover the next shift and she didn't want to refuse him. She called, asking me if we could keep the boys until midnight.

We were happy to keep them, but I insisted that they stay overnight. I hated to see them being woken up only to be dragged home at such a late hour. It would be the first night they ever stayed over.

Ray played off and on with them throughout the day and was tickled by their company. We put them at both ends of the sofa when it was time for them to go to sleep and Ray lulled them with an Italian bedtime song as they drifted off.

It was a long day for both of us but more so him than me. He tired easily and I could see he was exhausted. I suggested we both get some rest and went to bed.

He woke me a few hours later as he struggled to get up. I was in a dead sleep and angered that he wouldn't leave me alone. "What in the hell do you want Ray? Please, go to sleep." I begged.

He too was totally drained and didn't have an iota of energy but insisted that I help him over to see the boys. "Oh my God" I moaned. "I am not going to let you wake up those kids this time of night.

He persisted and promised not to wake them until I finally gave in. After helping him into the wheelchair, he directed me to sit him by the sofa next to the boys. He caressed their heads, then leaned over to kiss their faces and mumbled something to them. Turning his attention to me he touched my hand and spoke tenderly.

"Sophie, no one will ever love you like I've loved you. You know that, don't you? I'm still crazy about you after all these years."

In frustration I replied, "That's it. You woke me up for this?" "Yes" he said. "Now take me back to bed."

Had I known the significance of that moment, I would

have answered him differently. As I tried getting him onto the bed, his body started to collapse. I wasn't strong enough to hold his weight, so I guided him as gently to the floor as I could. I placed a pillow under his head and called for Peeps to come down to help me lift him back onto the bed.

Slumping from his weakening heart condition had become a regular occurrence during the last couple of months. And, it was getting worse, but it had never happened in the middle of the night.

Peeps lived on the fifth floor of our apartment building and he too was always a phone call away. I apologized for waking him up at 2:a.m. and asked for his help. I unlocked the front door for him and rushed back to the bedroom to comfort Ray.

I knelt next to him and told him to relax and that Peeps was on his way. He peered up at me and said with a smile, "I beat 'em, didn't I honey?"

I knew what he meant. He was losing the battle but had won the war of eluding the retaliation from the Cleveland mobsters and he was proud of that. I grabbed his chin and in a calmer tone, replied. "Yes you did Ferritto. Yes you did."

Peeps came through the doorway and stopped to joke. "Ray...what the hell are you doing on the floor this time of night?"

He shook his head laughing and bent over to help lift him. But Ray's body was limp. He looked at Peeps with the widest smile then closed his eyes.

His implanted defibrillator immediately sent a shock to his heart and his body bolted as it absorbed the electrical wave. "Peeps," I yelled. "He's not breathing." Frantically I called 911 as Peeps looked on in surprise at his friend lying there lifeless.

Then I heard Peeps sadly echo the words, "It's over Susan...He's gone." And I lost it.

The following days were more painful than I could ever have imagined. As tough as I was throughout my life, the one thing that I could never do was accept the losses of my loved ones. Denial set in and I was not up for the challenge.

The next day, the director notified me that the cremation was set for that following Friday. Even though it was five days after his death, I wasn't prepared for a memorial. In my mind the service would have finalized his passing. I couldn't do it. I don't remember ever feeling so inconsolable.

By the third day I was totally irrational. The funeral director must have thought I was some type of morbid lunatic when I arrived at the funeral parlor unannounced. I demanded that he remove my husbands implanted pacemaker and defibrillator and return them to me before his cremation.

In my highly emotional state, I saw these small metal electronic devices as my last tangible link to him. They had kept him alive for the last seven years and now they were going to help me keep him alive in my own sordid mind. After that, all I wanted was to be alone with our memories, our photos and Ray's ashes.

In hindsight, I realized that his ending played out the way he had wished. He often would tell the kids that the last thing he wanted to see before he died was their little faces. I'd get so mad at him for talking like that to them, but he'd do it anyway. It gave me a chill to know that he knew it was that time.

As the news of Ray's death became public that week, calls of condolences poured in from close friends and mob associates. One call in particular would send me over the edge.

The caller identified himself as an Associated Press reporter. He quickly offered his sympathies then proceeded to ask me if there was anything I wanted to say about Ray for his article. He was polite and explained that he had been given the assignment and with or without any statement from me, he had to put the news in print.

Normally, unless it was to my advantage, I would have hung up on any reporter. My husband and I would never have given them the time of day let alone a sentence or two. As a matter of fact, Ray would often spew obscene language at them so they couldn't use it for their articles.

This time though was much different. I wasn't in my right mind and became angry knowing that even in death the press was still going to persecute him. Jumping to Ray's defense, I instinctively blurted something back to the reporter. But as quick as I said it...I regretted it.

When the article broke, our neighbors were shocked to learn that this quiet elderly gentleman that they befriended had been a dangerous mob hit man. Until the cat was out of the bag, we were just a nice retired couple living in Sarasota. No one was the wiser. Now, they weren't speaking to me.

Ray's wishes were for his body to be cremated and his ashes placed at his mother's gravesite. He didn't want to put his family through a painful public memorial.

I was so distraught it took me a year following his death to do this. Ray's closest friends, Peeps and Bobby Fogel were kind enough to join me at this private little memorial at the cemetery in Erie. And still, I couldn't even bring myself to part with all of his ashes. I wanted to keep him with me always.

CHAPTER 35

There was little sympathy for the families of these mobsters. The public thought most mobsters got what they deserved. And, perhaps they were rightly so. But it was the families they left behind that would undeservingly carry the guilt and shame of it all.

Underneath it all Ray and I had both experienced those feelings that we had burdened our loved ones with our unspeakable acts. That was our biggest regret.

I had always known that my world would never be the same without my Ray. But, never did I realize just how far my emotions would take me. There was no one to understand my grief, nor anyone that I could open up to. I had never felt so vulnerable.

Imitation is supposed to be the highest form of flattery... or so I've been told. Consequently, in my case it became maddening. Since 1977, dozens of reporters, authors, historians and yes even fallen gangsters have taken a crack at portraying the mob's irrefutable desecration of the Cleveland regime's downfall. Each time a new version reared its ugly head over the years, it opened the old wound.

Here it was forty years later and the third anniversary of Ray's passing when I learned of an upcoming movie that was in production. It was about the life and death of "The Irishman."

I realized at that moment why I could never lift myself out of this mourning for Ray. The wave of interest from that era gone by was never going to cease. There was no closure that would put my mind at peace with all of it. And, it all came rushing back. My anger flared.

What finally struck me was the absence of Ray's side if the story. He never had a voice or a desire to bring up the ugly past. Now, I felt it was up to me to put our lives at rest. It was clear to me that I couldn't go forward with my life until I went back. But, most importantly, my motive was to defend his memory.

I wrote obsessively. The more I wrote, the more I remembered. And, the more I remembered, the more curious I became. In a haunting rage, I had written over a thousand pages. Sifting back through time was a daunting task and often disturbing. But, I was persistent. Even, stubborn at times when I was warned not to go public with his story. I continued to write every chance I had until the months turned into years.

Each time I read a Chapter, I would fall back into the painful realization, of how dreadfully and dangerously we pursued our lifestyles.

"My God," I thought to myself. Who were these awful people that I was writing about? Literally, after years of delving into the past, I felt so detached from that lifestyle. It was as if I were reading about someone else. And, I cringed to think that once upon a time this indeed was our reality.

How could we have plunged into these depths of sin without any remorse or conscience? What would cause people from good families to choose such paths of destruction?

Gradually, my focus began to change. After that, for me it was a matter of finding those answers.

By no means, did my revelations happen quickly. I had buried my sins from the age of about seven. But, as I peeled back the memories of time, a sick feeling came over me. And, the truth was about to set me free.

While prodding through some old photographs, I found one that was folded and taped closed. As I opened it I saw a picture of my little sister Yolande' in her lacy white communion dress. I didn't understand why it had been taped shut, but the picture itself was a little haunting.

I left it out on the dresser and on occasion would curiously stare at it. It was almost as though it was trying to tell me something. Then finally, out of the blue, it happened.

I had remembered being curled up on the floor hiding in

my closet. My communion dress was on a hanger above me and the crisp lacy veil had fallen off into my lap. I was clenching it crying, shaking and scared. As my memory unfolded my stomach began to turn. I could even recall the smell of dry cleaning solution that permeated the air. And I saw his face.

My mother had given me a pair of my father's trousers with a note attached for the local tailor. They were supposed to be altered right away. She instructed me to run down the street as fast as I could and give the pants to Mr. Chiappetta.

I didn't want to go. He was an ugly little man and I was scared of him, but my mother had given me an order and I had to obey. I thought if I could rush in quickly, leaving the trousers and the note on the front counter without him seeing me, that I'd be home free. But, when I shot through the front entrance, he was standing there with his tape measure loosely hanging from his neck. He glanced at me and a wave of delight came over his long wretched face. He reached out taking my arm and coolly stated, "Susie, my pretty little girl. Come with me…I have something for you."

Reluctantly I let him lure me into the back room like he had done so many times before. I was frightened and knew what was coming next.

He positioned me up against the old huge steam presser groping me from behind. His fingers were not where they should have been and I could feel his hot smelly garlic breath on the back of my neck. I felt a paralyzing pain and froze. This time he had gone too far and stole my innocence that day.

When he was finished, he pulled up his zipper and pressed a dime into the palm of my hand. He warned me not to tell anyone. And, to illustrate his threat, he reached up to grab the arm of the giant press and slammed it down hard. The machine released a loud hiss and the steam that shot out from it terrorized me.

The first thing I saw as I bolted out the door was our majestic holy sanctuary...St. Paul's Church. In my naïve mind, I believed God, "who sees everything" had just witnessed my most repulsive act of sin...and I was going to hell.

There was no place to rid myself of the shame until I hid in the closet that day when the veil had fallen into my lap.

Shortly thereafter, the day I was to receive my first Holy Communion finally had arrived. I was standing in the pew along other classmates with the nuns looking on when I began to feel sick.

The priest appeared at the altar and as he began the mass, my hands started to tremble. My mind was racing with pangs of guilt and shame. I felt dirty, impure and certainly not worthy of this holy sacrament that I was about to accept from God himself.

Sister Hildegard gestured it was time for us to file up to the altar for the ritual tasting of the bread and wine symbolizing the body and blood of Christ. I reluctantly performed my part in the ceremony and returned to the pew. And, as if I wasn't scared enough that God was going to punish me for committing mortal sins with that wretched little man, the fear of knowing He might strike me dead at any moment, terrified me.

Defying God's laws and receiving communion that day petrified me so much that I peed myself. I was praying that no one would notice the stream of urine slowly flowing across the floor. It was that moment when I put on the cuffs, and condemned myself to the fiery pits of hell. It was a back breaking burden, for such a small kid.

I subconsciously punished myself ever since. There is no way to erase the past or dismiss the unconscionable lifestyle I've led. But, I realized that I have found what I've been looking for all these years... "Me." That seven year old who was driven by the devil.

Aside the armchair psychology, I know that somewhere in there was a purpose. I honestly believe God does everything for a reason.

Every time Ray's story was publicized, it felt as though our lives were being emotionally violated again and again. A feeling or a place no one wants to be. But, despite the raging madness to give him a voice and defend his memory, it ironically has turned my life around. It was clear to me then. The bottom line...there is no defense.

AUTHOR'S NOTE

Never in my wildest dreams did I ever think that I would go forward with our most private lives and exposing our sins in such a public manner. But, my love for him and the obsession to defend his legacy far outweighed my silence. I truly feel it's the last gift I can give to him.

To the public he was a dangerous mafia enforcer, to the Feds he was their star witness and to La Cosa Nostra he was their "Comeback kid". But, for those of us who profoundly loved and cherished him, he was a son, a father, a brother, a grandfather, a husband and our hero.

You may love the Mob or hate its soul, but its lurid fascination will always remain. And, contrary to public belief and its critics, Raymond W. Ferritto was the only mobster in the history of La Cosa Nostra that has ever destroyed a leadership, lived to tell about it and rose to become a boss. I was his witness.

It's been said that Ray's particular breed of American Mafioso was born of a time and place that could never be duplicated, and they were rapidly becoming extinct.

And, as God is my witness, only when you are "Chin Deep" in cold cash, gambling, murders, contracts, violent betrayals, hookers, mobsters and death sentences can you be the judge.

CPSIA information can be obtained at www.ICGtesting.com
Printed in the USA
LVOW012232180613

339232LV00008B/70/P

9 780578 108292

MW01148430

THE
APOTHECARY'S
WIFE

KAREN BLOOM GEVIRTZ spent nearly three decades as a
professor of English at American universities, most recently
at Seton Hall University. Gevirtz earned a BA in English
at Brown University, where she was also pre-med and a
research assistant in a neurochemistry lab. She has a PhD in
British Literature and has received fellowships and grants
for her archival research. Internationally recognized for her
scholarship on women and writing in the seventeenth and
eighteenth centuries, she has authored academic articles,
chapters and several scholarly books, and co-edited a
collection of essays. She lives in New Jersey, USA.

The publisher and the University of California Press Foundation gratefully acknowledge the generous support of the Constance and William Withey Endowment Fund in History and Music.

KAREN BLOOM GEVIRTZ

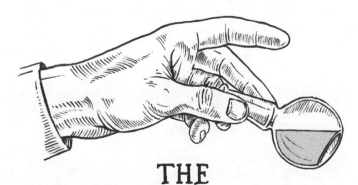

THE
APOTHECARY'S
WIFE

The Hidden History of Medicine and
How It Became a Commodity

UNIVERSITY OF CALIFORNIA PRESS

University of California Press
Oakland, California

© 2024 by Karen Bloom Gevirtz

First published in the UK in 2024 by Head of Zeus Ltd, part of Bloomsbury
Publishing Plc

Library of Congress Cataloging-in-Publication Data

Names: Gevirtz, Karen Bloom, author.
Title: The apothecary's wife : the hidden history of medicine and
how it became a commodity / Karen Bloom Gevirtz.
Description: Oakland, California : University of California Press,
[2024] | "First published in the UK in 2024 by Head of Zeus Ltd,
part of Bloomsbury Publishing Plc."—Title verso page. |
Includes bibliographical references and index.
Identifiers: LCCN 2024024443 | ISBN 9780520409910 (cloth) |
ISBN 9780520409927 (ebook)
Subjects: LCSH: Medicine—History. | Traditional medicine—History. |
Women in medicine—History. | Physicians—History.
Classification: LCC R145 .G48 2024 | DDC 610—dc23/eng/20240624
LC record available at https://lccn.loc.gov/2024024443

Manufactured in the United States of America

33 32 31 30 29 28 27 26 25 24
10 9 8 7 6 5 4 3 2 1

For Jessica,

who said, "What about Chawton?"

Contents

Introduction

This book began in a 400-year-old basement. The archivist of Chawton House Library said to me, "And of course, you'll want to see our copy of Blackwell's *Herbal*," and I replied, "Yes." I was not exactly being honest. I had travelled 3,000 miles to research how eighteenth-century women incorporated the Scientific Revolution into their daily lives, and "Blackwell's *Herbal*" was not on my to-do list. I did not even know what it was. But when a librarian or archivist suggests that you take a look at something, you say yes – and that was when the book that I thought I was writing ended and this one began.

"Blackwell's *Herbal*" was shorthand for *A Curious Herbal, Containing Five Hundred Cuts, of the Most Useful Plants Which Are Now Used in the Practice of Physick*, created by Elizabeth Blackwell between 1735 and 1739. A herbal is a compendium of medicinal plants made to be used and referenced; however, Blackwell made hers for show. It consists of 500 etched and hand-coloured pictures, 125 etched pages of information, and another dozen etched pages of front and back matter, including dedications and indexes in English and Latin. It is beautiful, in the same family of works as John James Audubon's *Birds of America* (1827) and Maria Sibylla Merian's *Metamorphosis Insectorum Surinamensium* (*Metamorphosis of the Insects of Suriname* [1705]). A *Curious Herbal* was also the first printed herbal by a woman that I had seen or heard of. Aside from being a remarkable work, two things about it struck me at that first reading. One was the number of eminent physicians, apothecaries, and Fellows of the Royal Society who had supported and encouraged Blackwell. They included Sir Hans Sloane, president of the Royal College of Physicians (RCP); Richard Mead, a leading physician of the early eighteenth century; Isaac Rand, praecentor of the apothecaries' guild teaching garden in Chelsea; and James Douglas, premier anatomist and man-midwife (obstetrician). It was very odd that Elizabeth Blackwell, an undistinguished Scottish woman married to a man arrested for bankruptcy, was connected with such an illustrious group.

The second thing that struck me as I read the *Curious Herbal* was this line: "The Herb Women sell the Leaves of the *Helleboraster*, or Bear's-foot, or *Sphondylium*, or Cow parsnep [*sic*], instead of this Plant, to those that are ignorant." It was the first mention of women other than as patient and to my disappointment, it was not sympathetic. It also had nothing to do with medication per se; Blackwell was accusing the "Herb Women" of an economic crime. Similar passages occurred periodically throughout the two volumes, all levelling the same accusation that the herb women were guilty of fraud and of preventing the "ignorant" from buying the proper herbaceous material from those who were honest and knowledgeable. It seemed absurd to me that anyone in 1735 would think that herb women competed with apothecaries and physicians in any way, but there it was. Blackwell's patrons were illustrious apothecaries and physicians; whatever she wrote had to be pleasing to them, perhaps articulating their views. Why was this group so threatened by these women? Why did they consider the threat to be economic?

The fact that I was asking those questions meant that there was something very wrong with the standard history of medicine, what I might call "the Triumph of Modern Medicine". That (his)story proceeds roughly like this: Once upon a time, ancient Greeks and Romans such as Hippocrates and Galen began to establish medicine as a field of knowledge and a form of practice, but everything remained crude until the Scientific Revolution, which brought in the scientific method, true knowledge, and the wonderful advances that continue to this day and from which humanity benefits, the end. One of this story's subplots is the triumph of modern medication: Once upon a time, medication was revolting and harmful because it was made by ignorant crones, whereas one of the wonderful advances of the Scientific Revolution was effective medication, which is what we have now, the end. There is nothing in either of these accounts of the past that has to do with money. These are "triumph" or "rise" histories, in which a revolution introduces something entirely new. Competition meant that "new" did not necessarily mean "better" to people in the 1730s.

Furthermore, *A Curious Herbal* showed that the medication being prescribed by physicians and made by apothecaries used the same organic materials as those used by ordinary people. The title page announced that the book depicted 500 "of the most useful Plants which are now used in the Practice of Physick". In case this was not clear enough, each entry about a plant informed readers why it would be prescribed and how it would be prepared, often citing renowned authorities in medical botany. On rare occasions, Blackwell relied solely on what "common folk" used a plant for; occasionally she cited both professional and common usage. It appeared that professionals and housewives alike used herbal ingredients for their medications. Could "modern" medicine have been perceived as superior? Yes, of course. Could it have been actually superior? It did not look like it. This led to another and particularly bothersome question. If the medications were the same, why did people stop getting treatment at home and start getting it from physicians and apothecaries? If money was an issue, as Blackwell's book suggested, how did the professionals get people to start paying for something that for hundreds of years they had been getting for free?

That is the central conundrum of this book. For centuries, ailing people got medication and treatment at home. Their medication was made by a member or a friend of the family, it was made from time-tested recipes and ingredients, and it was made right there. Furthermore, there was no charge. Then, ailing people started getting medication outside the home, travelling while ill to physicians or apothecaries. The medication that the patient purchased was made by a stranger from unknown ingredients according to an unknown recipe in a room that the patient was not permitted to enter. *The Apothecary's Wife* explains how, when, and through what means the Scientific Revolution catalysed the replacement of medications made at home with medications made by apothecaries and prescribed by physicians. This book also reveals that the Scientific Revolution transformed the entire concept of medication from a household item into a commodity, something to be sold and bought. An entire healthcare system – women's domestic medicine – was switched out for the system we have now – that is, for-profit medicine. There is nothing about the current medication system that is natural or eternal or inevitable. What exists was made by people at a certain time making certain decisions and doing certain things. We pay for medicine because we think of medicine as something to be paid for. We did not always think so. We choose whether to continue.

Therefore, *The Apothecary's Wife* is also something of an economic history. I explain in the coming pages that the Scientific Revolution and what became science and modern medicine have always been entwined with issues of personal and public gain, and with profit as well as benefit. Consequently, this book is not only a history of medicine but also a history of the economic system developed for the circulation of medication as a commodity. Such an economic system protects, normalizes, and obscures medication's commodity status. Powerful, dangerous aspects of it, such as unequal access to medication, the regulation of drugs but not of prescriptions, and the embracing of highly technical language (not to mention the fostering of educational curricula that do not prepare people to deal with that language) were knowingly built into it during its construction. These issues and the current global for-profit system are neither inevitable nor immutable. For-profit medication was created by choices; consequently, it can be retained, modified, or eliminated by choices.

This book is built on a tremendous body of material, only a small portion of which is visible in the reading. I have drawn on texts created by both men and women, including correspondence, diaries, recipe books, household budgets, personal accounts, plays, poems, sermons, narrative fiction, paintings, prints, tracts, treatises, textbooks, scientific articles, newspapers, advertisements, gardening handbooks, housekeeping manuals, herbals, pharmacopoeias, medical lectures, students' notes, annotations, inventories, prescriptions, municipal and parish records, guild archives, judicial papers, royal declarations, and legislation, both national and local. Although each chapter is built around two central figures, in fact readers will meet a whole range of people who lived and contributed to the transition. They will also hear the voices of long-dead people, including women. For millennia, women's lives were not well documented and as a result, finding them can be difficult. "When it comes to the lives of the other half of humanity," Caroline Criado Perez wrote, "there is often nothing but silence." The hundreds of surviving recipe books, fortunately, give them voice. These books speak of women's lives and worries – the ailments they treated, the meals they cooked, the children they bore or miscarried, and how they and their families grew and flourished or suffered. Every ailment afflicted a human being and concerned not only the sufferer but also the people who loved them and cared for them. Who to consult and where to get treatment could be life-and-death decisions; these were not academic issues for them any more than they are in this century. An account of such a watershed moment should include everyone who made that moment happen. This account does.

This book is not many things. It is not a book about how men are evil because they suppressed and oppressed women. Lived life is more complex than this simple binary and the historical record bears that out. Men and women participated in the Scientific Revolution, and men and women resisted it. Elizabeth Blackwell was not the innocent, unwitting stooge of Machiavellian physicians and apothecaries; *A Curious Herbal* was her idea and she genuinely advocated for what is sometimes called the New Science. *The Apothecary's Wife* is also not a diatribe against capitalism. For one thing, that would be hypocritical considering that this book is also a commodity. Instead, it is a critical analysis of one aspect of the development of Western capitalism, which itself has more than one strain. This book is not anti-science, anti-medication, or anti-"modern" medications. It is not advocating homeopathy or "natural" medications or supplements. Actually, it is not advocating anything. *The Apothecary's Wife* offers knowledge and insight about what happened in the past, and how and why it happened, so readers can better understand the present. The book is mine, the history is shared, and the choices are yours.

A few preparatory notes are in order. One concerns the term "Scientific Revolution". Scholars do not use it any more, having established in the last few decades that "science" in its current meaning did not exist until the start of the nineteenth century, and that there were numerous strands of innovative thought, not the single one implied by the singular "revolution". It is a convenient term precisely because it is so familiar and generally known, however, so I encourage readers to remember that it is used in a capacious sense. Another note concerns the idiosyncratic spelling and punctuation characteristic of the seventeenth and eighteenth centuries. With a very few, recognizable exceptions, texts are quoted in their original form. If a quotation appears to be gibberish, I recommend reading it aloud because sound often reveals the word when the eyes cannot make sense of it. In places where spelling might appear to be a typo, I have written [*sic*]. In places where writing was illegible, I have written [*illeg*]. Bad handwriting transcends place and time, and different periods in history also favoured different handwriting styles, some easier to read than others. There was a significant change in the type of handwriting at the end of the seventeenth century, which can be helpful when dating a document or recognizing the age of a writer. In some recipe books, for instance, entries start with one handwriting style and continue through at least one or two others, while in others, an occasional recipe from an older contributor appears among those written by younger women. Ordinary wear and tear also have their impact. One eighteenth-century recipe book I read had a charred hole through the middle of several consecutive pages. Not hard to guess what kitchen mishap caused that.

Place names posed another challenge. Before 1603, England (which controlled Wales and Ireland) and Scotland were separate nations ruled by different monarchs: the Tudors in England and the Stuarts in Scotland. In 1603, Queen Elizabeth I of England, a Tudor, died childless and her cousin, King James VI of Scotland, a Stuart, was crowned King James I of England. Between 1603 and 1707, England and Scotland were different nations governed by different parliaments, but ruled by the same monarch. In 1707, the two countries united "into One Kingdom by the Name of Great Britain". In this book, the term "British Isles" refers to the agglomeration of England, Scotland, Wales, and Ireland before 1707, while "Great Britain" and "Britain" refer to it after 1707. "Great Britain" specifically covers England, Wales, and Scotland. The term "United Kingdom" appears only in Part Two. I excluded Ireland from my research because, unlike the other countries, it was actively and deliberately exploited as a colony during this period and consequently has a very different history.

Rather than footnote every unusual word, which would be intrusive and cumbersome, I have included a list of frequently used medical and apothecary terms. These definitions are taken from the *Oxford English Dictionary*, medical dictionaries of the time, and explanations by contemporary medical writers.

ana	abbreviation for "of each" in a recipe
antiscorbutic	medication for treating scurvy
bolus	medicine in a round or globe shape
cataplasm	a poultice
cathartic	a purgative that works on the bowels
clyster or glister	an enema
compound	medication made of more than one ingredient
costive	constipated
decoction	a liquid medication made by boiling a small amount of medicinal substance in a lot of water
drachm, dram	a very small quantity of medication (apothecary measure)
electuary	medication made by mixing medicinal powder with honey or another sweet, sticky substance
emplastrum	medicinal paste or salve smeared on; sometimes used for "plaister" or "plaster"
flux	a substance flowing out of the body, including menses
fomentation	warm soft material soaked in medicinal liquid and applied to the body
jalap, julep	water with sweet syrup and medicinal substance dissolved in it
lithontriptic(k)	medicine that breaks up bladder and kidney stones
mead	a drink made with fermented grains and honey
meathe	spiced mead
menstruum	a solvent

officinal	official stock preparation made by apothecaries and prescribed by physicians
pectoral	medicine good for digestion or as an expectorant
plaister, plaster	cloth soaked in medicinal liquid and dried, to be laid on the afflicted area so that medication will sink in through the skin (also emplaister, emplaster)
scruple	one-third dram; apothecary measure
simple	a medicine made of only one ingredient
vulnerary	medicine for treating wounds

Part One

I

Kitchen Physic Is the Best Physic

T he scene: a richly furnished bedroom in England. Thick tapestries on the walls decorate and insulate, the latter function being especially important because there is no glass in the windows, which are themselves narrow and not very high. Hangings, possibly embroidered, on all four sides of the wooden bed and a canopy on top provide warmth and privacy. The bed enclosed by those fabric walls is occupied by a wealthy, powerful person who is unwell. Worse, the year is somewhere around 1250 CE. On the positive side, this ailing noble of medieval England has a physician on staff in the household. It is time for said physician to earn his salary and keep.

Summoned to the bedside, the physician asks a lot of questions: When did you start to feel ill? Can you describe your symptoms? What have you been eating and drinking? What colour is your urine? How many times have you had a bowel movement in the last twenty-four hours? At what date and time were you born? He also checks the patient's pulse, the colour of the tongue and the whites of the eyes, and palpates any body parts causing distress. Having collected the necessary information, the physician gets to work. He draws up his patient's horoscope because the sign and planet under which someone is born will have a significant influence on their treatment. He might have an almanac handy for reference. He consults tomes in Greek or Latin. Then he makes a diagnosis and gets to work. His remedy probably includes a procedure like bloodletting, applying leeches, or cupping. It will involve a medication, which he will make himself.

Even the thirteenth-century English patient knows that illness has to do with an imbalance of humours. The physician's job is to determine what humours are unbalanced, why they are unbalanced, and how to recalibrate them. This model of the body and role of the physician came from ancient Roman and Greek philosophers, primarily Hippocrates (*c.* 460 – *c.* 375 BCE), after whom the physician's oath is named, and Galen (129–210 CE). According to the Galenic model, the body has four humours and four elements; people are healthy when the humours and elements are in balance, and unwell when they are not. The four humours correspond to fluids in the body – black bile, yellow bile, blood, and phlegm – and to qualities: cold and dry, hot and dry, hot and moist, and cold and moist, respectively. Different humours predominate depending on gender and age. Young men are hot, old men are cold; too much phlegm in a soldier makes him a coward, too much blood makes him reckless. Medication helps the body reset its humours, perhaps by putting the body through a physical ordeal like vomiting or sweating, but sometimes in ways the patient cannot feel. Neither one drug nor one dose is likely to fix everything necessary. The physician – or at least his medications – will be needed by our ailing aristocrat for a while.

As it has been for centuries, medication is made from materia medica, which is roughly translated as the materials of medicine. The more unusual ingredients include spices, animal parts, bits of mummies, metals, gems, pearls, coral, ambergris, and dung. However, the vast majority of materia medica is herbaceous, and there are many medicinal plants to choose from. At least one of the physician's books in Latin is a herbal, an encyclopaedia of medicinal plants that explains what to use them for and how. All herbals, even in the third millennium, are descendants of *De Materia Medica*, compiled by a first-century Greek physician in the Roman army named Dioscorides.

As it is the middle of the thirteenth century and the only places that use printed material are Korea and China, the physician's herbal is written by hand. If it is illustrated, chances are that the illustrations are beautiful, possibly witty, but unhelpful in identifying the plants. This is where training and the local shops can be of help. The shops are owned and run by apothecaries, a fairly new occupation for the time. In the middle of the thirteenth century, apothecaries belong to the Guild of Pepperers, which imports and sell spices, most notably and obviously pepper. Generally, pepperers sell their goods wholesale and in bulk, while apothecaries are customer facing. This is not a hard and fast distinction, however, and a pepperer could also have an apothecary business. Apothecaries sell exotics like spices, which are among the most expensive substances in Western Europe, as well as wine and herbs. Some apothecaries also sell medicines. Anyone, including physicians, can get hard-to-find ingredients like cinnamon and nutmeg at the right apothecary. But to suggest that the apothecary himself has something valuable to contribute medically or medicinally would elicit laughter. You might as well ask the local wool merchant for healthcare advice.

Physicians serve a very small group; then as now, not many people are wealthy, let alone very wealthy. Thirteenth-century

London is an urban centre, but it has fewer than 80,000 inhabitants, a small percentage of England's population. Most sick people get their treatment at home from the trusted, expert female head of the family. Making medication is just one of her domestic responsibilities. Women run the household, which means supervising and doing tasks like cooking, cleaning, sewing, weaving, mending, repairing, carrying and delivering and nursing and raising children, washing laundry, making household goods like candles, carding wool, spinning thread, preserving food, making wine and brewing beer, and training children and servants. They also work in the fields or in the shop, look after farm animals like chickens and pigs, go to market to buy and sell goods, maintain the kitchen garden (which has vegetables and medicinal plants), and gather ingredients from around the countryside. Domestic space is a capacious domain ranging from the garden to the barn to the kitchen to the parlour.

The older women in the family teach the next generation of women the knowledge and skills to diagnose illness, make medication, and administer it. A housewife's remedies are highly personal: they have been used on people who were near and dear, they have been seen (or thought) to work at least to some degree, and they do not appear to have hurt anyone. Like the physician, the woman of the household uses herbaceous materia medica; unlike him, she would never use arsenic, mercury, ground emerald, bloodletting, cupping, and the rest of it. She does not have a mortality rate, either. Nor does she charge a fee. Women are trusted for a reason. As one popular saying put it: "Kitchen physic is the best physic." A woman with a particular talent for healing can serve a whole neighbourhood in exchange for coins, goods, or services. She is not likely to be accused of witchcraft – accusations of witchcraft have more to do with interpersonal conflict and anxiety about political, social, or religious instability than with the status of an individual in a community. Besides, good healers are hard to find. All in all, when it comes to medicine, it is better to be a sick farmer than a sick earl. The farmer is more likely to get relief and less likely to suffer or die from the medication provided at home by women than the earl is from the physician's professional treatment.

But suppose – since we are imagining – that a tear in the fabric of space–time allows our afflicted sufferer to cross into the next century in search of better treatment. Unfortunately for the ailing time traveller, summoning the physician in this century results in the same experience as it did in the last: he asks the same questions, does the same physical examination (if any), checks the pulse, draws up a horoscope, and spouts a lot of Latin and Greek before making a diagnosis and issuing orders for treatment. He also uses the same techniques: bloodletting, leeches, cupping, and medication made from materia medica. This remarkable consistency is fundamental to the system and philosophy of education at this time. The fourteenth-century physician is a product of scholasticism, the philosophy that all necessary medical knowledge is lodged with ancient writers, and that learning their insights is the only way to become a capable practitioner. Scholastics have great faith in the ancient authorities; if Galen said it, it must be so. Medical students attend lectures where they listen to someone read aloud books by ancient Greek and Roman authorities and frantically write down as much as possible verbatim.

In fourteenth-century England, not much has changed for women either. Another century has passed where they serve as the trusted, reliable medical authority for the majority. Although, like everyone else, the woman of the family believes that the body conforms to Galenic theory, she does not believe that whatever the ancients wrote down was correct or that knowledge and expertise depend on book learning. She has been trained at home and that education serves her people well. She makes medications in her kitchen using recipes that are handed down and time-tested. Never mind what Galen said – if his advice or anything else proves fatal, it is not used again.

That is one reason why domestic medication is more effective than whatever physicians are administering. Another reason is how women and physicians process their ingredients. Both use simples, which are liquids made from one ingredient like cloves or marjoram, and compounds, which are combinations of simples. Some medications are simples, some are compounds, and some are combinations of compounds. Physicians use simples far less than women do and they process their ingredients far more. Both groups, for example, recognize liquorice root's usefulness in treating several forms of respiratory ailments, an effect confirmed by twentieth-century laboratory analysis. How they use it, on the other hand, is quite different.

Suppose our ailing English patient has a respiratory disorder. A housewife would wash a handful of Hope leaves (probably hops) in "running fayre water", add a handful of pitted "great raysins", a "good stick of licguoris [liquorice] well bruised", and "a little orgomye" (probably agrimony); soak it all together; strain the liquid; add sugar; and have the patient drink some twice a day. The physician would transform the liquorice into a powder or pill or oil and combine it with any number of other ingredients similarly transformed. The wealthy time traveller's physician's order would look like this:

R. of the seds of white poppie. ℥.ss. gumme arabick, Amylum, and gumme tragacant. ana. ℥.j, ss. seedes of cucumbers, citrons gourds, melons, quinces. ana. ʒ.iij. burnt Ivory, iuice of licorace. ana. ʒ.j.ss. penidies, as much in weight as all the rest. Make a pouder, of the which minister daily everie morning. ʒ.ij with sirup of poppy or roses.

Translated, the prescription combines half a dram of white poppy seeds; five drams halved (two and a half drams) each of gum Arabic, plant starch, and gum tragacanth; three drams each of seeds from cucumbers, citrons gourds, melons, and quince; five drams halved of burned ivory and liquorice juice; and the equivalent weight of this mixture in pulvis (a medicinal powder). After grinding it all up together, four drams of the new compound powder are to be mixed with syrup of poppy or syrup of roses and licked up every morning. By the time the liquorice gets into the patient, it is so changed and so small a part of the whole that any medicinal qualities are greatly reduced, if not eliminated.

All illness takes second place to the Black Death, which strikes Europe in the middle of the fourteenth century. It begins in 1347 when a fleet of ships from Asia bearing plague victims arrives in Messina, Sicily, and shortly after, when another ship arrives in Venice. The plague quickly overwhelms the continent, kills one-third of the population, and lays human nature bare. Of particular concern to our sick time traveller is the response of physicians, which is disappointing at best. As a group, they are notorious for fleeing or refusing to treat plague sufferers. (They did not wear the famous beaked plague mask. That would come later.) Physicians are not unique in this regard but considering their profession, it is particularly egregious. Their descendants would do it again at the next major outbreak of plague 300 years later.

The Black Death is a turning point for the apothecaries. Until then, they had been evolving slowly into something distinct from the pepperers. The plague speeds up that process, and the physicians' failure to treat patients makes people turn elsewhere for prophylactics, cures, and treatments. Apothecaries are a logical choice because they sell herbs, spices, and other elements of the materia medica. Some apothecaries have already started to offer medical advice. After all, these shopkeepers have been selling their wares to physicians for some time, so they have knowledge of what the different herbs and spices can do.

The 1340s are no time to linger in, so imagine that the sick English aristocrat leaps forward another hundred years or so, to the middle of the fifteenth century. Looking out of the window, it is clear that London has recovered literally and demographically from the Great Plague: more than 100,000 inhabitants have stretched the city beyond its original walls. Henry VI and Margaret of Anjou sit on the throne, but not for long; Joan of Arc and the French armies have just finished drubbing the English; William Caxton has not yet imported his printing press; Martin Luther has not yet nailed his *Ninety-five Theses* to the church door; Vasco da Gama has not yet sailed around Africa into the Indian Ocean; and Christopher Columbus is a toddler. The art and science of medicine are still familiar to our unwell voyager. The fifteenth-century physician is still the product of a university, still a scholastic, still a Galenist, still drawing horoscopes to assist with diagnosis, and still designing treatment to rebalance a patient's humours. Bloodletting is still a standard procedure and medication is still made from materia medica.

The market for medical care is changing, however: male physicians are beginning to face real competition from male apothecaries. By the 1450s, although they continue to sell other items like soap, spoons, and wine, apothecaries are involved in making and selling medication. Frequently, they also offer medical advice. In London, apothecaries annually appoint two inspectors to make sure that every one of them is selling good-quality ingredients and compounds. Although they operate within the guild system, which means training apprentices to become journeymen (men no longer needing training but not yet proficient enough to be masters) and masters (men who have mastered the craft), paying dues and so forth, apothecaries are still not their own guild. Some of the guilds reorganized at the end of the fourteenth century; the pepperers, spicers, and apothecaries joined the new Company of Grocers ("grossers") for people who deal in bulk quantities ("in gross"). The Company of Grocers is not a good fit for apothecaries, a fact that is becoming more apparent over time.

The third type of practitioner (and the longest-standing one), the housewife, continues quietly and steadily to provide the best, most reliable treatment in England. If she has a garden, she is still growing medicinal plants like agrimony, columbine, elecampane, and hyssop. Everything grown at home has some value to health. As John Smith enthused in 1670, parsnips are "very useful in a Family, being good and wholsome Nourishment, and fatneth the Body much; the Seed hereof being drunk, cleanseth the Belly from tough Flegmatick matter therein". What cannot be grown at home is collected in the wild. Women teach each other where and when to find these ingredients: selfheal in meadows, sorrel in fields, butterbur on riverbanks, St John's wort from hedges and bushes, foxglove in country lanes, betony in the woods, moonwort in rocky pastures, and wild parsley on dunghills. If it grows within walking distance, a woman knows whether to use or avoid it.

Another journey through time brings the sick traveller to the middle of the sixteenth century. Mary I, daughter of Henry VIII, is on the throne. London has grown so far beyond its walls along the Thames that it has merged with Westminster, home to Her Majesty and the eponymous Abbey. The south bank of London – Southwark – has an arena devoted to bull-baiting and another to bear-baiting. In less than a decade, Mary I will be dead and the last of Henry VIII's children, Elizabeth I will ascend to the throne, but it will be another few decades before William Shakespeare takes the stage and has his first play performed. In the meantime, a revolution has just begun on the continent. According to the familiar so-called "Tale of the Triumph of Modern Medicine", before the Scientific Revolution – those centuries our ailing English aristocrat has just moved through – nobody knew anything about medicine and people had to resort to the foul concoctions of equally foul old women. Then modern science came along and revealed real cures. The foul concoctions were tossed away in favour of anti-biotics and the foul old women were charged with witchcraft and burned to death. All hail, the Scientific Revolution and the brilliant, brave men who made it happen.

Versions of this fairy tale have persisted for a long time, and it is time to replace them. Unquestionably, the Scientific Revolution was a period and a movement of tremendous change and many staggering achievements. No aspect of life went untouched: education, the body, politics, religion, gender, race, architecture, technology, the cosmos, and of course illness and health. Science's revolutionaries were also heavily indebted to that vital new technology, the printing press. It enabled the (comparatively) speedy mass production of anything involving words. Ideas could move from one end of Europe to the other with stunning rapidity for the times, and everyone could be sure of having exactly the same text. If a book or treatise could not be had in one place, like London or Madrid, it could be sent from Paris, Leiden, or Milan. Printed matter reached a much larger audience in far less time than any handwritten book, it could be available in many places all at once, and it was less expensive than a manuscript. From the very beginning, it was the most valuable and effective weapon that science's revolutionaries had. It arrived none too soon in England, around 1476, courtesy of William Caxton.

From medicine's point of view, the Scientific Revolution begins in the sixteenth century when the failures of Galenic medicine become too much for two very different men: Philippus Aureolus Theophrastus Bombastus von Hohenheim (c. 1493–1541), who took the name Paracelsus later in life, and Andreas Vesalius (1514–64). They have different frustrations and different solutions, but they both aim for comprehensive change. Born in Switzerland, Paracelsus is educated at a charity school where boys are taught mining, geology, and metallurgy. He attends universities throughout central Europe, earns a medical degree and, convinced that experience is a better teacher than books, starts travelling to learn as much as he can. By the time he returns to the Alps, he has formulated a revolutionary set of ideas. Paracelsus replaces scholasticism with observation and experimentation, rejects the whole humoural theory, maintains that disease infects a body from without, and promotes chemical medicine. He believes that diseases disable organs, which then produce poisons that cause illness. To cure the body's self-poisoning, the body must be dosed with poison (the theory that "like cures like"). As eighteenth-century physician John Fothergill understatedly wrote in his lecture notes: "The vegetables were more used by the antients [sic] than the Paracelsists." Galenists think that this approach is madness, if not murder, but Paracelsus argues that his medications are perfectly safe as long as the dosage is properly calculated.

This is Paracelsus's most significant impact on the history of medicine: the elevation of chemical medicine. He did not invent it, but his advocacy set chemical medication on the road to seeming superior to herbal medication. Strictly speaking, there is no such thing as chemistry in the fifteenth century, but there is alchemy, and Paracelsus adapts it to his purposes. Alchemists hold that matter consists of three building blocks: salt, sulphur, and mercury. Their interest lies in breaking down a compound into its building blocks to see how it was made, and then recombining those building blocks to make a better substance. Paracelsus advocates metals as medication because metals are excellent poisons with which to treat the body's self-poisoning. He adopts alchemy's techniques for working with metals (also sulphur and mercury) to create those medications. If that case of syphilis just will not go away, a little mercury should do the trick. All very logical for a revolutionary who, in the words of Allen Dubus, was "influenced by traditional alchemy, by medical theory and practice, and by Central European mining techniques".

Andreas Vesalius is also frustrated with Galenic medicine and scholasticism, in his case because of the frequent disagreement between what the authorities like Galen said about the human body and what he has observed for himself. He is not the first to confront this issue, but in the past, thinkers had come up with complicated solutions to reconcile authority and experience. Vesalius's solution is to reject a millennium and a half of tradition and learning. He concludes that the revered ancients were wrong about human anatomy and devotes years to dissecting human bodies and drawing everything he sees in meticulous, beautiful detail. In 1543 he publishes *De humani*

corporis fabrica libri septem, a literally and figuratively tremendous book that reveals what the human body actually
looks like from the surface of the skin down to the network of
veins and arteries. It still dazzles, five centuries later. Equally
stunning are the acts that produce it: Vesalius rejects the
ancient writers who had been relied upon for centuries and
trusts only what he can see and prove for himself. With *De
Fabrica*, Vesalius lays out a new method for identifying knowledge: observation, investigation, corroboration, repetition, and
dissemination. Begin by questioning everyone and everything,
perform observations or experiments and record the data, use
the results to forge an explanation of the previously inexpli-
cable phenomenon, get others to confirm the data, and then
share what was done and learned so everyone else can learn
what is true.

In England, our ailing time traveller can observe the influence
of these ideas by speaking with Sir Francis Bacon (1561–1626),
first at the court of Elizabeth I and then at the court of James
I. Bacon is inspired by the new method for identifying fact and
establishing knowledge. He imagines an ideal society in which
institutions exist solely for the purpose of making observations
and doing experiments, and asserts that knowledge should be
used to benefit humanity. His main interest in the New Science
is the relationship between reason and perception. As he points
out, the mind can affect the information gathered by our senses
– human sensory perception is limited and those senses can
trick the mind. Bacon offers several solutions to these problems. Beliefs and expectations, he insists, "must be abjured and
renounced with firm and solemn resolution, and the understanding must be completely freed and cleared of them". He
also holds that if at least one other reliable, unbiased person saw
it, got the same results from doing the experiment exactly the

same way, or calculated the same answer using the data, then the finding is fact rather than belief (or hope, or aspiration). In the middle of the next century, Robert Boyle will call this objective, observant person a "modest witness". Two hundred years later, the name for such a person will be "scientist".

By the end of the sixteenth century, proponents of the New Science are on an inventing spree. In addition to books, there are now microscopes (from 1590) and telescopes (from 1608). Technology supports experimentation, which allows humans to see how nature works and what it is made of. For physicians of the Scientific Revolution, experimentation first and foremost means dissection, which is a huge boon for obvious reasons. Between 1618 and 1628, William Harvey (1578–1657) dissects scores of creatures to discover that blood circulates through the body due to the contraction of the heart muscle. When he publishes *Exercitatio anatomica de motu cordis et sanguinis in animalibus* (*On the Motion of the Heart and Blood in Animals*) in 1628, it is a watershed event on the level of Vesalius's *De Fabrica*. Like Vesalius, Harvey reveals how the body actually works and like Vesalius, he exposes impossibilities in Galen's explanations. Also like Vesalius (and many other revolutionaries, scientific or otherwise), Harvey does not receive a wholly warm response to his work. Vesalius's mentor calls him a madman, while one eminent anatomist calls Harvey an "accountant".

On the face of it, the Scientific Revolution seems like the breakthrough that our English patient has been seeking. A whole school of physicians and apothecaries is forming around the New Science. They doubt or have rejected Galenic medicine, they are excited about the new emerging field of chemistry; they are dissecting, recording, publishing, and disseminating; they are writing and visiting like-minded colleagues throughout

Europe; and they are rethinking surgical procedures and medical school curricula.

The entire medical profession is also changing. In 1518, Thomas Linacre, Henry VIII's personal physician, persuades the king to grant physicians a royal charter, creating the RCP. His Majesty follows the charter with an Act of Parliament in 1523, putting the RCP in charge of medicine throughout the kingdom. "Medicines cannot be rightly used, but by them that understand the whole methode of Physicke," as Eleazar Duncan puts it. By the middle of the century, the College's physicians have established rules for licensing and standards of medical practice, and they are prosecuting those who do not meet them. From the beginning, although with irregular intensity over the years, the RCP prosecutes women within London and up to seven miles from the city who have established themselves as female physicians or practitioners of physic. Women, after all, are trained from girlhood to treat illness and make medication, their reputation is superior to that of the professionals, and there are many more knowledgeable women even in a city like London than there are university-educated physicians. Generally, the RCP is more willing to look the other way when it comes to women treating the poor at the request of parish officials, who are legally responsible for caring for the indigent; however, where a woman is a threat to reputation or income, she is chastised and forced to stop.

The apothecaries undergo a change very similar to the physicians. In 1617, Queen Anne's apothecary, Gideon de Laune, persuades the king to give the apothecaries a royal charter and make them a guild. The Company of Grocers, to which the apothecaries belonged, is furious; it means that some of their most affluent members are breaking off, with a consequent loss of revenue, power, and prestige. The RCP is also furious. The apothecaries are serious financial competition. Already they have been cutting into physicians' incomes by making and selling medication, touting their own expertise, and even treating patients. The charter given by James I does not help. He puts apothecaries in charge of medication, although physicians have already been in charge of medicine throughout the kingdom for the last century. So, to which group does medication belong? It is more than a question of territory and prestige. In addition to fees, by this point medication is a significant source of income for physicians and the primary source of income for apothecaries. The fight is about money and authority.

In addition to anti-woman prosecutions, things are changing for women during the sixteenth and seventeenth centuries. Men like Vesalius and Harvey exploited the advantages offered by the printing press, but the new technology is also a powerful tool for women in Europe. In Italy, Isabella Cortese (fl. 1561) publishes *I Secreti de la Signora Isabella Cortese* (*The Secrets of Mrs Isabella Cortese*) in 1561, the same year that Francis Bacon is born. Her book is full of recipes for compounding medication, making perfume, and performing alchemy. In France, the famous midwife Louise Bourgeois Boursier (1563–1636) publishes *Observations Diverses* (*Diverse Observations [of Medical Cases]*) in 1609. Bourgeois's expanded edition is published in 1617, the same year that the apothecaries become the Worshipful Society of Apothecaries. On the other hand, it is not possible to find a printed book by a woman about medicine or the New Science in England during the sixteenth and early seventeenth centuries. In fact, it is extremely difficult to find a printed book by a woman at all, and still harder to find one where authorship was confirmed. That is not to say that print culture in England ignores women; far from it. Male authors are writing books for women, some of them explaining how to do domestic things (mansplaining in print began early) and some of them praising women's authority. As Robert Green writes in 1592: "For my self if I be ill at ease I take kitchen physic, I make my wife my Doctor, and my garden my Apothecaries shop."

Despite the best efforts of Paracelsus and his followers, materia medica remains predominantly herbal, and gardening is still a vital domestic skill. Gervase Markham's *The English Housewife* (1615) has a section on raising medicinal plants, starting with how to care for and plant seeds, and another extensive section of recipes for medications. William Lawson's *The Country Housewife's Garden* (1618) is the first book dedicated solely to women's gardening. It is reprinted nearly twenty more times by 1695, making it a very popular, very common book throughout the century. Lawson recommends that women keep a separate garden for flowering herbs, which had primarily medicinal uses, and explains how to care for them.

Women are building their own, vibrant manuscript culture, with acknowledgement and respect for women's domestic medicinal authority at its root. After all, if it is not considered valuable, why go to the trouble and expense of writing it down? Late in Elizabeth I's reign, women start recording knowledge by keeping recipe books: blank books in which they write down their recipes for anything made at home, including food, drink, soap, face wash, ink, preserves, and medication. Every time the woman of the house has a recipe that she wants to remember, she writes it in the book. Women were already sharing recipes orally; now they are sharing them textually. A woman might write her own recipe in someone else's book, or vice versa, often at the owner's invitation. They also pass down these books to the next generation. Some women go on to inherit recipe books over a century old, and they still add their own recipes. Very quickly, the recipe book becomes an invaluable tool for women: a means of taking care of the home, a way to form and preserve community, and a deeply personal and deeply utilitarian possession.

One more particularly important development is taking place: European imperialism. While our ailing time traveller is moving through time and space between 1550 and 1650, the Portuguese, Spanish, English, and Dutch are slaughtering each other and the Indigenous peoples of the Spice Islands for control of the obscenely lucrative spice trade; establishing trading outposts along the coasts of Africa; colonizing the Americas; and killing and enslaving what will eventually be millions of people, turning the remaining inhabitants into captive markets for European goods. Spices once limited to the very wealthy (monarchs sent nutmeg as a wedding gift to each other) are creeping within the financial reach of less affluent, less powerful people. That means that more women are making recipes requiring spices. Knowledge of medications does not change, but the availability of expensive ingredients does.

All this is very promising, but the formerly medieval, long-suffering, much-travelled aristocrat we have been following has one last hurdle to clear before the Scientific Revolution arrives in Britain: civil war, which breaks out in the early 1640s. War is, to put it mildly, a significant obstacle to the development of intellectual thought and international trade, the national economy, the arts, religious toleration, and other key elements of a society. Combatants in the civil war are the Royalists, who believe that Charles I should rule and has God's mandate to do so, and the Parliamentarians, who believe that government should be controlled by elected representatives and that monarchs are subject to the law. Many Parliamentarians are Puritans, people who had been considered so crazy and subversive just twenty years earlier that they had to flee persecution to the howling wilderness of North America, where they established Massachusetts and began wiping out the Indigenous peoples. The Parliamentarians secure victory in 1649 when they execute Charles I, thus asserting definitively that man made (and unmade) kings. The fighting and appalling brutality continue briefly in Scotland and a little longer in Ireland, but England establishes a commonwealth in 1649 and a rough stability ensues. That is all the stability that the Scientific Revolution needs.

Much has changed since our patient took ill in the thirteenth century – at least, much has changed for the male professionals of healthcare. Physician and apothecary have become defined professions with guild status, jockeying for control of diagnosing illness, prescribing medication, and making and selling medications. Despite all their knowledge and training, they are fighting over a small pie; despite illness and injury being a constant of daily life, few people can or do pay physicians or apothecaries for care.

By comparison, little has changed for women. Even after four centuries, they remain the trusted source of most medical treatment in the British Isles. They are respected and reliable; their domestic medicine is always immediately on hand and free of charge; and their medications are time-tested and overall, equally or more effective and less lethal than those of their male, professional counterparts. Their domestic medicine is also available to anyone: if you are sick, you get treatment. In modern parlance, medication is a right. Women share their knowledge with one another and between generations, forming and maintaining personal connections and whole communities through the circulation of that knowledge and sharing of skills.

Women are the reason that physicians and apothecaries are not making more money or winning more respect.

But it is 1650. The Scientific Revolution offers new methods, new ideas, new technologies, and new opportunities. Everything is about to change.

2

The Countess of Kent's Recipe Book

6accdae13eff7i3l9n4o4qrr4s8t12ux. This is how Isaac Newton explained calculus to his friend Henry Oldenburg. If it seems confusing, take heart: Oldenburg did not understand it either. The numbers and letters are an encoded anagram of a Latin phrase, *Data aequatione quotcunque fluentes quantitates involvente, fluxiones invenire; et vice versa,* which translates to "Given an equation involving any number of fluent quantities to find the fluxions, and vice versa." Newton had not worked out all the kinks in his mathematical system and did not want someone to use his letter to Oldenburg to figure out calculus first, so he sent his explanation as... this. The eventual fight between Isaac Newton and Gottfried Wilhelm Leibniz over the invention of calculus was ugly. Partisans across Europe, including some of the most important and famous contributors to the Scientific Revolution, took sides while Newton and Leibniz fiercely and impolitely battled for credit. The argument lasted for centuries.

What does it matter who invented calculus? Isn't the point that it was invented? Those are not disingenuous questions;

those are questions about a fundamental principle underlying medicine and medicines: that knowledge can be private property. It can be owned, bought, sold, traded, or made freely available. Therefore, it matters a great deal who invented calculus because calculus and the credit for it not only belong to someone but can also be used as capital. Knowledge as private property was a crucial development in the Scientific Revolution and the engine that fired it. This concept was also an essential tool for male professionals' efforts to take the making and provision of medication from women, and to move it out of the home and away from the community – a story that starts in 1653 with Elizabeth Grey, Countess of Kent.

She would have been no ordinary woman of any age, but she was not quite as unusual for the seventeenth century as twenty-first century readers might expect. She was born Lady Elizabeth Talbot, daughter of Gilbert Talbot, Earl of Shrewsbury, and raised in the court of Elizabeth I. The Tudors believed in education for their daughters as well as their sons, and Tudor monarchs' courts were full of dazzlingly talented and skilled minds. Young Elizabeth Talbot was one of those gifted and fortunate women who received a spectacular education and became fluent in several languages. She was fascinated with new ideas and inventions, and became a patron of the arts at a young age. She was extremely intelligent, highly educated, fabulously wealthy, and a favourite of the queen – not a bad way to start her twenties.

In 1601, Elizabeth Talbot married Henry Grey, who became the 8th Earl of Kent in 1623, making her the Countess of Kent. Henry's most significant accomplishment appears to have been marrying Elizabeth. He hired a good manager for his estates, John Selden, and like many other noblemen sponsored a candidate for the House of Commons – again, John

Selden, who proved a very good choice. Henry Grey served one term in Parliament and two terms as Lord Lieutenant of Bedfordshire, but he always held that office jointly with another peer. He withdrew from political life after 1626 when he was forty-three and did little with his time. He never served the crown in a military, administrative, or diplomatic post; he had no particular talent like training horses or swordsmanship; he was not notably educated; he did not collect anything like art or ancient manuscripts; he did not write or compose anything; he did not make improvements to Wrest Park, the family seat; and he did not travel except from one house to the next. Henry did not impose much on his wife, either, from the very beginning. The Greys did not consummate their marriage for nearly a year after the ceremony, although they were living together, because Elizabeth did not want to. From her activities for the rest of their lives together, Henry made no objection to his wife going wherever she wished and doing whatever she wished.

Doing whatever she wished included carrying on an affair with the aforementioned John Selden, who was as unlike Henry Grey as possible. Selden probably met the earl and countess because he lived almost across the street from their London house in Whitefriars. His portrait at the Yale Law School shows a narrow-faced man with a large nose and sensitive eyes. He was not particularly handsome, but he was brilliant. As a politician, he was often consulted by members of the government to help develop policy. His work on law and the principles of government was required reading long after his death. He knew five modern languages (including French, Italian, German, and Spanish) and was familiar with nine ancient ones (including Old English, Hebrew, Chaldean, and Ethiopic), which must have appealed to the linguist in Elizabeth Grey. His love of literature must also have appealed; he personally knew John Suckling, Michael Drayton, Ben Jonson, and John Donne, and worked as a research assistant for Francis Bacon.

The earl and countess socialized with the most intellectual and intellectually adventurous people of the age. When James I succeeded Elizabeth I in 1603, the Countess of Kent joined his wife's court. In her portrait at the Tate Gallery, painted shortly after Queen Anne's death in 1619, Elizabeth is wearing mourning (see plate section, p.1). (It was Anne's apothecary, Gideon de Laune, who persuaded James I to make the apothecaries a guild.) The countess was also part of the inner circle of the next queen, Henrietta Maria of France, which included Théodore de Mayerne, personal physician to the queen; John Evelyn, noted botanist and Fellow of the Royal Society; John Pell, renowned mathematician and Fellow of the Royal Society; and Sir Kenelm and Lady Digby (about whom you will hear later on). The Greys shared many of their friends with John Selden and with Elizabeth's sister and brother-in-law, Alethea and Thomas Howard, Earl and Countess of Arundel and Lennox, including the Digbys, Ben Jonson (also a very good friend of Sir Kenelm Digby), and Sir Robert Cotton. Sir Robert learned Italian from John Florio, who had taught Elizabeth Grey, and owned the only known manuscript of *Beowulf*, which was almost destroyed when his library caught fire in 1701 (visitors to the British Library can see the charred edges of the pages). London was much smaller then, and the group of people with the same level of education who shared interests in learning was very small indeed.

When her husband died in 1639, the countess became even more independent and wealthy. She lived openly with John Selden and continued to socialize with intelligent, interesting people at the leading edge of cultural life. She conducted her own investigations into the workings of nature, a popular activity for educated male and female aristocrats at the time. (Her sister Alethea, who worked with Elias Ashmole, another member of the Scientific Revolution and founder of the Ashmolean Museum in Oxford, built and equipped her house, Tart Hall, so she could do experiments.) Elizabeth Grey acquired a reputation as a paragon of elite femininity: generous to friends and needy artists, uninterested in court intrigue, and occupied with the new, revolutionary ideas, although only at home. In contrast, Margaret Cavendish, Duchess of Newcastle, was also occupied with the new, revolutionary ideas but insisted on barging into male-only spaces and publicly rebutting men's ideas.

Notwithstanding her staggering wealth and scads of servants, Elizabeth Grey was the woman of the house – or in her case, several houses. For centuries, "woman of the house" was an executive position. Regardless of the resources and size of the family, from the lowliest labourer to the wife of an earl, the woman was expected to manage the household and look after her family's well-being. "Family" was not just blood relatives; in the seventeenth and eighteenth centuries, the term included servants, employees like estate stewards, apprentices, journeymen who lived with the master's family, and even tenants. A housewife was expected to keep the household accounts; the wives of tradesmen often also kept the business's books.

For the vast majority of women who did not have servants, daily life was an endless train of physical labour. Domestic tasks included cleaning (house, furniture, household goods, people, clothes, linen, and so forth), making clothing (spinning, weaving, sewing, knitting, and embroidering), repairing things or arranging for their repair, tending the kitchen garden, stocking the house with food (harvesting, drying, preserving, pickling, curing, candying, brewing, fermenting, and buying what was not grown or raised at home), cooking, bearing and raising children, caring for her spouse, and in agricultural families, caring for livestock and helping with the harvest. A widow would also be responsible for helping her children find suitable spouses, which in affluent, especially noble families could mean selecting the person for them. Regardless of marital status, every woman was also responsible for medication. As *The Ladies Dictionary* (1694) explained, the virtuous housewife's "Closet is stored with *Physicks* and *Cordials* prepared with her own *Skill* and *Industry*, to send to her poor Neighbours when they are sick or in pain". Gathering, storing, sometimes buying, and using ingredients was just the first stage; preparing medications "with her own *Skill* and *Industry*" was the next, and administering it the last.

The higher up the social ladder she was, the fewer of these tasks a woman did herself unless she chose to. Katherine of Aragon, first wife of Henry VIII, daughter of Queen Isabella and King Ferdinand, and one of the most educated women in Europe, made and embroidered Henry's shirts herself. A woman like the Countess of Kent would not peel potatoes or poach fish, but she would collaborate with the cook to design menus and develop dishes, supervise the housekeeper to ensure that the house was running smoothly, and check that the servants were doing their jobs and being treated properly. Household expenses were her responsibility, and those expenses could be complicated and extensive at each house. When the Duke of Beaufort undertook a six-week progress through Wales, the Duchess of Beaufort kept track of the expenses for a retinue of more than fifty people. Hosting an important visitor like the Duke of Beaufort required weeks of preparations by the female head of the house. Even changing residences could involve fearsome logistics.

Housekeepers were at the top of the servants' hierarchy and were expected to know everything about maintaining a house that a poor woman or tradesman's wife had to know. In *The Ladies Dictionary* (1694), the job description listed "Competent Knowledge in Preserving, Conserving, and Candying, making of Cates [cakes], and all manner of Spoonmeats, Jellies, and the like: also in Distilling all manner of Waters", as well as "competent knowledge in Physick and Chirurgery, that they may be able to help their maimed, sick, and indigent Neighbours; for commonly all good and charitable Ladies make this a part of their Housekeepers business". A noblewoman like the Countess of Kent would keep track of the medication supply in any of her houses as she would keep track of anything else, like the silver, the linens, or the amount of wine in the cellars.

To manage all of the information about what was or could be made in the kitchen, women kept recipe books. Previously, recipes were part of an oral tradition. Sometimes they took the form of rhyming verse because it was easy to remember. Jane Barker, one of the two central players of Chapter 4, includes rhyming recipes in *A Patch-Work Screen for the Ladies* (1723) as evidence of her protagonist's domestic excellence. "The Receipt for Welsh Flummery [a sweet, jelly-like dessert] / Made at the Castle of Montgomery," for example, sounds almost exactly like a recipe in prose:

Take Jelly of Harts-horn, with Eggs clarify'd,
Two good Pints at least; of Cream, one beside.
Fine Sugar and Limons [*sic*], as much as is fit
To suit with your Palate, that you may like it.

Three Ounces of Almonds, with Orange Flow'r-Water,
Well beaten: Then mix 'em all up in a Platter
Of China or Silver; for that makes no matter.

Written recipes and recipe books became popular around the end of the sixteenth century among women who were literate and could afford a large blank book, its binding if one were needed, pens, ink, and time. Even these requirements could be worked around: the first part of Mistress Honore Henslow's "book of surgerie and phisick" from 1601 was copied down by her servant, Andrewe Plowden, although the reason is not given. This period for recipe books roughly coincides with the second half of Elizabeth I's reign, just around the time that Elizabeth Grey, Countess of Kent reached adulthood. Recipe books contained the instructions for making household goods at home. Items like candles and ink, cosmetics like face washes and rouge, and foodstuffs like roast chicken, braised turnips, currant wine, pickled plums, and rum cake were all confected in the kitchen, so their recipes would be in a recipe book.

Medications were among these substances: cough drops, burn salve, elixir to reduce cramps, drinks to cure jaundice, poultices for cuts and blisters, and plasters for fevers were also made in the kitchen. Under C in the table of contents, one seventeenth-century book lists, in this order, one recipe for "chocolate puffs", one "for ye Collick", two recipes "for a Cough", and one each "for a consumption", "a good Cordiall", "a good cake", something called "spewsbry cakes", "for a cake", and "consumption". An early eighteenth-century recipe book (c. 1725) listed together recipes for baked goods, preserving fruit, and medication, including a treatment for strangury (frequent, painful urination in minute quantities at a time).

Anything having directly to do with the management of health – whether to restore or to maintain it – was made from a recipe; even an aristocrat like Elizabeth Grey, Countess of Kent, would need a book to keep track of the good ones.

As utilitarian, household objects, recipe books did not leave the home any more than mattresses and chamber pots did, but they were also deeply personal items and cherished family heirlooms. They had a far larger significance to individuals, to families, and to the larger society than just as collections of instructions for manipulating vegetables and meat. A woman treasured her recipe book. It was a valuable compendium of information. Tired of cooking carrots the same way? The recipe book would have several ways to prepare them. Someone in the family has an upset stomach? There would be at least a few recipes for remedies. Need an impressive dessert to serve guests? Or heartburn medication when that fancy dinner is over? Check the recipe book. The supply of wines is running low? A parent is going blind? The baby has worms? You can't get pregnant? There was a recipe for every concern, and if a woman lacked a treatment for kidney stones or a good way to cook venison, a female relative, friend, or neighbour would have one to share.

Recipe books were organic creations, always added to and amended. Physically, they were books of blank pages, many fairly large, and recipes were inscribed wherever the owner wanted them. That practice produced highly individualized recipe book organization, to put it mildly. As earlier examples suggest, some women just added recipes one after the other, so instructions for making pea soup could follow instructions for an earache treatment. In 1692, Mary Harrison wrote instructions "To make Barly Broth" right after those for "A Diet Drinke for the Wind". One eighteenth-century writer entered "To Roast

Hamm", "To make Ink", and "To make Black Salve" one after the next. Other recipe books were more ordered. Some women grouped recipes by kind: recipes for baking in one section and for preserving in another, or recipes for salves in one place, for cordials in another. Some women made a table of contents in the front, some kept one in the back, some had none at all. Sometimes recipes were listed in alphabetical order, although that did not inevitably offer much organization. Was that salve for gunpowder burn listed under S for salve, B for burn, or G for gunpowder? The answer depended on the woman who listed it.

Women were always in search of better recipes, whether it was a better way of pickling plums, a tastier fricassee of rabbit, or a more effective medication. They were empirics: people who used trial and error to reach conclusions. Burn medicines are common in recipe books, unsurprising for a population that spent a lot of time in the kitchen. Recurring recipes reveal family health over the years. A cluster of recipes for eye problems in one Mrs Johnson's recipe book reveals that she tried for more than a decade to find a successful treatment for her family's recurring eye problems. Empirics were not the same as empiricists, which early scientists took pains to establish. Empiricists observed or experimented on nature to understand how it works. Empirics were also not the same as theorists, the physicians who held a theory about the body's workings (like, say, Galenic medicine) and forged treatments in accordance with the theory and at times in discordance with observed reality.

The empiric method worked pretty well overall and far better than theoretical medicine like Galenism. It is not fair to judge anyone's success rates against major illnesses that have only just been (or have not yet been) conquered like smallpox, plague, or cancer. It is much more reasonable to judge success rates for other problems like heart palpitations, fever, irregular menses, jaundice, and fluid retention. If a member of the household told their wife, mother, aunt, or sister that they had a headache or a cut, there was a good possibility that they would get a remedy that actually remedied. At the time, Jesuit's bark or cinchona was used to treat fevers; in the twentieth century, chemists discovered that it contained quinine, which is good for treating malaria. The bark of the willow was used to reduce fever; it became the foundation for aspirin.

Useful recipes and up-to-date information tailored or tailorable to the needs of the family were all good reasons to value a recipe book, but the books offered far more than that. They created a community of knowers and promoted an ethos of sharing – the heart of domestic medicine. No woman, including the Countess of Kent, kept her recipe book in isolation. Women exchanged recipes all the time, whether casually, such as over the garden fence or during a chat at the market, or more formally, such as by invitation. They copied down recipes for food and medicines from dictation or asked the original source to write it in their books. Visitors and honoured guests could be invited to contribute a favourite recipe.

This practice of sharing and collaborating makes recipe books a place where the ordinary women of history, normally invisible and disregarded, become visible and vital. Over and over again, I have gingerly turned the first page of a recipe book three or four centuries old and fallen into the life of a woman, a family, and a community of friends and neighbours and distant relatives. A veritable flock of Mrs Hodgsons contributed recipes to Mildred Hodgson of Liverpool's book, including Mrs Hodgson from St Albans (about 180 miles distant), Mrs Hodgson from Ashbourne (about 65 miles), and Mrs Hodgson from "Crape Marsh" (possibly near Sheffield and therefore around 80 miles away). Even an unmarried relative, Miss Hodgson from Manchester (about 40 miles), contributed a recipe. Mildred also had visitors from far-off places. Her book includes recipes from Mrs Webb of Hillingdon, Mrs David of Calwich, Mrs Leigh of Greenhill, Mrs Mills of Norbury, and Mrs Pyshe of Noonham. A pair of surviving recipe books from the Wise family reveal that Prudence Wise's daughter-in-law, Mary, copied a long sequence of recipes into her own recipe book directly from the elder Mrs Wise's. The younger woman had already begun collecting recipes, but the addition of her mother-in-law's recipes early on offers a picture of the two women working together. Whether the copied recipes are a sign of harmony is another question.

Not every recipe was attributed or signed. After reading hundreds of sixteenth-century, seventeenth-century, and eighteenth-century English and Scottish recipe books, I found only one with every single recipe attributed to someone. To some extent, including a name depended on the personality of the person keeping the book or on the personality of the one giving the recipe. Contributions from a member of the landed gentry or aristocracy always included name and title, a practice that appears regardless of the century, place, or class of the book's owner. In some books, the contributor's name appears only at the recipe and not in the table of contents. The author who identified the source of every recipe wrote the name next to the binding, to the right or left of the recipe. Elizabeth Smith's recipe book, started in 1700, does not have a table of contents, but she wrote the title of "My Lady Greshame's Almond puddings" in larger letters and with a differently shaped quill than she wrote the directions, which makes the words stand out quite clearly. She did not have very many recipes from titled personages, so it's no wonder she showed it off.

What's startling is when a recipe from a physician or apothecary turns up:

Strengthening Plaister
♃ Rx Empt ad Herniam ℥vi
   Paracels
Diasaponis a ℋ℥ ss
℞ of extend sup AluCa
  Φ tergo

As I will discuss in Chapter 6, the inclusion of professionals' recipes was significant for a number of reasons. For now, the notable issue when professional language appears is how disruptive and intrusive it seems. The same holds for the appearance of someone professionally credentialled in a group of laypersons. No matter how distinguished the source or how many professional sources a book contained, the recipes from friends and neighbours far outnumbered them. Like people "of quality", physicians were always identified as physicians in recipe books. Apothecaries, who did not have the same social cachet because they were guild-trained rather than university-educated, were only sometimes identified as such, but the language of their recipes, like this one, often provides that information or at least strongly suggests the supplier. Even when a male professional's recipe was recorded in standard, written English, it often looked and sounded different because of its technical lexicon, such as the recipe for a powder to treat a toothache:

take [*sic*] red coral powderd 2 drames, Bole one dram, mastic half a dram, scutchinnel half a scruple, of burnd allum half a scruple, dragons blood half a scruple, Acorn cups A scruple, make all this into a fine powder & rub y^r teeth with it twise a week.

Elizabeth Smith's recipe for "The greater Palsie wat^r & also Apoplexye draught by Mr Mathias", another apothecary, was two or three times the length of all the other recipes in her book.

There has been little attention to these recipes from male professionals: how women got them, why women got them, from whom women got them, what a professional's motives were in allowing a woman to have them, or what the appearance of an apothecary's or physician's recipe in a woman's recipe book can tell us. At this stage in the story, I want to make clear two points. The first is that professionals' recipes were not always translated from the official apothecary code into English; the second, that women sometimes paid for the recipe, translated or not. The keeper of one seventeenth-century recipe book spent £100 for a recipe, a staggering sum for the time and roughly equivalent to £25,000 today. Part of what makes the appearance of a professional's recipe so shocking is that it is the equivalent of Isaac Newton's formula in his letter to Henry Oldenburg: the sign of a system in which knowledge is owned, bought, sold, and exchanged, rather than freely given. Prescriptions and professionals' recipes are Trojan horses, seemingly a gift to the woman but in reality an invasion of forces hostile to domestic medicine, women's knowledge, and women's community.

That is not to say that women did not recognize their recipe books as objects with value. A woman's recipe book was the ultimate training manual for future women in the family. The Johnson family began their recipe book at the end of the seventeenth century and only stopped keeping it at the start of the nineteenth. John Gibson began a book of medicinal recipes in 1634; Joan Gibson acquired it and started adding culinary recipes in 1669; and Joanna Gibson continued it, starting in 1708. One woman specified in her will that her recipe book should go to her daughter, suggesting that other relatives might try to make a claim. Another had the foresight to have her recipe book copied during her lifetime so she could bequeath one copy to her daughter and the other to her daughter-in-law. What went into that book was knowledge, and for the women who kept recipe books, knowledge's value lay in its use. Distribution was a vital element of use. Knowledge of useful recipes was meant to be shared with the community.

That point is underscored by the fact that the vast majority of recipes are undated, unsigned, and unattributed, not just in any given book, but throughout the genre. The many different handwritings for individual recipes in recipe books confirm that women often wrote in each other's books and without the need for credit. So even though Mrs Bodenham knew the recipe for "Lemond water" that she gave to Mrs Brooke, Mrs Bodenham did not own it. She never would have charged anything, let alone £100, for any of her recipes, no matter how effective or delicious. The Countess of Arundel and Lennox gave her sister, the Countess of Kent, her recipe for manchet, a very fine kind of bread. She certainly did not expect goods or coin in return. Recipes for food and medicine were circulated without restrictions, and the sharing of this knowledge bound women together across class, age, time, and space. Elizabeth Smith was not a countess like Elizabeth Grey, but they both needed recipes for medication to treat the people in their households.

This was how domestic medicine worked. These connections were far more than networks of knowledge transmission. They were personal and intimate. Every recipe was handwritten. Sitting down with a recipe book is sitting down with every woman who wrote in it. Handwriting styles changed significantly between the early seventeenth century and the mid-eighteenth century, so even an undated book offers evidence of when writers learned penmanship. Two recipes in two different styles from two different centuries next to each other in a recipe book tell a story of two different generations writing in the same book. Handwriting is also highly personal. Letters themselves – the size of a loop in a P or R or D, the height of an L or an I, the number of separate strokes used to make an M or W – introduce a new contributor of knowledge, even if her handwriting is all that can be known about her. Turning the pages of a recipe book is very often travelling through at least one woman's life. Her handwriting changes slowly from a young woman's steady, clear hand to the uncertain letters of arthritic fingers. Names or other hands recur frequently for a while, taper off, and disappear, as different women are more or less important or present in the recipe keeper's life.

For the owners of recipe books, leafing through the pages could remind them of mothers and grandmothers, sisters, cousins, aunts, and friends – women perhaps no longer there to share the kitchen with. A particular recipe might call to mind an event or a place, an occasion when women were gathered together to taste or write or tinker with a recipe. Those letters and words were placed on the paper by hands that stirred pots, turned meat, bathed babies, and wiped tears. Innumerable women left no trace at all that they ever existed, but recipe books provide evidence of thousands of women who formed communities and shared their knowledge to care for others and help one another.

Domestic medicine situated illness and treatment within communities, from households to neighbourhoods, from extended family to distant friends. A woman never treated sickness alone, a sufferer never ailed alone, and sickness itself was always personal and never solitary. The ten-year-old apprentice could expect the same medical care from the wife of his master as the forty-year-old master himself. The lady of an estate was expected to treat her impoverished tenant as well as her own new baby and her maid. Sometimes, a particularly talented woman would become the de facto "mediciner" for her community, the same way a woman could find herself the local midwife. She might charge people for medications in that case, but she was extremely unlikely to turn anyone away. If you did not have a penny, you might have eggs or be willing to chop wood. Recipe books were the fulcrum of domestic medicine's concept of illness, embodying sharing, knowledge, family, expertise, and connection.

That is why when *A Choice Manual of Rare and Select Secrets in Physick and Chyrurgery Collected and Practised by the Right Honourable, the Countesse of Kent, Late Deceased* was printed in 1653, no one was surprised that one of the richest women in England, the Countess of Kent, had a recipe book. A woman had responsibilities, even a countess. Everyone wanted to see what such a celebrity knew and did. *A Choice Manual* flew off the shelves and it was well worth the price. It was packed with cures for every condition from bad breath to vomiting. There were recipes for medicines to treat dog bites ("Take Ragwort, chop it, and boil it with unwashed Butter to an Ointment"), kidney stones (the herbs only work if picked in June or July), and tuberculosis (start with a live rooster).

It also had recipes for medicines to treat specifically female complaints. "For a dead Child in a Womans Body", the countess advised to "Take the juice of Hysop, temper it in warm water, and give it the Woman to drink" to expel the foetus. The next recipe, to ease frequent, heavy, or irregular menstruation, instructed readers to "Take a Hares foot, and burn it, make pouder of it and let her drink it with stale Ale." There were recipes for medicine to induce menstruation, to help a woman expel afterbirth, and to prevent miscarriage while travelling, a reasonable concern in an era before shock absorbers and road repair. If some of these recipes were used to induce miscarriage, they were labelled circumspectly.

Her ladyship's recipes were consistent with what male professionals could have prescribed, although there was so much variation in medications for conditions at the time that it would take a lot for a medication to seem truly bizarre or innovative. *A Choice Manual*'s recipe for heavy menstruation, for example, was essentially the same at Thomas Brugis's recipe in *The Marrow of Physicke* (1648) "To stop womens immoderate fluxe": "A Hares foote, and burne it to Powder, and drinke it first, and last in stale Ale, till you be whole." Like the Countess of Kent, Christopher Wirtzung recommended a drink with hyssop to expel a dead foetus, although he preferred wine over water and noted that vervain and myrrh work equally well. On the other hand, Wirtzung also suggested an "external application": "One may also hold before the privities swines bread, or cotten wooll made wet in the juice of the same: and to put it before into the bodie is also marvelous good for this purpose." Elizabeth Grey had a second recipe for treating "immoderate flux", which in contrast called for powdering date pits, cumin seeds, "Grains", and saffron together and serving a spoonful in warm malmsey, a kind of wine.

Holding "swine's bread" between a pregnant woman's legs is not likely to do very much; Grey's prescription of large doses of saffron, on the other hand, can induce contractions and cause miscarriage.

The second part of A Choice Manual provided recipes for edibles and drinkables served at mealtimes. Entitled "Most Exquisite Waies of Preserving, Conserving, Candying, &c.", it told the "true delighted gentlewoman" how to manage food-stuffs. These are not dainty recipes. "To sauce a pig" begins: "Cut off the head." There are elegant dishes, showing the reader how "To boyle Flounders or Pickerels after the French fashion" and "To roast a Pig with a Pudding in the belly", but most are far sturdier: "How to roast a Leg of Mutton", "How to roast a neck of Mutton", "How to stew a Rabbet", "A Potato Pie for Supper", and "To make Cheese-cakes". The book, in other words, really is for running a household. "To make a Pudding in haste" sounds like the kind of recipe a working parent might use and "To make a Leg of Mutton three or four dishes" is the sort of help a frugal housewife might value. A Choice Manual also has a large selection of recipes for preserving fruits and vegetables so they can be eaten out of season. "To keepe Quinces all the year" is followed by recipes for pickling (for instance, "Cowcumber", purslane, "Broom-bids", and oysters), preserving (including oranges, green walnuts, white quinces, red quinces, raspberries, gooseberries, mulberries, apricots, unripe white damsons, ripe damsons, white pippins, grapes, currants, and medlars), and candying (apricots, pears, plums, lemons, "Ringo roots", and "all kind of flowers in ways of the Spanish candy"). Both the method of cooking (boiling, stewing, roasting) and the ingredients (pig, pickerel, beef) were every woman's method. There was nothing remarkable about the recipes per se, with a few exceptions.

When Elizabeth Grey's recipe book was published, printed books of recipes for medication, cooking, or both had been around for a long time. There was Bullein's *Bulwarke of Defence Against all Sicknesse, Soarenesse, and Woundes,* which came out in 1562, as well as *Approv'd Medicines and Cordial Receipts* (1580) by Thomas Newton, *Prepositas His Practice* (1588) by "L. M.", *An Alphabetical Book of Physicall Secrets* (1639) by Owen Wood, and *A Pretious Treasury* (1649) by Salvator Winter and Francisco Dickinson. *A Proper New Booke of Cookery* (1575) not only provided culinary recipes but also listed which recipes were appropriate for which course; however, it did not offer any recipes for medication. *The Good Huswifes Handmaide for the Kitchin* (1594) was an impressive collection of cooking recipes in no particular order, while *The Widowe's Treasure* (1588) offered "sundry precious and approved secrets in Phisicke, and Chirurgery" and "sundry pretie practices and conclusions of Cookerie", all mixed together like any other recipe book. But these books were not written by women, and even anonymous books had no sign of a woman's hand anywhere in the composition. The purchaser of *The Good Huswifes Handmaide for the Kitchin* would assume that it had a male author because only men's work made it into print.

The Countess of Kent's *A Choice Manual* was unlike any of these books. It had all the features of a typical manuscript recipe book, with recipes appearing in the order in which they had been added: "A Medicine for the Stone in the Kidnies" is followed by "To make Horse Raddish drinke", "Sir John Digbies Medicine for Stone in the Kidnies", "An excellent Sirrup against Melancholly", "An excellent Receipt for the Plague", and then "An excellent Cordiall". Treatments for the same ailment are scattered throughout the book. Recipes

"For an Ague" are listed on pages 26, 131, 139, and 147; those "For a Stitch under the Ribs" can be found on pages 10, 59, and 95. *A Choice Manual* has a table of contents in the front, grouping the contents alphabetically: all recipes beginning with A are listed together, all recipes beginning with B are listed together, and so on. Like so many books of its kind, the principles governing the alphabetizing are a bit harder to identify. For instance, burns are one thing: "For burning with Gunpowder" and "For a burning with lightning" appear under B. However, bites are another: "For a biting of a Mad Dog" can be found under D. Like some other women, the Countess of Kent recorded which recipes were given to her by other people. The medication section includes "Dr Willoughby's Water" (under W), "Dr Stevens Water" (under S), and "Mr Ashley's Ointment" (under A). In the cooking section, the only recipe credited to someone else is her sister's bread recipe: "Lady of Arundel's Manchet".

All that distinguished the countess's recipe book from any other recipe book was that it appeared for sale in print, under her name, but this exception is everything. Transferring the Countess of Kent's recipe book into print and putting it on sale was a complete transformation of the recipe book. It made something public out of something private; something commercial out of something domestic; something mass-produced out of something individual; something common out of something unique. Turning a manuscript book into a printed book converted domestic knowledge that had been shared freely in a community of women into knowledge that could be obtained only by people with the money to pay for it – *A Choice Manual*, a symbol of domestic knowledge including medicine, had become a commodity. In one move, the Countess of Kent reversed everything intrinsic to her recipe book or to any recipe book. Impressive for a woman who had been dead for two years.

The person who turned her ladyship's private recipe book into public, saleable goods was not her ladyship at all, but a man named William Jervis. Not much is known about him except that later in life he called himself a physician and a professor of natural philosophy. The greatest mystery about Jervis is how he got his hands on the Countess of Kent's recipe book to begin with. None of the records of her household, her friends, or her extended family can account for him. It has been suggested that Robert May, a famous cook, gave it to him. In the seventeenth century, "chefs" were primarily men. They were called "cooks", but the job and the prestige were those conferred on chefs today and so was the gender bias. The person who ran the kitchen in an aristocrat's household was generally male. Robert May had been trained by illustrious English cooks (his father included) and had learned from a famous French chef in Paris. For fifty years, May cooked in aristocrats' households, including the Countess of Kent's. Maybe, the thinking goes, she left the recipe book to Robert May or he somehow wound up with it because they had worked together on the daily menus.

Maybe. It is hard to believe that the countess would give away her recipe book while she was still using it, and he was in her employ in the 1640s, when she was still hale and hearty. Would she have bequeathed it to Robert May, an unrelated male servant? Admittedly, May was very highly regarded as a cook. He was another acquaintance whom she shared with Sir Kenelm and Lady Digby. It is possible that she might have left her recipe book to Robert May if she had a particular fondness for him. Then again, he had not worked for her for nearly a decade when *A Choice Manual* was published in 1653. One thing is certain: whether William Jervis got the Countess of Kent's recipe book from Robert May or he acquired it by other means, Jervis was free to do with it whatever he thought best. And what he thought best was to turn a handwritten recipe book into a printed book attributed to a woman that he entitled, *A Choice Manual, Or Rare and Select Secrets In Physick and Chyrurgery: Collected, and practised by the Right Honourable, the Countess of Kent, late deceased. As also most Exquisite waies of Preserving, Conserving, Candying, &c.*

Jervis was a clever marketer. Celebrity sold as well then as it does now, and the Countess of Kent's name in the title guaranteed sales. (The title page of Hannah Woolley's recipe book, *The Ladies Directory, in Choice Experiments & Curiosities of Preserving in Jellies, and Candying Both Fruits & Flowers* [1662] stated that she "hath had the Honour to perform such things for the Entertainment of his late Majesty".) The first of anything – in this case, the first woman's recipe book to appear in print – is also alluring. The cleverest part of Jervis's title was the phrase "Rare and Select Secrets". The book claimed to contain things previously known only to the countess, rare knowledge that she kept a secret from everyone else. Once a secret is shared, of course, it is no longer secret. By printing a recipe book, William Jervis was exposing a woman's life, her experience and knowledge.

Furthermore, the knowledge in a woman's recipe book was the opposite of secret. It was meant to be shared and shared with anyone who needed or wanted it. Men were not prohibited from learning recipes, not even by cultural expectations, and there are enough recipes attributed to men to make the phenomenon unremarkable, if uncommon. Occasionally, men even kept recipe books, as was the case with the Gibson recipe book mentioned earlier. Physicians' notebooks offer instances of physicians consulting their wives for remedies when their own recipes or knowledge gave out. One son seized his mother's recipe book immediately after she died, despite knowing that his mother had willed it to his sister, because he recognized its value. It took a lawsuit for his sister to recover it. So when Jervis called the countess's recipes "Rare and Select Secrets", he changed their perceived identity from shared, shareable knowledge into knowledge not at all meant for sharing. In printing it, Jervis acknowledged that this knowledge had value. It was also knowledge taken from Elizabeth Grey by a man; knowledge that had been female and communal now belonged to a man as his private intellectual property.

The success of *A Choice Manual* was instant and catalytic. Two editions appeared in 1653, very unusual for the time. Within a decade, the printer Gertrude Dawson was putting out the fourteenth edition; the twenty-second edition appeared in 1726. *A Choice Manual* also led immediately to other, similar publications. *The Queen's Closet Opened* came out in 1655, attributed to Elizabeth Grey's friend, the Queen Mother Henrietta Maria, who was in exile. A look at the title page of *The Queen's Closet Opened* shows that it was the result of efforts by "W.M.", who was almost certainly male (scholars suspect that it was William Montagu, Her Majesty's steward). Another printed recipe book, *Natura Exenterata,* appeared in 1655, ostensibly authored by Elizabeth Grey's sister, Alethea Howard, Countess of Arundel and Lennox (she of the bread recipe). Alethea Howard also was dead when *Natura Exenterata* was published. The title page of the first edition declared that it was "Collected and preserved by several Persons of Quality", and the list of male and female contributors is extensive.

The title page of Owen Wood's *Choice and Profitable Secrets both Physical and Chirurgical,* printed in 1656, claimed rather grumpily that these "Secrets" were "Formerly Concealed by the deceased Duchess of Lennox, and now published for the use and benefit of such as live farr from Physicians and Chyrurgeons". If they were the duchess's originally, Wood did not mention it when the book first came out in 1639, the year the duchess died. Whether the recipes did or did not originate in a woman's recipe book, in the mid-1650s Wood certainly thought that putting a famous dead woman's name on it would be good for sales. The reverse was also true: people were learning that they would and should have to pay for a book full of recipes to make medicine and food.

To the casual observer, all these changes suggest that in the middle of the seventeenth century, women and written forms associated with them had cultural power. The wave of female-authored recipe books in print suggests that women were positively associated with "physick", that is, medication. It would seem that women's medicinal knowledge was now valued. Yes and no. *A Choice Manual* was capitalizing on the strong, positive cultural association of women and medication, while undermining it at the same time. Everyone knew that these women were terminally absent, whether by death or by exile. When it came to disseminating their knowledge and expertise in print, like publishing Elizabeth Grey's or Alethea Howard's recipe books, men controlled everything, men put their names on the book as well as the women's names, and men gained the profit from their publication. The use of insinuating titles perpetuated the conversion of women's ordinary, open knowledge into something unusual, exotic, and rare. Women's domestic medicine became knowledge that was "Too costly to wear every-day", as Beatrice puts it in Shakespeare's *Much Ado About Nothing*, and not "for working-days".

The surge of female-attributed printed recipe books in the

1650s was not an introduction into the mainstream of female knowledge and female methods for acquiring knowledge. Female knowledge *was* the mainstream, already freely circulating and circulating for free as women shared it with each other and used it to care for the people around them. Instead, printing women's recipe books moved those books and that knowledge into a male-controlled commercial sphere. Women's actual recipe books were organic, always growing and changing as women learned new things. Putting that knowledge into print froze it where it was at the moment of printing. William Jervis's *A Choice Manual* became an early salvo in the war against women for control of pharmaceutical knowledge and distribution. He acknowledged the power and authority traditionally granted women, their recipes, and their recipe books, but only to diminish them by sexualizing women's knowledge, by making it exotic and rare, and by nudging it into the male domain. He also branded the expert knowledge of food and medicine preparation in the book (which had been communal) as something secret that he had the responsibility to unlock – and to charge for.

The first printing of *A Choice Manual* in 1653 marks the moment when women's domestic knowledge began to acquire a different set of cultural associations. Women continued to keep recipe books until the nineteenth century, but over time and on the whole, recipes from professionals and from printed sources like newspapers began to appear more often, as I demonstrate later on. Men, on the other hand, produced the printed domestic recipe books, and the knowledge contained in those books belonged to the men who produced them. In the century between 1550 and 1650, fewer than thirty books with the word "recipe" or its variants in the main title went on sale, all of them authored or compiled by men. In the half century between 1650 and 1700, that number was closer to 100, the vast majority authored or compiled not just by men, but by physicians, apothecaries, and that emerging breed, scientists. In handbooks for housewives, which contained instructions and tips for responsibilities such as managing servants, keeping to a budget, setting the table, and comporting oneself virtuously, the recipe section shrank dramatically after 1650, with the medication portion of that section shrinking even more so.

Elizabeth Grey, Countess of Kent would probably have been furious with William Jervis. She had spent a lifetime asserting her independence and autonomy, and he was making use of her recipe book – her knowledge, her experience, her friendships, her learning – for his own purposes and without her permission. She used her wealth to help others and promote knowledge, skill, and beauty; Jervis used her recipe book to help himself and, while he was at it, to denigrate women's knowledge and skill. She was a patron: she made communities by gathering people together, inviting writers and artists to live at her house, people who she found interesting and exciting, who she thought would enlighten others. Jervis sold her book to thousands of individuals, who stayed individuals. *A Choice Manual* turned knowledge into property to be used to profit its owner.

Changing the association of recipe books from women to men was a vital beginning for the scientific revolutionaries. It still left them with everything that recipe books contained: recipes for beer-battered fritters and sauced young pigs, as well as recipes for treating jaundice and miscarriage. To separate what they wanted, medication, from what they did not, food, the New Learning's proponents were going to have to use another strategy. It would involve Sir Kenelm and Venetia, Lady Digby, piracy, two kitchens, a faked death, and a lot of inebriated snakes.

3

Chicken Soup and Viper Wine

Every day, Sir Kenelm Digby gave his wife Venetia, Lady Digby a glass of viper wine. He made it himself. He took a few dozen live, poisonous snakes, shoved them into a cask of wine, stoppered the cask, and let it sit undisturbed for a few months, until the snakes were dead and disintegrating. He might have strained the liquid before serving it, although his friend, Alethea Howard, Countess of Arundel and Lennox, did not recommend it in her recipe:

> Take eight Gallons of Sack which is the best Wine, and to that quantity put in thirty, or two and thirty Vipers; but prepare them first in this manner. Put them into bran for some four dayes, which will make them scowre the gravel and eathy [sic] part from them, then stop your Vessel or glasse you put them in very close until six months be past, in which time the flesh of the Vipers and vertue of them will be infused into the wine, although the skins will seem full, after which time you may take them out if you please, and drink of the wine when you please best to drink it.

A number of things about this story might raise questions for the modern reader. Why did Kenelm give his wife Venetia *viper wine*? *Why* did Kenelm give his wife Venetia viper wine? And why did *Kenelm* give *his wife* Venetia viper wine? These are not the same question, and they are all important. Answering them explains how another aspect of the change from domestic to professional medication took place: the separation of food from medicine.

So why did he give her viper wine? Viper wine was not as exotic in the seventeenth century as it is in this one. Physicians had been prescribing and administering it regularly to patients with skin conditions since Galen. Lecturing in 1635 on the treatment of tumours, Alexander Read recommended viper wine for leprosy. In 1675, Philip Bellon went even further, claiming in *The Potable Balsome of Life* that drinks made with vipers were useful for treating not only leprosy but also sexually transmitted infections, tuberculosis, fevers, and scurvy. A few years later, viper wine took on other powers: in *Pharmaceutice rationalis, or, An Exercitation of the Operations of Medicines in Humane Bodies* (1679), the distinguished physician Thomas Willis advocated viper wine for strengthening a man's "animal spirits", a use also endorsed by William Salmon in *The Practice of Curing* (1681). Additionally Salmon prescribed viper wine and occasionally viper powder (what he called "viperine medicaments") for convulsions, tremors, and somewhat para-doxically, "Paralytic Distempers". For good measure, he also agreed with Bellon that it could clear up leprosy. The poet John Donne even alluded to such medication in a sermon at St Paul's. Samuel Hartlib, who corresponded with all the great minds of Europe, recorded numerous recipes for viper wine in English, German, and Latin. The *Pharmacopoeia Londinensis*, the offi-cial compilation of medicinal treatments used by physicians and apothecaries, included a recipe for viper wine well into the eighteenth century.

Given its supposed ability to restore blemished skin and "the animal spirits", ordinary people often regarded viper wine as a combination of Botox and Viagra. In 1633, Francis Quarles wrote mockingly of "Viper-wines, to make old age presume / To feele new lust, and youthfull flames agin". John Jones, in his play *Adrasta* (1635), disapprovingly associated viper wine with witches and black magic because of its power to transform the body. Unsurprisingly, his play was never staged. It was even fashionable for a time for women at the Stuart court to take a glass regularly.

So there was nothing particularly exotic about viper wine. *Why* did Kenelm give it to Venetia? Perhaps she was physically worn out. She had five pregnancies in eight years. Their first child, named after his father, was born after she and Kenelm were married secretly in 1625. She went into labour after falling from a horse late in her pregnancy; to preserve the secrecy of her pregnancy and marriage, she delivered the baby at home with only her inexperienced maid to assist. Venetia and Kenelm's second child, John, was born in 1628, the day that Kenelm set sail for a two-year voyage to the Mediterranean. After receiving the news, Kenelm wrote Venetia from his ship that she could announce their marriage and then raised anchor, leaving her with two small children but without the financial, social, and personal support of a husband. After Kenelm returned in 1630, Venetia had three pregnancies in the next three years, two of which ended tragically. Her third child, a son named after his grandfather Everard, died within hours of his birth, and she miscarried twins in the seventh month. Small wonder if after so much physical and emotional battering Venetia's "animal spirits" were low.

Or perhaps Kenelm gave Venetia a regular glass of viper

wine to restore or preserve her remarkable beauty. Venetia Digby had been considered one of the most beautiful women in England since her teens. John Aubrey, a seventeenth-century diarist and biographer, called her "that celebrated Beautie". According to Aubrey:

> She had a most lovely and sweet-turned face, delicate dark brown hair. She had a perfect healthy constitution; strong; good skin; well proportioned; much inclining to a wanton (near altogether). Her face, a short oval; dark brown eyebrow, about which much sweetness, as also in the opening of her eyelids. The colour of her cheeks was just that of the damask rose, which is neither too hot or too pale.

Some of Sir Kenelm's biographers assume that he valued her stunning looks so highly that he medicated her to protect them. John Fulton claimed that: "To preserve her beauty, he threw his dynamic energies into experimenting upon her; inventing new cosmetics of dubious ingredients, nourishing her failing strength upon snail-soup and capons fed on the flesh of vipers."* Or his biographers imply that Venetia might have valued her looks so highly that she asked for something to do the job. Both scenarios are certainly plausible, but the evidence does not support either one. Actually, the evidence reveals that biographers and historians have gotten quite a lot wrong about their relationship.

---

* Feeding chopped-up vipers to chickens was supposed to make the latter even healthier to eat. Samuel Hartlib recorded that the Duke of Bavaria's personal physician prescribed viper-fed chickens for the duke, and His Grace was reputed "very vigorous in his health".

For one thing, there is no evidence that either of them ever valued her looks over her character. A fervent letter that Kenelm wrote her from college extols her mind and temperament, but says nothing about her physical beauty. Promising that he had only honourable intentions, he wrote, "you have too masculine a spirit to be frighted wth. shadowes, once you have duly surveyed and considered them". "My better Angell guided me to what I had reason to admire and love exceedingly," he averred, "And now in you, he sheweth me so many excellencies that I never was acquainted wth. before any woman, as I sweare Madame all former love wth. me hath bin but like an apprenticeshippe to teach me how to love and value you as I should." Writing after her death in 1633, his descriptions of Venetia lingered on her intellect, personality, and piety. In a letter to his brother, he wrote, "Indeed the greatnesse of her minde was beyond what ever I knew in any woman or man." "I have many times with exceeding delight heard her discourse seriously of other persons humors [*sic*] and actions," he recalled, "upon which she would make admirable strong observations, and hath often times made me acknowledge as undenyeable such things as, till she opened my understanding in them, I never fell to the consideration of, though I had had longer knowledge and more familiaritie with the parties than she had". In short, as he wrote defending her to a disapproving friend in Italy, "she was the best wife, the bravest woman, had the vertuousest and single soule and edified the most by her fine examples, of any woman that I have conversed with". Venetia herself does not seem to have been particularly vain, either. She was a model wife during her marriage (according to seventeenth-century expectations, of course). John Aubrey, who delighted in malicious gossip, wrote that she "carried her selfe blamelessly".

In fact, Venetia depended on her beauty for only a brief

period in her life, although admittedly it was a pretty scandal-
ous period. One thing to be said about Kenelm and Venetia is
that their relationship was always intense. They met when they
were teenagers. He was three years younger than she (fourteen
to her seventeen), but he was spectacularly smart and charming. It probably did not hurt that he was also tall and strong
and stunningly good looking. Kenelm's mother disapproved:
Venetia's family, the Stanleys, was more distinguished than the
Digbys, but they did not have much money. Considering that
Kenelm's father, Sir Everard Digby had been hanged, drawn,
and quartered for conspiring to blow up King James and
Parliament when Kenelm was three, it was pretty outrageous to
say that Venetia Stanley's family was not good enough.

Like many teenagers, Kenelm found ways to get around his
mother's disapproval. He wooed Venetia in person when possible and by passionate letters otherwise. She was not an easy
catch by any means. As he put it later, there was no lover who
"ever labored wth more passion in the gaining of [his beloved],
nor mett wth greater difficulties and oppositions". Eventually,
however, Venetia fell in love with him, and when he was seventeen, he persuaded her to exchange promises that they would
not marry anyone else (or be unfaithful to the other, for that
matter). It was a huge commitment for Venetia. She was at that
time of life in which a young woman did her best to marry a
titled, affluent man – preferably also young, handsome, and of
good character – and there she was, promising Kenelm that
she would not marry anyone else. She must have been madly
in love to make such a promise, because Kenelm was about
to embark on the grand tour. The grand tour was a standard
event for young seventeenth-century noblemen. With some
kind of adult supervision – a relative, a family friend, a tutor
– a teenager like Kenelm would travel around Europe, visiting

the sights, cities, and courts to gain polish, including fluency in several languages. It usually took at least two years, and a lot could happen in two years. But Venetia made the promise, and so did Kenelm, and off he went.

Things went wrong immediately. Not too long after he reached France, the young, charming, handsome Kenelm Digby was propositioned by Marie de Medici, the dowager queen of France, who was old enough to be his mother. People who said no to Marie de Medici tended to get into big and often fatal trouble, so Kenelm faked his own death and ran for it. The plan succeeded. Everyone heard that Kenelm Digby had died in France – including Venetia. Biographers including E. W. Bligh and Joe Moshenska claim that it then took her nearly two years to learn that Kenelm was alive, but that is so unlikely as to be impossible. Admittedly, seventeenth-century long-distance communication was far worse than such communication is now, but there was still plenty of interaction between England and Europe. Kenelm was not travelling incognito once he escaped from Marie de Medici, and he interacted on the road and at every stop with people who could have delivered a letter or a message. He was in Italy for more than two years, certainly enough time to write to her. After that, it was no secret that he was in Spain with his uncle, the Earl of Bristol, negotiating the marriage of the Prince of Wales. Kenelm, now in his late teens and having a glorious time in Europe, was just not making much of an effort to communicate with her.

As for Venetia, she was no idiot: she noticed. No longer feeling bound by a promise to Kenelm, Venetia became involved with at least one nobleman (although to what degree is a bit of a mystery). The story goes that when Kenelm heard, he flung himself on the floor, howling and crying at the betrayal. Oh, to be a seventeenth-century Englishman, when one could expect women to be chaste while one cheated on them all over Europe.

Kenelm and Venetia's relationship on his return was profoundly and irrevocably shaped by his silence on the grand tour. Unsurprisingly, although accounts vary of their reunion in London after three years, most agree that it was rocky. Male biographers of Kenelm have attributed both his and her standoffishness to her bad reputation, deserved or not, but that diagnosis only makes sense if Kenelm is not held responsible for his silence during those years. If he is held responsible – as he should be – her behaviour is perfectly rational and reasonable. Furthermore, when she finally agreed to renew their acquaintance, Kenelm tried to treat her like a courtesan. She required him to treat her like Venetia, the intelligent, thoughtful woman from a good family whom he had wooed devotedly and honourably, and all but promised to marry. For two years, they fought this battle. Kenelm swung between respect and contempt. Once, he snuck into Venetia's bedroom while she was sleeping, stripped, and climbed into bed with her. She managed to get him out of the bed, no small feat considering his size, strength, and undoubted resistance. One biographer maintains that Venetia berated him so soundly that he voluntarily leaped out of the bed, vowing "never again to do his love for her a disservice by being so forward and improper". Let us be clear here. The "disservice" was not to "his love for her" but to Venetia, nor is it "forward and improper" to climb naked and uninvited into a sleeping woman's bed to have sex with her. It is attempted rape.

Reader, she married him. But on her terms. In demanding that he acknowledge who she was and what she was due, Venetia reset the terms of their relationship and caused him to fall in love with her again. Once he began courting her in earnest, she fell in love with him again, as well. Admittedly, like many husbands of their time and class, Kenelm was not unswervingly sexually faithful. Nevertheless, their relationship was far more a partnership than his sexual infidelity would suggest. After their reunion in 1624, Venetia pawned, sold, or mortgaged her possessions to help Kenelm take up a prestigious post on a vital diplomatic mission. She supported his career and helped him win the approval of James I by encouraging his privateering voyage to the Mediterranean in 1626, even though she was pregnant with their second child. Kenelm sought Venetia's opinion and advice on everything. As he wrote his sons:

> I must confesse that her excellent temper in judging and great discretion in directing all affaires that was fit for me to consult with her (and I kept non from her that concerned my self) was the greatest guide and stay that I had in all my businesses [...] [S]he hath often turned my resolutions an other way, and hath mastered me with reason...

In a letter to his brother, he reflected: "That was the maine part of our happinesse, that we knew each others thoughtes as soon as we conceived them; we knew not how to reserve [any]thing from the others knowledge."

Venetia died suddenly in her sleep on the first of May 1633. Kenelm was shattered. He never remarried and wore mourning until his own death in 1665.* He had their entwined initials embroidered on the spines of his books. He wrote letters about

---

* Gossip later in his life accused him of having or trying to have an affair with a woman in France, and of opening marriage negotiations with a family. Even if true, the reality remains that at a time when remarriage was common, a young (for a time), handsome, wealthy, intelligent, charming man who could have remarried, did not.

her to their sons so the boys would know something of their mother as they grew up. At the time, however, his adoration manifested itself rather more idiosyncratically. After a servant discovered her dead in bed, Kenelm took plaster casts of her feet and face, and called in artist friends to paint her as she lay there and to compose a volume of poems in her honour. He also approached her death as one of science's revolutionaries and arranged a post-mortem. He was convinced that anatomy, the most developed branch of the New Science, would find the explanation for her sudden death.

What the New Science found was that her brain had turned to sludge. The cerebral cortex is not supposed to ooze out if the top of the skull is removed, but this is precisely what Venetia Digby's did. "When they came to open the head," Kenelm reported, "they found the braine much putrifyed and corrupted: all the cerebellum was rotten, and retained not the forme of braine but was mere pus and corrupted matter." Biographers have been rather casual about this bizarre finding; Moshenska does not speculate as to cause, and Michael Foster simply says that she suffered a "cerebral haemorrhage" overnight.

From a medical perspective, there is sufficient evidence to explain not only why her brain melted but also why she drank viper wine. What killed Venetia Digby? A stroke, but not in her sleep that morning. As a research team explained in 2021, "Scientists have known for years that the brain liquefies after a stroke. If cut off from blood and oxygen for a long enough period, a portion of the brain will die, slowly morphing from a hard, rubbery substance into liquid goop." The process is called "liquefactive necrosis" and that kind of necrotic (dead) tissue is toxic to adjoining tissue. In other words, liquefactive necrosis is internally contagious. Although the brain creates a barrier between damaged and healthy tissue after a stroke, toxins still slowly escape to kill off more and more healthy brain cells until, as researchers explain, "Liquefied brain tissue eventually will result in an empty cavity in which healthy brain tissue once existed." Precisely what witnesses observed at Venetia Digby's autopsy. How long does it take from the initial damage – that is, the stroke – to reach this stage? It can take months. In fact, the doctors performing Venetia's autopsy told Kenelm that the "decay they found there was not the worke of short time", and that "though the braine be the cause of sensation through the whole bodie, yet it hath none in it selfe", so she would not have felt it decaying. A stroke followed by liquefactive necrosis explains why Kenelm would have been giving her viper wine every day for a protracted period of time, although the exact period of time has not been established. As the dead brain tissue poisoned Venetia's remaining healthy neurons, she became increasingly debilitated. The viper wine was administered to revive her sinking "animal spirits". Eventually, the liquefying necrosis killed her, leaving the cerebral sludge that poured out when her skull was opened.

So that takes care of *why* Venetia drank viper wine every day, and why she drank *viper wine*. What about the fact that it was *Kenelm* who took care of the medication? The answer to this question is one of the keys to the Scientific Revolution's success at overthrowing domestic medication. Until the Scientific Revolution, food and medication were grouped under one heading because they were both made from recipes. They shared processes, equipment, materials, and the space in which they were made. Contributors to the Scientific Revolution like Sir Kenelm Digby changed the entire concept of medication, distinguishing it from food and claiming it for themselves. Where food and medication had belonged together because they shared processes, by the middle of the eighteenth century, food and medication belonged apart because they were different products. Kenelm and Venetia Digby's marriage – their division of tasks, of equipment, of knowledge, of space – shows that transformation as it took place.

When it came to domestic responsibilities, Venetia was very much in charge. As her appreciative husband put it, "She was exceeding careful and vigilant over the domestike affaires of her family, and ordered them very wisely." She gave orders the night before as to what she wanted the servants to do, and before she dressed or breakfasted in the morning, she went through the house to make sure everything was in order. Kenelm, unlike many men of his class and time, understood the difficult realities of that work. "To performe this part as it ought to be, requireth great sufficiency and stayednesse," he told his sons, "for although few of these affaires seeme to be very weighty, yet they are so many and so troublesome and of such several natures that all together they are very cumbersome and pressing."

Like other women, Venetia Digby had her own recipes. Although her recipe book has not been found, her recipes appear in books written by others. For one unidentified friend, "Ven. Stanley" provided a recipe for "A Water to Cleare Hands & Face":

Take a quart of fair water, a pint of white wine the juice of 4. Lemons, put therein Beanblossoms, white lilly Blossoms, Elder blossomes, of each one handful, put to it 4 whole Daizy roots 4 marsh mallow roots, 2 or 3 Branches of wild tansy as much ffuemitorie the weight of 2^{d} in Camphire, put all these in an Earthen pott, sett it in warm Ashes all night in the morning strain it through a peice [sic] of white Cotton, put it in a narrow mouthed glasse, sett it in the heat of the sea[?] 3 or 4 dayes, if there bee any pimples or rednes in the face take a quantitie of water in the glasse & steep the white dung of an hen in it one night then strame [sic] it through a Cloth, wash your face wth this morning & night, if your hands, add three or 4 bruised Almonds this is a most excellent water. prob.

The attribution to "Ven. Stanley" rather than "Ven. Digby" shows that she had the recipe before she was married, presumably from another woman. Recipes for cosmetics were common in recipe books. Venetia's recipe for "A Water to Cleare Hands & Face" is on the same page with "To make Breath sweet" and "A Powder for teeth", for example, and the book also contains recipes for removing smallpox scars, freckles, and sunburn. In her recipe book, Lady Sedley collected treatments for "a redd face", freckles, thinning hair, and yellowing teeth (herb and wine toothpaste).

Venetia was in charge of the household, which made them partners: Kenelm performed experiments during their marriage and she made all his work possible. For one thing, he had full access to the kitchen and anything else domestic he needed. For another, he talked with her about whatever he was thinking. Venetia's role in Kenelm's scientific endeavours and the domestic dimension of his work have been overlooked both by writers interested in Kenelm and by writers interested in the development of science and medicine. Although Sir Kenelm Digby is often recognized as an important player in the beginning of the Scientific Revolution in England, his community is described and defined as a group of men performing intellectual and experimental investigations: for example, the political theorist Thomas Hobbes, philosopher René Descartes, chemist Robert Boyle, and mathematicians Marin Mersenne and Pierre de Fermat. Kenelm was one of the earliest members of the Royal Society. Even before Charles II gave it a royal charter in 1662, when it was still a group of like-minded male investigators, Kenelm presented his own research to the other members in a paper entitled *A Discourse Concerning the Vegetation of Plants*. He had given papers all over Europe by then, starting as a young man while visiting Italy.

In reality, Kenelm's scientific circle was not all male, not all academic, and not based on the one-way transmission of knowledge from scientist to audience. After Venetia died, Kenelm became part of a group of people who shared recipes and were interested in the Scientific Revolution. Yes, that group included Robert Boyle, but it also included Boyle's sister, Katherine Jones, Lady Ranelagh, a respected chemist and political operator. The names of several other members of the group should also be familiar: Elizabeth Grey, Countess of Kent, and her sister, Alethea Howard, Countess of Arundel and Lennox. Samuel Hartlib compared the efficacy of Elizabeth Grey's "Powder" with that of Kenelm Digby's. Robert May, who cooked for Elizabeth Grey and might have had a hand in *A Choice Manual*, not only cooked for Kenelm Digby but also included him among the five dedicatees of May's own cookbook, *The Accomplisht Cook* (1660). (Kenelm was also close to John Selden, the Countess of Kent's lover.) Kenelm and the Queen Mother Henrietta Maria were good friends, sharing recipes and talking about cooking (even queens learned the domestic arts; royal they might be, women they definitely were). Apparently, he was considered an expert in making viper wine. Like a community of women, Kenelm's community shared recipes, not just for preparing food, drink, and medication but also for transmuting substances (alchemy) and understanding the components of substances and how they interacted (chemistry).

Kenelm had another connection to members of this group: like Elizabeth Grey and Alethea Howard, his papers were printed after his death without his permission. In his case, they were printed for sale at the direction of George Hartman, Kenelm's laboratory operator, who assisted him with experiments or performed them under his direction. Where the Countess of Kent's recipe book, *A Choice Manual*, was printed as a recipe book, however, the printed books with Sir Kenelm Digby's name are more amphibious. In some ways they look like recipe books, but in others they definitely do not. They have indexes or tables of contents, for example, they print recipes one after the other and only sometimes in logical order or logical grouping, and they are divided according to function – recipes for candying in one section, for medication in another.

Furthermore, like many housewives, Kenelm collected multiple recipes for the same substance. Ninety-eight of the first 103 recipes in *The Closet of the Eminently Learned Sir Kenelme Digbie Kt. Opened* (1669) are for meath and metheglin (variations of mead), fermented medicinal drinks used when someone was "feeling poorly", so to speak. Many of the culinary recipes in his books also use conventional recipe language. For instance, in *Two Treatises* (1669), three pudding recipes in a row – "To make excellent Black-puddings", "To make White Puddings", and "To make an excellent Pudding" – begin with "Take", and the recipe for white pudding warns that the "small-guts [...] are to be cleansed in the Ordinary manner; and filled very lankley; for they will swell much in the boiling, and break if they be too full".

Also like an ordinary recipe book, many of the recipes came from people Kenelm knew, such as "Sweet-meats of my Lady Windebanks" and "Mr Webb's Ale and Bragot". Several of those people served in the court of Henrietta Maria, the queen mother, where Kenelm was an officer starting in the 1640s. Her Majesty shared her own recipes – "White Marmulate, the Queen's Way", for instance – and gave advice on roasting meat: "The Queen useth to baste such meat with yolks of fresh Eggs beaten thin, which continue to do all the while it is rosting." Kenelm also recorded recipes for dishes she was served, such as "Portugal Broth, as it was made for the Queen". The recipe for "Portuguez Eggs" begins: "The way that the Countess de Penalva makes the Prtuguez [sic] Eggs for the Queen, is this."

Language like "the way that" and "was made thus" is not like the usual instructions beginning with "Take" or "Put". Instead, such language elevates the process to be equally important or more important than the product. "Pressis Nourissant" begins "The Queen Mothers Pressis was thus made," for example, and "The Queens ordinary Bouillon de santé in a morning, was thus." This rhetorical difference is not minor. Once recognized, Kenelm's interest in process appears everywhere, so much so that the books seem less like recipe books and far more like laboratory notebooks. Women's recipes begin with directions, almost always the word "Take". Kenelm's are not so regular. Many of his recipes combine instructions with source when they begin: "My Lady of Monmouth boileth a Capon with white broth thus," for example, or "My Lady Homeby makes her quick fine Mustard thus..."

When Kenelm persuaded "Master Webbe, who maketh the Kings Meathe" to show him how the King's Meathe was made, he recorded not just the recipe but also the entire event as a narrative. "The first of Septemb. 1663. Mr Webb came to my House to make some for Me," he began, adding commentary along the way: "I am not satisfied, whether he did not put a

spoonful of fine white good Mustard into his Barm,* before he
brought it hither, (for he took a pretext to look out some pure
clean white barm) but he protested, there was nothing mingled
with the barm, yet I am in doubt." Kenelm must have suspected
that Mr Webb was not going to give him the actual recipe,
hence the invitation to his house so he could watch the procedure (and even then Mr Webb appears to have been less than
straightforward). One of the clearest statements of Kenelm's
interest in process is the recipe for "Slipp-coat Cheese", which
begins "Master Philipps his *Method* and *proportions* in making
slippe-coat Cheese, are these" (emphasis added).

Kenelm's own process is often part of the recipes. There is
his eagle-eyed account of watching Mr Webb make meath,
of course. The rather smug recipe in *Two Treatises* for
"Hydromel as I made it weak for the Queen Mother" concludes, "Thus was the Hydromel made that I gave the Queen,
which was exceedingly liked by every body." (Hydromel was
a kind of laxative that used water and honey. It suggests a
considerable level of intimacy, not to mention gastric distress,
that "every body" used Sir Kenelm Digby's hydromel at some
point, although Kenelm was also prone to bragging.) When
he records "My Lady Bellassises Meath", the recipe begins:
"The way of making is thus. She boileth the honey with
Spring-water, as I do, till it be cleer..." Kenelm himself shows
up quite a lot in *Two Treatises*. Explaining one of his recipes,
he announces:

> I have found it admirable for the Brain, the Eye-sight, the
> Heart, the Stomach, and all languishes Diseases and decays

* Barm is the layer of yeast forming at the top of malt drinks while they
ferment.

of Nature, and causeth a little gentle breathing, scarce amounting to swear: When you take it in a morning, it gives you a wonderful severity of brain and cheerfulness of humour in languishing Diseases.

Every now and then, his humour appears: "Into this liquor put two ounces of good old Venice Treacle." Good old Venice Treacle indeed.

While the contents of the books printed and sold from Kenelm Digby's papers make classification challenging, the titles reveal how experiments and recipes were being used by science's revolutionaries. Hartman printed the first book from Kenelm's papers in 1668, with the permission of Kenelm and Venetia's sole surviving child, John Digby, and crediting himself ("GH") as translator. The book was entitled *Choice and Experimented Receipts in Physic and Chirurgery: as also Cordial and Distilled Waters and Spirits, Perfumes, and other Curiosities, Collected by the Honourable and truly Learned Sir Kenelm Digby Kt.* Since the title announces that it contains recipes, it would seem to be a recipe book. On the other hand, the recipes are "experimented", which suggests that there is something scientific going on. It was usual for recipes in "Physick", that is, recipes for medicinal treatments, to appear in recipe books. However, recipes for "Chirurgery", the physical aspect of medical care like amputation and excising growth, were not usual to recipe books. Furthermore, there were plenty of printed and private books of recipes dedicated solely to medicinal treatments, and "cordials" and "waters" could have medicinal value. On the other hand, *Choice and Experimented Receipts* also has instructions for making perfumes and "Distilled Spirits" (not to mention that intriguing category, "other Curiosities"), which are for domestic use. The title does not definitively classify the book, nor do the contents. It is a platypus: definitely something, but not like anything.

The next year, George Hartman had another volume of Kenelm's records printed for sale: *The Closet of the Eminently Learned Sir Kenelme Digbie Kt Opened: Whereby is Discovered Several ways for making of Metheglin, Sider, Cherry-Wine, etc. Together with Excellent Directions for Cookery, as also for Preserving, Conserving, Candying, etc.* Readers of the previous chapter may notice the similarities of this title with the titles of other recipe books, although Hartman eschewed the titillating innuendo. *The Closet of the Eminently Learned Sir Kenelme Digbie* does not use the word "recipe" (or "receipt") anywhere on its title page. Although the book is full of recipes, it avoids that term. Instead, Hartman replaced the word "receipts" with the phrases "Several ways for making" and "Excellent Directions for Cookery". Here is a recipe book that is not a recipe book, even though it contains only recipes for food and drink.

Hartman saw a second book into print in 1669: *Two Treatises, By the Honourable and truly Learned Sir Kenelm Digby Knight. The one, Of Choice and Experimented Receipts in Physic and Chirurgery; as also Cordial and Distilled Waters and Spirits, Perfumes, and other Curiosities. The other, Of Cookery, With several ways for Making of Metheglin, Sider, Cherry-Wine, etc. Together with Excellent Directions for Preserving, Conserving, Candying, etc.* Hartman combined both books into a single one, creating something that looks like a standard recipe book with medicines in one part and foodstuffs in another. The trick is in the eye-glazing subtitles. They underscore the distinction between the recipes for "Physic and Chirurgery" on one hand and those for "Cookery" on the other. The title for the combined book, *Two Treatises*, emphasizes that two complete works are bound together; it is not one whole work with two sections. *Two Treatises* is itself an odd title. Calling a collection of recipes a "treatise" makes a claim for coherence and unity, not to mention a purpose and a thesis, that a recipe book does not have. The title transforms the collection of recipes into something from the intellectual and traditionally male aspect of culture. Using the title *Two Treatises* is also a clever marketing strategy, as it was the title of a well-known publication of Kenelm's from the 1640s that addressed theological issues. Hartman's *Two Treatises* from 1669 is another amphibian, neither one genre nor another but something in the middle of its development.

The titles to Kenelm's posthumous publications reveal that there was a great self-consciousness about how to classify his work. Kenelm – a man – could have recipes for medicinal substances for use in "Physick and Chirurgery", but when it came to edibles and drinkables, he had "ways" and "directions". It was women who had recipes for cider, cherry wine, and roasted venison. The publication of Kenelm's recipes reflects a growing distinction between medication and comestible. The recipes are in separate books, and the language for titling and describing the contents of each book is different.

Two Treatises was never reprinted. After 1669, the two parts were printed and sold separately. *Choice and Experimented Receipts* (primarily medicinal treatments) was reissued in 1675, and *The Closet of the Eminently Learned Sir Kenelme Digbie* (primarily cookery) came out in 1671 and 1677. In 1682, Hartman again made use of his late employer's papers to produce *A Choice Collection of Rare Secrets and Experiments in Philosophy, as also Rare and unheard-of Medicines, Menstruums, and Alkahests; with the True Secret of Volatilizing the fixt Salt of Tartar. Collected And Experimented by the*

Honourable and truly Learned Sir Kenelm Digby, Kt. The title page also announced that this collection was "Hitherto kept Secret since his Decease, but now Published for the good and benefit of the Publick". It was printed again that year as *A Choice Collection of Rare Chymical Secrets and Experiments*, and in 1683 as *Chymical Secrets and Rare Experiments in Philosophy*. The evolution of the titles for Kenelm's books from 1669 to 1683 reveal that big changes were taking place in the composition of what was considered the best medication – chemical medication was growing in prestige and replacing organic medication. That is a subject for Chapter 6, however; I am pointing it out here only in passing. For now what is of interest is the change from "Choice and Experimented Receipts" in 1669 to "A Choice Collection of Rare Chymical Secrets and Experiments" in 1682. "Choice" has to do with the collection, not the recipes; the adjective "Experimented" has become the noun "Experiments".

Kenelm's posthumous works offer a timeline showing how the proponents of the Scientific Revolution drove a wedge between food and medication, gendering each side of the divide. This separation contributed to reconceptualizing the body and health. Until the middle of the seventeenth century, men like Kenelm and Francis Bacon conducted experiments with food as food, but as the Scientific Revolution progressed food was increasingly excised from scientific investigation. Before about 1650, books about maintaining health often discussed diet and sometimes referred to it explicitly in their titles. Tobias Whitaker may have been prompted by wishful thinking to pen *The Tree of Humane Life, or, The Bloud of the Grape. Proving the Possibilitie of Maintaining Humane Life by the Use of Wine* in 1638, but others were more practical. Sixteenth-century titles, for example, included *An Introduction into Phisycke,*

with an Universal Dyet (1545) by Christopher Langton and
The Olde Mans Dietarie (1586) by Thomas Newton.

At the same time that "physic" was evolving into a category
that did not include diet, domestic medicine was evolving into
a category that was primarily about food. The phrase "kitchen
physic" changed meanings between 1650 and 1740. Initially,
the term referred to workaday, reliable medication. In *A Pisgah-
sight of Palestine* from 1650, Thomas Fuller wished upon a
frail, older man "good kitchin-Physick, carefull attendance, and
serious meditation on his latter end". In 1677, however, the distinguished Scottish physician Matthew Mackaile explained in *A
Short Treatise, Concerning the Use of Mace, in Meat, or Drink,
and Medicine* that his work was "particularly recommended
unto such of the Female Sex, as are most studious, only of the
Diecteticall part of Medicin (commonly called Kitchin Physick)
it being chiefly of that nature, and most properly belonging
unto them". Thomas Tryon capitalized on the success of his
first book, *The Good Housewife made a Doctor* (1692) with
A Pocket-Companion (1693), which contained extracts from
The Good Housewife and claimed to provide "A plain Way
of Nature's own Prescribing, to Cure many Diseases in Men,
Women and Children, by Kitchen-Physick only". By the end of
the 1730s, "kitchen physic" meant a healthy diet, either for preserving health or helping a patient regain strength after illness.
In his manual for midwives, *The Midwife's Companion* (1737),
Henry Bracken prescribed his own medication to stop heavy
bleeding after childbirth and recommended "Kitchen Physick"
once the bleeding stopped, to help a woman get back to strength.
Two years later, William Dover asserted that "Kitchin Physick
is the best medicine" for staying healthy. Viper wine when you
are ill, chicken soup to keep you well.

At the same time that these changes were taking place,

commercial household manuals were shrinking women's responsibility for medication. Early books aimed at women mentioned both comestibles and medication in the main title. There was *The Good Hous-Wives Treasurie. Beeing a Verye Neccessarie Booke [of] the Dressing of Meates. Also Sundrie Medicines* in 1588 and *A Closet for Ladies and Gentlewomen, or, The Art of Preserving, Conserving, and Candying. Also Divers Soveraigne Medicines and Salves*, printed nine times between 1608 and 1636, an impressive sales record. John Partridge, whose books ran to many editions apiece, sold *The Treasurie of Commodious Conceits, & Hidden Secrets. And May be Called, the Huswives Closet, of Healthfull Provusion* in 1573 and *The Widowes Treasure, Plentifully Furnished with Secretes in Phisicke and Chirurgery for the Health and Pleasure of mankinde. Hereunto are Adioyned, Sundry Pretie Practises and Conclusions of Cookerie* in 1586. *The Treasurie of Commodious Secrets* was reprinted until 1637 and the more titillatingly entitled *Widowes Treasure* was reprinted until 1639, when it competed with a hot new title, *The Ladies Cabinet Opened, Wherein is Found Hidden Several Experiments in Preserving and Conserving, Physicke, and Surgery, Cookery, and Huswifery*.

Compare these manuals for women to those at the end of the period. In 1723, John Nott, a celebrity chef of his day, put out *The Cook's and Confectioner's Dictionary: Or, the Accomplish'd Housewife's Companion* for the "Use of you *British Housewives*, who would distinguish yourselves by your well ordering the Provisions of your own Families". Nott also considered it a "necessary Companion also for Cooks, &c, in Taverns, Eating-Houses, and publick Inns, and not an unnecessary one, for those who have the ordering of noble tables". About a decade later, another celebrity chef, John Middleton, produced *Five hundred new receipts in cookery, confection-ary, pastry, preserving, conserving, pickling; and the several branches of these arts necessary to be known by all good housewives.* Neither book has any recipes for "physick". Charles Carter's *The Compleat City and Country Cook: or, Accomplish'd Housewife,* a sumptuous collection of "Several hundred of the most approv'd receipts in Cookery" and fur-nished with forty-nine illustrations, was in its second edition in 1734, and mentioned almost as an afterthought that it also had "two hundred" recipes for standard family injuries and ail-ments, including several for treating "the Bite of a Mad Dog". Just a few years later, "Mrs Sarah Harrison, of Devonshire" issued an expanded edition of *The House-keeper's Pocket-Book And Compleat Family Cook* (1739). Although it claimed 700 culinary recipes, *The House-keeper's Pocket-Book* only contained "many" aids for treating family health problems. Furthermore, these aids were "excellent Prescriptions" that had been taken from other physicians' books rather than "receipts" or "recipes". Where later printed housekeeping books men-tioned recipes for physic, those recipes were almost always in the back, in small print. Some recipe books divided food recipes from medication recipes, and some recorded the latter in the second part of the book. The consistency of this place-ment and the very literal shrinking of the space in the books given to those recipes attests to the removal of medication from women's responsibilities and the emphasis on edibles and drinkables instead.

The change of space in housekeeping manuals reflected a change in domestic space. As women's responsibilities changed, so did the places that belonged to them. The kitchen and the garden were the most obvious domestic spaces affected, but the whole notion of "domestic" was impacted: after all, if "making and administering medication" belong to others, they no longer belong to "domestic". As medication and food went their separate ways – or were perceived to be separate entities – the kitchen lost its function as a place for making medicinal goods.

The changing physical architecture of Digby households epitomizes this evolution. Initially, Kenelm began experimenting on food in the kitchen of the house in Charterhouse Square in Clerkenwell, where he and Venetia lived with their children. As a widower, Kenelm was more peripatetic, and his children usually stayed with his mother or at school. Wherever he lived, however, he created experimental space. Immediately after Venetia's death, Kenelm moved to Oxford and maintained a laboratory in his lodgings. The inventory shows that it was stocked with, among other things, several furnaces, a "Reverberating Calcining Oven", numerous glass bottles, tongs, and grinding implements. It also had "His New Oven to bake pies in". When Kenelm lived in Paris, he also maintained a laboratory, and when he lived in Covent Garden in London at the end of his life, his house had two kitchens, one for experiments and one for preparing food. (His friend Alethea Howard, who was exponentially richer, built herself a whole separate house in London for conducting experiments and making medications from recipes.) Kenelm even established space for performing experiments when he was a prisoner in the 1640s.

Over his lifetime, his household staff reflected the redistribution of space that came from the growing division between medication and experiment on one side and food on the other. Initially, he and Venetia employed a cook, who occasionally assisted him or got out of the way. In Oxford, he had laboratory operators to help him conduct experiments who were separate from his household staff, including Hans Hunneades.

When Kenelm returned to London, he employed a cook for the cooking and a laboratory operator to assist with the experiments, Anne and George Hangmaster, respectively. George Hartman also worked with Kenelm in this house. The point is, at the start of the seventeenth century, Kenelm like so many other experimenters was highly dependent on domestic space, specifically female domestic space, for room and equipment to undertake his experiments. By the end of the seventeenth century, kitchens and laboratories were beginning to be distinct spaces, the one belonging to women like Venetia Digby (had she survived) and Anne Hangmaster, the other belonging to men like Kenelm Digby, George Hangmaster, and George Hartman.

For men interested in experimental science, this was a gain: the laboratory was a whole new space belonging to them. For women, whether they were interested in the New Science or in keeping intact the lives and limbs of their families, it was not. As women lost their responsibility for medication, their role in the household – and therefore their authority – shrank. And as the kitchen took on a more limited function, its role in the household also shrank. The concept of "domestic" shrank accordingly. Without medication, "domestic" lost a whole realm of responsibility and its outward, community orientation. As the idea of "domestic" contracted, family life also contracted and communities increasingly consisted of discrete units banded together and less and less an organic, syncretic whole.

If the kitchen was one front in the battle to separate food and medication, then the garden was another. Medication was almost entirely organic at the start of the Scientific Revolution, and many if not most of its ingredients were grown at home, just like most and often all ingredients for meals. The garden was vital to the survival of the household, which made it domestic space and women's responsibility. As "FB" explained in *The Office of the Good House-wife* in 1672, the housewife is responsible for the "Cure & Charge of the Families health"; therefore the "good House-wife must have a good share in the oversight" of the garden – by which "FB" actually meant all of the oversight. Even queens were expected to manifest responsibility for gardens. In the middle of the seventeenth century, the Queen Mother Henrietta Maria had a garden planted for her that included artichokes, a fashionable new plant.

For centuries, every household that had the space for it, had a garden. Maps of grand estates show that they usually kept their kitchen gardens out of sight, as the great botanist John Parkinson advised. In urban neighbourhoods, people grew household necessities in the areas behind and between houses. Seventeenth-century maps of cities such as London and Bristol show that in many neighbourhoods, gardens were standard; guilds maintained gardens beside their meeting halls and, in London, garden sheds were so common that they turn up frequently in the records for crimes such as burglary or selling illegal substances.

Most kitchen gardens were outside of cities, however. Every inch of a kitchen garden's space was used, including the walls, and every plant had a purpose: to attract and feed bees, to feed people, to supply fragrant floor coverings, to make soap or other household goods, to treat ailments, illness, and injury in humans and animals, and so on. John Smith, an early agricultural scientist, calculated that the ideal small estate should include a three-acre "garden of herbs and roots" divided equally between a "Kitchen Garden" and a "physick-garden". Caring for the home garden demanded from the woman of the house a tremendous amount of knowledge, skill, labour, and time. Unsurprisingly, housewives maintained their own storehouse of knowledge, seeds, and tools. As they did with recipes, they shared cuttings, seeds, gardening tips, and so on.

Like cookery books and housekeeping manuals, printed gardening books written specifically for women began to appear in the seventeenth century. The very first gardening book for women, *The Country Housewife's Garden* by William Lawson, first went on sale in 1618 with a companion volume for men, *A New Orchard and Garden*. It sold outstandingly well, particularly after Gervase Markham acquired it and started churning out editions. Other gardening books followed. "FB" devoted fourteen pages of *The Office of the Good House-wife* to caring for the kitchen garden, and another seven to "the Garden of Pleasure" (plants notable for colour and scent). *The Accomplisht Lady's Delight in Preserving, Physick, Beautifying, and Cookery* (1675), sometimes mistakenly attributed to the cookbook author Hannah Woolley, included "The Lady's Diversion in Her Garden", which provided instructions for maintaining the family gardens and ornamental greenery around the house and concluded with a month-by-month planting and garden maintenance schedule. *The Office of the Good House-wife* also provided a month-by-month planting schedule and detailed instructions for beekeeping because, "If the greatest part of the profit of a Farm depend upon the keeping of Cattle: I dare be bold to affirm, that the fruitfulest thing that can be kept about a Countrey-house, is Bees." The *Woman's Almanack, for the Year 1694* begins with a monthly calendar for maintaining the orchard and gardens, and caring for bees.

Lawson's vocabulary in *The Country Housewife's Garden* reflects organizational thinking before the Scientific Revolution. He called everything a herb: artichokes, chamomile, coriander, featherfew (or feverfew), fennel, lilies, lovage, parsnips, poppies, and so on. This general definition makes sense when you think of the root (association intended) of the word "herbaceous". Lawson's instructions organized the housewife's garden based on the frequency of harvest and replanting: the "durable" garden bloomed every year, while "that which is [for] your Kitchens use, must yield daily roots". The ingredients for food and medication were grown together because the two products belonged together, but the truth was that distinguishing between an edible and a medicinal plant was often impossible. Some plants promoted health, others had a medicinal effect but were eaten at meals – were they medicinal or culinary? Both.

By the middle of the eighteenth century, however, gardening instruction for women had little to say about maintaining medicinal plants. Small wonder. In 1651, Nicolas de Bonnefons wrote *Le Jardinier François* (*The French Gardener*) for a female audience, and his conception of the garden was female. When John Evelyn, a member of Samuel Hartlib's circle and a founding member of the Royal Society, translated *Le Jardinier François* into English in 1658, however, he re-gendered it male. Over the next few decades, gardening books increasingly addressed male readers and increasingly dismissed women's contributions. In *The Art of Gardening, Improv'd* (1717), John Evelyn's son Charles stated that the "curious Part of Gardening in general, has always been an Amusement chosen by the greatest of Men". The "Management of the Flower-Garden in particular, is oftentimes the Diversion of the Ladies", Charles explained, but only "where the Gardens are not very extensive, and the Inspection thereof doth not take up too much of their Time". In his view, "the fair Sex" needed "Encouragement" to take up gardening. Although Henry Stevenson addresses "Gentlemen and Ladies" at the very start of *The Young Gardener's Director* (1716), every other page, including the title page, uses male pronouns; he states that he designed the book for "young men" to carry around in a pocket.

By the late 1720s, gardening books were directed at men. Stephen Switzer's *The Practical Kitchen Gardener* (1727) never considered that a woman might be involved in maintaining the kitchen garden. His and other authors' texts reinforced women's exclusion from gardening by requiring the kind of erudition only available to men, such as knowledge of botanical experts, ancient writers, and Latin. "I can't help considering a good Gardener both as a philosopher and a politician," Switzer wrote. Richard Bradley's *New Improvements of Planting and Gardening* (1717) was *Both Philosophical and Practical* and therefore only comprehensible to men – women, of course, did not have the education (or the brains) to understand it. By 1739, the incomparably named Batty Langley was arguing that the "Pleasure of a Garden depends on the variety of its Parts" and asserting that "all the most useful elements of Geometry" were "necessary to be understood by every good Gardener", regardless of whether the garden was for aesthetic enjoyment, growing fruit, or supplying the kitchen.

European imperialism was vital to efforts to assign medication and physic gardens to men – another way in which imperialism and the Scientific Revolution conspired together. As Europeans arrived and strengthened their presence in Asia, sub-Saharan Africa, the Americas, and the Caribbean, they encountered flora that they had never seen before. These plants became an object of fascination and a commodity. The potential for new medicinal treatments was exciting and the desire to have the latest exotic item from distant locales is only human. Boasting the most extensive collection of exotic plants became fashionable among those with the money and space. Plants became commodities; collecting became a serious international business. The Dutch established nurseries in South Africa to feed the collecting craze for plants gathered from around the Indian Ocean. (In 1668, the Dutch cemented their hold on that region by obtaining the last of the Spice Islands in exchange for an island at the mouth of the Hudson River. History had the last laugh.) The English finally caught up with the Dutch in terms of horticulture in 1681, when George London and Henry Wise founded London and Wise's, the first plant nursery in England. As Richard Pulteney wrote in *Historical and Biographical Sketches of the Progress of Botany in England: from its origin to the introduction of the Linnæan system* (1790), "The growing commerce of the nation, the more frequent intercourse with Holland, where immense collections from the Dutch colonies had been made, rendered these gratifications more easily attainable than before." The popular frenzy for collectable plants was also partly inspired by Mary II. Before returning to the British Isles as queen in 1688, she and her husband, William of Orange, had collected rare specimens from around the world. When she moved back to the land of her birth, in addition to a Dutch husband, she brought the latest horticultural technology. Thanks to the Scientific Revolution, starting around the middle of the seventeenth century, people also started collecting plants for intellectual or research purposes. Others, like John Goodyer, William Coys of Stubbers, Edward Morgan, and William Sherard, a diplomat, had the time, money, and interest to establish impressive gardens and often amass equally impressive libraries about horticulture. By the end of his life, Goodyer had learned the medicinal properties of many plants and was providing "simples" for people in his neighbourhood. In other words, he had turned into a housewife.

Men like Goodyer and Morgan and women like Mary II were not scientists. The Scientific Revolution not only encouraged the deliberate collection of plants and knowledge but also developed a methodical approach to the botanical world. Science's revolutionaries wanted to organize and make use of these new plants, this new knowledge, and this expanded view of nature. Pulteney approvingly noted that domestic peace and international trade fostered the interest in collecting rare plants, and "from all these happy coincidences, science in general reaped great benefit". Botanists were part of the New Science's active, international network through which knowledge, ideas, equipment, results, and even seeds and plants were exchanged. They endlessly catalogued and recatalogued as new herbaceous life became known to Europeans. John Ray developed one way of classifying plants in the late seventeenth century; Carl Linnaeus developed his Linnaean taxonomic system in the early 1730s.

Collectors and botanists formed clubs that met regularly at coffee houses such as the Temple Coffee House and the Rainbow Coffee House in London. Members corresponded, exchanged seeds and samples, commissioned each other to find rarities, and wrote papers for scientific journals like the Royal Society's *Philosophical Transactions*. Even Sir Kenelm Digby, who was not a plant collector, gave a paper on *The Vegetation of Plants*. Unsurprisingly, with the very rare exception, these people were men. Furthermore, many of the most dedicated investigators and collectors of new flora were Fellows of the Royal Society, the organization founded in 1662 to promote the New Science.

Many of them were also medical men. Physicians Sir Hans Sloane, Alexander Stuart, and Richard Mead, for example, and well-known apothecaries like Isaac Rand, Samuel Doody, and James Petiver all were Fellows. Petiver also made a fine living selling seeds and samples from his collection. Another Fellow of the Royal Society, James Sherard, trained as an apothecary and later also received a medical degree; his garden of exotic and medicinal plants at his estate in Eltham was famous. The private plant collector William Sherard was his brother. When William died, he endowed a professorship in botany at the University of Oxford, with the condition that the professor should be chosen by the RCP. James Douglas, the most prominent obstetrician of his day and a central figure in Chapter 6, published papers on plants in *Philosophical Transactions*. He also read papers to the Royal Society on the curative properties of different plants and trees, the discovery of a new kind of narcissus, and the cultivation of "English saffron", an ingredient in organic medications.

A notable exception to this boys' club was Mary Somerset, Duchess of Beaufort, whose spectacular wealth, intelligence, and interest made her a vital contributor to the development of botany in the late seventeenth century. She was so important that Richard Pulteney, who neglected to mention Queen Mary's work at Hampton Court, named Somerset among the most significant early botanists. She obtained thousands of cuttings, plants, and seeds from across the globe; what she could not get through personal connections, she commissioned from agents. One shipment from Barbados had to be divided and transported on five different ships because the specimen containers were so large and so numerous. The Duchess of Beaufort was committed to the Scientific Revolution in botany. She received *Philosophical Transactions* to keep up with the latest discoveries. She identified, classified, and catalogued everything she collected; kept illustrations of her samples; and hired her own assistants to help with her work. She also exchanged ideas, materials, and the results of experiments – including her own – with men including Sloane, Petiver, Ray, and William Sherard.

The duchess became interested in botany after learning of

Joseph Glanvill's recommendation to study nature through the scientific method as a way of treating depression. She exemplifies the convergence of the woman's domestic responsibility to create treatments for family ailments, the idea that medication is organic, and the New Science. Unfortunately, she is an exception who proves the rule: the New Science's male revolutionaries determinedly established that studying plants, medication, and medicinal plants was their business. (After her death, Charles Evelyn generously conceded that the Duchess of Beaufort "thought it no Diminution to concern herself in the directing Part of her Gardens" and called her the "greatest Example of Female Horticulture", which was a "most pleasant and agreeable Employment".) Gardens created by proponents of the Scientific Revolution were scientific gardens. These were spaces that belonged to men, were maintained by men, and served male interest in knowledge. They were not spaces whose primary function was to sustain a household through the care and feeding of its members.

Unsurprisingly, there was a simultaneous surge of academic interest in medicinal gardens. Almost the moment that Andreas Vesalius published *De Humani Corporis Fabrica* in 1543 and kicked off the Scientific Revolution, medical schools across Europe began establishing gardens of medicinal plants. The University of Pisa established Europe's first physic garden in 1544; the University of Padua followed in 1545. From there, academic medicinal or physic gardens for training physicians spread rapidly. The University of Valencia established a position for teaching medicinal compounds and a teaching garden to support the curriculum in 1567. The University of Leiden began its famous physic garden, the Hortus Botanicus (better known as the Hortus) in 1577; in France, Montpellier broke ground in 1595 and Paris in 1596.

Across the English Channel things got going a little later. John Gerrard's efforts at the end of the sixteenth century to establish physic gardens for the barber-surgeons' guild and for the University of Cambridge came to nothing. In London, the RCP aspired as early as 1587 to start one, but there are no documents proving that it existed until 1651. Edinburgh's apothecaries and College of Surgeons together founded a physic garden in 1656. As for educational institutions, the University of Oxford began its physic garden in 1621, but the other great educational institutions of the British Isles did not follow suit until after 1650. The University of Glasgow established a physic garden in 1704 and the University of Cambridge, clearly not in the vanguard, finally broke ground in 1762.

From at least as early as the late 1500s, during Elizabeth I's reign, some physicians and apothecaries kept personal gardens to supply materia medica, but it was hardly a system for training apprentices. The apothecary's apprentice had a lot in common with the daughter in a household. He had to learn what parts of what plants processed in which ways produced which medications, and he had to learn to recognize medicinal plants in a garden and in the wild. To provide a thorough, standard, reliable education in materia medica to their apprentices, in 1673 the Worshipful Society of Apothecaries leased a small plot on the Thames to use as a teaching garden. The Chelsea Physic Garden is still there, a bright, beautiful island in the middle of Chelsea.

From its beginning, the physic garden was a product and a tool of the Scientific Revolution. The apothecaries created administrative and teaching positions: the *Horti Praefectus*, who oversaw everyone and everything at the physic garden; the head gardener; and the demonstrator, who taught the apprentices. Its earliest officers were active in the New Science. James Petiver and Isaac Rand were the first two demonstrators. Rand also served as *Horti Praefectus* for nineteen years. Samuel Doody was the head gardener from 1692 to 1706. His immediate predecessor, James Watts, established a partnership between the physic garden and the Hortus at the University of Leiden that outlasted individuals and provided both institutions with invaluable seeds, samples, and information. In the scientific spirit of technological innovation, in 1680 the apothecaries built England's first greenhouse to keep alive delicate plants from foreign climes. Mary II was so impressed that she added a greenhouse to the gardens at Hampton Court to protect her exotic plants. To foster research and learning, the apothecaries also established a library for books about materia medica, botany, and gardening. Any member could use them after getting permission from the *Horti Praefectus*. And, of course, there was the collecting. Head gardeners collected almost fanatically.

Another aspect of the apothecaries' physic garden that was tied to the Scientific Revolution was the collaboration of the apothecaries and the physicians to establish and maintain it. Before 1650, the two professions competed for patients, money, and control of medication, and in truth this competition did not vanish with the end of the Civil War. Far from it. Nevertheless, significant members on both sides shared two vital interests: the Scientific Revolution and taking over medication from women. The physic garden was a powerful tool in promoting both in one go. When the Worshipful Society of Apothecaries was in danger of losing the land on which they planted their garden, the organization turned to Sir Hans Sloane for help. While buying his estate in Chelsea, Sloane purchased the physic garden's land and leased it to the apothecaries for five pounds and delivery of fifty samples to the RCP every year. The lease still runs, although the terms have changed slightly.

Interest in medicinal plants united the apothecaries and the physicians, and Sloane's arrangement eliminated competition for knowledge and materials. The relationship was reinforced by the close ties with the University of Leiden. Many of the Fellows of the Royal College had been trained at Leiden's prestigious medical school and in its spectacular Hortus, while the apothecaries and the Hortus exchanged materials and information. Long after Sloane and his colleagues – including Mead, Rand, Petiver, Sherard, Douglas, and Doody – were gone, the Chelsea Physic Garden brought together physicians and apothecaries in the scientific pursuit of botanical medicine. The collaboration and like-mindedness regarding the physic garden intensified over the late seventeenth and early eighteenth centuries. By the 1730s, physicians often attended dinners at Apothecaries' Hall and regularly were guests at the "public" herbarizing for apprentices in July. Herbarizings were monthly summer expeditions into the countryside led by master apothecaries. One important use for the guild's official barge was to transport apothecaries and their apprentices down the Thames on these occasions.

It was at the dinner following the public herbarizing in July 1734 that the RCP and the Worshipful Society of Apothecaries agreed to support another scheme promoting their superiority: Elizabeth Blackwell's *A Curious Herbal*. Blackwell (1707–58) proposed to make a beautiful, two-volume herbal for commercial sale – a luxury item, a boutique publication – that showed off the spectacular extent of apothecarial knowledge while linking it with the New Science. Her plan was brilliant and innovative: she organized the images and the information so each one and the book as a whole appeared methodical, but she also rendered the images and information visually compelling. Her proposed target was not women as a whole, but "herb women" – that is, women who competed with apothecaries by selling medicinal herbs. All those women who could afford to buy the print sets or complete volumes remained unoffended, but they were also directed towards male authority.

The apothecaries and physicians embraced Blackwell's proposal, publicly announced their support, and gave her unlimited access to the physic garden. Over the next four years, despite extreme weather, two pregnancies, the deaths of both infants, the hostility of the head gardener, the theft of her work by rival printers, and a deadbeat husband who sold all of her etched copper plates (even the unfinished ones) to settle his debts, she produced 500 etchings of plants and another 125 etched information pages. All in the service of the apothecaries and physicians' campaign against domestic medicine and the women who practised it. When she died in 1758, a group of physicians and apothecaries arranged for her burial next to Sir Hans Sloane in Old Chelsea Churchyard as a mark of respect.

Elizabeth Blackwell was also the only woman permitted in the physic garden. A woman could be brought to the garden as a guest, but they were not allowed into the garden on their own. The *ne plus ultra* of professional physic gardens, the apothecaries' garden in London was thus also the antithesis of domestic medicine's medicinal garden, which was female space. Domestic medicine's garden belonged to the home and was literally next to it; commercial medicine's garden was educational and professional space, physically separated from the home. (Elizabeth Blackwell and the head gardener lived across the street from the physic garden; they both commuted to it.) Domestic medicine's garden was female space; the professional physic garden was male space. Domestic medicine's garden was open to the household; the professional physic garden was off limits except to authorized professionals. And of course, women were allowed in domestic medicine's garden but banned from the professionals' garden.

Kenelm and Venetia Digby's married life together was short and sometimes tempestuous, but it also encapsulated the transformation that the Scientific Revolution wrought on food and medication. Initially, Kenelm's experiments and Venetia's space, the kitchen, literally and metaphorically overlapped. As Kenelm continued his experiments after Venetia's death, he increasingly separated one space – the laboratory where experiments were conducted – from the other – the kitchen where recipes were followed. And while Kenelm himself did not necessarily distinguish medication from food as cleanly in life as he appeared to in death, the posthumous publication of his work promoted and attested to a cultural distinction between the two and a re-gendering of medication from female to male.

The whole process, of course, took longer than the span of Kenelm's life and the life of editions of his notebooks, but it had succeeded by 1740. Printed housekeeping, gardening, and cookery books for women had little or nothing to say about women's role as medicine makers and everything to say about women's role as food providers. Medicine had been disentangled from food, or maybe reconceptualized, and associated with men. Although in practice plenty of women continued to grow physic gardens and make medicine to treat their families, friends, and neighbours, the cultural associations had been rearranged. Elizabeth Blackwell's *A Curious Herbal* (1737/39) glorified the scientific approach to medication, promoted its connection with physicians and apothecaries, and denigrated women as medicators. The work itself, its purpose and supporters, and its success all testify to the reconfiguration of food and medication between 1650 and 1740. Had the Digbys lived a century later, Kenelm would have had to become an expert in chicken soup, not viper wine, if he wanted to take care of his beloved Venetia.

4

Proscriptions, Prescriptions, and Poetry

What do you call a woman physician? That depends on when and where you are asking. If the year is 1674 and the place is England, the answer is "Mrs". If the year is 1675 and the place is England, the answer is "Medicatrix". At least, that is what Mary Trye would tell you. If the year is 1685 and the place is England, the answer is "Doctor" – according to Jane Barker. By the middle of the eighteenth century, the answer is "an impossibility" or "a freak of nature".

A rose by any other name might smell as sweet, but titles matter, and starting around 1650, the meaning of certain medical titles changed significantly. What did it mean to be a physician? What did it mean to be an apothecary? A barber? A surgeon? A barber-surgeon? What did it mean to be licensed to practise medicine? Some of the change had to do with the profession itself: what knowledge or experience was required of or expected from someone to justify the title "physician", "apothecary", "barber-surgeon"? Some of that change had to do with the project of commodifying medication. A medication marketplace does not just require medication as a saleable object. It also requires people to buy it and sell it. Both groups have to be created, but to maximize profit the former has to be infinite and the latter has to be very small. Titles were vital for this project, and no title was more important than "prescription".

Mary Trye and Jane Barker show how and why the prescription system developed into a powerful economic engine. So, let us start with Mary Trye, medicatrix. Biographical facts about Trye are few and far between. She was born in 1642, lost both parents in 1665 during the Great Plague of London, married twice, gave birth to at least one son, lived for a few years in Warwickshire, and returned to London in 1674. Her father, Thomas O'Dowde, trained her to make medication and she became his assistant sometime before she was eighteen. O'Dowde was a fervent proponent of the Scientific Revolution and of chemical medication in particular. He introduced his daughter to the New Science, teaching her to value experience and experiment as well as study. He also trained her in one of the Scientific Revolution's discoveries, chemical medication.

The reason why anyone knows about Mary Trye is because in 1675 she published a small book entitled *Medicatrix, Or The Woman-Physician*. In *Medicatrix*, she claims that she is writing to defend her father as well as the validity of chemical medicine from the aspersions of Henry Stubbe, a Fellow of the RCP. The two parts of the book map out her strategy: rebut Stubbe's argument and extol her father's skills and knowledge in part one, expose the problems in Stubbe's brand of medicine and promote the virtues of her father's brand of medicine in part two. Henry Stubbe is an example of the opposition that the New Science faced. The standard story of the Scientific Revolution has physicians seizing upon the new knowledge and methods, with which they modernize the practice of medicine, create effective treatments, and kick those ugly, warty, cackling crones to the kerb. In reality, some physicians, apothecaries, barbers, barber-surgeons, midwives, and other "irregular practitioners" seized upon the Scientific Revolution, and some did not. The members of the medical community who became science's revolutionaries often became Fellows of the Royal Society; at the very least, they read the Society's journal, *Philosophical Transactions*. Not all Fellows of the Royal Society belonged to the Worshipful Society of Apothecaries or the RCP of course, and most definitely not all guildsmen of the Apothecaries or Fellows of the College approved of the Royal Society: vide Henry Stubbe, Fellow of the RCP, opponent of the Royal Society, and ardent advocate of phlebotomy and studying the ancients like Aristotle and Galen. For someone like Dr Stubbe, someone like Thomas O'Dowde – or much, much worse, Mary O'Dowde Trye – would be quite threatening.

Stubbe was an ideal straw man. He had attacked O'Dowde publicly and had a reputation for vociferous opposition to the New Science. He was also a relatively safe target for a woman with the audacity to publicly attack a man. In 1674, he was drinking heavily and not well respected. Furthermore, although he had published plenty of attacks in the past, he had not published any recently; Trye was provoked by "some Papers [that] came to my hands, subscribed by Henry Stubbe Physician at Warwick". Private papers such as Stubbe's "private Notes and Manuscripts I have by me", even those circulating among a group of interested readers, would not have required a public refutation. Furthermore, the timing is suggestive: "upon my coming to London in October last [1674], being inquisitive after the advance of Chymystry, so desirable by all sorts of

People, some Papers came to my hands". So, after living in Warwickshire for a few years, Mary Trye returned to London and investigated whether the environment was favourable for a woman to establish a practice in chemical medicine. In an answer to her enquiries, someone gave her Stubbe's papers. Perhaps that someone gave them to her with the advice to use them to write against Stubbe and thereby establish herself; perhaps someone gave them to her and she saw the opportunity on her own. Regardless, the papers – private, unpublished – were her opportunity to get her name out to the public and to display her credentials as a medicatrix.

When it comes down to it, however, *Medicatrix* is not about O'Dowde, Henry Stubbe, the Royal Society, or chemical medicine. The book is about herself; she is the eponymous medicatrix, the woman physician. People with a shop put up a sign to indicate where to find them and what they did ("at the sign of the wig", "at the sign of the wheel", and so forth). Trye's book was her shop, and the sign over the door was the word "medicatrix". The term comes from a Latin phrase *Natura corroborata est omnium morborum medicatrix*, which roughly translates as "Nature reinforced is the best treatment for all diseases." The passage appears with slight variations in medical writing throughout the seventeenth century, most often in the final decades. It is attributed to either Hippocrates or Jan Baptiste van Helmont, the most significant contributor to chemical medication after Paracelsus. The word "medicatrix" displays her erudition, but Trye uses it to signal that she is part of the Scientific Revolution, that she uses chemical medication, and that her medications grant her the ability to strengthen nature's curative power. Trye was the first person to use the word as a title for a human practitioner; she invented and conferred it on herself to explain who and what she was. From its title page, *Medicatrix* is not only a declaration of principles, which is bold enough, but also a confident assertion of a self-fashioned identity.

Trye establishes her credentials in ways that her readers would have recognized and approved of. She claims the stereotypical female qualities that help her seem authoritative and rejects those that do not. She reminds readers from time to time that she is a loving daughter behaving with appropriate filial devotion when she defends her father. She anticipates charges that her tract is just stereotypical female chatter (according to one adage, "A woman's tongue wags like a lamb's tail") by promising "to avoid Prolixity, which is a crime we Women are commonly guilty of". Repeatedly, she performs modesty by protesting her inability to judge or make sense of something. One can almost imagine a demure murmur and slyly downcast eyes when she writes, "Now whether Mr. Stubbe be not as conceited in this particular as ever Cicero was, I must leave to those that are proper to judge." Trye also displays the virtues of thoroughness and rigour. "I have given the Reader, this Historical account, not only that he see I have read in History," she explains, "but that I may mind him of the vast difference, between wit and wisdom, truth and errour, justice and interest."

In fact, she delves deep into Stubbe's past, analysing his actions and how he characterizes himself. She uses Cicero's interrogation techniques to challenge Stubbe's self-representation as a well-known, prolific author. "Where hath Mr. Stubbe lived all this while?" she asks. "At Jamaica; or where are his famous works extant, and victorious Books exposed to Sale? For I am inform'd, the Author himself, with most Book-sellers in this City, is not known; and the Books themselves scarce with any to be had; so that I am satisfied, the Generality of this

Kingdom never heard his name, much less saw him." She shows off her own knowledge of chemical medication and her connection to men, such as in her alliance with the Royal Society.

Trye's characterizations of O'Dowde and Stubbe establish her own integrity, dedication, skill, and courage. When Stubbe and other physicians fled the plague, she and her father remained. Consequently, Stubbe saved no one, her father saved vast numbers of the public, and Mary saved members of the public and her own family. Her fearlessness appears also in her attacks on Stubbe and his like-minded colleagues, calling him names (for example *medicus*, "the Great Oracle Mr Stubbe", "the Tinkling Campanelle", "the Quacking Parrot"), mocking his accomplishments ("O prodigious!" she snorts at one point), and accusing him of being more talk than substance. "Learning will fit a Man for that Profession, but a diligent and indefatigable Elaboration must perfect it, Medicines when obtained, one may in a reasonable time learn to apply," she writes, "but how to obtain those Medicines, I verily think is a question beyond Dr. Stubbes's Study." She, however, has the combination of education and experience vital for serving the ill:

> Yet I do say, Learning in it self, is only preparatory, not perfect, a proper progress and tendency, in order to the Art of Physick, not the Perfection and Consummation of that Art: A Man may read and Author, and yet not understand a medicine [...] And as I am not satisfied, That every Author that writes of Medicines understands them; so I am as well assured, That a Man may sleep many years at the Fountain of Learning, and yet awake no Physician: Medicines are the Marrow and full Perfection of a Physician, and those are hard to be attain'd...

These are the qualities of a physician, and as *Medicatrix* makes clear, she has them. She knows what medicinal treatments should be used for what ailment, and equally important, she knows how to make those treatments herself. She is a chemical physician. A medicatrix.

As a declaration of self, Trye's book is stunning. It does not just assert, it displays her equality with physicians and apothecaries. It rejects the accepted ways to fulfil the requirements for a licensed or guild membership: studying at a university (she did the reading on her own), being fluent in Latin (Who needs it? She read excellent translations), apprenticing to a member of a guild (she apprenticed to her father, who was a master chemical physician), gaining experience (she assisted O'Dowde and treated people herself), learning what medicines treat which illnesses (she was apprenticed to O'Dowde), and learning how to make those medicines (again, apprenticed to O'Dowde).

Furthermore, *Medicatrix* is a declaration of competition, and as such quite alarming. Her justifications for writing – I am a good daughter vindicating my wronged father; I am a charitable, knowledgeable person seeking to help people; Henry Stubbe is a cowardly quack who must be slapped down – enable her to promote herself and her medications. "Mr. Medicus hath forc'd me to tell the World, in answer to him, what Remedies I can afford them, and what good I can do them," she complains. Yes, right, of course it is Henry Stubbe's fault that she must tell everyone how effective she and her medications are. The last eight pages of *Medicatrix*, entitled "An Advertisement of Dr. O. Dowdes Medicines, and the Authors", list medicaments that Trye sold for several common, painful afflictions, including gout. Between this section and the end of her treatise, Mary Trye included a two-page postscript, in which she challenges

Stubbe "to an experimental Tryal" to prove that what she has said is true. Like the opening, the language of the postscript tends towards the formal challenge ("I am and shall be ready to maintain" and so forth), another way of making Trye's position more male than female.*

Mary Trye and *Medicatrix* highlight two related problems that accompanied the challenge of commodifying medication. The first was excluding women and their medication from the medication marketplace. The second was shifting the culture so the professional's medication was the one that everyone sought. The prescription system solved both of these problems. Prescriptions had been around for centuries. From the mid-seventeenth century onwards, professionals used them to create an economic system: the physician got money for writing the prescription and the apothecary got money for filling it. Legally, only a physician could write a prescription and only an apothecary could fill one, which should have restricted participation in the system to men. The physicians and apothecaries of London wrangled with each other over the privilege of diagnosing and prescribing, but they united when it came to women's exclusion from the system.

The prescription told the apothecary what medication was required, including the ingredients and their quantities; the dose to be taken, how often, and in what form; and the duration of the medication's use. Until well into the twentieth century, it was

* Trye was not the only woman in London challenging someone to a duel. That same year, Hortense Mancini, Duchess of Mazarin, and Anne, Countess of Sussex, engaged in swordplay one night in St James's Park, wearing only their nightgowns. The duchess had left her much older, insane husband in France and so could do as she pleased, but the countess was hauled off to their estate in the country by her husband, who was, in the words of a future monarch, "not amused".

standard for the apothecary (or druggist, chemist, or pharmacist) to make up the medication themselves. The doctor wrote the prescription for a medicinal compound and the apothecary either knew what ingredients were required or followed the instructions in the script. He would then mix it together and dispense the compound to the patient.* In addition to the legal restriction, the prescription system excluded women and other untrained people by virtue of its elaborate code. Medical students learned it in their courses; notebooks reveal that they even took notes in it. Apprentice apothecaries learned it from their masters.

The situation with women and guilds was messier than it was with women and universities, where they were forbidden. Some guilds in some towns at some point admitted girls as apprentices, and some granted women the "liberty" or "freedom" to act as a member if they proved their knowledge and skill. Esther Dudley, a widow, was "admitted into the freedom" of the coopers' guild because her father was a cooper. Some guilds allowed widows to take over the business and some also allowed widows to take apprentices. It was difficult to remain ignorant when the shop was inside the house and the wife of the guildsman was also keeping the books and caring for the apprentices. Nevertheless, women's part in guilds, including the apothecary guilds in London and beyond, was not consistent or sizeable enough for them to be real participants in the prescription system.

Measurements were the first level of the cypher. Dry

---

* This is how Mr Gower nearly poisons Mrs Blaine's little boy in the film *It's a Wonderful Life* (1946). (Fortunately, despite not being trained as a pharmacist, twelve-year-old George Bailey manages to read the word **POISON** written in giant letters on the bottle and prevent disaster.)

ingredients such as powders were measured in grains, indicated with "G" or "gr"; scruples (℈); drachms (ʒ); ounces (℥); and pounds (lb). Occasionally, there was a call for "handful" or "pinch", symbolized as "M.j." and "p", respectively. Wet ingredients were measured in minims, indicated with "♏"; guttes or drops (gtt); drachms (ʒ); ounces (℥); pints (O); quarts (ɑ); and gallons (C). Yes, that's correct: both wet and dry substances were measured in drachms and ounces. Pints were abbreviated "O" because another name for a pint was octuarius, and gallons were signified with "C" because another name for a gallon was congius or "congy", as it was sometimes pronounced. Numbers were written as Roman numerals (i, v, x), except if the i was on the end of the number; then it was written as j. Thus 1 was written i, but 2 was written ij and 6 was vj. Often the "v" after an "i" was written as "ÿ", however, so 4 might be iÿ. To indicate half of an amount, the writer could use "ss" but much more often used "β", which was faster and easier to write (especially with a quill). Half a scruple had its own name: an obol, which mercifully was written "obol". Most of the time, however, half a scruple would be written as ℈iβ. There were also measurement shortcuts. "Ana" indicated that all the ingredients in a list should be added in the same quantity; "p.ae." meant that the product should be divided into or administered in equal portions.

Students and apprentices had to learn the symbols and abbreviations for different elements, metals, and transformed metals, as well. The symbols came from alchemy, which was the starting point for the modern discipline of chemistry and for chemical medication. Salt, for example, was written as ϴ, sulphur was 🜍, and philosopher's sulphur was 🜎. Other common symbols included mercury (☿), silver (☽), and antimony (♁). Latin supplied the vocabulary for a medication's effect, such as astringent (closing a wound), pectoral (an expectorant), or sudorific (provokes sweating), although the ordinary housewife had a chance of recognizing words like these even if she did not use them herself. When it came to the forms that medication took, however, there was a shared lexicon. Medical terms such as clyster (enema) or linctus (medication to be licked off a spoon) were also household terms found in recipe books as well as in physicians' and apothecaries' records. Put together, a prescription often looked like gibberish. Take this one, written by an apothecary in 1740:

Sal. Vol. Oleos ℥ss Spt. Lavend. c. ℈i
Tinct. Castor. ℈ij. Misic.
xxv Drops to be taken Morning and
Evening in a Glass of white wine and
water;   ad. Vertigineum

Who could understand this? Certainly not the patient, their family, neighbours, or friends. Hopefully their vertigo went away, at least.

The *Pharmacopoeia Londinensis* was the last layer of code. Although one apothecary, Nicholas Culpeper, went rogue in 1650 and translated it into English so housewives could use it, the official editions remained in code, and for some time, in Latin. Furthermore, the *Pharmacopoeia* did not indicate quantities or processes. The apothecary who was instructed via prescription to make Æthiops Mineralis would read, "Rx Mercurii crudi, Florum Sulphuris, ana partes aequales. Agitentur in Mortario vitreo, cum pistillo virtreo, donec Mercurius evanescat": mix equal amounts of mercury and flowers of sulphur in a glass mortar with a glass pestle until the mercury is fully integrated.

But how much mercury? How much flowers of sulphur? The apothecary often knew offhand; some compounds were so common and made so frequently that it would become almost automatic. Knowing this, some physicians wrote "Pharm Lond" on their prescriptions to tell the apothecary to follow the instructions in the *Pharmacopoeia*. Otherwise, the prescription would tell the apothecary exactly how the physician wanted it done.

There was a significant potential for error in this system. Doctors have always been famous for bad handwriting, so reading a prescription was difficult enough without having to remember the meanings of the abbreviations and symbols. After all, quantity mattered a great deal with ingredients. Some were fairly benign no matter how much was ingested, but others such as poppy or foxglove could be fatal if taken in the wrong amounts, and killing one's patients was definitely contraindicated. The potential for disaster was worth it. The code enabled the professionals to indicate that their medicines were fundamentally different from those made by women, and to hide when their medicines actually were not.

At the start of the Scientific Revolution, most medication, regardless of who made it, came from organic materials, primarily plants. If the primary ingredients for making medicine could be grown in anyone's back garden or picked up along the side of any local road or river, and if they were often prepared the same way to make the same treatment, then there was not much difference between the ingredients of an apothecary's medicine and the ingredients of a housewife's medicine. Not much or none. That was not something the professionals wanted anyone to know, and the code hid it. As historian Patrick Wallis puts it:

Knowledge of many such substances was widely diffused, and formed part of the skills expected of women in particular. Yet in the apothecaries' and druggists' hands, these commonplace materials somehow also became expensive and exclusive, a transformation of muck into brass that seemed to many a uniquely, and unjustifiably, profitable enterprise.

"Capiscum" sounds so much more impressive than "pepper". So does "Borrago floribus caerulis et albis" for blue and white borage flowers. True, apothecaries occasionally used exotic ingredients that ordinary women would not be able to find or afford. In addition to "Powders of Viper" and snake's skin, a list of unusual materials compiled by Robert Pitt in 1703 included "Bezoar-stone", pearl, gold, silver, gemstones, mummy (ground-up bits of mummies – yes, really), pike's jawbone, swallow's nest, "the Bone in the Heart of a Stag", rabbit and boar ankle bones, elk and "ounce" hooves, and "the Horns of the Elke, Buffalo, Rhinoceros, Unicorn". Pitt was not an anomaly. John Quincy also included unicorn's horn and "bone of a stag's heart" in *Pharmacopoeia Officinalis & Extemporanea* (1724). Imperial expansion ensured that there was always a new, hard-to-get substance from a distant corner of the earth that might be said to have medicinal properties. "These are some frontier plants as it were, that cannot with any certainty be ranked amongst ither [sic]," one medical student recorded in his lecture notes, but they were still included in the lecture on medicinal botanics. Tobacco, coffee, the "Magellanic Bay-like tree", the "India Berry tree", and the euphoniously named "Gamboodge tree", for example, were used to cure everything from cancer to leprosy to lice to sexually transmitted infections.

Unfortunately for the professionals, imperial expansion also meant that it got easier and easier for ordinary people to acquire those exotic substances (except perhaps unicorn horn). Quincy noted in *Pharmacopoeia Officinalis & Extemporanea* that although Pliny thought red coral was "found only in the Indian Seas", in fact "we have it now from many parts of the Mediterranean, and Naples is a great Market for it." By the end of the seventeenth century, a woman's recipe might call for cinnamon, nutmeg, or ginger whether she was baking a cake or making a bolus. The code, however, preserved the mystery of a prescription's ingredients. What's in a name? Profit, my girl. Profit.

Then there was "human skull". In 1724, John Quincy explained disdainfully in *The Complete English Dispensary* that it "has obtain'd a Place in Medicine", although "more from a whimsical Philosophy, than any other account". The philosophy might have been whimsical, but many professionals and housewives accepted it. In *The Marrow of Physicke* (1648), Thomas Brugis recommended "Oyle of Mans Skull" for epilepsy, instructing his readers to "buy this Oyle of the Chemists". If a chemist was not available but a skull was, unlikely as that seems, Brugis also had a recipe:

> The Skull of a man that hath been dead but one yeare, and bury it in the Ashes behinde the fire, and let it burne untill it be marvellous white, and so well burned that you may breake it with your finger; then take off all the uppermost part of the Head to the top of the Crown, and beat it as small as is possible, then grate a Nutmeg, and put to it, then take Dogs blood, and dry it, and make Powder thereof, and mingle as much with the other Powder, as the Powder weighes, and give it the sick to drinke, both when

he is well, and when he is sicke, first, and last, and it will help him by Gods grace.

As in professionals' books, "skull" turns up rarely in recipe books, but every now and then a recipe calls for the skull of a man – sometimes specified as "a dead man", as if one could get a man's skull under other circumstances. To make lozenges, one recipe required coral, pearl, amber, crab eyes, crab claws, hartshorn, ivory, mistletoe, and "Man's skull". Hartshorn and mistletoe were rare but not bizarre ingredients; everything else, especially the skull (hopefully), was. Recipes did not always require the whole skull, fortunately. Another woman's recipe, this one for "Convulsion and fitts" of a pregnant woman, begins: "Take one ear off dead Mans Skull yt was never buryed." Frankly, it is unlikely that anyone at home actually made any of the recipes requiring pieces of a dead man's head. A woman need not have believed in its curative properties to collect the recipe, however; recipes involving "dead Mans Skull" had a titillating "eew" factor even then.

The fact is, a prescription was really a recipe, a truth that the professionals did not want their customers to realize. Part of their project was to replace "recipe" with "prescription" in the general lexicon. For centuries, professional makers of medication used the word "recipe" far more often than "prescription". The word "recipe" was substantially more common in printed medical materials than "prescription" until the last few decades of the seventeenth century, when they began to switch places. In 1701, for example, an anonymous author of *The Present State of Physic* extolled physicians' "prescriptions"; George I used the word in his 1721 proclamation on medicine.

The transition was not just about swapping one male-associated word for another female-associated word. By the

1730s, "recipe" denoted the list of ingredients and procedure, while "prescription" referred to the document presented to an apothecary or to the product. *The Generous Physician*, printed in 1733 and attributed to Sir John Colbatch, Fellow of the RCP, offered "The Best Receipts in English, and Directions how to use them, adapted to ordinary Capacities" on its title page, but the preface concludes with the assurance that "No Prescription is embarrass'd, or Ingredient invented, to bring on an Application to a Physician." In Daniel Bellamy's comedy *The Merry Swain* (1739), a sighing lover asks a cynical friend for his "Receipt" to cure love, and on receiving it exclaims, "I like your Prescription." The shift to "prescription" was a shift in focus to the product and away from the process indicated by "recipe". By 1740, *A New General Dictionary* defined "prescription" as "the appropriating proper remedies to particular diseases goes by this name; also the medicine itself".

Built into the concept of a recipe was the idea of communal knowledge. Recipes were supposed to be shared with others. In contrast, prescriptions were built on the idea of knowledge as property, so they were extremely limited in circulation. To the great delight of the RCP, in 1721 George I issued a proclamation "Commanding Apothecaries to follow the Dispensatory lately compiled by the College of Physicians of London", although he permitted some variation: "except it shall be by the Special Direction or Prescription of some Learned Physician". Mary Trye subscribed as much as any proponent of the Scientific Revolution to this view of knowledge and medication. She touted her own cures in the "Advertisement" section of *Medicatrix*, but she did not say how they were made. After extolling her training, knowledge, and skill, the book ends with a catalogue of goods. The whole thing is an advertisement, not just the last eight pages. She had to promote her ready-made medications, however, because as a woman she could not write prescriptions.

One of the diseases that Mary Trye discusses in *Medicatrix* is gout. Gout is a highly painful condition caused by uric acid crystals building up in the joints, most often those of the big toe. It feels something like a herd of sea urchins wedged between two bones and set on fire. James Gillray painted its portrait (see plate section, p.4). Gout was a "disease of the rich" because it was caused by a fatty, sugary diet and sedentary lifestyle. It was also considered a man's disease because women's diets contained less alcohol (and because menstruation was thought to purge women of some of the toxins that caused gout). When Queen Anne was diagnosed with gout as a young woman, probably for lack of a better explanation for her ailments, the diagnosis implied that there was something unnatural and unwomanly about her, an unsurprising accusation of any female monarch, but especially pointed given her inability to provide an heir to the throne.

There was quite a demand for gout treatments because none of them seemed to work. In his book *The Attila of the Gout* (1713), the surgeon John Marten called it "the great uncertainty in which Physicians fluctuate as to the true Method of Cure", or as Jane Barker wrote, "The sturdy *Gout*, which all *Male* power withstands". A seventeenth-century adage put it more astringently: "The Physician is blind at the Gout." Hermannus Vander Heyden advocated cold water, Roger Dixon used "Sol Triumphans, or Horizontall Gold" (whatever that is), and Benjamin Welles recommended purges and phlebotomy.

Handbooks of medication listed multiple substances or recipes that could ease or cure gout. The *Pharmacopoeia Londinensis* of 1702 suggested among other materials powdered bear's breech, the roasted roots of Hounds Tongue, oil of ebony, guaiacum, germander, the fat or marrow of a dog, the gall of a puppy mixed with vinegar, and the flesh or excrement of a cat. Many of the *Pharmacopoeia*'s ingredients contribute to the gout medications in Fuller's *Pharmacopoeia Extemporanea* (1714). His "Arthritic ale" included guaiacum and germander, as well as avens roots, agrimony, sage, betony, raisins, sassafras, ground pine, "Hermodactyls", "Dodder of Thyme", "Stechas Flowers", and "Wort". For gout, William Salmon recommended alabastrum unguentum, made with red briar, white wine, rue, chamomile, powdered alabaster, fennel seeds, oil of roses, wax, and five egg whites. Mary Trye sold "A Medicinal Milk, an Aural Tincture, Two sorts of Radiant Pills. A Purging Potion, an Extract against the Gout, A Cordial Potion; and for outward application, Two Unguents, the one White, the other Green, and my Golden Balsamick Spirits", all of which removed gout pain "in Three or Four days".

Treatments for gout appear in women's recipe books, although they are considerably rarer than medications for less class-dependent afflictions, such as cough, burns, cramps, headache, eye trouble, and labour pains. Some gout treatments made a more credible attempt than others: one called for harvesting the root of a male peony during a waxing moon in May to wear at one's waist. One type of gout medication was meant to be ingested, a convenient delivery method for an ailment that made the afflicted place unbearably sensitive. 'Mary Courthop's recipe for a gout drink mixed "venice [*sic*] Turpintine" with egg and milk, for example, while Lady Sedley's cocktail combined turpentine, wax, wine, rose water, and salad oil. "Turpentine" was then what it is now: a thick, resinous oil made from the terebinth, a kind of tree. These days it is used for strengthening horse's hooves and creating a shiny coating over paint.

There were also topical treatments for gout because like burns and acne, it involved the skin and flesh, but anything that had to be smeared on, such as an ointment or a salve, was of very limited use because the place was so sensitive. A more comfortably applied treatment was a plaister, a very light cloth that had been soaked in a compound of melted fat or wax and medicinal substances such as herbs, and then dried. The cloth (also called searcloth, serecloth, or cerecloth) would be laid over the swollen area; its healing properties would sink into the skin as body heat melted the wax and released the herbal compound. According to a late seventeenth-century recipe book compiled by Mary Granville and her daughter, Anne Granville D'Ewes, "Mrs Badge's Plaister" required both "white Rosin" (resin) and "the best yellow bees wax" as a solution for the rest of the ingredients. Plaisters could be made in bulk by preparing a long length of cloth from which pieces could be cut as needed (as Lettice Pudsey advised, "role up the seare cloth: & keep it for your use").

Such gout treatments were often part of a multi-cure medication. Lady Sedley's powder, to be consumed by the spoonful for "three dayes following fasting", was good "For the Dropsy in the Womb, or in the feet, or for the Imposthume in the Stomach or Gout in the Stomach, or for any evill". Lady Barkham's "oyntmt" was good "for aches: gout, pyles, swellings, bruses: spraynes, the Kings Evill: and divers other grevances". Lady Gifford's cerecloth treated "gowt" as well as "aches: [and] greene wounds", and could "strengthen broaken bones", while another recipe for a "serecloth" was to be used "for any ach in any place: broken bones: for the gout proved: it doth seldom fayle to ease the gout". As medicine and chemistry evolved according to the Scientific Revolution's principles, the idea of a panacea – a medicinal philosopher's stone – became, also like the philosopher's stone, increasingly fantastical. Perhaps desperation suggested that a medication that did other things could also cure gout, or vice versa. Perhaps a cure for gout retained the mythical status of the philosopher's stone because it proved so elusive.

In 1685, bookseller Benjamin Crayle advertised in the back of one of his books for sale that "Dr. Barker's Famous Gout Plaister" could be purchased at his shop in Fleet Street (look for the sign of the lamb). The back pages of a volume of titillating narratives seems like an odd place to hawk medication, but it was common practice to use that part of a book as an advertising section. That is one reason why Mary Trye listed her own medications for sale at the end of *Medicatrix*. Crayle also advertised Monsieur Blegny's "Venereal Water" in the back of *England's Heroical Epistles* by Michael Drayton, along with a long list of books, some of them on the same topic, such as *Philaxa Medicina, The Queens Closet Opened* (which I discussed in Chapter 2), and *New and Curious Observations on the Art of Curing Venereal Disease* by Monsieur Blegny. *The Queens Closet Opened* was also one of the books advertised in *Delightful and Ingenious Novells* with "Dr Barker's Famous Gout Plaister".

For five shillings per roll, the Famous Gout Plaister "infallibly takes away the pain in Twelve Hours time, with the Paroxysm of the Distempter, and in time may effect a perfect Cure". Twelve hours might not sound particularly efficacious, but relief in any amount of time would have been appealing. Besides, some remedies claimed to take even longer. "The Duke of Portland's gout powder" took two years. Similarly, the high price for Barker's "gout plaister" is not so very exciting. Five shillings was five times the amount usually charged for advertised medication, equivalent to roughly two days of wages for a labourer. However, labourers did not get gout: rich people did, and rich people could and would pay a premium to ease their agony. Besides, a whole roll of plaister provided multiple doses.

What is outrageous about "Dr Barkers Famous Gout Plaister" is that Dr Barker's first name was Jane. Then again, Jane Barker was an outrageous person. As a teenager, she sent a perfidious ex-suitor a pair of horns on his wedding day, "in the Presence of the Bride and all the Company; as also several Emblems and Mottos on the Subject, the Horns being fasten'd on a Head-band, as a sovereign remedy for the Head-ach, to which marry'd Men are often very subject, especially those who marry Town-Coquets".

It was not surprising that she knew a great deal about medication. She grew up in the country and had the conventional upbringing of a landed gentleman's daughter, as recipes for punch, flummery (a sweet dessert, often in the jelly family), and chicken soup in her novel, *A Patch-Work Screen for the Ladies* (1723), attest. She learned reading, writing, mathematics, and the requisite domestic skills and knowledge for marriage within her class, including how to treat the ailments and injuries of a family and its dependents. She was taught about medicinal plants and worked in the kitchen, learning to transform those ingredients into salves, pastes, cordials, boluses, tablets, electuaries, fomentations, and glisters. When a medication did not work, she and her mother would have asked friends, neighbours, and tenants for other recipes, and would have experimented with their own to find one that did. As a girl, Barker modelled herself on Clorin, the title character in a popular play, *The Faithful Shepherdess*, who healed the other characters of illness, injury, and heartbreak.

Barker knew much more than domestic medication, however. She was also up to date with the Scientific Revolution's methods and discoveries, thanks primarily to her own fierce determination and secondarily to her older brother, Edward, who studied medicine at Oxford, Leiden, and Paris. Initially when Barker asked him to share his knowledge, Edward refused, claiming that he could not teach anyone who did not know Latin. So she set about learning Latin – from Edward: "I got my Brother, who was not yet return'd to *Oxford*, to set me in the Way to learn my Grammar, which he really did." However, "thinking it only a Vapour of Fancy" that she wanted to study medicine, he expected her to give up when the Latin got difficult. He underestimated her. She stuck with it, and Edward Barker kept his word: he taught her what he had learned whenever he came home. As she described it in her semi-autobiographical narrative *A Patch-Work Screen for the Ladies*, "[M]y brother continued to oblige my fancy," and "assisted me in Anatomy and Simpling, in which we took many a pleasing Walk, and gather'd many Patterns of different Plants, in order to make a large natural Herbal". In a poem to him on his medical studies in France, Barker lamented that in his absence:

> Nothing at present wonted pleasure yields,
> The *Birds* nor *Bushes*, or the gaudy *Fields*;
> Nor *Osier* holts,* nor Flow're banks of *Glen*;
> Nor the soft *Meadow-grass* seem *Plush*, as when
> We us'd to walk together kindly here,
> And think each blade of Corn a Gem did bear.

Under Edward's tutelage, she obtained the latest medical knowledge. "I made such progress in Anatomy, as to understand Harvey's Circulation of the Blood, and Lower's Motion of

* An "Osier" is a kind of willow tree.

the Heart," she wrote proudly, explaining that "My Time and Thoughts were taken up in Harvey, Willis, and such-like authors."

These authors were advanced knowledge for anyone, and certainly for a woman at the end of the seventeenth century, but she had Edward and she had Latin: "my Brother help'd me to understand and relish [them], which otherwise might have seemed harsh or insipid". William Harvey's *Exercitatio anatomica de motu cordis et sanguinis in animalibus* (1628) revealed that blood circulated through the body, a tremendous breakthrough. It had been translated from Latin into English in 1653, but she was probably reading Edward's copy and he probably had it in Latin. "Willis" refers to Thomas Willis, who was a founding member of the Royal Society and authored *Cerebri anatome, cui accessit nervorum descriptio et usus studio Thomæ Willis* (1664) and *Pathologiæ cerebri, et nervosi generis specimen in quo agitur de morbis convulsivis, et de scorbuto* (1667), on brain anatomy. She must have read those and the 220 pages of Richard Lower's *Tractatus de Corde* (1669) in Latin because none was translated into English until the 1680s.

Edward Barker died unexpectedly after a short, intense fever. He was twenty-five. Jane was twenty-three, and devastated. Eulogizing him, she called Edward "him [who] my Soul ador'd with so much pride, / As makes me slight all worldly things" in grief. He left behind a personal library, papers, and notebooks from his medical studies, materials that no one in the family wanted or cared about except Jane. Initially, she turned to his books and papers for solace, although "No Book or Paper cou'd I turn over, but I found Memorandums of his Wisdom and Learning." Over time, her interest in studying medicine revived and she used everything that Edward had amassed over the course of his medical education – "those Books, on which I had seen my Brother most intent" – to complete hers.

Barker was very aware that this background made her a hybrid of new and domestic medicine, and her writing celebrates her multifaceted body of knowledge and practice. Although her most recent biographer, Kathryn King, calls Barker's view a "confused, shifting, and contradictory play of scientific under-standings", she was not at all confused. She was forging a radical union of the New Science and the old, domestic, female-associated model of medicine. Consider Barker's description of making a herbal with Edward: "we took many a pleasing Walk, and gather'd many Patterns of different Plants, in order to make a large natural Herbal". Women would have needed to know medicinal plants, especially those that grew in the vicin-ity, and walking around the countryside gathering plants was part of a woman's tasks. Those walks might have been pleasant – one hopes so – but taking "many a pleasing Walk" to gather "many Patterns of different Plants" is an undomestic way of representing them. Herbals themselves were increasingly the tools of science's revolutionaries as they attempted to list and sort everything in nature. In Barker's hands, female knowledge and skills are equal partners with male knowledge and skills.

Barker's overlap of male-associated New Science and female-associated domestic medicine is most pronounced when she discusses medication directly. Putting anatomy and "sim-pling" together as the two subjects she studied with Edward, for example, pairs the Scientific Revolution's discoveries with traditional medicine's methods. A "simple" was a medicinal liquid made from a single organic ingredient. Simples and simpling were foundational to both domestic medicine and professional medication; much of early medical chemistry went into developing simples from inorganic materials such as mercury and sulphur. In her poem "On my Mother and Lady W. who both lay sick at the same time under the Hands of Dr. Paman", Barker contends that Dr Paman's "great *Art*" lies in his medications, his "best Receipts", the part of physicians' practice that doctors shared with women. Barker's fervent wish for Dr Paman is that no apothecary should mess with his recipes: "Nor to bad Druggs let Fate thy Worth expose, / For best Receipts are baffl'd oft by those."

Confident in her knowledge and skills and unsurprisingly still unmarried, Barker took her talents to London. Big-city newspapers like the *London Gazette* and smaller periodicals such as the *Ipswich Journal* and the *Newcastle Courant* were full of advertisements for medication and remedies such as *Eradicatorium Arthiriditis*, Pectoral Drops, or the enticingly labelled Royal Purging Cordial. Asthma, headache, rheumatism, deafness, infertility – newspapers boasted cures for them all. Barker was aware of the dangers of quacks, people selling substances with purported rather than actual curative powers. As she wrote in her poem "On my Mother and Lady W. who both lay sick at the same time under the Hands of Dr. Paman":

> Nor let no Quack intrude where thou do'st come,
> To crop thy Fame, or haste thy Patients doom;
> Base Quackery to Sickness the kind Nurse,
> The Patients ruine, and Physicians curse...

She was no quack, however. Domestic medicine's recipes were time-tested; as far as she was concerned, there was nothing speculative or fraudulent about them. Furthermore, Barker also had an up-to-date medical education, thanks to her brother Edward. So off she went, and by 1685 she was selling gout medication under the name of Dr Barker.

There was no need for a woman advertising her medication to hide behind a title, false or otherwise. Plenty of women used their own names when advertising their medical expertise or treatments. A full name was not even necessary; "Barker's Famous Gout Plaister" would have sold just fine. For Barker as for Mary Trye or any man, the title was a statement of identity, of credentials. After all, what entitled a man to call himself "Doctor"? She had read what her brother had read, she knew what her brother had known, she cured people's ailments like her brother had, and Edward had been a doctor. Ergo, she was a doctor. But Barker went further. She prescribed medications to be made by others. Even better: those others then filled her prescriptions. And sometime in the early 1680s, probably not far from St Paul's Cathedral in London, she recorded this triumph in a gleeful poem entitled "On the Apothecary's Filing My Bills Amongst the Doctors". Jane Barker had written a prescription and an apothecary had taken it for the real thing, a prescription written by a licensed male physician. It was bad enough for the nascent prescription system when apothecaries learned prescriptions for different illnesses through filling physicians' orders. As Gallypot announces in *Physick Lies A-Bleeding*, "I can write a Prescription as well as any of 'um all, I learn'd that the first thing, by reading Doctors Bills in my Shop." Jane Barker was not an apothecary, however; she was a woman, which was so much worse, and such behaviour was an outrage. It would have been had anyone found out, anyway.

Barker did not consider herself *equivalent* to a physician. As she wrote in "On the Apothecary's", she had joined their ranks – she *was* a doctor:

I hope I shan't be blamed if I am proud,
That I'm admitted 'mongst this Learned Crowd;

To be proud of a Fortune so sublime,
Methinks is rather Duty, than a Crime...

It is an important distinction. As she sees it, she has not fooled
anyone into thinking that she is both a physician and male. She
has been "admitted" to the "Learned Crowd", who themselves
"exalt and own our Fame", and "gain'd this mighty place /
Amongst th' immortal Æsculapian Race". As she puts it
succinctly about the apothecary's action, "This tis, makes me
a famed Physician grow." Nor is she accepting her triumph
with demure decorum. "But with this honour I'm so satisfy'd, /
The Antients were not more when Deify'd," she crows, calling
her admission to the company of physicians (the "Aesculapian
Race") "a Glory that exceeds excess" and "transcends all
common happiness".

  In addition to doing something that the men could do – that
is, write a prescription – Barker did something that they could
not do: prescribe a gout medication that worked. "The sturdy
Gout, which all Male power withstands," she explains, "is overcome by my soft Female hands." (Mary Trye made a similar
claim in 1675.) Considering the number of people and how
badly they suffered, Barker saw her success in biblical terms:

  Not Deb'ra, Judith, or Semiramis / Could boast of
  Conquests half so great as this; / More than they slew, I
  save in this Disease.

  She also compared her joining the ranks of physicians to
"Saul [who] 'mongst Prophets turn'd a Prophet too". It was
not enough to be as knowledgeable and skilled as a physician if
one were also female. She complains that "Some Women-haters
may be so uncivil, / To say the Devil's cast out by the Devil"

when a woman's medication worked, but patients felt differently: "so the good are pleas'd, no matter for the evil". If the medicine works, what does it matter who made it?

It matters a great deal if the emphasis is on the medication rather than on the healing. Mary Trye referred to Henry Stubbe's "dis-ingenious and inhumane Brethren, that care not what becomes of Sick [*sic*], or any thing else, so they can support their own Grandieur, Profit, and Interest". Jane Barker recognized that the exclusion of women from the prescription system had everything to do with money. As she cynically explained in "On the Apothecary's", "Thus Gold, which by th' Sun's influence do's grow, / Do's that i'th' Market Phoebus cannot doe" ("Thus Gold, which by the Sun's influence does grow / Does in that Market what Phoebus cannot do"). The rising sun resembled a gold coin, but it did not have money's power in the drug market. It was a not-so-subtle jab at the very uncelestial motives of the professionals. Phoebus Apollo was the Greek name for Apollo in his charioteer-of-the-sun aspect, and Apollo was also the God of Healing. The God of Medicine, Asclepius – or as Barker spells it, "Aesculapius" – was his son. She uses the same terms in other poems, such as when she calls her late brother's colleagues "the Apollo's of thy noble Art" and that "Gallant Aesculapian Crew". Describing her early ambitions to study medicine, she wrote, "Thus I sought to become Apollo's darling Daughter." In "On the Apothecary's", Barker unsubtly asserts that neither Phoebus Apollo nor anything divine had a whit to do with "That Market". Anyone who cares about healing will agree with her that "so the good are pleas'd" is all that matters, but the priority for professional healers is money.

The prescription system was not established overnight, of course. It took time, for example, for "prescription" to replace "recipe" in the popular imagination and vocabulary. Barker, it will surprise nobody to learn, eschewed the word, instead celebrating Dr Paman's "Receipts" and her own ("On the Apothecary's"). It also took time for the professionals' mystery medication to seem as good as, if not better than, women's domestic medicine. "How oft, when eminent physicians fail, / Do good old womens [sic] remedies prevail?" asked James Bramston in 1733. "Of Graduates I dislike the learned rout, / And chuse a female Doctor for the gout." Not everyone accepted exclusion and obfuscation as the foundation for a system of medication, either. "Sophia, a Person of Quality" argued that "Reason is absolutely unlimited in her jurisdiction over mankind; we are all born to judge of what concerns and affects us, and if some cannot use the objects of sense with the same facility as others, all have an equal right to them." Knowledge, including the New Science and prescription codes, cannot be "diminish'd by communication". Everyone benefits when everyone contributes to the search for "Truth and knowledge"; those attempting to keep women away from the sciences are interested only in themselves.

There were practical ways of resisting. A raft of books began to appear in the late seventeenth century that explained the meaning of apothecaries' symbols, translated medical terms, and helped people buy medication or ingredients for medication from apothecaries. William Salmon, a prolific producer of medical and housekeeping manuals, included a dictionary of medical terms and a list of tools for making medication at home in the back of his *Family-Dictionary* (1696). The second edition of John Quincy's *Lexicon physico-medicum: or, a new medicinal dictionary; explaining the difficult terms used in the several branches of the profession, and in such Parts of Natural Philosophy as are introductory thereto: with an account of the Things Signified by such Terms* (1722) included a chart of apothecaries' symbols. Pages like these disappeared from these kinds of books, however, not only because the opponents of secrecy faded away but also because women were increasingly discouraged from dealing with illness at home (see Chapter 2). The separation of medicine from food, women, and the kitchen is reflected in and effected by printed materials, from the amount of space allotted to and the kind of medicinal recipes in housekeeping manuals to the inclusion of lexicons and charts to the definitions of words.

Trye and Barker were part of the rearguard action being fought for women's traditional position. In promoting their own expertise, they emphasized that their knowledge came from and with the approval of men. Trye justified publishing *Medicatrix* by claiming filial virtue: she owed it to her father, good girl that she was (although she called herself his "only child" rather than his daughter). Barker gloated in verse, but it was unpublished verse. Her published works – the semi-autobiographical narrative trilogy – emphasized her brother's role. The two women exemplify the union of what the professionals were trying to divide into separate and very unequal spheres. They also illustrate the variety encompassed by the term "Scientific Revolution". Trye was married with children, part of the Scientific Revolution, and skilled in chemical medicine. Barker was single without children, part of the Scientific Revolution, and skilled in organic medicine.

Readers know how this story ends: the prescription system became the method for getting medications with the best reputation, elevating prescription medication over homemade or store-bought. The system thickened the cloud of mystery around professionals' medications and made the unknowability of medicine's components one of its positive features. Jane

Barker's triumph "upon the apothecary's filing her bills among the doctors" demonstrates just how difficult it was to enter into the prescription system's closed course as early as the 1680s. She is indeed the exception that proves the rule.

Trye and Barker had one more thing in common. Both worried about what impact commodifying medication would have on people who could not afford it. Barker praised Dr Paman for being "mightily approv'd, / Both by thy Patients, and the Poor belov'd". Excluding women from the prescription system was bad enough; persuading people that women's treatments were useless, dangerous, or fatal not only destroyed the viability of a set of medications but also helped to destroy the system for distributing them. Without domestic medicine, what would happen to the people who could not afford to enter its replacement, the commercial system? Well-to-do, erudite men brawled over the answer to this question, but readers can safely turn to Chapter 5.

The smaller Tobacco.

Eliz. Blackwell delin. sculp. et Pinx.

1. Flower.
2. Seed Vessel.
3. Seed Vessel open.
4. Seed.

Nicotiana minor.

(*above left*) "Haw-thorn" (no. 149) from Elizabeth Blackwell's *A Curious Herbal*, vol. I, 1737. Note the seeds and cross-sections, as well as Blackwell's signature (bottom left): "Eliz. Blackwell delin. sculpt. et Pinxit" (Elizabeth Blackwell outlined, etched, and painted this image).

(*above right*) Professionals and their bad reputation. Thomas Rowlandson or follower, *Death as an apothecary's assistant*.

(*left*) Lady Elizabeth Grey, Countess of Kent, painted by Paul van Somer, *c.* 1619. The Countess is likely wearing mourning for Queen Anne, with whom she was close. The low neckline was fashionable for women of the time.

Early eighteenth-century recipe book, owner unknown.
The recipes on these pages (for nursing, giving birth, cooking, and livestock)
demonstrate the variety characteristic of these books.

Life-sized family portrait of Sir Kenelm Digby (1603–1665) with his wife Venetia
Stanley (1600–1633) and their two eldest sons, Kenelm (1625–1648) and John
(1627–1673), by Anthony van Dyck, c. 1632. Venetia might have been pregnant when
she sat for this painting, because she gave birth to George in January 1633.

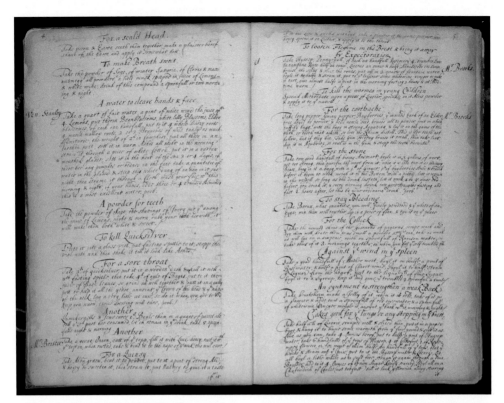

Venetia Stanley's recipe for face wash (left side). Seventeenth-century recipe book, owner unknown.

"De la Vipère" from *Histoire générale des drogues* by Pierre Pomet (1694).

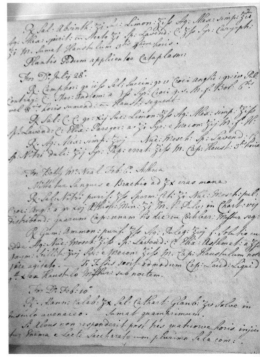

A page from a medical notebook with Dr John Huxham's prescriptions for several patients. When one set of prescriptions fail, the physician tries another. Mid-eighteenth century.

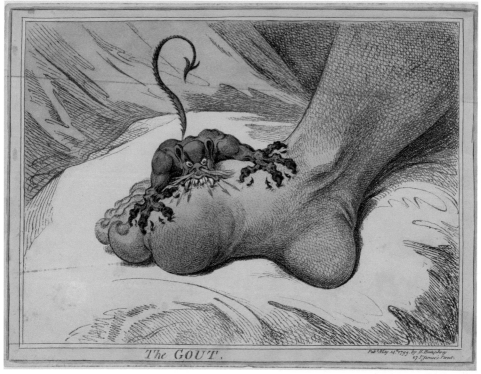

The Gout by James Gillray (1799).

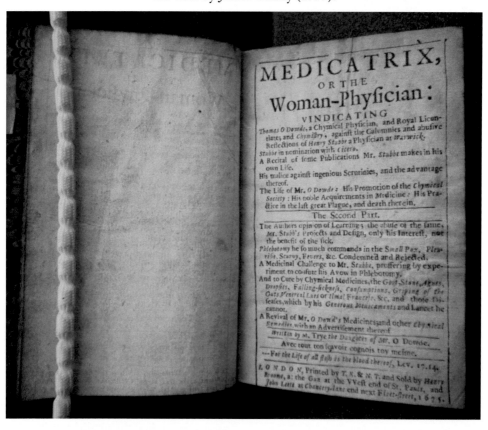

Mary Trye's *Medicatrix* (1675) prepared for a twenty-first-century reader.

A woman's numerous domestic responsibilities. John Shirley, Frontispiece to *The accomplished ladies rich closet of rarities* (1687).

Seventeenth-century illustration showing the well-known overlap in women and men's knowledge and skills. *A man and a woman demonstrating the process of fermentation and distillation in alchemy.*

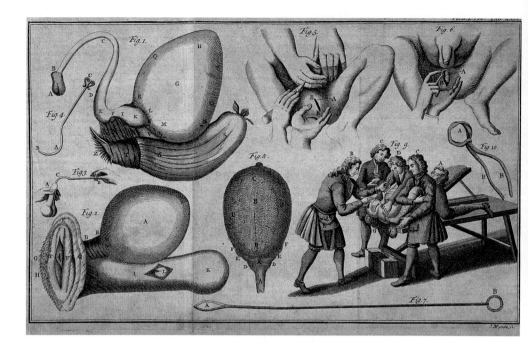

(*above*) A surgeon performing a lithotomy on a patient who is being restrained by three assistants, with five other anatomical illustrations by J. Mynde (1743).

The Company of Undertakers by William Hogarth (1736).

After Pietro Mainoto, *The apothecary making up a prescription, his wife holds a recipe for him…* (Eighteenth century).

English delftware drug jar with the coat of arms of the Worshipful Society of Apothecaries. First known image of Apollo, God of Healing, on an apothecary jar. In English, the Society's motto reads: "I am spoken of all over the world as the one who brings help."

Small jar for an apothecary shop to store ecphractic (laxative) pills (1700–1740).

Interior of a pharmaceutical laboratory (1747). The chemist and assistant
work in the well-equipped back room. The shop where their products
are sold is visible through the doorway.

Advertisement for iodised salt.
Early twenty-first century.

Portrait of Dr Frances O. Kelsey,
3 May 1965.

"Was Once a Science, Now's a Trade"

Why is it that some people cannot get medication because they cannot afford it? It is easy to assign responsibility to corporations, but there is an even deeper reason why access to medication, including life-saving treatment, is not available to everyone. Take the case of insulin. In 2018, the Kaiser Family Foundation released a study showing that one in four adult Americans with type 1 diabetes had rationed their insulin at least once because they could not afford to buy enough at a time. That figure included people with health insurance. Rationing insulin means taking less than the required dose to stretch your supply longer, and in case you are wondering, yes, that can be fatal. Five years after these data were announced, in 2023, Americans witnessed a flurry of activity at the state, federal, and corporate levels. The Attorney General of California brought suit against the insulin manufacturers "for driving up the cost of the lifesaving drug through unlawful, unfair, and deceptive business practices". A federal law went into effect capping insulin prices for some low-income people using Medicaid, a federal health insurance programme. Two senators proposed a bipartisan bill to cap the price of insulin for everyone, regardless of their insurance status. The three corporations responsible for 90 per cent of manufactured insulin reduced their prices. That is quite a lot of change for one fiscal quarter. These actions did not make insulin available to everyone; they made insulin unavailable to fewer people. But suppose the outrage did not manifest in lawsuits and legislation that focused on insulin as a commodity? In other words, suppose the perceived problem was not the price of insulin but that insulin had a price?

That was the problem facing those practitioners who were commodifying medicinal treatments during the late seventeenth and early eighteenth centuries. They recognized the significance of putting a price on medication: some people would not be able to pay, which could only have a bad outcome. They talked about what should be done, and sometimes argued or came to blows about it. In the end, they knowingly chose to value profit over human health and life and deliberately worked not only to validate and normalize that value but also to render it invisible, a given.

Medical professionals had been balancing the conflicting virtues of getting paid with giving charity to the poor at least since the Middle Ages. After 1650, the dilemma became much more acute as physicians and apothecaries worked to commodify medication. Following outbreaks of smallpox and plague, especially the Great Plague of 1665–6, the issue became urgent. The existing methods for connecting the impoverished with medical treatment were obviously utterly incapable of handling demand during crises, with horrific results: mass graves, bodies in the streets, unchecked contagion. Either professionals would incorporate into the system a method for enabling the poor to get medication, or professionals would continue to build a system that placed profit over access. As Dr Samuel Garth put it in his poem "The Dispensary" (1699), medicine would be either a "Science", dedicated to the acquisition and deployment of knowledge, or a "Trade", dedicated to producing goods and acquiring income. The professionals chose the latter, legitimizing and normalizing the idea of people dying so other people could maximize their income.

A rehearsal for this crisis had taken place in the sixteenth century. When Henry VIII declared himself the head of the Church of England so that he could annul his marriage to Katherine of Aragon and marry Anne Boleyn, he dissolved the monasteries and convents. Cloistered communities tended their own well-being, of course, but for centuries as part of their charitable mission they also provided care to travellers and the local community, especially the impoverished. The Benedictine Rule emphasized care for the sick. Monasteries and convents of all orders had their own physic gardens, which usually would be tended by a monk or nun appointed to be the herbalist. There were cloistered communities all over England in the sixteenth century, so by eliminating them, Henry VIII also eliminated one of the two medical resources available to the vast majority of his subjects. Individual practitioners declined to fill the void that the king had created. It turned out that given the choice between caring for sufferers who could pay and those who could not, professionals preferred the paying kind.

Even if no one had anticipated this thoroughly unsurprising outcome, someone should have warned His Majesty that a tiny number of individuals could not replace an entire network of healthcare. At any rate, Henry VIII was irked. The result was legislation known as the Herbalist's Charter of 1542, officially labelled 34 & 38 Henry VIII c.8. Because "the surgeons admitted [they] will do no cure to any person, but where they shall know to be rewarded with a greater sum or reward than the cure extendeth unto", Parliament authorized local unlicensed, untrained experts to practise medicine "for the ease, comfort, succour, help, relief, and health of the king's poor subjects, inhabitants of this realm, now pained or diseased, or that hereafter shall be pained or diseased". Consequently, the act announced:

> It shall be lawful to every person being the king's subject, having knowledge and experience of the nature of herbs, roots, and waters, or of the operation of the same, by speculation or practice [...] to practise, use, and minister in and to any outward sore, uncome [sic], wound, apostemations, outward swelling, or disease, any herb or herbs, ointments, baths, pultess [sic], and emplaisters, according to their cunning, experience, and knowledge in any of the diseases, sores, and maladies beforesaid, and all other like to the same, or drinks for the stone, strangury, or agues, without suit, vexation, trouble, penalty, or loss of their goods...

The Charter empowered and protected a much larger group than the professionals comprised, which was good, at least in theory. It did not create a system to replace the one that the king had obliterated, which was not so good. In the next century, and using the Scientific Revolution rather than royal prerogative, the professionals eliminated the remaining resource for ordinary people, and like Henry VIII, put nothing in its place.

In effect, the Herbalist's Charter conferred royal approval and legal protection on the practitioners of domestic medicine. In earlier chapters, I showed how domestic medicine was built on and nurtured a set of values, among them that knowledge should be shared and shared without strings or cost, and that people who needed treatment should receive it, also without strings or cost. Women from the top of the social scale down to the poorest woman who could fulfil this role made sure that everyone in the household and their dependents (servants and tenants included) got care. When Anne Clifford, Countess of Dorset, Pembroke and Montgomery heard that her mother was ill in London, she immediately sent a servant with "certain cordials and conserves" to help her mother recover. John Shirley's *The Accomplished Ladies Rich Closet of Rarities: Or, The Ingenious Gentlewoman and Servant Maids Delightfull Companion* (1687) addresses women in every class, but the first chapter, on making medication, is aimed at gentlewomen in particular. It instructs this audience "how to Distill and draw off such Waters from Herbs, and other Cordial matters, as may contribute to the preservation of health, and wherewith a Gentlewoman, being furnished, may be instrumental in saving the Lives, or at least in doing good to her poor Neighbours".

Domestic medicine created and preserved communities. It supported the now-obsolete definition of "family" as the people who lived together in a household, from the lowest stable hand to the master of the house. Under the system of domestic medicine, illness was a communal experience. For healers, domestic knowledge of medications was common knowledge in the sense that women shared it and expected to share it. As I discussed previously, recipe books connected women across time and space: across backyard fences, villages, counties, regions, England, Scotland, classes, and generations. No one owned that recipe for an effective eye wash any more than she owned that recipe for pear tart. It was so much a part of culture that literature could use the interaction as a marker of virtue. In the narrative *The Wandering Beauty* (1698), the heroine Arabella sees a baby with "bad" eyes and offers a cure to the mother (it works).

Nor did the ill or injured suffer alone. They were attended by members of the household and, when necessary or helpful, by members of the extended family or community. Pregnancy and childbirth were viewed the same way, as one long experience involving women of the family and community. The welfare of a family was affected by the health and well-being of its members – the death of a father or mother could send the household plummeting into destitution – but it was also a question of ethos. One person's illness was everyone's concern. Domestic medicine's values were cultural; they were organizing principles of social practice and structure for everyone. It was the way people understood what it meant to be in or out of health. If a labourer complained to his buddy that he had a strange rash on his arms, the buddy would ask if he had shown the rash to his wife. That is just what one did.

It was not a form of charity. True, a great deal was made of charity in Christian Europe. Individuals were exhorted to be charitable. However, charity involves a vertical distribution of resources, one in which virtue accrues to the resource-rich individual choosing to part with some of those resources. Domestic medicine involved the lateral circulation of resources. Sick people needed treatment; sick people received it. Recipes passed from equal to equal to empower the recipient. If you do not think of knowledge as private property, or of something like burn salve as a commodity, you do not worry about losing or gaining property from giving or withholding it. When it came to medicinal recipes, sharing was more than a norm. It was an expectation and an obligation.

In fact, "I think myself obliged to send it" is how Mary

Huntington explained sending a medicinal recipe to John Locke on 5 January 1699. That is the John Locke who wrote *An Essay Concerning Human Understanding* and *Two Treatises on Government*; coined the phrase *tabula rasa*; helped draft the English Bill of Rights; provided the foundation for the American Declaration of Independence, Bill of Rights, and Constitution; and who was himself a practising physician with his own recipes. Mary Huntington was the wife of one of Locke's old friends, and her letter was precipitated by the news that he was having breathing problems. She had the recipe for a good cure and "as I desire your Health (which I most heartily doe)," she wrote, "I think myself obligd to send it". Properly deferential to "the Great Philosopher and Physician of the Age", as she called him, Huntington began her letter by noting that Locke did not need her advice, writing, "We have a proverb, sir, of carrying coals to New Castle," but she continued defiantly, "and I am now going to act it." And although she ended her letter with an apology – "If I be impertinent, I beg your pardon" – the apology itself ended with "but if it should have the blessed effect I wish it, then I'll not ask you to forgive". Considering that she was confident in the cure, and considering that she sent the letter, she could not have been too worried.* In fact, her recipe might well have eased the philosopher's respiratory distress. It called for brewing liquorice and figs in "Spring Water" and drinking the mixture "in a wine glass". Laboratory analyses have confirmed that liquorice, an

---

* Huntington did not lack for determination. When her husband Robert Huntington died in 1701, she badgered his colleague, the distinguished Oxford scholar Thomas Smith, to write his biography until Smith caved in to her demand in 1704.

ancient treatment for chest congestion and phlegm, really does work. Figs appear to have anti-inflammatory effects.

Domestic medicine was not a system for treating the penurious ill. It could not provide care for everyone, but it could offer a set of values. Instead, the hierarchical thinking of charity shaped the initial organized responses to the sick, impoverished population. The first earnest, effective governmental attempt to create a system for tending to the medical needs of the impecunious came in the form of the Poor Law of 1601, often referred to now as the Old Poor Law. It was aimed at people who were truly desperate, who had nothing – no home, no food, no family or acquaintance to help, no income, nothing. Until the nineteenth century, the Poor Law required all parishes, urban and rural, to collect fees from residents to pay for food, employment, and medical care for those unable to provide it for themselves. Parishes paid weekly pensions to residents who proved need.

Urban parish overseers sometimes established a workhouse, where desperate indigent people could live and work, perhaps get some education, and obtain medical care supplied by a hired surgeon and apothecary. The first workhouse in Birmingham, established in 1727, employed three practitioners. Workhouses were generally inundated with people desperate for treatment. It was a significant financial burden for a parish, and the cost skyrocketed over the seventeenth and eighteenth centuries. Additionally, each parish negotiated (or did not) the price of medical care and specifically of medications. When the RCP offered to supply medications for the price of what it cost to make them for one year to the Bishopsgate Street workhouse, the Worshipful Society of Apothecaries outbid them by proposing to supply medications to the workhouse for three years for free. It was a great deal for the apothecaries, who burnished their reputation, and for the Bishopsgate parish officials – but only for the Bishopsgate parish officials.

Beyond the Poor Law, there was a patchwork of methods for providing care for those who could not afford it. After the dissolution of the monasteries, church hospitals sometimes continued under different management. In Gloucester, for instance, three hospitals – St Bartholomew, St Margaret, and St Mary Magdalen – came under the control of the city government, called the Corporation. The same happened to St Catherine's in York. Small parishes and the governments of smaller cities and towns often hired a medical man to treat the indigent in addition to his regular business, or arranged to recompense certain providers (apothecary, surgeon, or physician) for doing so. In the parish of Alfriston, one Richard Alcorn was reimbursed by "Mr Brooks" for, among other things, "17 powders", "8 papers", "18 Drops", "six bolusses", and "an oyly mixture", as well as for "opening the swelling on Martha Asten's hand" and a "visit & bleeding" for Thomas King. Especially in the hinterlands, "wise women" were paid to handle lesser ailments and injuries. Occasionally, individuals in towns and cities across England formed "friendly societies", which functioned like health insurance: everyone in the group paid in, and when someone needed care, the fees would be paid from the kitty. Further afield in the countryside, it was not uncommon for landowners and clergymen to obtain medical training so they could care for the neighbourhood.

And of course, there was private charity. To borrow from Tennessee Williams, the impecunious ill had always depended on the kindness of strangers. In towns outside London, professionals sometimes attended individuals without fee, while in some places, apothecaries banded together to provide care or medications for the local poor. Guilds might take charitable action. St Thomas's and Trinity Hospitals in York wound up in guild hands. In London, St Bartholomew's Hospital, established in 1123 and famously known as St Bart's, and St Thomas' Hospital, established in 1173, were still operating on their own in the seventeenth and eighteenth centuries. Britain also was dotted with establishments founded by very wealthy individuals: hospitals to care for those unable to care for themselves – usually because of age, poverty, or both – and almshouses for the homeless. These institutions tended to be small, averaging about twelve residents. Thomas Oken's Charity in Warwick maintained almshouses for six people. The Wolborough Feoffees and Widows' Charity in Devon provided housing and a tiny annual stipend to a small number of widows; the Yerbury Almshouse in Wiltshire housed six widows and provided each just under four pounds per year. Thomas Gouge devoted an entire book, *The Surest & Safest Way of Thriving* (1673), to biographical sketches of self-made men who exemplified charity, such as Mr John Walter, a draper, who built two almshouses in London. As Lady Lucy says to Sir James Courtly in Susanna Centlivre's play *The Basset Table* (1705), "That Superfluity of good Manners, Sir James, would do better Converted into Charity; this town abounds with objects."

Private or "voluntary" hospitals, funded by a group of benefactors paying an annual subscription, also began to appear in the early eighteenth century. The anonymous author of *The Present State of Physick and Surgery in London* (1701) noted the endless demand for this kind of succour: "The Governours of our Hospitals, who give their charity in directing the charity of the Foundings in their respective Houses, where the health of some Hundreds is provided for, cannot observe the calamities of many Thousands without concern, and their Endeavour to promote their relief." In London, for example, the Westminster

Infirmary was founded in 1719, Guy's Hospital in 1724, St George's Hospital in 1733, and the London Hospital in 1740. The Glasgow Town Infirmary opened in 1733, staffed by volunteers from the local Faculty of Physicians and Surgeons; benefactors and staff physicians paid apothecaries for the necessary medications. Bristol opened its voluntary hospital in 1737 with a full medical staff, and Aberdeen opened its first voluntary hospital in 1740.

Organizations like these had a limited impact, even the Charterhouse, the most significant private charity in the British Isles. It was established in London in 1611 by Thomas Sutton, who was outrageously wealthy, spectacularly connected, and extremely well liked. Sutton bequeathed a London property, Howard House, and an ample endowment to establish and maintain a combined retirement home (hospital) and boys' school. Sutton directed that eighty pensioners and forty students should be provided for, an outrageous number in comparison with most charitable hospitals, almshouses, and schools of the day, and he left a magnificent real estate portfolio to fund it. The education provided for the boys was famously good. In the short play *The Triumvirate* (1719), the character Harlequin assures his friend Scaramouche that "I have Latin and Greek enough left, since I was a scholar at the Charterhouse." To qualify for the retirement side, pensioners had to be old and fallen into poverty through no fault of their own after they "had lived active and useful lives in conditions of prosperity and comfort". To be admitted, a pensioner had to be nominated and accepted for admission by a Board of Governors. He was guaranteed a fully furnished private room, board, and medical care and could remain at the Charterhouse until death.

Sutton's network and awe-inspiring wealth ensured that his institution was well provisioned. In addition to the reigning

monarch, his or her spouse, and the heir to the throne, the
Charterhouse's Board of Governors included the Archbishop
of Canterbury, the Bishop of London, the Bishop of Ely, three
other bishops, the Lord Chancellor, the Lord Chief Justice,
and four privy councillors. The large staff included a physician, who received a salary and a house on the grounds, and
a gardener, whose responsibilities included providing vegetables and fruit for the kitchen, and herbal plants for making
medicaments. The physic garden must have markedly alle-
viated expenses because when the soil became irremediably
overworked in 1731, bills for medication (not to mention vegetables and fruit) increased.

Medication was an imposing expense for every charitable
organization; considering that the Charterhouse's two popula-
tions were schoolboys and older, infirm men, it was probably
formidable. Like the governors of other institutions, such as
the Westminster Infirmary, the governors of the Charterhouse
determinedly attempted to control the cost of medication by
harassing the apothecaries who required payment. Between
1700 and 1712, the board challenged every set of bills submitted to them by James Petiver, apothecary to the Charterhouse.
Petiver was an impressive figure in his own right, not only
a successful apothecary but also a Fellow of the Royal
Society and one of the most prominent botanists of his day.
The RCP had written in strong support of his appointment.
Nevertheless, the governors did not trust him. Petiver recorded
that on 12 July 1710, William Hempson, the registrar of the
Charterhouse, reported that in response to Petiver's petition
to be reimbursed for the medication he made, the governors
"referr'd it to their next Meeting in full Assembly & Order'd
yᵗ in yᵉ meantime Dr Goodall shall examine yᵉ bills & give his
opinion as to yᵉ Reasonableness of yᵉ Price of ye Physick".

To his credit, the physician of the Charterhouse always supported Petiver. In 1703, Dr Charles Goodall held the post, and on 29 February of that year he wrote the governors that "I have compared these Bills with those directed by me & am satisfied they were accordingly delivered." His letters all said the same thing and almost in the same words. March 1708: "I have Carefully lookt [sic] over ye Prices of Mr Petiver Medicines relating to ye Pentioners of ye Charterhouse & do find them valued at lower rates then to his other Patients & lower then the late Apothecary Mr Holme did rate some of them," while in 1709, Goodall wrote only "The Truth of these Cases I do attest & know." More was required of him in 1712, after the governors balked. "May it please y^r Honours," he wrote on 14 June, "There having for these 2 or 3 Years last past been several very Malignant & Dangerous Fevers & Small Pox in this House & a great Number of ye Schollars infected with ye Itch," as well as "Violent Convulsive Collics, Stranguries" and "other stubborn Cases too long to trouble your Honours with", it was logical that James Petiver's bills should be higher than expected. In 1712, Petiver recorded in his notes for the Charterhouse that Goodall had told the governors that Petiver's bills were fair, and that Goodall had reiterated that he, Petiver, was charging the same or even slightly less than the previous apothecary to the Charterhouse, Mr Holme.

The next physician to the Charterhouse, Dr Henry Levett, also attested to Petiver's honesty. After reviewing the records, Levett confirmed that Petiver had done exactly what Dr Goodall had ordered and at a reasonable price. As for his own prescriptions, Levett was "satisfied yt all these medecines were delivered with Care & according to Order", a phrase he used again in his June 1714 letter to the governors. The governors were fortunate, however ungrateful they may have appeared.

The Westminster Infirmary went through long periods of difficulty with apothecaries; during one tumultuous eighteen-month period, it hired and fired three of them.

The Charterhouse's governors were also probably aware that the medical staff of charitable institutions sometimes used the institution that employed them for their own ends. After all, private and voluntary hospitals usually were staffed with professional men who knew each other. Alexander Stuart and William Wasey, future distinguished Fellows of the RCP, shared a casebook for their patients at the Westminster Infirmary between 1723 and 1724. Samuel Garth sent several insolvent, ailing patients to Hans Sloane bearing notes requesting Sloane's help in procuring treatment for them. In one, Garth asked Sloane to "gett this poor Maid" into Christ Church Hospital; in another, he wrote, "I beg you'll be so charitable to gett this poor woman into some Hospital." (Garth was not always so kindly. He asked another friend to "doe [sic] an action of Charity" for the bearer of the letter, "this miserable slut".) A pair of letters in the Sloane Manuscripts at the British Library even shows one physician to the Charterhouse daringly attempting to evade the dragonish governors.

The letters record an exchange between one Mary Burley of Reading and the physician Dr Henry Levett about her son's condition.* The reply letter was penned by "J.P.", that is, James Petiver, from his shop in Aldersgate Street, under the sign of the White Cross. The correspondence centred around Mrs Burley's son, who had suffered a terrible blow to the head some

* As of this writing, the British Library identifies the physician as Dr Charles Goodall, but this is an error. The letters are dated July 1713, when Goodall had been dead almost a year. Either he was a miraculously dedicated physician or the addressee is Dr Henry Levett, his successor.

weeks earlier. On the morning of the letter, his anxious mother wrote: "My Son have this day A very bad fit; being taken in yᵉ morning with a great payn whare [sic] yᵉ blow was, & so sick & faint with it that he could neither stand nor spake for a very Considerable time." She reported that she "gave him to open him as soon as he could take it an infusion of rubarb [sic] & lickirish; and when that came to work with him; he had ease". That is, Mrs Burley gave her son a drink of rhubarb and liquorice, and once he began to feel its effects, his condition improved, although "he is very weake and faint, as he allwaies is after such a fit". The effects were in the purgative line: powdered rhubarb was used as a laxative (and yes, it works), while liquorice (as Mary Huntington knew) is an expectorant. Mrs Burley may have administered it as a liquid or "juice" given her term "infusion". Apparently young Burley's caregivers thought to purge him until his brain injury healed. Unsurprisingly, it was not working.

Mrs Burley's appeal did not come out of the blue. Levett had treated her son for the injury before. As she explained, "I was in hopes to have hard [sic] from you before now I rit by last Tuesdays post to acquaint you how he was" because "he is faln back for want of proper things to take", that is, Levett's prescribed medicine. As politely as urgency allowed, she entreated him for a reply: "I bag [sic] I may hear from you as soon as posable." To ensure that she received any medication sent from London, Mrs Burley included detailed instructions for posting it: "yᵉ Apothecary may direct to me in London strete in Reading; yᵉ Reading coach goes out every day from yᵉ b[illeg] & Tun inn in flete strete & from yᵉ white hors [sic] in fleet strete." The illegible word and repetition hint at her distress.

James Petiver wrote the answer:

Madam

I sent yr Letter to ye Dr as you directed, who has prescribed
him a purging Electuary to take 2 or 3 times a weeke if
Costive, & yt he would have him come up to Town if
worse, because he cannot prescribe so well for him at
yt distance Nor will ye Governors pay for ye Physick or
Advice wch is given out of House In ye interim wt he has
now & later Ordered is very proper for him to take & I
heartily wish him ye good Effect of them who am

    Madam yr humble servt to command

J. P.

Aldersgate Street [*illeg*] Juli [*sic*] 7. 1713

It was not uncommon for a physician to entrust the apothecary
with a prescription and the explanation for how the patient
should take it. Petiver's extra reassurance ("In ye interim
wt he has now & later Ordered is very proper for him to
take") demonstrates familiarity with physicians' recipes and
a respectful relationship with the doctor, not to mention
consideration for a terrified mother. Mrs Burley also might
have found relief in having used domestic medicine to do what
the professional medicine would do ("costive" was a medical
term for constipated). That she relied on a London physician's
advice and medication, however, shows how much professional
medicine had gained on domestic medicine by 1713.

There is one odd element to this letter. The recommendation
to bring Mrs Burley's son to London to be treated in person,
logical as it sounds to someone reading this book, was not a
given. (Prescribing without examining the patient will come
up again in Chapter 7 because quacks encouraged patients

to self-diagnose.) But Levett had two motives for asking
Mrs Burley to come to "Town": to see the patient for himself
and to get the Charterhouse to pay for the treatment. Hence
the warning about the "Governors", the explanation of paying
for a consultation and the prescription, and the mention of the
"House".

These methods of connecting impoverished sick people with
medication were insufficient to the demand. The more that
access to medication depended on money, the less access there
was. Looked at one way, this was and is a significant moral
issue. A real number of people who could not pay for treatment
became sick, maimed, debilitated, or dead. A system that with-
held medication from those who needed but could not afford it
was a system that accepted the deaths of some people so other
people could profit. This was the moment, as they were commodifying medication and creating an economy around it, for
professionals to devise a mechanism ensuring access for everyone. They knew it, too. They even discussed what to do, as well
as whether to do anything, to ensure everyone could get treatment. In the end, they let the opportunity go by. Instead, and
rather reminiscently of Henry VIII, medication's commodifiers
let the hierarchical practices and values of charity continue as
inadequate suppliers of care for those who could not afford it. It
was perfectly fine if those who already had acquired more and
more, and if those who had not did not experience a change in
situation.

Just who were "the poor"? It is a capacious category. "Poor"
describes people who had nothing: no means of feeding, shel-
tering, or clothing themselves. Generally lumped in with this
group was another, who might be called the "solvent poor".
People in this class worked jobs, resided somewhere, and
had food and clothing to some extent. When the Scientific

Revolution arrived in the British Isles, the solvent poor also
had domestic medicine and, in some areas, apothecaries.
Apothecaries had a pretty good reputation for caring about
the lower classes and the indigent. For one thing, they did
not leave during outbreaks of plague or smallpox the way
the wealthy (and physicians) did. During the Great Plague of
1665–6, apothecaries remained in London, while all but a very
few physicians left. True, an apothecary's living was inseparable from his shop and its stock, neither of which could be
packed up and moved, so it is perhaps not so surprising that
they stayed put. But the shop also bound its apothecary to a
neighbourhood, making him a member of a community with
established relationships with his customers. These connections were particularly strong in rural areas or small towns.
In Coventry, for example, the apothecary Abel Brooksby was
elected mayor in 1672. Apothecaries had some ability as well
as incentive to match the price of their medications to their
customers, to fit the micro-market that they served. It was not
unusual for apothecaries to provide medication on credit, in
fact. That economic flexibility ensured that more people could
get medication and nurtured a market for the apothecary's
goods. A poor family might not be able to afford a physician,
but they might be able to afford an apothecary.

  Physicians did not have a reputation for caring about the
impecunious. Like the members of other guilds, physicians
everywhere depended on income generated as individuals; in their case, consulting and diagnosing fees. The more
famous the physician, the higher his fees. In the late seventeenth century, the pre-eminent London physician Dr John
Radcliffe charged up to £20 for a house call, roughly equivalent to £4,000–£6,000 in the early twenty-first century. At the
time, 94 per cent of the population earned less than £100 per

year; less than 1 per cent had more than £500, the minimum required to maintain a genteel lifestyle. When the protagonist of *Physick Lies A-Bleeding* (1697), Mr Trueman, is handed the bill for his wife's treatment, he grumbles that "I do suppose to be genteel, I must give you a crown." Plague or smallpox could erupt in any urban centre (the plague could even be tracked as it swept across continents, nations, or cities), and when epidemics struck, those who could afford to, fled. Of course, those who fled tended to be the people who could afford a physician, so unsurprisingly, physicians fled with them. Individual physicians might have a reputation for generosity, compassion, or benevolence, but between the paucity of physicians overall, the absence of physicians at times of crisis, and their being expensive, the stereotypical doctor was not imbued with generosity or fellow feeling.

So what happened? Scotland offers examples of what might have been. One of the first actions taken by the Royal College of Physicians of Edinburgh, founded in 1681, was to establish a dispensary that provided free medical care to the poor. Initially that treatment took the form of house calls, but after 1705 it took the form of an outpatient clinic at the Edinburgh College's headquarters. From its inception, the Edinburgh Dispensary was staffed by two physicians elected by their peers to serve for twelve months. It was funded at first by fines paid by the membership for assorted infractions, and then as part of the College's entrance fee. Medication still had to be paid for, but not by those receiving it. The Glasgow Town Infirmary technically belonged with its attached workhouse, but in fact it functioned separately. Volunteers from the city's professional medical organization staffed both infirmary and workhouse, and an apothecary provided the medications out of his own pocket. Sometime around 1740 this position was given a salary, some of which was to cover the price of materia medica and whatever else was needed.

These were not the only ways that professionals responded to the question of whether the poor could get access to medicinal drugs if they could not pay for them, nor were any of them the one that became embedded in the medication economy. For that, we can turn to London: the story of events there is the tale in miniature. In London, different guilds responded quite differently to the Scientific Revolution. The Worshipful Society of Apothecaries as an entity adopted the Scientific Revolution's principles, methods, and fascination with tools and technology. The guild saw an opportunity to reduce the cost of materia medica for its members and to create reliable sources of revenue. From its inception in 1611, the Worshipful Society of Apothecaries recognized that controlling a member's expenses increased the profit margin, and also made it economically more feasible for him to attend the lower classes. The London guild built a laboratory at its guildhall, possibly as early as 1623, to train apprentices and to make in bulk supplies for members to buy from the guild and sell in their shops.

After the Great Fire burned it down and two-thirds of London with it, the Worshipful Society of Apothecaries rebuilt the hall with a large laboratory in the cellar and commercial ambitions in mind. Opened for business in 1672, the laboratory quickly became, as historian Anna Simmons puts it, "one of the earliest sites in England for large-scale drug manufacture". In this way, the laboratory suppressed the cost of medicinal simples and compounds, and also enriched the guild as a body. By 1680–1, the laboratory was so useful that it was turning a 30 per cent profit. In large part because of their manufacturing capacity and the consistency of their mass-produced compounds, in 1703 the Worshipful Society of Apothecaries won a highly lucrative contract to supply the medications for the Royal Navy, a contract that the organization held for more than a century. In 1673, the London apothecaries acquired what became known as the Chelsea Physic Garden and started growing many of the necessary herbaceous, arboreal, and floral ingredients for their medications, giving them even more control over prices. This strategy also benefited apothecaries outside London. They too could buy the complex and chemical compounds from the London guild's laboratory, expanding their materials, following the latest medical developments, and keeping their prices suited to their own local markets.

While the apothecaries were making use of the Scientific Revolution's emphasis on technology and innovation to establish an economic foundation for their guild, the physicians were not. When they rebuilt their headquarters at Warwick Lane after the Great Fire of London in 1666, they added an anatomy theatre that became internationally famous but was not designed to produce revenue for the College. Generally speaking, proponents of the Scientific Revolution gathered at the Royal Society once it was chartered by Charles II in 1662. Some of the Royal Society's Fellows were apothecaries: James Petiver, for one, and Isaac Rand, who directed the Chelsea Physic Garden. A significant number of the Fellows belonged to the RCP, such as Hans Sloane, Alexander Stuart, and Richard Mead. But on the whole, the RCP was slower to accept the Scientific Revolution and the medical revolution that came with it. Warwick Lane was not the place to hear a paper on the most recent anatomical discovery.

Broadly speaking, then, the primary provider of medication (apothecaries) and the two main providers of treatment (apothecaries and physicians) did not engage in the kind of creative thinking that might counterbalance their efforts to take full control of medication and to eradicate domestic medicine. The literature of the time shows that when push came to shove by the end of the seventeenth century, neither group was willing to give up any way of making money, even in the interests of saving lives or ameliorating suffering. Neither group was willing to risk any future part of the medication market, either; they directed the conversation and shaped the vocabulary around the question of the poor's access to medication, hiding the real values under their choices and deflecting attention from those values and choices onto other actors.

Until the 1690s, the apothecaries of London and individual benevolent physicians were left to treat ailing people who could not pay a doctor's fees. Before that, the RCP had made several feints at an outpatient clinic, which they called the Dispensary, to be staffed twice weekly with physicians donating their time. Discussions in the College in 1670 and 1687 petered out, the latter producing only an order to the Fellows to donate some of their time to treating the poor, an edict that changed no one's behaviour. When the College brought up the idea in 1675, they approached the apothecaries about providing the medications for the Dispensary, but their tone was not conducive to partnership: "Not doubting but that the Company of the Apothecaries will suitably comply with our just and real intention and désigné of serving the public in affording medicines pre scribed by us to such poor at rates answerable to the lowness of their condition." Unsurprisingly, the apothecaries did not choose to suitably comply, and so yet again nothing happened. Inertia is remarkably comfortable when the money is coming in.

Things changed at the RCP in the mid-1690s. In 1695, the governing committee of the RCP convened a subcommittee, called the Committee of Medicines, to investigate the feasibility of the Dispensary. On 30 October 1696, the minutes for the College's governing committee record that "A Scheme of a Charitable Design was offer'd to this Committee, from ye Committee of Medecines, & Read," after which the "Scheme" was "Refer'd" to the College's officers. To avoid the arguments that had scuttled earlier plans for a dispensary and in the spirit of "it is better to ask forgiveness than permission", in November 1696 the Committee of Medicines simply took up a private subscription to fund a dispensary and went ahead without putting it to the College for a vote.

The success of this private plan gave the Committee of Medicines courage on 21 December 1696 to propose putting a subscription to the general membership. They had already found a location for the Dispensary and arranged the terms, leaving the general membership with little traction for objections. In April 1698, the RCP opened the Dispensary's doors at their headquarters in Warwick Lane. Cue trumpet fanfare! The poor were saved! Previously, as one anonymous partisan put it, illness was the "ruine of the Poor, who beside the pain and dread event of the Disease, are under the fear of spending their whole Substance, in one sickness, and being absolutely undone". The Dispensary, however, "is the greatest Relief to the Poor, who have the best advice, and the best Physick at a very small Expence".

That last phrase – "at a very small Expence" – reveals that unlike, say, the Edinburgh College's Dispensary, the London College's Dispensary was not designed to provide access *for* the poor; it was designed to provide access *to* the poor. And "the poor", solvent or insolvent, were a vast market. Physicians also encouraged their middle-class patients to buy their medications from the Dispensary. The unnamed pro-Dispensary narrator of *The Present State of Physick & Surgery in London* urged his acquaintance to purchase them there. The supposedly charitable institution not only preserved but in fact promoted medication as a commodity. It also violated the College's Charter, which permitted physicians to inspect apothecaries' stores but not to make their own medication, as well as the apothecaries' Charter, which granted only apothecaries the right to make and purvey medication. The RCP knew it; committee minutes reveal that the Committee of Medicines reviewed the apothecaries' Charter in 1695. Dress up the Dispensary in benevolence and spritz it with the perfume of sanctity, however, and that attempt to seize part of the medication market – a very, very bad action – appears to be a very, very good action. Claiming benevolence covered the reality of the Dispensary and offered a deceptive justification.

The ensuing fight over the Dispensary not only pitted apothecaries against physicians but also pitted physicians who opposed infringing on the apothecaries' Charter against those who embraced it. Some opponents argued that each profession should do what it was trained to do, and that the different practitioners could and should work together for everyone's benefit (even the patients). As Mr Trueman of *Physick Lies A-Bleeding* states, "I am for employing every Man in his own way, the Doctor for Advice, the Apothecary for Medicines, and the Surgeon for Wounds, et cetera." Others were infuriated by the financial implications. William Salmon pointed out in 1696 that the goal of the physicians was "in plain English, to Monopolize all the Practise of Physick into their own hands". Sounding very much as if he had been reading John Locke's *Second Treatise on Government* (1689),* Salmon argued that

---

* "And reason, which is that law, teaches anyone who takes the trouble to consult it, that because we are all equal and independent, no-one ought to harm anyone else in his life, health, liberty, or possessions." John Locke, *Second Treatise on Government*, 2.6.

"a Monopoly [is] wonderfully prejudicial to the Lives, Liberties, Estates and Properties of the good People of England", especially the impoverished: "I hope the Mercies of God are such to the poor People of this City, that he will never permit" it. The battle over the Dispensary exemplified the thinking and actions that justified refusing medication to those who could not pay for it, regardless of the outcome. Although the combatants realized that there was a genuine problem of access to medication, they did not work to solve it.

The fighting was fierce; at one point, a brawl actually broke out at the RCP headquarters in Warwick Lane. Admittedly, physicians appear to have been a pugnacious lot at this time. Dr John Woodward and Dr Richard Mead once drew swords over an argument about the efficacy of a medication. When Woodward slipped and fell, Mead ended the fight by sneering, "Take your life!" To which Woodward retorted, "Anything but your physic!" A fist fight between two physicians at Child's Coffee House in 1734 made the news. As *The Universal Spectator* lamented, "Where shall we seek for Unity and Love / When Brother *Doctors* civil Discord move?" Fortunately, although less sensationally, both Dispensarians and anti-Dispensarians fought primarily in print, using the idea of caring for the poor to nurture the idea of medication as a commodity and thus to hide their prioritizing profit over access.

The most significant of those works was Samuel Garth's poem "The Dispensary", from which the title of this chapter is drawn. By the time Garth was writing those letters to Hans Sloane about "needy sluts", he had become wealthy and famous because of his medical practice and literary talents. His patients included dukes, duchesses, lords, and ladies, as well as Queen Anne's husband, Prince George of Denmark, and her successor,

George I. Garth's good friends among the literati included Joseph Addison, Richard Steele, William Congreve, Lady Mary Wortley Montagu (who brought inoculation from the Ottoman Empire), and Alexander Pope. He was considered the literary heir to the acclaimed playwright and former poet laureate John Dryden, a reputation encouraged when he arranged Dryden's funeral procession and burial at Westminster Abbey in 1701. Garth's own death in 1719 was so notable that newspapers reported it.

The timing of Garth's arrival on the scene and the resumption of the dispensary project by the RCP is suggestive. Garth did not receive his medical degree until comparatively late in life: in 1691, when he was thirty or thirty-one. After that, his medical career took off. He was admitted as a licentiate to the RCP (a step below Fellow) in 1692 and as a Fellow in 1693. Whether before or after he was made a Fellow, Garth and Sloane must have discovered an ally in the other; the dates suggest that Garth's admission to the RCP was based in part on his willingness to support Sloane in the debate over establishing a dispensary. In 1695, he joined the Committee of Medicines, uncoincidentally chaired by Sloane, and was among the first subscribers to the project. When the original proposed lease fell through, Garth was part of the group that took the new lease – on rooms at the RCP, thus giving the Dispensary a home and the RCP another form of income. He and Sloane remained close friends until Garth's death.

Garth used "The Dispensary" to frame the war as a battle between the benevolent and competent (the physicians) on one side and the venal and incompetent (the apothecaries) on the other. He cannily targeted a general audience and his poem proved hugely successful. To maintain control of the terms of the contest, he frequently revised and reprinted the poem to keep up with developments; it was reprinted with "corrections" three times in 1699 alone. Garth told his story in six cantos. In the first canto, the deity Sloth is awakened from his slumber at the RCP's hall in Warwick Lane by the sounds of people building the Dispensary. Since Sloth just wants to sleep, in Canto II he recruits the goddess Envy to help him end the project. She assumes the form of Colon, the most recent warden of Apothecaries Hall, and goes to alert Horoscope, another prominent member of the Worshipful Society of Apothecaries, to the Dispensary. Horoscope is so upset that he faints, but he is revived by his assistant, Squirt, who uses the "steam" of a urinal as smelling salts. In Canto III, Horoscope summons the apothecaries to their guildhall to decide on a response to the physicians (called the "Faculty"). The discussion is cut short when the laboratory under the Hall explodes. A disreputable crew of physicians and apothecaries meets in the next canto to conspire against the Faculty and destroy the Dispensary. Canto V recounts the battle between apothecaries and physicians, fought with medical instruments and bodily substances, until the goddess Health, also known as Hygeia, intervenes. In the final canto, she brings one of the physicians to the Elysian Fields to get the great physician William Harvey's instructions on how to resolve the battle. Harvey utters his lament that everyone cares about money and nobody cares about learning, and tells them how to resolve the conflict.

In Garth's representation, there is nothing inherently problematic about the Dispensary. The apothecaries are incited to opposition by Envy, an emotion for which the physicians cannot be held responsible. Attributing their opponents' objections to a personal flaw is a very tidy trick for sweeping away the physicians' wilful violation of the apothecaries' and physicians' Charters. It also neatly places the blame for the conflict on the apothecaries: if they were not so envious, everything would be fine. At the same time, it is disingenuous of Garth to identify the cause of the apothecaries' ill will as envy because the poem does not in fact depict the apothecaries as envious. Instead, they are deeply concerned about having their secrets exposed. At the apothecaries' meeting in Canto III, Ascarides the Elder wails, "Suppose th'unthinking Faculty unvail, / What we, thro' wiser Conduct, wou'd conceal." They also resent losing the sole right and power to wipe out humanity. As Colocynthus explains:

> we [are] the Friends o' Fates, / Who fill Church-yards, and who unpeople States, / Who baffle Nature, and dispose of Lives

(One wonders if Garth is turning on the apothecaries the adage "The young physician fattens the churchyard".) And of course, they are more interested in money than in anything else, including their patients' lives. Horoscope, for instance, "knows that to be rich is to be wise".

On the whole, Garth's anti-Dispensarians, apothecary and physician alike, are appalling specimens. Colon, the former Warden of the guild, is "shrill" and "in Morals loose". His brain is "empty", while "Hourly his learn'd Impertinence affords / A barren Superfluity of Words". Horoscope "fancies that a Thousand Pound supplies / The want of twenty Thousand Qualities" and Squirt is inordinately concerned with urine. There are "Two Brothers nam'd Ascarides" who "Both had the Volubility of Tongue, / In Meaning faint, but in Opinion strong." Querpo, an anti-Dispensarian physician is a "worthless Member of the Faculty". As for his colleague Carus, his "Spirits stagnate", his blood is "chill" and "sluggish", and his mind full of "lazy Fogs". He is, Garth writes, a "brainless

Wretch". Mirmillo, a physician who confabulates with the apothecaries in Canto IV, is positively lethal and proud of it. "Whilst others meanly ask'd whole Months to slay, / I oft dispatched the Patient in a Day," he brags. Garth also implies that Mirmillo is attracted to men – he "Seal'd the Engagement with a Kiss, / Which was return'd by th'Younger Askaris" – a serious accusation in a highly homophobic time.

In fact, Garth accuses both Dispensarians and anti-Dispensarians of greed. Their battle in Canto V only halts when "Apollo interpos'd in form of Fee". Like Jane Barker in her poem "On the Apothecary's", discussed in the previous chapter, Garth relied on the association of Apollo and the sun to accuse physicians of wanting those little gold discs a little too much. "Some members of the Faculty there are," Askarides the Elder notes, "Who Int'rest prudently to Oaths prefer." Elsewhere, the narrator describes a scene of:

> grave Physicians at a Consult met; / About each Symptom
> how they Disagree, / But how unanimous in case of Fee

Physicians even believe that they have a "right to assassinate" when it comes to money.

All this – the meetings in guildhalls, the satiric descriptions of apothecaries and physicians, the battle fought with syringes and gallipots, the intervention of deities such as Envy and Hygeia, and so on – is a Trojan horse. Both sides are greedy, both sides chase after fees, and whoever has this motive, Garth indicates, is wrong. Nor does "The Dispensary" ultimately justify the Dispensary on the basis of apothecarial inferiority, a frequent claim by Dispensarians: Canto V's battle is a draw. But the poem also does not justify the Dispensary on the basis of serving the poor, either. They only appear as two passing allusions, one on the usefulness of workhouses, the other as fawning praise of William III's compassion.

Instead, the poem justifies the clinic in the name of the Scientific Revolution. Garth bookends the narrative with laments that physic has abandoned the New Science. It is no longer interested in discovery and knowledge for improving the treatment of illness. After the Great Fire of 1666, Garth points out that the College's hall in Warwick Lane was:

Rais'd for a use as noble as its Frame;
Nor did the learn'd Society decline
The propagation of that great Design;
In all her mazes Nature's Face their view'd,
And as she disappear'd, they still pursu'd.

Garth is talking about the study of the body through anatomy, that is, using the methods and principles of the Scientific Revolution. Following his allusion to the famous anatomy theatre ("a use as noble as its Frame"), Garth spends a long time devotedly enumerating the most famous breakthroughs in physiology. Much research remains to be done, he points out, especially in the connection between the flesh and consciousness: "we wait the wondrous Cause to find, / How Body acts upon impassive Mind". Unfortunately, "we" will be waiting for a while: "But now those great Enquiries are no more" and "The drooping Sciences neglected pine". Physicians "ne'er rifle her [Nature's] mysterious Store, / But study Nature less, and Lucre more". As William Harvey puts it at the end of the poem, "what was once a Science, now's a Trade". The whole story is boxed in by a lament that the noble medical profession has abandoned the Scientific Revolution for commerce – "trade".

Garth is not bemoaning the replacement of knowledge with

coin. Like other sons of the Scientific Revolution, he sees profit (in this case, "Lucre") as part of scientific discovery. His explanation of "How Physick her lost Lustre may regain" collapses money and learning into one. The College's penury prevents it from contributing to the New Learning; the solution is to get money for that noble endeavour through the Dispensary. To have a dispensary, however, the Charter must be changed. Via Harvey, Garth urges his colleagues to apply to the king, William III, to rewrite their Charter because that will facilitate medical research. "To him", Harvey/Garth orders Celsus/the physicians:

> you must your sickly state refer,
> Your Charter claims him as your Visiter.
> Your Wounds he'll close, and sov'reignly restore
> Your Science to the height it had before.

For Garth, this is the public statement of the Dispensary's purpose: to make the RCP sufficiently solvent that they can do more New Science. Providing free medical care for the poor never enters into the poem. Not once.

Garth was an enthusiastic adherent of the Scientific Revolution. That is not to say that he did experiments or published medical studies or any of the expected things from a revolutionary, because he did not, although Hans Sloane got him made a Fellow of the Royal Society anyway. Rather, he fully ascribed to its principles and methodology, and believed in its possibilities. Even after his death, Garth was associated with the scientific method. An anonymous tract from 1744 used the poet–physician in a satire of *Siris*, a posthumous work by George Berkeley, Bishop of Cloyne that endorsed tar water as a panacea. In *Siris in the Shades*, the ghosts (or "shades") of two medication purveyors in Hades ask Samuel Garth to judge the validity of each man's claim to have sold an excellent medication. Their argument is really an attack on Bishop Berkeley's tar water. Garth's ghostly opponents say things such as: "I do not pretend to understand Logic, for my Part; but I look upon *Tar-water* to be good in Fevers, because the Bishop of *Cloyne* has said so. ---And this has more Weight with me, than all your Arguments put together," following scholasticism's emphasis on authority over experiment. Having read *Siris*, Garth's shade concludes that he does not rate it very highly: "For, though I have read the Book, such a studied Want of Perspicuity, and such a methodical Want of Method, seems to run through the Whole that, I confess, I am not much the wiser for it." To which the second contestant offers the kind of retort that would strike horror into the breast of any scientific revolutionary: "Well, Sir, you may reason as long and as learnedly as you please, upon the Folly of trusting to Universal Medicines and the Retailers of them; but depend upon it, that we *Empirics* shall still have the Multitude on our Side." Garth sounds very much like his "Dispensary" self when he replies: "I grant it, Sir; and for this plain Reason, because it is much easier for a Man to surrender himself up to the Guidance of any Pretender to Medicine, than to be at the Pains of examining his Pretensions by the Light of his own Sense and Understanding."

There were those who saw access to medical care as a problem requiring a systemic change, who placed the Scientific Revolution's values and methods at the heart of a new vision for a medication system. In 1689, Hugh Chamberlen also proposed a method for expanding access to medical treatment designed to promote the New Science. Chamberlen belonged to the famous family of Chamberlens who invented the forceps and kept it a secret for nearly a century (*c.* 1600 – *c.* 1725) to command high obstetrical fees. The family exemplifies the interest in tools and technology, the privatization of knowledge, and the use of knowledge for personal gain baked into the Scientific Revolution. Chamberlen's idea for what he called a "more compleat practical Constitution of Physic" was published as *A Proposal for the better Securing of Health. Humbly offered to the Consideration of the Honourable Houses of Parliament.* It looks like an early version of the UK's National Health Service. In his view, too few people had access to any part of professional medical care, let alone the full range from diagnosis to cure: "as Physick is now managed", he wrote, "not only the very Poor, but meaner sort of Tradesmen and their Families, Servants, and Misers, deter'd by Physitians Fees, and Apothecaries Bills, have little or no Benefit by Physic". In his system, everyone would receive treatment: "all Sick, as well Poor as Rich, shall be Advised and Visited, when needful, by Approved, Skillful Phisicians, and Surgeons; and furnished with necessary Medicines in all Diseases". It would be paid for with a hearth tax graduated to each family's income, with additional charges for treating "the Pox", for attending labour and delivery, and for operations for "the stone". By "each House", Chamberlen meant "every Individual Person of the Family, as well the Lodger and Servant; as Master, Mistress, and Children". "It's proposed to serve all the Families," he explained. "Rich and Poor, Little and Great, within the City and parts adjacent, much better and cheaper than at present, with Visits, Advice, Medicine, and Surgery."

At first, Chamberlen's public health system appears to share a great deal with domestic medicine. Everyone can get good, reliable treatment regardless of who they are. "Household" is defined broadly to include everyone regardless of status. Food and drink are as vital to preserving health as medical care is to restoring it. Chamberlen advocated revising or passing laws "against the Sale of unwholesome Flesh in the Markets", "that Wine not [be] Sophisticated", "that Bread may be well Baked" and "Beer well Brewed". (He also advocated for public sanitation: "the Houses and Streets well cleansed from Dirt and Filth".) The foundational perspective of his proposal, however, is very different from domestic medicine's. There are no women, for one thing, only male professionals. His plan is based on laws, not on an ethos that holds the culture together. Legislation protects food and drink, those important components to health. He wants to reduce or eliminate "Epidemical and Contagious Distempers" and reduce the number of deaths, but because "To preserve Health and save Lives, is always a Public Good, but more especially in time of War." In other words, we need to preserve public health so we can send strong men into our armed forces – "food for powder", as Shakespeare put it. Health and treatment serve a function: to expand the empire, to protect the nation, to ensure a sound economy. They are not rights or part of daily life.

Chamberlen had the advancement of science in mind, at least. One advantage to his plan, he wrote, was that "Physic and Chyrurgery will be extreamly [*sic*] improv'd, and in little time, by the multitude of Experiments, recording of Observations, and mutual candid Assistant of the Members, come near to a Demonstration." Expanding access to medicine and medication does more than take care of the vulnerable members of society. It expands the number of people available for experimentation, observation, and the demonstration of results. London and its environs would be the largest colony of laboratory mice at any time in history.

Hugh Chamberlen's plan was never enacted, and the RCP closed the Dispensary by 1726. Personal charity, including

individual apothecaries, private organizations, and the parish
continued to provide medication and medical care for the poor,
solvent and insolvent alike. Despite all the discussion and the
recognized need, the commodification of medication did not
feature any real attempt to adjust the system to provide access
for the poor. Discussing this topic, however, and the way it was
discussed deflected attention from and normalized what was
actually happening: profit was being elevated over life. As "A
Chymist in the City" caustically noted:

> If these Gentlemen had not made so great a noise about
> the Poor, and shewn such great industry in inviting to
> buy their Panaceas, one might have believed something
> of their Generosity. But Mankind now adays [*sic*] are not
> so immoderately desirous to serve one another, much less
> those that have most need.

6

The Laboratory on Cheesewell Street

It is the early eighteenth century, you are passionately dedicated to the Scientific Revolution, and the dead elephant that you purchased has been delivered to your front lawn. You wanted to know all about elephants, but now that the thing is right there in front of you, you are having second thoughts. Dissecting an elephant may not be a one-man job after all. Also, your wife is furious. If you are Hans Sloane and this is London, the solution is obvious. You need James Douglas, the premier anatomist of the day. Besides, he has dissected a flamingo; the man's unshakeable.* Off goes a gracious invitation to your colleague to share in your good fortune. Unfortunately, James Douglas is no fool and he has anticipated you, stopping by to view the rotting pachyderm when you are not home just in case you extended this very invitation. The elephant's "enormous

---

* Douglas published "The Natural History and Description of the Phoenicopterus or Flamingo; with two Views of the Head, and three of the Tongue, of that beautiful and uncommon Bird" in the Royal Society's journal, *Philosophical Transactions* vol. 29, no. 350 (31 December 1716).

bulk quite frightens me from medling with its dissection," he replies. Sorry.

Douglas was not just the best anatomist of the early eighteenth century. He was also a leading obstetrician and a profoundly curious, deeply committed contributor to the Scientific Revolution. As soon as he earned his medical degree from the University of Rheims in 1699, he joined the corps of physicians at the leading edge of the revolution. He returned to London to practise obstetrics with the famous Chamberlen family, whose interest in tools and technology for enhancing human ability had led to their famous, secret obstetrical instrument, the forceps. Douglas took stunningly detailed case notes and, whenever possible, performed post-mortems. He shared his expertise through papers at the Royal Society, publications, and correspondence with other researchers around Europe, as well as training and mentoring young physicians. He was one of the first to give anatomy lectures out of his home to educate the paying public. The Company of Barber-Surgeons awarded him the Gale Osteology Lectureship for 1712 and the Arris Muscular Lectureship in 1716 to teach the apprentices. As Helen Brock, one of his twentieth-century biographers, understatedly put it, Douglas was a "worthy inheritor of the new approach to science and medicine, all his work being characterized by careful observation and the testing of traditional beliefs against new discoveries". He was the very model of a scientific revolutionary.

When he became interested in medication, he sought an expert in chemistry for help. Chemistry was in the process of evolving from alchemy, roughly defined as the belief and practice that every substance in the cosmos could be manipulated until it yielded the pure element or elements at its heart. Alchemy gave the emerging science the ideas that substances can be reduced to their component parts and that breaking down and recombining substances can yield an improved product. "Chymistry, is an art that doth both teach and inable us (for our exceeding good and benefit) seperate [*sic*] Purity from Impurity; Exalt and advance what God and Nature hath given us, to a farther and higher Perfection than we receive it indewed with," Richard Fletcher wrote in 1676. With any kind of substance, he explained, once its "essential purities are separated" from it, those pure substances "make it plain enough by their powerful effects, that it is to this state they ought to be reduced, before they work with Efficacy". Alchemy also provided chemistry with equipment and a set of techniques for transforming substances: boil, distil, pulverize, dry, burn, melt, and so on. The Scientific Revolution provided chemistry with a methodology – the scientific method – and a way of thinking.

Before this chapter goes any further, two interrelated but non-synonymous terms would benefit from definitions: chemical medicine and medical chemistry. "Chemical medicine" has several meanings. The term applies to medication made through chemical processes. That means transformations – many transformations – using fire and water and so forth. Consistent with the belief inherited from alchemy that everything could be purified and the pure version is always better, a compound or an ingredient was not just boiled once; it was boiled until it left only a residue, reconstituted, and boiled again three, four, perhaps nine or ten times. "Chemical medicine" also applies to Paracelsan medicine, which relied on metals and minerals. Paracelsus rejected theories of health and disease inherited from Hippocrates and Galen because those theories often clashed with evidence of the senses. His revolutionary and therefore supposedly more correct theory contended that malfunctioning organs caused illness, and medication's purpose was to poison or drive out the substance that was making the organ malfunction. A number of people spotted the problem with deliberately poisoning the patient to make them well: dosage was everything, and dosage was extremely hard to judge. A little too much lead and your patient will be beyond curing. Nevertheless, both aspects of "chemical medicine" caught on: medication created through certain ("chemical") processes that often used metals and minerals, and the school of thought that endorsed this kind of medication.

"Medical chemistry" is chemistry used in the service of medicine, especially to improve medication. Just as Paracelsus's ideas attracted many people dissatisfied with the ancient models of medicine, the possibility of repurposing alchemical methods to improve medical care attracted adherents who were looking for new types of medications. Medical chemistry's primary quest during the seventeenth and eighteenth centuries was to identify the curative component of any medicinal material. That goal is not the same as creating or discovering a medicinal substance. Take aspirin, for example. It comes from willow bark, which was known as far back as Sumer as an analgesic, antipyretic, and anti-inflammatory. Between 1826 and 1828, several individuals and groups used chemistry to extract salicin and identify it as willow bark's medicinal essence. In other words, chemists isolated a substance that everyone knew must be there from a plant that everyone knew about. It took another decade for chemistry to do anything more. Chemists transformed salicin into salicylic acid in 1838, turned it into acetylsalicylic acid in 1853, and finally made it into a powder patented and sold by the Bayer company in 1899. Chemistry did indeed contribute something: the transformation of salicin into a more effective compound. Just not during the Scientific Revolution.

In the seventeenth and eighteenth centuries, however, proponents of the Scientific Revolution thrilled to chemistry's possibilities. They believed that it could improve the pharmacopoeia, creating more effective, less dangerous drugs for sufferers. It could create a class of drugs based on transformed substances that women could not reproduce. It could establish all-male spaces and it could make them seem more important than female-associated spaces. Last but not least, because chemistry was new and a product of the Scientific Revolution, its improved medication would promote science and vice versa.

Initially, the home provided everything the chemist needed, including a woman (unless she was also the chemist) with experience and knowledge about the tools, technology, and processes. Many households also had a stillhouse or stillroom. Initially used to make simples – that is, to process herbaceous materials like roots, bark, leaves, flowers, and seeds into liquids with medicinal qualities – by the eighteenth century the space was used to make all household liquids, such as cordials, medicinal waters, wines, and perfumes such as rose water. Stillhouses came with stills of course, as well as plenty of flat surfaces, all kinds of nifty equipment, and furnaces. The inventory of Charles Allington's kitchen in 1731 included:

> four brass porridge potts, two copper coffee potts, one chocolate D., iron grate, shovel, tongs, poker, fender, two tables, one brass warming pan, one pewter cullender, two pewter quart potts, one two quart pott, two pints eight blood porringers, dresser and shelves, one large bell mettle mortar, one small brass mortar and pestle, six chairs, a halfe quarterne pint and halfe quarterne measures of pewter, brass scales and weights...

The "Brewhouse" had "one large copper and iron grate, to the same one large mash pott and all other brewing vessalls".

Standard materials for a kitchen of the time.

There were a number of problems with using the kitchen to perform chemistry experiments, however. Kitchens and still-houses were constantly in use, so anyone wanting to do more than tinker with a specific recipe (think Sir Kenelm Digby when he was starting out) had to create a separate place with the same capabilities. Some chemists did not have a well-equipped kitchen, especially if they were bachelors. Besides, chemistry is smelly, not to mention occasionally explosive. It is best done in a place that cannot burn down. Early chemists turned to apothecaries, who had the necessary equipment and space, and who (especially in Oxford) allowed meetings or demonstrations in their shops after hours. Individual apothecaries began to imitate the Worshipful Society of Apothecaries of London and to build their own laboratories to provide medication in bulk.

Eventually, borrowing apothecaries' shops proved impracticable, and the laboratory was born. Peter Stahl, for example, needed his own laboratory in Oxford to help him teach chemistry. Isaac Newton had a laboratory; so did Samuel Pepys, now more famous for keeping a diary. Robert Boyle, once called "the father of modern chemistry", had laboratories at different residences during his life. Charles II had two laboratories: one at the palace of Whitehall, the other at St James's Palace. A chemist, like a housewife or a cook, might employ one or more assistants, who either helped the chemist or did the work under their direction. Advertisements for private "laboratory operators" began to appear in late seventeenth-century newspapers, such as the one in the *Collection for Improvement of Husbandry and Trade* in 1695: "One that has practiced Chimistry some Years, desires to serve a Chymist, or some Gentleman, that for his Diversion keeps a Laboratory." Laboratory operators could put such a position to good use. Like George Hartman with Sir Kenelm Digby's laboratory notebooks, John Headrich, "formerly Operator to Dr. Richard Russell", used his previous position to tout his book *Arcana Philosophica; or, Chymical Secrets* (1697).

The laboratory had some bad press to overcome initially. Sceptics of the New Science latched onto experiments as signs of foolishness or credulity. Thomas Shadwell's play *The Virtuoso* (1676) and Aphra Behn's *The Emperor of the Moon* (1687) very successfully satirized experimental science with protagonists who obsessed over pointless experiments and missed everything going on literally under their own noses. The silliest things in the plays happened in the laboratories, of course, as when Shadwell's Sir Nicholas Gimcrack tries to learn to swim by lying atop a table and flailing his limbs. In *The Emperor of the Moon*, after discovering that he was tricked into believing that two suitors of his daughter and niece are the Emperor and Prince of the Moon, Behn's Doctor Baliardo exclaims:

Burn all my Books, and let my Study Blaze, / Burn all to Ashes, and be sure the Wind / Scatter the vile Contagious Monstrous Lyes.

By the first decade of the next century, however, laboratories had lost a great deal of their mystique. When Susanna Centlivre satirized the New Science in her play *The Basset Table* (1705), she attacked it for using incomprehensible language and excluding women. Centlivre's female protagonist, Valeria, is an eager and intelligent observer and experimenter who keeps a laboratory in her home. Her suitor, Ensign Lovely (it is the eighteenth century, stage characters had names like that), admires both her and her experiments. "Oh you Charm me with these Discoveries," he says as an aside. Valeria's father, Sir Richard Plainman, is the villain of the piece, throwing her laboratory equipment out the window and forcing her to marry the man of his choosing. "You and your Will may Philosophize as long as you please, Mistress, but your Body shall be taught another Doctrine, – it shall be so," he sneers. "Your Mind, and your Soul, quotha! Why, what a Pox has my Estate to do with them?" Of course Valeria winds up with Ensign Lovely, who she loves as much as he loves her. As Centlivre's successful play indicates, by 1705 the laboratory is not the cultural oddity; a woman working in it is.

Medical chemistry was also established by then in its effort to identify the mechanisms of curative substances. When James Douglas, that model of a scientific revolutionary, wanted to know in 1723 what made medication work and whether it could be improved, he hired "Mr Durham's Laboratory in Cheesewell Street" to analyse "Chymical p.tions made by my order". The laboratory is long gone, but Douglas's "Cheesewell Street" was "Cheswell Street" on contemporary maps and "Chiswell Street" on maps today. Amazingly, however, the laboratory notebook survives. It does not look like much, just a slim, leatherbound book, but it contains the records of ten years of chemical experiments performed in Mr Durham's laboratory. True to the New Science's aspiration to objectivity, Durham kept meticulous records in a detached tone. With considerable *sangfroid*, a note at the bottom of one report warns future experimenters that "the Crucible ought to be pretty large, and take care that no charcoal get into the Crucible otherwise the matter will flame most furiously and fly out to some distance. this [*sic*] was our fate and perhaps that might have done harm to the Tincture." Sometimes, however, Durham proved human, as when he effused over a "glorious colour". The chemists of the day might not have known what they were doing or what they had made, but they could still feel wonder and delight.

Douglas first requested an analysis of wormwood, which makes good sense. It was used to treat a wide variety of ailments. According to Elizabeth Blackwell's *A Curious Herbal* (1737), the "Leaves & Tops" of wormwood "purge Melancholy Humour, provoke Urine, restore an Appetite that is lost by Drinking", and "are good against the Disorders of ye Stomach, vomiting and Surfeits: they strengthen the Viscera, kill Worms, & are of service in Dropsies, Jaundice, tertian & quartan Agues". Dr George Cheyne used wormwood to treat Prudence Wise's husband's "not intermitting" fever, and Prudence's own recipe for "Lady Nottingham's Oyl of Charity" for "scalds and burns" required it. Dorothy Rousby used wormwood in medicines for scurvy, rickets, and general aches and pains. The London apothecary John Doody treated digestion problems with it. Who would not wonder what made wormwood effective for treating so many different conditions?

So at Douglas's order, Durham's laboratory attempted the task:

> We put 20 pounds of Wormwood into a large Copper still with a sufficient quantity of Water, fixing and luteing to it a large Copper head with a Leaden pipe to which fixes into the Worm, then setting under it a Seperatory [*sic*] glass vessel filled with cold Water, we put Under it a pretty strong fire once it begins to Work, and then we kept such a degree of heat as made it come over in a pretty full stream, the oyl that came over first was somewhat clear or yellowish but soon after it became black and thick, the Operation was begun about 11 ockloak [o' clock] and finished at 5 in the afternoon.

The Oyl was easily seperated from the Water in a glass
funnel the oyl being higher than the water by allowing
ye Water to run out we catch'd the oyl in the neck of the
funnel.
We had of a black thick oyl 1 ounce.
The water that was of the still was of a fine red tincture
and excessively bitter, so that I believe we might have got
from it an extract and probably a fixed salt.

After six hours and after someone – probably the apprentice
– tasted the mysterious red water that was left in the still, Mr
Durham had no idea what they had made. Page after page of
the notebook is the same: the laboratory operator describes
what remained at the end of the procedure, but he could not
identify it or say what it could do, if anything. One report ends
with: "We put the first lotion of the Antimon. Diaphor: into
an earthen pan in the sand heat and in 2 days time evaporated
it to a dryness and got ʒiÿ of a Salt." Salt of what? What is it
good for? No idea. The rest of the page is blank. Analysing oil
of fennel seeds, the recorder concludes, "the Oyl was seperated
by a Glass funnel and then passed thro a little cotton to free it
from a whitish froathy substance that comes over in distilling
all seeds we got ʒiss of it," "it" being the unknown "whitish
froathy substance". All they can be certain of is that it appears
every time they distil seeds.

The laboratory records of others follow the same form:
detailed narrative of procedure, description of resulting substance, non-conclusion. When Daniel Coxe tested tobacco
in his laboratory, "The oyle being separated from the Spirit
a young man that was present tooke the 6th or 8th part of
a drop on the tip of his tongue whose unpleasant tast [sic]
though it made him immediately spit forth most thereof." Then

the handy young man (probably another apprentice) got dizzy for two or three minutes and nearly fell down, after which the tobacco oil "did almost prove Emetick bellicating his Stomack as he affirmed, in a very troublesome manner; the vertigo and rachings [sic] to vomitt continued almost a ¼ of an hour". "I was deterred by his example from prosecuting this Experiment by triall on my selfe or on other persons," Coxe wrote without irony. He was nothing if not resourceful, however, and:

> having procured a lusty Cat, I put one drop of this oile into her throat, who immediately thereupon (as neer as I could guess w^{in} a minute or two) was taken with a staggering & fell down on her back where shee was grievously afflicted with Convulsions; I willing to Save the Catts – life [sic] reared her on her legs & endeavoured to keep her in motion.

At first the cat was stupefied, then she revived and began running around, and finally she took "a great leap fell down stone dead, without sense, pulse, or motion [illeg] the Trunk of her body and her limbs going as pliant as a rag". It has to be said: curiosity killed the cat. It also demanded a post-mortem. "As soon as I was satisfied that the cat was really dead, my Curiosity prompted me to open the body, and enquire what alterations the poison had made therin," Coxe adds. "As soon as I opened the skin my nose was saluted with ungrateful steams perfectly resembling the smell of the oyle." Otherwise, he concludes, there was nothing of note. Tobacco remained part of materia medica, although one hopes that no one attempted to prescribe oil of tobacco after that.

It did not go unnoticed that nobody was learning much. "How little do we really know of the action of other bodies on ours?" demanded George Martine in 1740, "And yet how readily do we at the very first pronounce all purges to act indiscriminately, differing only in their various stimulating forces?" But proponents of the New Learning were undaunted. In fact, the enthusiasm for chemical medicine drove a shift towards Paracelsan medicine. Metals, elements, or compounds with one or both comprise the majority of the experiments ordered by Douglas of the Chiswell Street laboratory. All but two of the experiments between number thirty-six through seventy-nine, the final one, analyse forms of sulphur, tartar, and different kinds of salts. Over the years Douglas's prescriptions became more chemical. On 24 August 1711, for instance, Douglas ordered a laxative for a patient:

Rhubarb. ℥iÿ
Curr: ℥vi ℥i. M

It was an electuary – a sweet, medicinal paste – of powdered rhubarb mixed into a kind of currant and potassium jam. A decade later, Douglas's prescriptions looked like this:

Elect: Antiepilept.
R. Ead: valer. sylv. ante
quam Caulem edatcolect
pulv. ℥iÿ. Cinab: Antim:
℥i. Cinab: Antim: ℥i.
syr. Caryoch: 9:f. f:
El:

This electuary had a herbal component – "valer. sylv", or wild valerian (which Douglas wrote a paper about for the Royal Society) – but it also used a lot of cinnabar and antimony. By the end of his life, Douglas's personal *Catalogus Pharmacorum* included a "Catalogus Chymicorum" section as large as the catalogue of organics.

Other physicians' records confirm this shift. Between 1706 and 1709, the medications given to Sir William Millman's family were more often organic than Paracelsan, but not exclusively so. Medicaments included "prepared" pearl, Conserve of Athermes, and "Red Led plaister" as well as "Peny royall water", "Strong Cinnamon and Plantane water", "Syr[up] of Cowslips", and everyone's favourite, "Frog Spawn water". Eventually, some physicians' prescriptions only used metals and minerals. To make "the Pill", Dr Huxham instructs:

> Take Quicksilver make an Amalgama with p: ae. Regulus Antim. Mastielis [?] & pure Silver adding a proportionable Quantity of Sal. Ammoniac. Distill off the Mercury by a Retort in a glass Receiver then with the Quicksilver make a fresh Amalgama with the same Ingredients. Distill again & repeat the Operation nine or ten times then dissolve the Mercury in Spirits of Nitre put it into a Glass Retort & distill to a dryness calcine the Caput Mortuum 'till it become of a Gold Colour, burn Spirits of Wine on it & keep it for Use.

There is a lot of metal in the Pill. A lot. True to chemistry's alchemical origins, the mercury, antimony, and silver are combined, distilled, and recombined many times with sal ammoniac, which is a compound of ammonia and chloride, and spirits of nitre, a combination of water and nitric acid. Huxham's recipe notes directly link medical and chemical knowledge. "It is impossible for any one that does not attend the Process to Specify the precise dose," he wrote, "because the Medecines [*sic*] will be stronger or weaker as the Process is conducted. In general 30 Gr. Of the Antimonial Powder, & one grain of the Mercurial Powder is a moderate Dose, tho sometimes more or less is required."

Chemical medication had impressive commercial value. Unlike organic medication, it seemed obvious that it could not be made at home. The ordinary housewife was unlikely to own all the necessary equipment for making chemical medication, nor was she likely to be able to get hold of the materials required. Mercury the plant could be grown in a garden; mercury the metal could not. Her location (Was she urban or rural? What grew in her area? What was sold nearby?), weather (Was the spring too wet or too dry for certain herbs or flowers to grow?), and season (not a lot of fresh sage in January) also affected stock and therefore medical capability. Paracelsan medication did not have to wait for chamomile to grow or borage to flower. Its practitioners did not have to depend on the overseas trade for nutmeg or tamarind, either. From a sales point of view, chemical medication was new, mysterious, unavailable at home, and consequently eminently lucrative.

In the mid-1660s, practitioners led by Thomas O'Dowde (Mary Trye's father, last seen in Chapter 4) attempted to found a Society of Chemical Physicians and petitioned for a charter as a College of Chemical Physicians. Had they succeeded, they would have competed directly with both apothecaries and university physicians for patients and money (what "The Dispensary" mockingly deified as "Fee"). Sceptics of the self-styled "chemical physicians" viewed them as economic opportunists rather than true devotees of the healing arts, a view reinforced by the fact that many of the signatories were self-taught, untrained, and "illiterate", that is, they could not read Latin. Despite what appears to have been genuine belief in chemical medicine for some, the petition to form a new society failed and no economic or professional wall was built around chemical medicine.

The even bigger, game-changing issue was normalizing chemical medicine, regardless of why or whether it worked. As ever, without demand, supply is just the stuff lying around the house. Proponents argued for chemical medicine's place in education. As early as 1651, people like Noah Biggs were urging universities to add chemistry to their curricula. The pharmaceutical forged in a laboratory, Biggs proclaimed fervently, was "true medicine". Universities hired professors or endowed chairs to teach the newest methods and findings in physic, anatomy, and chemistry. At the same time, popularizers began working on the public. Readers were inundated with books such as George Starkey's *Natures Explication and Helmont's Vindication. Or A short and sure way to a long and sound life: being a necessary and full apology for chymical medicaments* (1657) and Peter Shaw's *Philosophical Principles of Universal Chemistry* (1730). George Wilson's *A Compleat Course of Chymistry* (1703) even included explanations of how different kinds of furnaces worked. It sold out three print runs in its first year. The great chemist Nicolas Lémery's *Course of Chymistry* was published in French in 1675; it appeared in English in 1677 and was reprinted in 1680, 1686, and 1698. A posthumous edition came out in 1720.

Chemists offered public lectures in chemistry, often in coffee houses, and sometimes expanded their impact by publishing those lectures in a collected set. (Coffee houses were busy places in the seventeenth and eighteenth centuries. Patrons could get a newspaper, conduct business, see patients, and hear a lecture on chemistry or Newtonian physics, for instance.) Distinguished physician John Freind's lectures on chemistry became available in 1712; John Quincy's lectures were so popular that, like Lémery's *Course of Chymistry*, they were published post-humously in 1723. Following the publication of his book *Philosophical Principles* in 1730, Peter Shaw published his lectures as *Chemical Lectures* in 1734. By the end of the 1730s, the public was hooked. When a "Laboratory [was] fitted up at St. James's [Palace] for the Use of his Royal Highness the Duke, who is going thro' [*sic*] a Course of Chymistry" in 1738, it made the *London Evening Post*.

Women could learn about chemistry, but only to some degree, and they were not encouraged to think of themselves as chemists. From one point of view, it was logical for women to learn chemistry and chemical medicine: alchemy and chemistry obviously overlapped with women's domestic work. The marvellous transformation of materials happened every day in kitchens where beer was brewed, milk became butter, meat was browned, and bread rose – never mind the medications that were made. Then there was the principle of it. As the author of *The Summary of Chemistry* explained in 1712, "It may indeed be a Crime in Politicks, but never in Good Manners to aim at a General Advantage; and hereby Ladies (if they please) are not exempted from attaining the Intelligence and Knowledge of Arts." Only a boor would exclude ladies from the "Knowledge of Arts". He also makes it a matter of national interest: knowledge of the sciences is "a Happiness which renders French Ladies particularly famous, where Sciences and Philosophy are made Natural to them, by being written in their Native Language; and sure it is but a barbarous part to debar that to others which we so much seek after our Selves".

It is not a matter of enabling women to set up their own laboratories and experiment with sulphur and mercury, however. Normalizing chemical medicine meant delegitimizing the old

and replacing it with the new. The rhetoric around cooking
and chemistry made divisions between them. "Consider our
Bread, our Beer, Wine, Meat etc. Or whatever can render our
lives happy or satisfactory: And you will find it in one degree
or other to pass under the hand of Chymistry, and its various
Operations, or Preparations," Richard Fletcher wrote. So far,
so good. But he credits Nature, not women, with the use of
chemistry to produce food, drink, and medicine. Women's tasks
– making food, "Extract[ing] any thing from her Physick",
and so on – he assigns to Nature. Fletcher also depicts Nature
as "Diseased" and weak, unable to complete her domestic
round without the help of male physicians. "For of Necessity",
Fletcher concludes, "either the Physician or Nature must officiate, or act as Chymist." His formulation and language retain
a female doer, but she is an abstraction rather than an actual
female, and even then the female abstraction (Nature) cannot
do her job without the assistance of a male physician.

The impact on women appears in their recipe books, a
place where medication, cookery, and process converge. As
a body of work, these texts show signs that women began
to replace their own modes of thinking and measuring with
those of male practitioners. No switch was flipped, no single
transformation in recipe books occurred. Put together the different kinds of change, however, and broader transformation
appears. For one thing, increasing numbers of recipes from
physicians or apothecaries started turning up in recipe books
over time. It is a bit tricky counting contributions from apothecaries because unlike physicians, apothecaries did not have
a special title to distinguish them from ordinary people, and
men did contribute to women's books. I have erred on the side
of caution here and counted someone as an apothecary only
when specifically identified as one.

Conservative estimates notwithstanding, the change in recipe sources was real. When Elizabeth Strachey began her recipe book in 1693, contributors included friends like Mrs Langton and family such as "My Mother" and "Aunt Clarke". Starting around 1727, the book began to include recipes from professionals. Prudence Wise's book, which spans roughly the same years as Elizabeth Strachey's, also follows that pattern. The first recipe from a physician does not appear until page seventy-seven, and then it is one that was in circulation among her friends. After that, physicians' names begin to appear frequently, some of them because the man himself contributed a recipe or two. "Mr Beaumont a Duguist [sic]" gave her "Doctor Meads prescription" for treating "an intermiting [sic] feavor", and a whole slew of physicians' recipes came to her from friends a little later: "A Receipt from Dr Ratcliff by Mrs Aislaby – for a Flux" and another "From Mrs Aislaby also", as well as "Doctor Palmers Electuary for the Stone or Gravell – from Mrs Greville December the 19th 1731", for instance. Some recipes seem to have come directly from the physician, as when she recorded "Doctor Mead Prescriptiosed [sic]" and "From Dr Cheney at Bath. February 1731." Sarah Draper's book includes recipes in different hands, including "For a Cough or Hoarseness" about forty pages into the book: "From 4 to 12 Drops of Balsam of Sulphur on moist Sugar now & then. As the Balsam is made of different Qualities by the Chymists, it might be necessary to ask them." There are several explanations for an increasing presence by professionals, but they all come back to the same point: over time, the family decided, consciously or not, to depend more on a male professional.

Another trend seems to have begun roughly around the 1720s: including medicinal recipes from print sources. Strachey started her recipe book in 1693; in the 1730s she added "ye following Receipts [...] out of *Salmons Practical Physick*" and "Dr Mead's Method & Meison for ye Bite of a mad Dog taken out of Farley's News Paper August ye 30 1735". Two recipes clipped from newspapers, one of them dated from 1747, were inserted at the end of the book. The owner of another recipe book slipped in a page from a printed book providing a "Method for Reviving Drowned Persons" (strip the body, lay it in front of a fire, and rub it all over with salt). In a number of cases, women treated a recipe from a physician the same way. Anne Selden copied into her own book the recipe for "Dr Lacocks Milk Water" given by "Mrs. Willoughby". Recipes given to her by physicians or apothecaries, however, she kept on the original paper pressed between two leaves. Another keeper of an eighteenth-century recipe book did the same, storing Dr Thompson's recipe "To keep the Body open" between the first two pages. In these cases, the recipes coming from outside the book owner's circle are treated as foreign objects. They are not recipes, they are prescriptions.

Recipe books also show that women began adopting chemical medicine's vocabulary. The recipe book is a genre; in earlier chapters I discussed how it has its own textual conventions, elements that all recipe books share. For example, recipe titles often specify what the recipe is for – "An approv'd Powder to prevent miscarriage", "For ye Gout", "An Electuary for the palpetations of yᵉ Heart", "A Poultis for a sore Brest", "To make Wallnut Water for all malignant Diseases, or Poyson, or Surfett". Where the purpose is not in the title and it is not a common compound, such as "The Gray Ointment", the usage often comes at the end: "Approv'd for a Burn or a Scald". Instructions begin with a command, usually "Take"; provide the ingredients and their amounts as they go; and conclude with how to use the medication. "Let the Patient drink from half a Pint to three Pints every morning—according to the strength of the disorder," orders one book.

Some recipes provide dosages. Many of the recipes in one book from the early eighteenth century come with different dosages for children than adults, as well as for children of different ages. Abbreviations are rare and measurements are domestic: a handful, a "pennyworth", a pint, "as much as will lie on" a coin or the point of a knife, and so on. The further towards the middle of the eighteenth century the recipe books get, however, the more likely that professionals' terms will turn up. Ingredients are measured in drachms and scruples, the quantities sometimes written in longhand and sometimes with the symbol. One early book has apothecary symbols and their meanings at the top of the first page. Another recipe book refers to "Chemical oyls" for a set of ingredients that do not sound particularly chemical: "oyl of Lavender, Sweet Marjoram, Rosemary, Chymicall Oyl of Nutmeggs & oyl of Nutmeggs by Expression, & oyl of each half an ounce". Sarah Draper included antidotes for poisoning by different chemical substances – arsenic and oxalic acid are the first two – where there was extra space at the bottom of a page. Arsenic and oxalic acid are not the sort of thing lying around the ordinary eighteenth-century home, and they are toxic, if not fatal, for humans. Hopefully, she did not record antidotes because she had experience with poisoning.

The lexicographical invasion also takes more obtrusive forms. Prescription form begins to make its way into later recipe books, even if the recipe is all in English and does not use any code. After copying a recipe from Mrs Hyde "For a Strain" ("A penny worth of oil of Saint John wort, as much of oil of Exeter, as much of oil of earth worms" – that is the whole thing), the owner of an eighteenth-century recipe book recorded "For an Ague":

Take ½ a pint of Ale
a quart^r of a pint of Carduus water,
½ a pint of mint water,
Two pugils[?] of Sena,
Tamarrinds [*sic*] as much as a large nutmeg, boil all these together, over a gentle Fire till it be ½ a pint, & drink it an hour before ye fit comes.
If it be for a Child, ½ this, for a Man, or woman all of it.

When a prescription appears, it can be a startling intrusion. In one seventeenth-century recipe book, a recipe in full apothecary code for a "Strengthening Plaister" has been squeezed in at the bottom of a page. In fact, the juxtaposition of domestic and chemical can cause a bit of whiplash. On one page of a book at the RCP in London, the owner wrote this recipe:

To cure a sore Breast
Rx. Empl: de Panis cum ♉rio ℥
Somnj ferj theraic ʒij
Take of ye Emplaisyer of Frogs wth Mercury two Ounces.
Opium ʒii mix y^m & make a plaister for ye Breast.

On the facing page, she wrote this one:

An approv'd medicine to procure deliverance of a dead Child
Take 3 Dragon Roots & stamp y^m & divide & bind to ye hollow of ye Feet:

These recipes are both likely to fail, but they are very different approaches to medication. As in the top recipe, ingredients like mercury start turning up in women's recipes that are meant to be made. Elizabeth Smith, who began her book in 1700, used flour of brimstone as part of a treatment for asthma (brimstone is a type of sulphur; flour of it means that it has been turned into powder). In a later recipe book, a contributor has copied a recipe for "an ague" with measurements in ounces and drams (written out), as well as "Steel prepared with Sulphur half an Ounce". Such recipes indicate that women saw Paracelsan medicine – or just chemical medicine – as legitimate, equal to, and possibly better than the organic recipes that had been passed down for generations. Recipe books suggest that the idea was making its way into the cultural psyche, including into theirs.

Household accounts offer another view of these developments. Generally speaking, accounts reveal a lot about a family – consider the family that used up a half pint of gin three times between 14 and 23 March, for example – and they offer evidence that women turned increasingly to professional help and prepared medication. Allowance must be made for specifics, of course. Lady Doyly incurred an impressive set of charges for professionally made medication between August 1688 and May 1689, suggesting that she was unable or disinclined to rely on herself or her housekeeper for what appears to be innumerable ailments.

But accounts like Anne Brockman's, which span decades of married life, bear out this change. In the early days of her marriage, Brockman bought more ingredients for medication than she did prepared treatments. On 24 February 1700, she purchased eight ounces of liquorice, four ounces of anise seeds, and two pounds ^{of} runing [*sic*] Treacle, and on 17 April she bought them again: "2 lb ½ of Treacle" and a pound of liquorice. In May 1704, she bought carduus seeds and centaury, both used in herbal medication. She was still regularly buying liquorice, anise seeds, and centaury in 1721, but the amounts had increased considerably: in July alone, she purchased six bunches of centaury. Similarly, in 1701 Brockman bought "1 ½ ʒ of Syrop of popyes" and "3 drams of pouder of Corrall", and "10[?] ½ of lenitive Electuary" in 1704. She regularly purchased anise seed water. By 1721, however, "Hysterick water" was appearing frequently in the accounts. Perhaps the Hysterick water was for her – payments for nursing care that year, including a poignant payment to a nurse for helping to wash Mr Brockman, suggest that her husband was incapacitated and that she was running the household and managing the family's extended affairs – a very stressful situation.

Fortunately, the elevation of chemistry and chemical medicine did not establish Paracelsan medicine as "the way" to understand health, illness, and medication. Promoting chemical medicine changed perceptions of medication, however. Highly manipulated ingredients, such as those resulting from multiple transformative steps, came to be seen as the most effective ingredients. Because those manipulations, those transformations, could only be performed in a laboratory, the laboratory became the best site of medication manufacture. Laboratories were not domestic space (the very thought!), not kitchens, and therefore not female space; laboratories were separate from the home and were therefore male space. The residue of Paracelsan medicine's moment in the sun was the perception that medication is not made from natural or organic substances. Drugs for treating illness are made by men, in a laboratory, using special processes, and involving mysterious substances that are not – repeat, not – grown in a garden or anywhere else.

Katherine Jones, Lady Ranelagh, the most important woman in early chemistry, would have been outraged, and not only because she was a woman. Like James Douglas, she was a committed soldier in the Scientific Revolution, but she had a great deal more money and influence than he did. She used her wealth, social position, and influence to advance the New Science, especially to support chemistry. She herself was a chemist with her own laboratory at home in London in which she did her own quite serious and intelligent experiments. Ranelagh worked with and among other great scientific revolutionaries of her time such as Samuel Hartlib, Henry Oldenburg, the botanist John Beale, chemists Daniel Coxe and George Starkey (both of whom we have met in this chapter), physician and neuroscience pioneer Thomas Willis, and yes, Sir Kenelm Digby. Ranelagh was crucial to the brilliant career of her brother, Robert. She helped him establish several of his laboratories by sending equipment to him in the country, helping him settle at Oxford and set up his laboratory there, and allowing him to build a laboratory onto the back of her own home when he moved to London. It was quite a thing to do in the very fashionable neighbourhood of Pall Mall, but she also hired Robert Hooke as the architect, so it was probably quite elegant. For the rest of their lives, she and Robert occasionally performed experiments together, and they developed a medication for children with rickets that used copper.*

Lady Ranelagh brought together the new and the old. As a gentlewoman, she had been trained in domestic medicine, and she took her responsibility to provide treatments

---

* I have been unable to find evidence of its effectiveness.

and care for the sick and injured of her family and dependents very seriously, becoming renowned and respected for her knowledge and skills. Collecting medical information in the 1650s, Samuel Hartlib noted that she had told him that "Walnut-honey (or the rindes of Walnut) is a most excellent and soveraigne Remedy against a sore throat," adding that, like many women with a household, "My Lady Ranalagh [*sic*] hath store of it." She and Elizabeth Grey, Countess of Kent discussed and exchanged medicinal recipes. She was a protective mother; her concern for her children sometimes meant challenging diagnoses or treatments when they conflicted with her own judgement and knowledge. She raised her daughters to do the same, training them to treat their families while also keeping up with medical developments. Ranelagh's extended family sought her advice and often received medications from her when ill. So did others to whom she was not related, including the royal family. She and Thomas Willis were among those who attended the Duke of Kendal, the infant son of Charles II's heir, James, Duke of York, when the baby was fatally ill, and she was one of the few who read the autopsy report. She also attended the little Duke's grandmother, Lady Clarendon, in her final illness.

Overall, Ranelagh's medical practice drew on both domestic and chemical medication. She depended on her own skill and knowledge but was willing to consult experts; she used her own recipes as well as theirs. Indefatigable in pursuit of good cures, she once exerted tremendous pressure on a Dublin practitioner to give her his recipe for treating kidney and bladder stones because her friend Samuel Hartlib suffered from "the stone" so badly. Their correspondence indicates that despite Monsieur Fontaine's resistance, she still extracted almost everything from him. What mattered to her was whether a medication worked, not what it was made of or where it came from. Practically and idealistically, Katherine Jones, Lady Ranelagh was both a person and a sign of the Scientific Revolution's possibilities.

She was neither the first nor the only woman with an interest in alchemy/chemistry and medicine. Her mother's generation (Elizabeth Grey and Alethea Talbot, for instance) had also been interested in alchemy and the first stirrings of chemistry, and women in Europe were already publishing works on chemistry, such as Isabella Cortese's *I Secreti Della Signora Isabella Cortese* (1595) and Marie Meurdrac's *La Chymie Charitable et Facile, en Faveur des Dames* (1656). Rather, Ranelagh is significant for proving that scientific principles could be reconciled with those of domestic medicine. On a practical level, she demonstrated that the pharmacopoeia could include any medication that worked, and that all medication should and could be tested for efficacy. Combining domestic and chemical medication was a logical step, and Katherine Jones, Lady Ranelagh showed how possible and effective that synthesis could have been. The crucial point is the "where" of medication. Despite the seeming compatibility of domestic and chemical medication, the two were firmly differentiated on the basis of where and how they were made. Even if you did not use metals, if you made your medication with chemistry's processes and, even better, did so in a laboratory, that medicine had legitimacy (efficacy is another matter).

Dr James Douglas and Katherine Jones, Lady Ranelagh shared a commitment to the Scientific Revolution and a deep belief that its methods and ideals could be used to improve humanity's condition. Both saw chemistry as a valuable tool for understanding the world and helping others. Instead of reconciling chemistry, medical chemistry, and domestic medicine, however, the Scientific Revolution's acolytes went in an oppo-site direction, using chemistry and medical chemistry together as an opportunity for profit and control – of medication, of the market, of education. Most physicians and apothecaries, like James Douglas, continued to depend more or less on organics while focusing the culture's – and the paying public's – atten-tion on synthetics. Chemical medicine's primary usefulness at the time was as an opponent to domestic medicine, another way of separating women and medication and rewriting cultural norms and expectations. Medical chemistry nurtured aspira-tions that it could not achieve; it did not improve medication during the seventeenth and eighteenth centuries. Nevertheless, by the middle of the eighteenth century, chemical medicine's image as the "best of all possible methods and treatments" loomed too large in the cultural consciousness to be dismantled without concerted, communal effort.

7

The Doctoress's Cure for the Stone

Bladder stones are painful. Really, really painful. They are so agonizing that before anaesthesia and antiseptics, people willingly subjected themselves to surgery to have them removed, and if voluntary organ surgery without anaesthetic and with a high mortality rate does not indicate just how unbearable it was, it is hard to imagine what would. After seventeenth-century diarist Samuel Pepys survived his procedure on 26 March 1658, he hosted an annual dinner party to celebrate the anniversary of the excruciating event. The stone was on prominent display.

The seventeenth and eighteenth centuries called Pepys's affliction simply "the stone", and it was appallingly common. Lithotomy, the surgical procedure to remove stones, was first developed centuries before Hippocrates, in the fourth century BCE. By the middle of the seventeenth century, two primary methods of lithotomy had been developed, the lesser (incision through the perineum) and the greater, or higher (incision through the belly). Fortunately, the Scientific Revolution precipitated the development of better techniques: the "lateral" method, developed by a French priest, and the "high" method, developed by John Douglas, brother of Dr James Douglas (discussed recently in Chapter 6). By the late eighteenth century, a medical student might receive several lectures on bladder stones and the appropriate surgical procedures. Alexander Gordon recorded in his notes that Alexander Munro, physician and professor of anatomy at Edinburgh University, described in his lecture different ways for operating on men and women. Dr Munro also passed around examples of bladder stones when he spoke on surgical interventions, warning his students that it was vital when making incisions into the bladder to be alert to bladder stones' variations in size and shape. Regardless of method, speed was vital. The great surgeon William Cheselden was renowned for being able to complete a lithotomy in just over one minute (once, in fifty-four seconds). Assistants were equally vital: someone had to hold down the patient. John Douglas used seven assistants in his operations.

First, however, the surgeon "searched" the patient. This he did by inserting an instrument called a staff up the patient's urethra and into the bladder. Its purpose was to confirm that there was at least one stone and its location – ideally, the surgeon might even get a sense of the size – so when the doctor went in, he knew exactly where he was going and what he was looking for (see above: speed). Doctors were more casual about searching than about operating. Edward Nourse, a Fellow of the Royal Society and a respected member of the barber-surgeons' guild, reported that he searched one "Mr Gardiner" at Childs Coffee House, which was indeed a coffee house. Mr Nourse did so "in the presence of several Physicians & Surgeons, who likewise felt for the stone". Happily for Mr Gardiner, although he had complained of bladder stones previously, he had none at this examination and was spared the knife.

Unsurprisingly, medicinal treatments were highly preferable. John Moyle, author of *Chirurgus marinus: or, the Sea-Chirurgion* (1702), instructed aspiring ship's surgeons to treat patients with medication and offered recipes for healing abraded ureters, easing pain, and dissolving stones. Among other recommendations, Stephen Blankaart's *The Physical Dictionary* listed goosegrass, marshmallow (a plant), and swallow grass for the stone. An abridged list in the 1702 *Pharmaceopoeia Londinensis* of plants, trees, and fruits useful for treating the stone included alehoof, turnsole, liverwort, ash bark, asparagus, burdock, balsam, pennyroyal, bayberry, lemon, beans, birch bark, broom, furze, spikenard, chickpeas, figs (dried or green), eglantine, eringo, galangal, goatsbeard, gooseberry, marshmallow, melilot, onions, pellitory of the wall, ragwort, saxifrage, smallage, swallowroot, tarragon, toadflax, and wild cherries. *The County Physician* (1701) recommended that its readers "Take a Nutmegg and cut it into four quarters, and steep it in good Sallad Oyl, 24 hours. Take a Radish Root, slice it and steep it in good white Wine, eat a quarter of the Nutmegg in the morning, and drink a little of the Wine above it, and fast two hours thereafter."

Personal recipe books were full of recipes for "the stone". One recipe combined "1 Gallon of Gascon Wine Ginger gallangall Cinamon Nuttmegs, grains, Cloves, Mace, illnesseeds fennel Seeds Caraway Seeds of Each 1 Ounce Sage red mint Rose leaves time Pelitory of Spane Rosemary wild time Chamomile Lavender each 1 handful" for a miracle drink that cured (among other afflictions) bad breath, infertility, head colds, and bladder stones. A slightly later recipe book recommended drinking up to three pints of a "strong decoction of black Currant leaves or in Winter, when the Leaves can't be produced, the small Buds peculiar to that Tree". Lady Sedley collected several recipes, among them "The Duke of Monmouth's Receipt for the Stone", "A Most Excellent Pill for the Stone or an ulcer in the kidneys or Bladder, or bloudy water. Approved by Able Physicians", and "Docter Jacob of Canterbury medicine for the Stone".

Naturally, printed recipe books also had them. *A Choice Manual* (1653), attributed to Elizabeth Grey, Countess of Kent, offered six: five under "A Remedy for a Fit of the Stone" and one from Sir John Digby. Readers could still find recipes for treating the stone almost a century later, testament to how often it afflicted people and how truly horrific the pain was. Charles Carter's *The Compleat City and Country Cook: or, Accomplish'd Housewife* (1732) did not encourage women to make and dispense medication, but it did advise women that birch wine treated "inward Diseases as accompany the Stone in the Bladder". Printed compilations of physicians' prescriptions, which began to appear around the turn of the eighteenth century, also offered many recipes. *Dr. Lower's and Several Other Eminent Physicians Receipts* (1701) listed seven for "stone" – the book actually offered nine. Other ailments might be permitted to vanish from the housewife's capabilities, but not kidney and bladder stones.

Desperate people will try anything, however, and ready-made nostrums abounded. There was the Tinctura Mirifica, which "infallibly cures the STONE and GRAVEL, whether in the KIDNEYS, URETERS or BLADDER, and also the Strangury, Stoppage of Urine, and all Heat, Pain, and Difficulty making Water" with just one dose and "in a Minute". And there was "The famous POWDER lately found out", which was advertised in the *Daily Courant* and "so much better than Tippin's Water (which hath had such a Name these several Years for that Distemper)". Anthony Daffy claimed that his Elixir Salutatis could cure kidney stones as well as gout, colic, diarrhoea, tuberculosis, and "ptisick". The Grand Specific cured kidney stones, as well as everything from incontinence to blockage. (It also reversed debilitation from "tedious or ill-manag'd Cures of the Venereal Disease, or from Self-Pollution, inordinate Coition, etc.") *Fog's Weekly Journal* in September 1737 tactlessly (or perhaps waggishly) placed advertisements for rival medicines, the Pulvis Salutis and Tipping's Cordial Liquor, next to each other on the page. According to its maker, the Pulvis Salutis could cure "Jaundice, Dropsy, Rheumatism, Fits of the Mother, Heart-burn, Agues, Fluxes of Blood, Internal Ulcers, Pains in the Head, Stone, Gravel, Palsy, Leprosy and King's Evil [Scrofula]", as well as "Burning or Malgnant Fevers". Tipping's Cordial Liquor was sold as a "wonderful and speedy Dissolvent of the Stone, which cures the Strangury and Ulcers in the Kidney and Bladder, and speedily relieves the Colick, Gout, Rheumatism, Palsy, and all Chronical Distempers" that also restored strength to "debilitated Limbs" and eased "all intermitting Fevers, Hectick and Consumptive Cases". Readers of the *Athenian Gazette* learned that "Mrs. Norridge, [who] now lodges at the Blew Ball in Exeter-street in the Strand" was selling an "infallible Powder for the Stone and Gravel" originally made by her father from a secret recipe that he bequeathed her.

There were no regulations about where these medicines could be sold, either. Anthony Daffy initially peddled his homemade Elixir Salutatis at Robert Clavell's printing shop in London. The "famous, little, ITALIAN BOLUS" that supposedly cured "Venereal Disease" was available at the "Flaming Sword the Corner of Russel Street, against Will's Coffee-house, Covent Garden". A "Chymical Liquor" for treating eye problems was available by appointment only, "at the Gentle woman's at the Two Blue Pots in Haydon-Yard in the Minories, London".

A stroll through late seventeenth-century London offered endless opportunities to buy a cornucopia of healing concoctions from printers, booksellers, bakers, hosiers, toy sellers, chocolate makers, postmasters, grocers, and linen drapers, at coffee houses and taverns. Enterprising nostrum makers also sold their wares in other cities. One advertisement assured readers that its elixir was "sold by some one Bookseller in most Cities and great Towns in England, and in the chief Coffee-houses in and about London". Customers could purchase Dr Bateman's cure for gout in Newcastle-upon-Tyne, Northampton, and London, while those in London, Bristol, and Gloucester could get "The Famous Specific INJECTION or LOTION" which "intirely [sic] destroys and carries off all Venereal Contagion".

There were fortunes to be made in this developing medication market, and plenty of people made them. In the eighteenth century, one of the most famous purveyors of quack medicines was Joshua Ward. (I am using the term "quack" to refer to medication that is not made by or for physicians and/or apothecaries. It encompasses medication that the seller truly believes will ease suffering or cure ailments all the way to compounds that the seller is using solely to get money.) Ward's personal story illustrates how volatile the social, economic, scientific, and medical systems were in the first half of the eighteenth century. Legend has it that as a young man, he became an MP under dubious circumstances. Ward duly presented himself to take office, the powers that be ruled that he had committed fraud, and Ward hotfooted it to France before he could be arrested. What is better documented is that Ward found a place among France's abundance of quacks, frauds, and hucksters. Two Englishmen, Sir Thomas Robinson (a future member of Parliament) and John Page (a future Secretary of the Treasury), met Ward and his medicine in Paris. Shortly thereafter, Ward was pardoned. He returned to England, bringing with him the first version of his miraculous elixir.

In London, Ward wasted no time advertising Ward's Pill and Drop. He even hired people to claim to have been cured by them. Between advertising and word of mouth, Ward very quickly built a very large, very enthusiastic client base. He opened a store for selling his goods (as opposed to a shop, where he would have made and sold them). Customers flocked to it and a cadre of women sat outside it crying up his goods. His clients included Lord Chesterfield of furniture fame, the author Henry Fielding, the historian Edward Gibbon, and George II. (The story is that His Majesty dislocated his thumb and Ward wrenched it back into the socket; after both pain and temper subsided, the king endorsed the charlatan.) Unsurprisingly, Joshua Ward very quickly became famous and rich. He expanded his products to include a "blue pill", a "purple pill", a "red drop", a "white drop", haemorrhoid cream, headache medicine, the lovely sounding "liquid sweat", a "Purging Powder" for swollen limbs, eye drops, and a medicine for treating gonorrhoea that was injected. Injection needles were not nearly as small or as sharp as they are today, and plungers did not depress as quickly; an injection would have felt not unlike being stabbed with a blunt pencil. That this medication had a market testifies to Ward's reputation (and people's desperation).

Ward cannily legitimized himself with ostentatious performances of benevolence. Promised George II's patronage for returning the royal thumb to the royal socket, Ward had himself installed in His Majesty's almonry office so he could dispense his cures to the poor for free. With this glow of charity about him, Ward then used his financial success to establish a hospital for the ailing indigent and a house within the City of

London, on Threadneedle Street, to serve more as a clinic. As "Philo-Chemicus" ironically explained, "pretending a Public Charity, or the universal Good of Mankind" conferred the "Authority" to practise medicine even in the absence of training or a medical licence. Or as Ward often pointed out, he could not be a conman because a conman would never be so generous with money (and product) to the poor.

There were plenty of sceptics, especially about the Pill and Drop. The poet Alexander Pope mocked Ward for having neither proper training nor reliable medications. "He serv'd a 'prenticeship who sets up shop," Pope wrote, but instead of serving an apprenticeship, Ward experimented on test subjects: "Ward tried on puppies and the poor, his drop." Sir Charles Hanbury Williams, a member of Parliament with a larger talent for invective than for oratory, wrote two bitter poems in which he satirized both man and Pill. Poetry was a popular medium for seventeenth-century and eighteenth-century critics, and poetic attacks appeared in the newspapers of the day. One poem in the *Universal Spectator* addressed "Egregious Ward", sneering "you boast with success sure, / That your one drop, can all distempers cure" before listing cures that it had failed to perform. In another issue, an untalented but enthusiastic critic of Ward's wrote, "'Tis plain Ward's nostrums arn'td [sic] dispensed for money all," warning readers that "I fear, instead of Tartar's Cream and Scammony, / You'll catch a Tartar [a shrew], and find all a Sham on ye." The *Universal Spectator*'s readers were neither the first nor the last to be unpersuaded by really bad poetry, but the effort was there to change Ward's medicaments from fashionable to embarrassing.

A more substantial attack was launched by physicians, apothecaries, and Fellows of the Royal Society. After all, the phenomenon of Joshua Ward and his miraculous Pill and

Drop was exactly the kind of phenomenon that the Scientific Revolution aimed to eliminate. Ward kept the formula for his Pill (and everything else he sold) secret, but the New Science valued knowledge sharing. Ward made extravagant claims for the Pill's efficacy, but medical professionals had established that there was (alas) no universal panacea. Ward made a virtue of his ignorance, proclaiming his complete lack of medical and chemical knowledge as loudly as he proclaimed the virtues of his medications. Secrecy, illogic, and a complete disregard for, if not active devaluing of, hard-won facts, insights, and methods, was bad enough. The real danger that Ward's Pill posed to those who took it was appalling and horrifying. Starting in 1734, physicians, apothecaries, and other proponents of the New Science applied the scientific method to Ward's most popular medication to establish what it was, how it worked, and whether it was safe.

Not coincidentally, the popular press was the primary field of combat. In July 1734, early in Ward's ascent to fame and wealth, a short piece in the *Gentleman's Magazine* warned readers that Ward's secret formula was not a secret to the physicians and furthermore, the reason why the public could not get such a treatment from them was because men like Sir Hans Sloane thought that it hurt rather than helped patients. When in November and December the *London Evening Post* and the *London Daily Post* offered testimonials of the Pill's efficacy, other newspapers printed furious rebuttals. The *Weekly Oracle* began publishing a series of long articles by an unnamed physician in which the author examined the credibility of Ward's claims. The "Operation of all these *Antimonial Vomits*, is so very precarious, that no Man can be absolutely certain how they will turn out," the anonymous author warned, underlining the "Hazard and Uncertainty of their Operation, and the manifest

Danger that must frequently attend upon many of those who think proper to venture on them". The author acknowledged that he had "given many Pounds of *Crude Antimony*", but he distinguished himself, a medical professional, from those who knew nothing of the "Remedies they recommend, much less of the Diseases for which they recommend them, and less still of the human Frame which is to grapple with them". In a subsequent instalment, he assessed which diseases the Pill really could cure, quite nicely informing his readers that Ward's Pill could cure none of them.

The unknown author's goal was to educate the public to protect them from the worst dangers of Ward's Pill. Having pointed out that it was dispensed by someone who knew nothing about chemistry, disease, or anatomy, he listed the types of people who should not under any circumstances take it. Or, as he put it, "I thought I might do an acceptable Piece of Service to the Publick, if I laid down some Cautions in Reference thereunto." He also made it difficult for Ward to object to these "Cautions" by claiming that the "Dispenser of them to necessitous Persons, will not be displeased" because of course, "the more Good he can do with them, without any unhappy Accident supervening, the great Applause to him, as well as Esteem for his Remedies". This attempt to limit the number of people injured or killed by Ward's Pill addresses the self-interest of both parties involved in the medication marketplace: the seller (Ward, in this case) and the buyer (the patient).

A more aggressive, protracted campaign was waged by a partnership between the *Grub Street Journal* and several members of the medical (or medicinal) community. A document in the British Library's Sloane Collection reveals that as early as 13 August 1734 a team, perhaps of physicians, apothecaries, or Fellows of the Royal Society, performed several chemical analyses of Ward's Pill, including examining the crystals under a microscope, heating a ground pill, and combining a ground pill with another substance to catalyse a reaction. "The conclusion is this," they reported, "that it can be nothing but the glass of Antimony powder'd, colour'd wth cinnab[ar]: and made up with Gum: for no praparation [*sic*] of Antimony but the glass will do to so small a dose." Just to make absolutely sure, however, "We have try'd ours uppon several people, and find our perfectly to coincide in the operation, & to produce the same effect." (Remember that Ward's Pill usually made people vomit or gave them diarrhoea.)

Later that autumn, Dr David Turner performed his own analysis and wrote a lengthy letter to the president of the Royal Society, Dr James Jurin. Like Philo-Chemicus and the anonymous writer in the *Weekly Oracle*, Turner proved that Ward's famous Pill was a form of antimony that was known to be toxic. Deeply concerned that the public was paying for the privilege to poison themselves, he begged Jurin to pressure the government into banning the use of antimony in over-the-counter medications. When the letter did not work, Turner turned to the press to alert the public and pressure Jurin. His treatise, *The Drop and Pill of Mr. Ward, Consider'd*, was subtitled *In an Epistle to Dr. James Jurin, Fellow of the College of Physicians, and of the Royal Society*. Dr Jurin and the Royal Society did not take any action, but the *Grub Street Journal* did. The newspaper printed excerpts of Turner's letter to Jurin, including twelve case histories of people who had taken violently ill or died from the Pill. Two weeks later, the newspaper featured a letter of support from another physician, and two weeks after that, a second one. Admittedly, this issue first printed an exuberant defence of Ward and the Pill (even eighteenth-century newspapers ran on advertising), but by following it with the serious, knowledgeable letter, the editor gave the professionals the last word. When Ward provided a rebuttal, it consisted of *ad hominem* attacks on Turner, assertions that he had evidence supporting his claims (but none of the evidence itself), excuses (some of those who died were already "at the point of death", for example), "what-about-isms" such as, "He says nothing of all those incurables who die in the operation of his own medicines, and those of his brethren, tho' ordered by the most learned and experienced," and most ridiculously, that he did not have time to write a "true and candid relation of the good and bad effects" of his medications. Mr Ward might indeed have been busy, but he was not too busy to write a riposte taking up one full sheet of the newspaper and two-thirds of another.

Enter Joseph Clutton, apothecary. He was born in Worcestershire in 1695 and apprenticed at the age of fourteen to the apothecary Benjamin Morris. Not unusually, he married the daughter of another apothecary, Richard Morris, who was likely a relative of Benjamin's. Mary Morris Clutton was not only well educated but also trained as an apothecary. Joseph stipulated in his will that she should take over the business until their son, Morris, was of age, and letters to her were addressed to "Mrs Clutton, apothecary". Joseph Clutton was interested in chemical medication from the start of his career. In 1730, he bought from two "druggists" their lease to a sizeable property in what would become Coldbath Fields, part of Clerkenwell. The lot included "a Shed a Countinghouse" and, most desirable, an "Elaboratory with other conveniences for the making of Chymical preparation", such as "Potts Glasses Furnaces Grates Barrs Goods Utensils & things". Clutton also purchased the right to build a street directly to his laboratory from the main thoroughfare. In 1739, he became the supplier of the chemical bases for medications to Hampshire County Hospital. (When he died in 1743, Mary took over the contract.) His apothecary off Dorrington Street in Holborn was at the sign of the Bell and Dragon.

Although in time Clutton's son, Morris, and Clutton's apprentice, Thomas Corbyn, would turn the business into a chemical medication supplier, Joseph Clutton himself was a sincere adherent of the New Science, passionate about the developing field of chemistry and its ability to benefit humanity through medication. His attack on Joshua Ward and Ward's Pill was intended to destroy Ward's credibility and promote the New Medicine and the New Science. He was pushed to act after Ward brought suit against the *Gentleman's Magazine* for defamation instead of producing evidence to refute their claims. That act told Clutton that Ward was more interested in silencing his critics than he was in vindicating himself with evidence. As Clutton wrote, initially Ward "seemed inclin'd to appeal to the Publick, if not upon medicinal Theory, yet at least upon Fact and Experiment: But he quickly grew weary of this manner of Trial". So the apothecary did what any modern, scientific thinker would do: he collected data to establish the Pill and Drop's safety and efficacy, and he conducted a series of experiments on Ward's Pill to determine its ingredients. He published his findings in 1736 as *A True and Candid Relation of the Good and Bad Effects of Joshua Ward's Pill and Drop.* He had a great deal to say. It was 122 pages long.

Ward was not just a competitor of Clutton's: he challenged in a very high-profile way the nascent medical establishment and even more alarmingly, the entire Scientific Revolution. Ward's claims and strategies in the late 1730s touched on all the points that proponents of the New Medicine were trying to overcome. Ward argued that there was nothing special about medical education or training, and made a virtue of his lack of either. He contended that there was nothing mysterious or special about effective medications. He used chemical medications like the professionals did, but discredited their analyses and therefore the scientific method. Ward ostentatiously cared for the poor, filling a gap created by the commercial system that physicians and apothecaries were building. He claimed his own data and brought out his own disinterested witnesses, some of them of high rank. In short, Ward was saying that chemical medication worked better than that crazy organic stuff that women made, but you did not need to be one of the elite in education or apprenticeship to make or use it. The knowledge was available to anyone. Furthermore, you did not need this testing mumbo jumbo to come up with great cures.

A True and Candid Relation was not Clutton's first time in the lists against Ward, although in their first engagement he signed himself Misoquackus (he might also have been some of the other anonymous critics of Ward and his medication). In A True and Candid Relation, Clutton states that since Ward has declined to defend himself and is instead suing the Grub Street Journal a second time ("yet he has given us no Notice of Trial" [emphasis added]), he, Clutton, "shall therefore proceed in my first innocent Intention of informing Mankind, by Examples and Facts, how violent and dangerous his Medicines are". Clutton's attack was very simple: Joshua Ward did not care about anyone's welfare, he only cared about making money; he aggressively preyed on people, especially the poor; and he sold poison under the name of medication. Clutton's method for making this argument was a model of the Scientific Revolution's thinking: he destroyed Ward's credibility while justifying his own, and he discredited Ward's evidence while providing an avalanche of his own, reliable evidence.

It was a duel, Clutton brandishing the New Science against Ward wielding emotion, and as duels are, it was personal. For one thing, Clutton understood that he had to be the Scientific Revolution's ideal, the Modest Witness. For another, Ward had gone after him by countermanding Clutton's instructions to a mutual patient and sending people to Clutton with stories of miraculous cures from Ward's treatments. So Clutton emphasized his own scientific character: disinterested, working for the good of humanity, transparent with method and conclusions, knowledgeable, and reliable. Had Ward's Pill "done, or would it do, but ever so little more Good than our common Medicines, I should have been as ready an Advocate in promoting it", he contends, but "I cannot, however, be just to my first Principles, of being *honestly concerned for the publick Good*, if I cease to publish some farther Discoveries on this Head" (original emphasis). He even provided the recipes for one of his treatments. As for Ward, Clutton showed him as greedy, predatory, ignorant, and secretive, taking care to use Ward's own words to do so. Over and over again, for instance, Clutton recounts how someone has become ill from one of Ward's concoctions but is urged by Ward to take more of it.

Character alone is not evidence, however. At best, it can establish or reinforce the credibility of the evidence. In addition to proving throughout *A True and Candid Relation* that Ward was trustworthy, credible, and interested only in the good of humanity (in other words, the ideal scientist), Clutton provided a tsunami of evidence. One kind was case studies: accounts of real people and what really happened to them when they took Ward's medications, especially the Pill. To demonstrate a scientific willingness to entertain data that challenged his conclusions, Clutton provided several accounts that people gave him of their own cures. "A poor woman came" to his shop, he reports, "to tell me she was better by taking of Ward's Medicines" and a man from Greenwich tells Clutton that Ward's "Medicines" had cleared up "scorbutick Breakings out about his Arms". Clutton then called that evidence into doubt. The "poor woman" admits that "some Woman persuaded her to come and tell me so" and the man from Greenwich "evaded that Question" when Clutton asks "who sent him to me". After Clutton says that "those who sent him were much in his Debt, for coming so far in such bad Weather", his visitor "compos'd his Countenance, and took Leave". In some cases, Clutton showed how signed affidavits attesting to Ward's miraculous cures were falsified, compelled, or bribed into existence.

Then there was the case of the woman who "had a Wolf in her Stomach, and was used to devour four or five Pound of raw Meat at a time, but was now cured of it", a story that a friend of Clutton's was told when the friend went to Ward's office. "A Surgeon of Note had it from *Ward* himself, that she eat two Legs of Mutton at a time," Clutton writes, before calculating the weight of the average leg of mutton in London. He concludes, tongue firmly in cheek, that "It must not be a small Wolf in her Stomach, which could devour either ten or five Pound of raw Flesh, and therefore this must be a very remarkable Cure."

In contrast to these dubious accounts, Clutton provided two large sets of cases whose sources were reliable, that is, verified either by Clutton himself or by other credible authorities. These cases were appalling, recounting profound suffering, permanent disability, or death. Clutton himself dealt with people who were determined, in his opinion, to kill themselves by using Ward's medicines. "Three or four of my own Acquaintance" took Ward's medicines "for slight Ailments; two of whom had like to have been kill'd, and apply'd to me for Assistance."

Friends and colleagues shared their experiences; even Clutton's laboratory assistant had been devastated by Ward's treatments.

Also helpful, the *Gentleman's Magazine* had been collecting and publicizing horror stories, which Clutton retold (giving full credit to his source). For example, Hester Staps (aged forty-five) took Ward's Panacea to treat her "small scorbutic pimples, which used to break out spring and fall". The first dose "vomited and purged her time beyond numbering", but since the Panacea was supposed to cure vomiting and diarrhoea, Hester took two more doses. She lost her appetite and developed a migraine, fever, respiratory illness, "continual griping pain in her bowel", and depression (no wonder), after which "a most violent leprosy" broke out "all over her body" and she began to shed "scales". Finally, she "miserably wasted away" and died. John and Daniel Wooten, both in their mid-30s, took Ward's Drop for nearly two months despite getting sicker, and Daniel then took one of Ward's Pills. Unfortunately, "Daniel's pill burst a vessel within him in the working, and forced up a quantity of blood." He and John survived only another five days. James Frettwell, a forty-nine-year-old carpenter subject to dizzy spells, took Ward's Pill and then his Liquid Snuff, developed swelling in his face, and became violently insane before dying several days later. "Mrs. Magee's daughter", a five-year-old with a rash, took three doses of Ward's medication and was dead by morning, and Mrs Riely's three-month-old died in her arms immediately after Ward gave the infant Liquid Snuff.

There is something sensational about this kind of evidence, however, and Clutton took care to it shore up with other, less titillating kinds. In response to Ward's taking credit for a drop in the mortality rate for 1734, Clutton provided an analysis of the Bills of Mortality that showed no change in the mortality rate to those who suffered from the ailments that Ward claimed to cure. Corroborating experts appear throughout *A True and Candid Relation*, such as Pierre Dionis, the renowned French anatomist; Nicolas Le Fèvre, brought to England by Charles II for his expertise in chemical medication; and Nicholas Lémery, an apothecary and chemist who was one of the first to propose the idea of acids and bases. Clutton also refers to other experts at the time that he was writing, such as the surgeon William Cheselden and the physician Richard Mead. Others, like J. Mason, surgeon, or Francis Dalby, apothecary, reveal the wide network of knowledgeable apothecaries and physicians within which Clutton worked.

Because the chemical composition of Ward's Pill was vital to the argument against it, Clutton also walked the reader through the chemistry and the procedures by which he analysed the Pill. He defines the kinds of antimony and explains, one by one, how each is made. He proves the presence of arsenic in Ward's pills by explaining that:

Men of Learning generally agree, that of all the Ways to find out the Virtues of Medicines, the two following are the chief; the first is to strictly observe their Effects, the other, to trace them back to their component Principles.

The former of these two Ways we have gone through in the preceding Cases, and laid before the Reader both the good and bad Effects of the *Pill* and *Drop*. By comparing these with what Authors of the greatest Credit say of the Effects of Arsenick, I think is the fairest Way to prove that Arsenick is in *Ward's Pills*...

This is not prose for specialists but for the lay reader, the people who are taking Ward's so-called medicines on the strength of word of mouth and perception rather than on evidence and reason. Consistent with the founding principles of the Scientific Revolution, *A True and Candid Relation* states what it is going to do and how it is going to do it. "I shall therefore observe this Method in the following Sheets," he announces early on, and then provides a numbered outline of his argument. There are guidelines along the way, such as "all things divided into three classes", "I shall now in the 3d place shew, that this *Nostrum* is a poison," and "Having informed the Reader what *Cobalt, Arsenick* and *Zaffer* are, we shall proceed." All vocabulary is defined, all processes are explained, no foreign language (ancient or modern) is used, and every step is identified along the way.

The full breadth of Clutton's argument appears best by looking holistically at *A True and Candid Relation*. Taken together, the sections establish that Ward does not have a consistent recipe for his medications. Early on, Clutton shows that the Pill's weight varies greatly, which means that production is not standardized. Part I of the treatise, Sections I and II, show how Ward uses antimony in his medications. The case studies have similar symptoms (primarily vomiting and diarrhoea); Clutton's chemical analysis reveals the presence of antimony. In Section III, the centre or fulcrum of the argument, Clutton uses Ward's defamation suit against the *Gentleman's Magazine* to justify the extensive reprinting in Parts I and II. He also uses the suit to protect the never-before-seen argument in Section I and Section IV, its parallel in Part II. Part II of the treatise, Sections IV and V, uses the same structure and method as Part I, except to show how Ward also uses arsenic in his medications. The case studies in Part II share a set of symptoms, but in addition to vomiting and diarrhoea, sufferers experience muscle spasms, swelling, numbness and paralysis, paranoia, and madness. If treated for open wounds or intestinal disorders, the sore or excretions acquire profoundly foul smells. (People who lived with pit toilets, chamber pots, and horse dung in the streets were driven out of the room by the odour. That's bad.)

What does this mean? For one thing, apothecaries and physicians knew that antimony and arsenic are both very, very bad for people, probably (hopefully) one reason why Paracelsan medicine never really caught on. The "five known preparations of *Antimony*", Clutton explains, "for their violence and harsh manner of working, are but very rarely prescribed by physicians". One grain of "Algarott", the fifth preparation, "is so rugged and harsh, working upwards and downwards, with so much pain, and such uncertainty with all, that it is seldom or never prescribed". Yet Ward used "Algarott" in his Purging Sugar Plumb, a medication designed for children. As for arsenic, Clutton provides only case studies of fatalities, including post-mortem results. It was alarming that Ward was using these metals at all. It was even more alarming that he did not control how much of either he used, and that there was very little predictability as to which he was using. In other words, there was no consistency in his medications. He did not have a recipe. If there was no recipe, then Ward was just throwing cheap materials together and selling them under assorted titles. Clutton says as much – in fact, he says that quacks do it all the time. Antimony is cheap and easy to procure, so "Ignorant and bold quacks generally make these articles the basis of their packets." He explains precisely how the profit margin works: metals like antimony "are all suitable for Quacks in that respect, the Chymist selling after the rate of 40 grains of the two latter a penny, and 480 grains of the 3 former for the same money. So there are 480 doses for a penny." Antimony is also useful because ingesting it makes people so sick that they "feel they have somewhat for their money".

Clutton's ally, the *Grub Street Journal*, used *A True and Candid Relation* to continue attacking Joshua Ward. An unknown poet wrote:

> In this bright age three wonder-workers rise
> Whose operations puzzle all the wise.
> To lame and blind, by use of manual flight
> Mapp gives the use of limbs, and Taylor sight.
> But greater Ward, not only lame and blind
> Relieves, but all diseases of mankind
> By one sole remedy removes, as sure
> As Death by arsenic all disease can cure.

"Mapp" refers to Mrs Sarah Mapp, who had a short but highly successful career setting broken and dislocated bones, and "Taylor" is Dr John Taylor, who achieved fame as an oculist. It was not quite fair to attack Mapp like this, as unlike Ward's and Taylor's businesses, bonesetting had no room for quackery: either the bone set or it did not, and everyone could tell just by looking at the injured person. Unsurprisingly, there was a great deal of reluctance in some quarters to trust her, not least because she was female, highly successful, and ostentatiously enjoying it. For example, Hans Sloane was very cautious about acknowledging her effectiveness even when presented with irrefutable evidence of it. In a letter dated 18 November 1736,* he corroborates an

* The spelling and punctuation of this letter are so idiosyncratic that I have modernized and corrected them enough to be comprehensible to a modern reader who is not Sloane's correspondent.

account that his correspondent had heard about Sloane's step-granddaughter:

> M^{iss} Isted was carried to Epsom, to Mrs Mapp for many
> disorders in her joints being awry. This [journey] was kept
> a secret from me lest I should be averse to such a trial,
> [Miss Isted] being my late wife's granddaughter. I saw for
> that reason none of the operations nor meddled save in
> taking care of her after she came up with Mrs Mapp on
> account of a dangerous colick which I do not attribute
> to ye operator. After she was free from the danger of
> the colick, I left her to Mrs Mapp's care. I believe she
> [Miss Isted] had received benefit by her, but she is not
> yet got out of her [Mrs Mapp's] hands. She herself told
> me she gathers strength every day & her friends that
> she is straight although one leg is shorter than the other
> by being 14 years contracted. Mrs Mapp by relation of
> credible persons has replac'd bones both in the ankles
> & shoulders wch have been out of their places & I think
> is now in London removed from Epsom. You have here
> a plain short account of my knowledge & belief in this
> affair who am
>
> Your most obedient & most
> humble servant
>
> Hans Sloane

He is fair: he speaks from medical expertise, not prejudice, about Miss Isted's colic, and after he has treated her for the colic, he allows Mapp to take over the case again. Still, he is careful not to endorse anything; in the original document, the word "certainly" is crossed out and replaced with "by relation of credible persons". Disrepute clung to Sarah Mapp, and she remained the sort of practitioner who was satirized in public and consulted by respectable people in secrecy, if at all. Sloane's letter preserved the distinction between himself, a real physician, and her, a bonesetter. After all, many women learned of necessity to set bones – it was the kind of thing that happened in families. Sarah Mapp had the nerve to attend strangers and charge for it.

The line between quacks and legitimate practitioners was easy to blur. William Hogarth, recognized in his time as one of the most important visual artists of the period, skewered physicians as well as Ward, Mapp, and Taylor in his print "The Company of Undertakers" (see plate section, p.6). Taylor has one eye closed and is holding a cane with a Freemason's eye, as if his eye has jumped from face to cane; Mapp is bloated, cross-eyed, clutching a bone for a cane, and dressed like Harlequin; and Ward has half his face shaded, also like a carnival figure. Both men are snuggling up to Mapp, who is staring directly out of the frame at the viewer. Hardly complimentary. However, below them, unobserved by the trio, is a cluster of twelve wigged, cane-wielding physicians. They are facing in all directions as if in confusion; most of them are fleshy, except for two who look rather cadaverous. Hogarth has framed the whole scene with a coat of arms and unscrolled across the bottom the motto *Et Plurima Mortis Imago*: "The many images of death." For Hogarth and popular conception, everyone in the frame, quack or professional, grotesque or respectable, is an undertaker, an image of death – someone who helps the ailing and injured into their grave.

Hogarth was not wrong that, on the whole, neither the professionals nor the quacks offered anything truly curative.

Nor was he wrong that commercial medicament dealers were taking advantage of a market that the physicians and apothecaries were busily establishing for their own gain. Clutton's *A True and Candid Relation* cut this Hogarthian knot. He distinguished between the fraud and the professional by showing the audience exactly how scientific medicine worked so they could compare it favourably to the often illogical and never proved promises of individuals like Ward. He also showed the difference between treatment by people you know and the invisible, unavailable quack. Reliable, effective medication was medication obtained by someone the patient could meet in places associated with that someone's authority. In the case of physicians, prescriptions for medications were obtained through an in-person visit, so the sufferer could trust that they had been seen, literally and medically, and they could trust who saw them, the physician. Patients who so desired and could afford it could be attended at their own home. One frantic writer warned his physician that:

> If this note finds you at home, I will call on you now. If it does not, I must beg you to us, to morrow morning, the person on whose account I have already given you so much trouble: and who is so very dear to me. Her pains are returned upon her, and have been for these 3 days, with cruel violence.

House calls were private only in a relative sense. The patient was attended by family, servants, sometimes friends, and sometimes other medical professionals. Visits could be followed by still further visits, but as previous chapters also demonstrate, a great deal of medical business was conducted by correspondence between the patient's representative and the physician or apothecary. One son wrote about his mother to the attending physician, and the message was delivered by the patient's daughter. "Sir", the anxious letter began:

> My mother is much the Same as when yr honour See her. She had a very Bad night, & is Exceeding sick att her Stomach, She swells much in her Bode, & take but Little water, & her Breath, for most part is very Short. She take the oyle's Surrup often, but has not took of the other Since yesterday in the After noon, it is so bitter, & heats her mouth, which is always dry. i [*sic*] beg Sir you will tell my Sister what you think of my poor mother and yr honour goodness to her very much adds to the many obligations already laid on Your humble Servant Jas Keill

Mrs Keill's health was a matter for the household, involving two children who knew quite a lot about her. They were responsible for conveying and receiving all medical information.

Professionals also acted in the public eye. They made use of their journeys from patient to patient to advertise their skill and authority. Clothes, servants, servants' clothes, and equipage were all displays of success. Dr John Radcliffe, the most successful and respected physician of his day, carried a gold-headed cane. When he died, the cane went to Richard Mead, his protégé, who by then was the most successful and respected physician of *his* day. The cane was handed down from one generation to the next, until it was finally retired as an object sacred to the RCP. Physicians also made use of a public forum to display their skill and knowledge. By the early eighteenth century, medical consultations with physicians often took place in coffee houses. Grouchy Dr Radcliffe frequented the Bull's Head Tavern; his successor Dr Mead preferred Batson's Coffee

House. Part of what made Sarah Mapp so outrageous was that she held consultations at the Grecian Coffee House.

Occasionally, depending on the physician and the apothecary and the nature of their working relationship, an apothecary might spend some time with a physician at the coffee house. As Clutton's case studies indicate, by the 1730s apothecaries could also be sent for, like physicians. Primarily, however, apothecaries were tied down because they had stock, the material for making medications. So apothecaries used their shops to proclaim their honesty and skill, and their medicines' efficacy and safety. The development of the shop as a place of commerce, sociability, and authority was central to the development of Western capitalism. The apothecaries were part of this trend as medicines and the substances to make them became commodity and capital.

Apothecary shops generally shared certain features. The shop was divided into two zones: the public, commercial zone where people handed over prescriptions and talked with the apothecary and assistants, and the private, operating zone where most of the ingredients, including the really rare ones, were stored and where all medication was made. (This operating zone was one of the reasons why early chemists met in apothecaries' shops.) From the middle of the seventeenth century, apothecaries developed the public area into a place that testified to their skill, knowledge, and honesty. There were boxes, jars, canisters, and bottles of all sizes, designed for a wide range of functions and made from an array of materials, from ceramic to wood to glass. These were displayed on floor-to-ceiling shelves all around the shop and sometimes even over the door. The front room of one late seventeenth-century apothecary held twelve barrels, one large box, more than 160 small boxes, thirteen syrup glasses, 130 gallipots, another eight regular pots, sixty-five bottles, and eighty-two parcels of medicinal substances. Some apothecaries had equipment in the front room for performing simple procedures, such as making pills or grinding up ingredients, giving customers a sense that the apothecary had nothing to hide and impressing them with his skill and knowledge. As historian Patrick Wallis explains, the "design" of the shop "functioned alongside other contemporary sources of customer reassurance, such as the vendor's reputation". In contrast, the majority of quack medicinal cures were not sold in person by their maker or in a place dedicated to healing the sick.

It might seem paradoxical, but the unseen space or spaces, such as back rooms or yards for brewing the really noxious stuff, were equally important for distinguishing professionals' endeavours and medicines. For one thing, it helped them differentiate their work from women's work in the kitchen, where everything was visible and known. For another, even though customers were forbidden these private, professional spaces (as opposed to the public, professional front room), customers knew where they were and who worked in them (see plate section, p.8). Advertised medications, on the other hand, were concocted often by unknown operators or in unknown places. The historian of science Penelope Corfield explains, "By the Georgian era, secrecy was a technique or hallmark of quackery." It was certainly both defence and offence in the drug market. Professionals who had their doubts about an advertised medicine could demand that the inventor of the medicine reveal their ingredients so others could test its true effectiveness. The ostensible logic was that if the medicine were legitimate, its purveyor would have nothing to hide; they would have no qualms about someone objective testing it to make sure it worked. Having the secret out, however, would significantly if not completely undermine the seller's control and profits.

One attack played out in the advertisement section of the *Daily Journal*. Apothecary John Moore's long advertisement for his highly effective "antiscorbutic" was followed directly by a highly sceptical, anonymous letter. "Whereas you seem to promise chymerical Wonders from your never-failing Antiscorbutic," the author sneered, "I beg you would satisfy the Public how the Scorbutic Salts are to be discharged without Sweats, Stool, or Urine, lest we should be apt to imagine this but an amusement to the world." He concluded, "Your Answer to this is expected, or your Silence will be taken as a secret Indication that you are conscious of your Error." It was the proverbial rock and hard place. Either John Moore explained all, allowing everyone else to make his medicine, or he said nothing, proving himself a quack.

Women were in an even more precarious position. Some widows were permitted to continue running their husband's apothecary shop, others were not. There also were women among the ranks of healthcare providers in London and in provincial towns. Readers have already met Mary Trye, Jane Barker, and Mary Morris Clutton, for example. The Cluttons' apprentice, Thomas Corbyn, finished his training with "Ann Burrell, Apothecary" and Mary Pardoe. Anglican bishops and archbishops also could license men and women, married and widowed, to practise midwifery, surgery, and medicine. Mr and Mrs Smith of Knutsford in Cheshire had three licences among them: surgeon and physician (him) and midwife (her). According to David Harley, in some rural dioceses women could only be licensed to practise midwifery, but in others women could also be licensed as surgeons and physicians. Episcopal licences were very difficult to come by; however, the Bishop of London licensed three women in 1727, one in 1728, and one in 1730.

Readers may remember from Chapter 5 that professionals, such as those belonging to the RCP, were generally content to let women care for the poor, the indigent, or the exceedingly rural ill. Women who posed more of a threat by treating paying patients, however, were not tolerated. Someone in Cuerden, Lancashire (population 401 in 1666) had a local woman, Mrs Garlick, charged with practising medicine without a licence. After twenty years of treating people in her London neighbourhood, Mistress Wilkenson was reported by a Fellow of the College. She was warned to stop practising and her husband had to pay a bond as surety that she would indeed cease. Sometimes, a case proceeded without the involvement of a spouse. Margaret Gibson, wife of Richard Gibson, was hauled up in front of the RCP's Board of Censors for giving medicine to Philip Chickering. She contritely confessed and was "admonished". Susan Lyon, the widow of an apothecary, was simply forbidden to practise and had to close the shop. Some women resisted. Accused of giving medication to ailing people, Elenor Woodhouse avoided punishment by disappearing into the depths of London, where she could not be traced.

Anything to do with medication was a particularly egregious transgression. Susannah Dry was imprisoned for selling it. The RCP warned Mistress Goodcole three times, then brought charges against her for making and distributing it. When the surgeon William Foster was charged with advertising his medication, he immediately pointed the finger at his wife, although he also contended that she had done a lot of good with it and "injured none". Like Mrs Gibson, the Fosters were "admonished" and ordered never to administer medication again. They also were forced to hand over Mrs Foster's recipe. A medication that safely and reliably cured people of chlorosis, a form of anaemia that turns people greenish yellow, was of great interest to the RCP.

Joanna Stephens was not nearly so tractable when it came to her safe, reliable cure for the stone. Ultimately, it took an Act of Parliament to get her to turn it over. In the mid-1730s, her medicine for the stone was sweeping London and Paris. A cure that did not have a mortality rate for an agonizing condition? Yes, please. Physicians, apothecaries, and medical-minded men on both sides of the Channel recognized that "Mrs Stephens Medicine for the Stone" could have a huge therapeutic impact. They also recognized that it posed serious financial and medical competition. Complicating the problem, Joanna Stephens's gender and seemingly unmarried state made her a threat to the gender definitions that they had been working so hard to establish. She was an outrage. She was alarming. She was also the perfect target: a woman – better, an unmarried woman – with no important social connections.

In 1737, Stephens acquired a nemesis: David Hartley. Hartley himself had suffered from the stone, so he knew first-hand how excruciating it was. He also had been cured of it – or so he thought – by Stephens's medication, so he also knew first-hand how effective it was. He wanted her recipe for the professionals, and he wanted Joanna Stephens out of the way. Chemical analysis might enable him to steal the recipe, but it would not put her out of business. His plan? Take the medication away from her by making it public property. In his first major publication, *Ten Cases*, he wrote bluntly that "My design in printing these Cases and Experiments is to engage the Publick to purchase the Discovery of these Medicines of Mrs. Stephens." In March, an announcement appeared in the *London Evening Post*. Signed by David Hartley, it proposed raising £5,000 from the public to give to Joanna Stephens in exchange for the recipe to her "Medicines for the Stone". He put it in terms of benevolence. In *Ten Cases*, he had taken a leaf from Joseph Clutton's book, writing: "But the Benefit which many Persons have plainly received from them in painful and dangerous Cases and my Opinion of their Efficacy in dissolving Stones of the Kidney and Bladder would render me inexcusable, if I did not use my best Endeavours to make them of general Service." In the *London Evening Post*, he explained that "at present the good Effects of 'em are confined to a few Persons only" because Stephens could not mass-produce it. "But there are in all Parts of the World great Numbers of Persons afflicted with the Stone, and whose Condition entitles them to all possible Compassion and Relief," Hartley lamented, and those poor souls deserved access to the medicine. Compassionately, Hartley acknowledged that the owner of the recipe should not "forfeit her whole Subsistence, by imparting a Secret of so much Importance to Mankind". This medicine, after all, was how Mrs Stephens earned money to live, but he promised in his proposal that Joanna Stephens would not be the loser.

It was a good performance, but in reality Stephens was far down the list of people or things that Hartley cared about. His proposal begins, "The Credit of Mrs. *Stephens*'s Medicines for the Stone, has of late been so much established, that many Persons of the first Distinction have thought them worthy of their Protection and Encouragement, and have desired that some Method might be take to make 'em public." Observe how Mrs Stephens does not come into this scenario. The passive voice of "has been so much established" means that someone else, not Stephens, has proved the medication's value. It is a disingenuous choice of tense as Hartley had recently published a tract with case studies – he means that *he* has "so much established" the medication's "Credit". Hartley goes from that point to what "many Persons of the first Distinction" want done with the medicines; Stephens's desires do not enter into his thinking. When Hartley does acknowledge her, it is to contend that she is incapable of handling the responsibility or demand ("herself not being able to make up for a large Number"). His connection to the medication, his perspective, others' interest, and Stephens's unworthiness all come together when he explains his purpose. "I have used my best Endeavours," he writes, "ever since I have been acquainted with the Value of the Medicines, first to dispose Mrs. Stephens to part with the Secret, and then the Publick to make her a proper Gratification for it." Stephens is the selfish loner; he is the benevolent, scientific member of society: "I have desired the Advice and Assistance of my Friends in every Step that I have taken."

As for the proposed "proper Gratification", it was designed to render her dependent. As Hartley explains a few months later in *An Account of the Contributions for Making Mrs. Stephens's Medicines Public*, Stephens would not actually receive the £5,000. That money would be given to one Mr Drummond, a banker. With every thousand pounds raised, Mr Drummond would buy annuities in the South Sea Company, and the portfolio would be held in trust for Stephens by a group of men, including Hartley himself and his partner, Peter Shaw. Once the trustees had raised and invested the full sum, Stephens would hand over her recipe for them to test, receiving in exchange the interest on the account until the professionals pronounced it cure or quackery. If they decided that the medicine was truly effective, Stephens would receive the annuities. If they decided that it was not, the money would be returned to the donors. What Hartley did not mention, of course, was that if the medicine were discredited and the money returned to the contributors, Joanna Stephens would be left with nothing except a bad reputation.

Hartley was trying to separate Stephens from her medicine, her income, and her good reputation, and to reattach all three to men. As he contended in the initial proposal, her medicine "may have many other Uses and Applications", but only "when in the Hands of Physicians" as a "leading Principle in their Reasonings upon the human Body". Hartley's approach also made the legitimacy of Stephens's medicine contingent on its meeting the standards of the New Medicine and the New Science. Her medicine had to be validated by observation and repeated testing by respectable, qualified, male professionals. Its operations had to be explained in chemical and biological terms. Hartley's plan was not about distinguishing male medicines from female medicines. It was designed to do the opposite: claim a successful female medicine for the male professionals.

Stephens held out against Hartley's pressure for months. After his initial salvo in March 1738, he kept her intransigence before the public eye with a stream of articles in newspapers. He appealed to the public to contribute to the fund to recompense her. He published the list of illustrious subscribers, implying that Mrs Stephens had some nerve refusing people of such importance. Sometimes he accused her of asking for an unreasonable sum of money, sometimes he said the amount was his idea and only fair. He rebutted the objections to his proposal in *An Account of the Contribution for Making Mrs. Stephens's Medicines Public; with Some Reasons for It, and Answers to the Most Remarkable Objections Made Against It.* He petitioned Parliament to pay the money, arguing that her medication was vital to the national good. When Parliament agreed to foot the enormous bill, he made much of that.

Stephens finally caved in December 1738. A collection of physicians, surgeons, and apothecaries recruited four test subjects who were suffering from the stone to take her medicine for different periods of time. To confirm the success of the treatment, groups of physicians examined each man, sometimes more than once. "Henry Norris, of Leather-Lane, aged 55", for example, was searched by "several Physicians and Surgeons" at St George's Hospital, who agreed that he had a bladder stone. After taking Stephens's medicine for four months, he returned symptom-free to St George's Hospital, where eight surgeons and physicians agreed that he had been rendered stoneless, so to speak. Sixty-seven-year-old Peter Appleton initially was searched by "Mr. Sharp" as well as "Dr. Pellet, Dr. Nesbit, Dr. Whitaker, and Dr. Hartley", all of them agreeing that he had a bladder stone. When he returned after five months, he had the pleasure of having a staff inserted up his penis and into his bladder by Mr Sharp and "Thirteen Physicians and Surgeons [...] at Child's Coffee-house in St. Paul's Church-yard", but "no Stone could be found". All four of the men passed their stone and achieved considerable relief. The cured patients then testified before a group of physicians and peers, after which the group approved Stephens's payment. Then the recipe appeared in newspapers from London to Edinburgh, slowly making its way into recipe books.

One of the test subjects was the same Mr Gardiner who appeared earlier in this chapter with Edward Nourse. In 1741, Nourse published a research paper on Mr Gardiner in the preeminent scientific and medical journal of the day, *Philosophical Transactions*. (His cover letter began, "Permit me to lay before you the bladder of Mr. Gardiner.") The article was also one of the very few of that time with an illustration: a fold-out engraving by the artist Elizabeth Blackwell, who had just completed the stunningly beautiful, magnificently erudite, two-volume book of medicinal plants entitled *A Curious Herbal* discussed in an earlier chapter. Nourse's medical and academic treatment of the case of Mr Gardiner and his bladder stone exemplifies the thoroughly scientific methodology with which David Hartley and his colleagues approached the testing and gathering of data. It also highlights what Joseph Clutton knew: that case studies made better drama than they did data. The *London Gazette*'s account of Mr Gardiner had a clinical tone, but it was a narrative all the same. All four case studies were narratives, with the gripping quality of a well-told story, however short.

Like the concurrent newspaper campaigns against Ward and his Pill, Hartley's newspaper campaign focused on the human angle. Unlike those efforts, chemical analyses appeared in publications that attracted a smaller audience. From mid-1739 to late 1740, four men – David Hartley and Stephen Hales of England, S. J. Morand and C. J. Geoffroy of France – not only deconstructed Stephens's medication but also established what made it effective and how those ingredients could be used more effectively. Morand and Geoffroy gave papers to the Académie des Sciences and then published their results. Hartley and Hales followed Clutton's example, publishing their results in tracts that also included case studies. Like Clutton, all four men could determine what went into the medication and deduce how it worked. Like Clutton, they all did so without the recipe. So much for Hartley's claim in 1737 that he needed the recipe to know what he was ingesting: "It is easy to see how much concerned I am to know what these Medicines are which I take daily." More evidence, if more were needed, that his relentless effort to pry the recipe for her medication from Joanna Stephens had to do with money and competition.

On the rare occasions that it is told, the story of Joanna

Stephens usually ends here, with the publication of her recipe and the destruction of her business. It is a convenient conclusion for anyone trying to lessen her significance rather than write accurate history. For one thing, although Joanna Stephens relinquished her recipe, it was not on Hartley's terms. Instead of waiting for the money to be raised by contributions, which was a dodgy proposition, Stephens was paid in one lump sum by Parliament after the results of the testing appeared in print. Furthermore, she was paid in pounds, not in stock. For another thing, Joanna Stephens did not vanish after this episode. Her name remained attached to the recipe even after it became public. It appeared under her name in recipe books, including apothecary books. Even Hartley continued to credit her for the recipe, recommending to "The Right Honourable The Lady Frances Shirley" in 1751 that she have "Mr Roberts an Apothecary in Pall Mall, at the Golden Mortar" make it for her. Furthermore, Joanna Stephens continued to practise medicine for another thirty-four years. The record of her burial on 17 November 1774 at St Paul's Church in Hammersmith identifies her as a "Doctress". It does not identify her as a widow. As the entries on either side of hers are for women identified as "widow", one of whom was also a "Shopkeeper", it seems that Stephens supported herself as a medical provider until her death at age eighty-two. What she did not do, however, was rebuild her business as a purveyor of over-the-counter medications – not under her own name, at least. If she sold medications, she must have used a different name or no name at all.

What, then, of Joshua Ward and his Pill? Financially, Ward cannily diversified his sources of income, building up his saltpetre and chemical works. Reputationally, he was unaffected by the efforts of men like Joseph Clutton. The satire *Siris Among the Shades* (1744) that teased Samuel Garth also took a moment to mock the "celebrated Pill and Drop", but that brief allusion was all. When Parliament finally passed a bill in 1748 to regulate over-the-counter medications, it excepted Ward *by name*. His fate was the opposite of Joanna Stephens's. Parliament named each of them in legislation, but to protect Ward and his business and to destroy Stephens and hers.

How to explain it? Ward was famous; Stephens was famous. His medication had an international following; so did her medication. The most powerful people in society, religion, and government believed in his Pill. The most powerful people in society, religion, and government believed in her medicine. There was ample evidence that his drugs did irreparable harm and could be fatal, but people kept taking them. There also was ample evidence that Ward knew the damage that his pills did, yet people continued to trust him. There was ample evidence that Stephens's treatment restored people to health, and that she was doing a great deal of good with it, yet she was stripped of her recipe and seemed to disappear. Chemists like Clutton established and published the recipe for Ward's Pills, but everyone kept buying them. French and English chemists found the composition of Stephens's medication and her recipe was made equally public, but it did not have the same staying power.

The explanation, of course, is that Joanna Stephens was a woman. Hartley and the British scientific community succeeded by taking advantage of that fact: they treated her recipe like domestic medication. They ignored or overlooked the fact that their analyses proved that Stephens's medication was more than effective; it was an intelligent compound, chemically speaking, with ingredients such as soap and eggshell that acted on the body in different ways to make the dose work. They certainly did not credit her with knowing chemistry or practising medical chemistry. Hartley and the men who followed him also used the ethos of commonality that underpinned recipe books to de-commodify Stephens's medication. They printed her recipe in the newspaper to show that unlike chemical medication (of course), Stephens's treatment could be made by anyone with a kitchen. At the same time, readers had to pay for the privilege of obtaining Stephens's drops, pills, or liquid from an educated, trained apothecary or physician. It was 1740, and medication from a professional was a commodity.

Actual regulation had a long way to go, but by the end of the 1730s, a nascent system was in place. Experts in chemistry and medicine ran human trials and chemically analysed a medication's components to establish its safety and effectiveness. They used print to distribute their findings, explain their views of the drug, and affect the market. From its inception, regulation was influenced by gender considerations. It also had a strong economic component. Approving substances expanded revenue opportunities and disapproving substances eliminated competition. The process strengthened the connection between medication makers (i.e. apothecaries), and medication prescribers (i.e. physicians).

If our ailing time traveller from Chapter 1 jumped forward one more century, from 1650 to 1750, they would hardly recognize the world. The concept of medication, the system for making it, the system for distributing it, and its components had changed profoundly. A time traveller jumping backward from the twenty-first century to 1740 would be appalled at what was offered, but the idea of paying for it? Well, of course.

Part Two

Part Two

Ripples and Reflections

There is far, far too much to say about the global medication economy to attempt to cover it all, so Part Two has modest goals: to demonstrate how the developments and decisions of the seventeenth and eighteenth centuries (that is, Part One) manifest in the twentieth and twenty-first centuries, and to suggest ways in which domestic medicine has much to offer.

To begin this discussion, consider these three couples: insulin and lenalidomide (trade name Revlimid), thalidomide and aducanumab (trade name Aduhelm), fezolinetant (trade name Veozah) and sildenafil (trade name Viagra).

Insulin and lenalidomide are lifesaving medications, one for diabetes and the other for cancer. A century ago, insulin's developers attempted to ensure that only non-profit entities would benefit financially from insulin. One of the scientists, Frederick Banting, reportedly said, "Insulin does not belong to me, but to the world." His view has been shared by other significant contributors to medicine. Jonas Salk, who developed the dead-virus polio vaccine, and Albert Sabin, who developed the live-virus polio vaccine, refused even to attempt a patent.

Salk asked, "Can you patent the sun?" and Sabin announced, "It is my gift to the world's children." In a system where knowledge can be private property, however, recipes for medication (including chemical formulae and molecular structures) can be owned, guarded, bought, and sold regardless of what the medication does, including if it saves lives. And whoever owns the recipe controls the price and with it, access, which in turn affects health, suffering, and survival for many.

Despite Banting's highly quotable line, readers of Chapter 5 know that insulin became a golden goose for several pharmaceutical corporations, who had to be forced to make it available to more people. Government and popular pressure surely had a role in this change, but so did plain old competition – Walmart and Sanofi each announced their own brand of low-cost insulin in 2021. Eli Lilly's agreement in 2023 to lower prices included an immediate, significant price decrease for users of their insulin. In a use of punctuation deserving of a gold medal, reporters Jen Christensen and Betsy Klein neatly used a dash to show how Eli Lilly's benevolence covered and facilitated an attempt to acquire a larger share of the market: "The company said that its price changes should make a difference, but more is needed to help all Americans with diabetes – 7 out of 10 don't use the company's insulin." Joshua Ward would have been proud. Such a lovely cloak of benevolence with which to hide self-interest.

Like insulin, lenalidomide was synthesized to treat people with a specific disease, in this case cancer, and it is extremely effective. Also like insulin, in the United States it cost a fortune, had a history of frequent, large price hikes, and was unaffordable for many patients. The Celgene Corporation, the company that made it, charged US$215 per pill when it was approved in 2005; by 2019, the price was US$713. Bristol Myers Squibb bought Celgene later in 2019 and began charging US$763 per pill. The next year, the federal government began an investigation, which revealed that lenalidomide's price had been repeatedly raised solely to increase corporate profits, which in turn increased executives' bonuses. Summarizing the congressional testimony of Celgene's former chief executive officer, Mark Alles, Representative Katie Porter said, "So to recap here, the drug didn't get any better, the cancer patients didn't get any better—you just got better at making money." Well, of course. In the United States, pharmaceuticals circulate in a system where medication is first, foremost, and always a commodity, where its purpose is to generate income rather than to restore or preserve health. Like the scorpion in the fable, it is the nature of the system to pursue monetary gain regardless of the damage wreaked by that pursuit.

Unlike other countries, the United States has protected the market and the corporations often and paradoxically at its own figurative and literal expense. The Congressional committee found that "Celgene targeted the U.S. market for price increases while maintaining or cutting prices for the rest of the world. One presentation described the U.S. as a 'highly favorable environment with free-market pricing.'" In fact, the US market alone provided over half of Celgene's global profits between 2005 and 2019. Americans pay more for most medications than people do in other countries; in 2022, 10 per cent of Americans purchased their medications abroad in an effort to reduce costs.*

One reason for this difference is that other governments

---

* The Trump administration even proposed a programme to encourage Americans to buy medications from other countries rather than engage with pharmaceutical companies about the American market.

negotiate the price of medications with the pharmaceutical companies. Even after the US federal government authorized the largest purchaser of pharmaceuticals – itself – to negotiate drug prices with corporations in 2022, other methods for profiting from medications remained untouched. It took a year for those negotiations to begin and when they did, they involved only ten medications. Once the new prices were agreed upon, they were not scheduled to go into effect for another three years. Furthermore, the legislation limited negotiations to a certain number of medications each year, leaving the cost of hundreds of drugs unaffected. In short, the market that I described in Chapter 4 – that closed circuit between apothecary/drug maker and physician/drug prescriber, with minimal opportunity for interference or intervention by other parties – remained intact in the wake of the legislation. So did the decision to prioritize profit over others' quality or quantity of life.

Pharmaceutical corporations use other strategies to maximize their profit that descend from or are the same as those used in the seventeenth and eighteenth centuries. In the United States, every new invention, even if it is still at the idea stage, can receive a patent, a government assignation of ownership (see Chapter 2 on the privatization of knowledge). It is a crime to copy something under patent, such as a battery or a medication, but not after twenty years, when the patent expires. Joanna Stephens and quacks such as Joshua Ward knew that keeping secret the medication's formula is a key to financial success. If nobody knows how to make it, nobody can sell a rival drug. In 1725, an anonymous satirist explained that British medication makers:

> purchase a Patent under the Great Seal for the Sole making, using or vending such a Machine, Preparation or Commedity [*sic*] [...] for a certain terms of Years, on

condition that he then publishes it to the World; a sure way of saving their own Money, whatever the Subjects may suffer in the mean time for want of such a Publication.

In this millennium, pharmaceutical corporations follow this practice by tweaking the molecular structure of a medication to obtain a new patent on an essentially unchanged drug, thereby extending their monopoly and increasing profits. As Matthew Harper explained in *Forbes*, "drug companies file patent upon patent to try to extend the life of a single drug—turning to litigation to try to stifle generics". His language shows how supporters of Big Pharma view medication. About Bristol Myers Squibb, the company that bought Celgene and raised the price of lenalidomide to US$763 per pill, he wrote sympathetically:

> The company used court cases to delay generic versions of cancer drug Taxol and BuSpar. Generic Taxol was delayed for years. Keeping the copycats off the market made Bristol hundreds of millions of dollars and hurt generic drugmakers like Ivax and Watson Pharmaceuticals. But while this was going on, Bristol spent [US]$2 billion on a cancer drug from ImClone that wound up being delayed, watched the prospects for hypertension drug Vanlev sink on new clinical data, stuffed its inventory channels and saw generics eat away at its market share for many top drugs.
> The result: Despite its vigorous defense of its patents, Bristol Myers [Squibb] had to cut its earnings estimates for 2002 in half.

Oh no, not that. Harper does not address patient safety or benefit in his analysis, which makes sense if medication is a commodity used to make money, not something to benefit humanity. William Salmon had a point in 1698 (and Chapter 5) when he wrote that "a Monopoly [is] wonderfully prejudicial to the Lives, Liberties, Estates and Properties of the good People".

So let us return to the example of lenalidomide. After the congressional hearings and the committee's scorching report in 2022, the US price of lenalidomide increased. Why not? Even if any or all of the testifying executives felt shame or embarrassment when members of Congress showed them up as extortionists, there was no external incentive to act on those emotions and plenty of external incentive to keep on doing what they were doing. As a publication from the National Academies of Science, Engineering, and Medicine unironically put it, an "inherent conflict exists between the desire of patients (and society) for affordable drugs and the expectations of – as well as legal obligations to – corporate shareholders and other investors in biopharmaceutical companies". "Inherent conflict" indeed. Near the end of that congressional hearing, Representative Ayanna Pressley charged that "the lack of access to affordable lifesaving medicine is an injustice. It represents an act of economic violence, and an attack on the basic principle that health care is a fundamental human right." But healthcare cannot be a human right in a society that commodifies medication. A commodity *by definition* cannot be a privilege inhering in the human being or conferred by a government on all its citizens. Turning medication into something to be bought and sold in the seventeenth and eighteenth centuries involved a tremendous shift in values, and compromised medication's identity as a fundamental right of all human beings. When Dr Samuel Garth from Chapter 5 and those like him did not create access for those who could not pay, they reinforced that change.

Pharmaceutical corporations have a point that it takes a long time and a lot of money to develop a new drug. In the United States, approval takes one route, through the US Food and Drug Administration (FDA). In the European Union, there are four routes to approval, each for a different type of medication, circumstance, or combination of the two. Most drug approval processes involve four primary steps: the development of a drug, animal and clinical (human) trials by the drug developer to establish safety and effectiveness, expert review of the data gathered by the drug developer, and a decision by the regulatory agency. The process is easily summarized, less easily accomplished. The US National Institute of Child Health and Human Development states baldly that "The clinical trial phase can take years to complete." From some perspectives, the most significant thing about the drug approval process is that it is so complicated, time-consuming, and expensive. From another perspective, a long, rigorous process is warranted because history is replete with pharmacological disasters that damaged, destroyed, or outright killed adults, children, and foetuses.

Thalidomide is a global example of that peril. At present, it is used to treat leprosy and cancer, but its first appearance on the medication market in the 1950s was catastrophic (cancer researcher A. Keith Stewart called it "Shakespearean in scope"). Thalidomide was developed in the early 1950s by Chemie Grünenthal, a West German pharmaceutical company, as a sedative, and it was prescribed primarily to women. (This phenomenon is another instance of medication used to silence women, but that issue is much too large to be handled properly in this book.) According to Chemie Grünenthal's extremely inadequate testing, thalidomide had no side effects and could not be overdosed. The accidental discovery of additional uses, especially for morning sickness, made the drug even more lucrative. Companies around the world quickly bought the rights to sell the medication in their own markets. For the purveyors of thalidomide, it practically rained money. At the same time, two troubling phenomena appeared. The first was that adults who took thalidomide for a long time developed nerve problems in their extremities. The second was that physicians observed a shocking rise in the number of babies born with underdeveloped or missing arms, legs, feet, toes, hands, and fingers.* According to Sir Harold Evans, "Depending on the day it was ingested, a single dose of thalidomide could kill babies in the womb, degrade their organs, or lop off limbs." By 1960 the international medical community was circulating research papers showing a connection between thalidomide and these children.

At the same time, the American pharmaceutical company Richardson-Merrell (now Sanofi)† applied to the FDA for approval to sell thalidomide in the United States. Richardson-Merrell had already manufactured 10 million pills before applying for the FDA's approval, and their method for evaluating its safety was to distribute 2.5 million pills to physicians to give to their patients and see how they did. Patients and many of the physicians had no idea that Kevadon, as Richardson-Merrell labelled thalidomide, was not yet approved in the United States. At the FDA, Frances Oldham Kelsey and her team – Lee Geismar, chemist, and Jiro Oyama, pharmacologist

---

* Other physiological malformations, such as extra fingers or toes, partial or complete deafness or blindness, and injury to internal organs often resulting in death shortly after birth, also occurred.
† Although Richardson-Merrell passed through several acquisitions to become part of Sanofi, I am using the company's name at the time to avoid confusion with the present company. Sanofi did not exist during this time.

– rejected the application because of an absence of data on the medication's safety. She and the company went back and forth for months – Merrell submitted gibberish and meaningless numbers, Kelsey demanded real data and rejected the application, Merrell attacked Kelsey and submitted more gibberish and meaningless numbers* – until autumn 1961, when the research evidence of thalidomide's effects on adults and foetuses become impossible to ignore or deny. Chemie Grünenthal and the other companies took it off the market, even Merrell in March 1962. Around the world, thousands of adults had suffered irreparable nerve damage, and thousands of pregnancies had miscarried, ended in stillbirth, or resulted in infants with severe malformations and impairments. In the United States, the numbers were far lower thanks to the FDA's refusal to approve the drug.

The thalidomide disaster is important to this study for two main reasons: what happened, and how it is recounted and therefore represented. Chemie Grünenthal produced a substance through chemical experimentation and then went looking for a medical application, which was standard practice up to that time. That practice should sound familiar: it is what the chemists and chemical physicians from Chapters 4 and 6 had been doing. Physicians' ready acceptance of the drug makers' claims can also be traced to the Scientific Revolution, which built into Western medicine the concept that drugs are made from secret formulae in laboratories, places where ordinary people cannot go. The circulation of research papers establishing the connection between thalidomide and birth defects, stillbirths, and

---

* Kelsey's husband, Fremont Ellis Kelsey, PhD, called parts of the application "an interesting collection of meaningless pseudoscientific jargon apparently intended to impress chemically unsophisticated readers".

miscarriage was also put in place by the principles and practices of the Scientific Revolution, and the circulation of those findings did exactly what it was supposed to do. Other aspects of the crisis are the result of the New Science's tying together of knowledge and gain: science used to make a profitable object and to justify or promote that object, and purveyors of medication working with prescribers of medication for their mutual profit. When science's function to provide benefits conflicted with its function to provide profits, in the case of thalidomide it was the former that gave way until 1960. Greed was not the only force that enabled the thalidomide disaster. Other values and practices that were built into science (and its offspring, medicine) during the elimination of domestic medicine and its replacement with modern or for-profit medicine also made it possible.

In the United States, the story of thalidomide is recounted as a David v. Goliath story, a tale of a heroic novice who triumphed over an evil empire (Evans called it the "imperial power of American business"). Kelsey was indeed courageous and unyielding in the face of tremendous pressure. She was also a woman in her forties who had dealt with plenty of sexism and who was rightly confident in her knowledge and skills. She had a doctorate in pharmacology from one of the finest research institutions in the United States (the University of Chicago), which she had earned under the supervision of one of the most distinguished pharmacologists of the day, E. M. K. Geiling. Additionally, she had an MD from the University of Chicago – which she earned while married and bearing and raising two children – and had practised medicine for several years. She kept up with the latest research and corresponded with others in the field. She held to the principles of the New Science and the New Medicine: observing, experimenting, analysing the data, and drawing a conclusion from the data, all in a way that someone else could replicate, and she did it for the benefit of humanity. She was, in fact, a woman extremely well qualified for her role and consequently imbued with the power of knowledge and expertise.

Nor does it diminish her achievement to point out that she did not do it alone. The image of the individual genius in the laboratory is not how science (or medicine) is done. Kelsey had a team precisely because each one brought their own expertise in a relevant field to the drug evaluation process. She made the final decision, but their input shaped that decision. Kelsey also sought the expertise of pharmacologist Fremont Ellis Kelsey (her spouse, as it happened), who worked at the National Institutes of Health (NIH) and concurred with her analysis of Richardson-Merrell's application. The British physicians and apothecaries of the early and mid-eighteenth century would have agreed with Kelsey that Richardson-Merrell's claims about their "super drug" were dubious at best. Like Stephen Hartley (but not, unfortunately, Joseph Clutton), she had the support of colleagues and powerful institutions. When F. Joseph Murray, the executive at Richardson-Merrell in charge of the drug, complained to her boss, Ralph Smith, Smith told him that Kelsey had the full support and weight of the FDA behind her. She did exactly what she was supposed to do as a scientist and physician, and the scientific community (which includes the medical community) did exactly what it was supposed to do.

But Frances Oldham Kelsey also defied three centuries of science. She did not just want data establishing the medication's safety for patients. She had done considerable research in teratogens, substances that cross the placenta from mother to foetus, and studied embryology. She wanted data proving that thalidomide was safe for pregnant patients, and she wanted data proving that it was safe for their foetus. In one way, this was good science, but in another way it was deviant science. Kelsey rejected the idea of a "universal subject", a human being whose responses to medications (or anything) were shared by all other human beings. The "universal subject" came out of the Scientific Revolution, which pushed women out of sight as much as possible when it redefined and took over medication. Difference, women's bodies, and women's experiences were all erased as much as possible. Kelsey brought women's bodies back into everyone's awareness and into the centre of the discussion of a medication that was – oh, right – given to women, and for a – oh, right again – specifically female experience. She and Dr Helen Taussig, internationally renowned as one of the pioneers of paediatric cardiology, ensured that the development of the foetus and the children who were born was also recognized and accounted for. Kelsey made women's bodies, women's experience, and the foetus they were making central to the analyses of thalidomide – not only visible but also vital.

There is some truth to the adage that the more things change, the more they stay the same. After thalidomide, governments around the world, including the United States, revamped their criteria and processes for medication approval. Drugs must undergo rigorous testing. Patients must be informed if the drug they are taking is experimental and must be given the choice whether to participate in clinical trials – what is called informed consent. Nevertheless, the regulation of medication inevitably continues to conflict with the commodification of medication. Agencies such as the FDA and the European Medicines Agency have "fast tracks", routes that certain drugs can take if they are so urgently needed that final rounds of testing can be deferred until after their release. (There are also emergency authorization protocols for medications such as the initial coronavirus disease 2019 vaccines.) The example of aducanumab, a drug proposed for treating patients with Alzheimer's disease, is the reverse of thalidomide, and reinforces the old lesson that regulation requires both science and the will to heed it.

Health Canada, the European Medicines Agency, and the United Kingdom's Medicines and Healthcare products [sic] Regulatory Agency all rejected Biogen's application for aducanumab because the data about its efficacy were inconclusive and showed the possibility of life-threatening and fatal side effects. The FDA, however, ignored the recommendation of its own review committee to reject the application. Ten out of eleven members of the committee voted against it (the eleventh voted "unsure") but aducanumab was approved, and for a larger patient pool than it was designed for (although this was changed later). Three committee members resigned and the subsequent investigation by the Office of the Inspector General found that the FDA used (deliberately or de facto) its "accelerated approval pathway" to allow pharmaceutical companies to avoid completing their safety and efficacy testing. The FDA had gotten too close to the corporations that it was supposed to be policing and regulating. All the Inspector General's Office had to do was read *Forbes*: Robert Hart reported that Roche was "the latest pharmaceutical company to court the regulator in the wake of following its controversial fast-track approval of Biogen's Aduhelm [aducanumab]". Regulators are not supposed to be woo-able, but the FDA had signalled that it was.

The gender imbalance in science, technology, engineering, and medicine (frequently shortened to "STEM") has been increasingly publicized and addressed over the last few decades, but unfortunately it is only one consequence of the Scientific Revolution's construction of gender to define and establish science and medicine. The last pair of medications, fezolinetant and sildenafil, demonstrate other consequences of removing and barring women from the medication marketplace. Fezolinetant was created by Astellas Pharma to reduce moderate-to-severe hot flushes (sometimes called hot flashes) in perimenopausal women. It is the only drug of its kind, unless Bayer wins approval for elinzanetant. In 2023, fezolinetant was approved by the FDA and was undergoing review by the European Union, the United Kingdom, Switzerland, and Australia.

Perimenopause, which can last up to a decade, is the stage during which menstruation slowly ceases due to a lowering of hormones, particularly oestrogen. Menopause is the stage after menstruation has stopped; loss of oestrogen causes a seemingly infinite number of other health problems during this stage. Up to 80 per cent of perimenopausal women experience hot flushes, which can interrupt ordinary work and daily life. According to one study, between 10 and 20 per cent of women rated their hot flushes "near intolerable". Hot flushes also have a cascading effect, disrupting sleep and concentration, which in turn affect physiological and mental health, memory, social interactions, and the ability to perform paid and unpaid work.

Until recently, however, the question of economic productivity and menopause was characterized by researchers as a "quality of life" issue, as if the hours of work lost have nothing to do with paying for food and shelter, or with an employer receiving the employee's best work. In reality, the financial impact of debilitating menopause symptoms hits individuals and families as well as corporations and national economies. By one calculation, the US economy loses almost 2 billion dollars per year. More than half of the world's population is biologically female and every single one who survives long enough – not at all a foregone conclusion in many places – will experience menopause. That is a lot of people, a lot of families, a lot of local and national and global economic impact. So it is a good thing that researchers have been working so long and assiduously to treat erectile dysfunction (ED).

The first medication to treat ED, sildenafil (Viagra), was approved in the United States and Europe in 1998, a quarter of a century before fezolinetant. As with thalidomide and many other medications, sildenafil's effectiveness at treating this condition was an unexpected but very welcome discovery. Since then at least two other prescription medications for ED have hit the market, and generic forms are also available. Medications like sildenafil treat ED, a condition in which an adult man cannot get an erection or maintain it sufficiently for sexual activity with or without a partner, by enabling the patient to get and maintain one. ED is caused by conditions such as diabetes, certain kinds of injury or surgery or treatment, and ageing. ED itself does not prevent someone from working, but a root cause, such as a heart condition or cancer treatment, or a psychological response to ED, such as depression, can have that effect.

Without minimizing the impact of ED on those suffering from it, the choice by researchers and corporations to address it before giving attention to any of the effects of the perimenopause or menopause makes little fiscal or pharmacological sense. Economically speaking, more people are affected by menopause than by ED, so the market is greater. Medically, hot flushes themselves impair functioning, so medication for it addresses the actual health problem. Because ED is often a symptom of a serious underlying ailment that requires treatment, medication for it does not address the real health problem.

Furthermore, one could argue that the psychological distress caused by ED is itself the product of definitions of masculinity.

If so, then addressing those definitions as well as attitudes towards ageing would be more helpful and wide-reaching for treating the psychological response to ED than restoring the ability to maintain an erection long enough for penetration. The word "dysfunction", for example, suggests that the penis is not working properly, but if inability to maintain an erection for a certain period of time is a natural effect of ageing, then perhaps the condition when caused by ageing deserves a different name. Menopause is not "menses dysfunction" after all. But to return to the pharmaceutical makers and distributors – despite the size, scope, and permanence of the market and the impact of a medication for hot flushes, researchers and corporations invested in ED, and more than once. That repeated decision suggests that it is not the condition so much as who suffers from it that guided the decision.

The amount and relative timing of medications for ED and for the hot flushes of menopause are more than the artefacts of sexism. They are also the products of a particular form of sexism rooted in the appropriation of medication by male proponents of the New Science. "Medicine carries the burden of its own troubling history," Elinor Cleghorn writes. "The history of medicine, of illness, is every bit as social and cultural as it is scientific." As science's revolutionaries pushed women out of certain figurative and literal spaces and into smaller ones, women became less and less figuratively and literally visible. Then and now, problems of access, patient credibility, and quality of treatment are compounded by race, ethnicity, class, and sexual identity. In 2021, the overall maternal mortality rate in the United States was 32.9 deaths per 100,000 live births (a 40 per cent increase from 2020), by far the worst of the industrialized countries, which average 12 deaths per 100,000 live births. The maternal mortality rate for American Black women, however, was 69.9 deaths per 100,000 live births. The degree of disparity in the United Kingdom was comparable.

Frances Oldham Kelsey's demand for studies assessing the risk of thalidomide to women and pregnant women shocked Richardson-Merrell's executives because nobody had thought about the female body as its own being – a blindness that, as extensive research shows, continues in clinical trials in the twenty-first century. It is not a coincidence that "Veozah" sounds a lot like "Viagra": the name capitalizes on the associations raised by the sounds (V-vowel-vowel-hard consonant-ah) and rhythm, and also suggests an equivalence between the drugs. Nevertheless, Veozah's arrival on the market twenty-five years after Viagra is a signal of just where women's physiological debility rates in comparison with men's. Anyone who is not the universal subject can be a deviation or a deviant, but they cannot be someone with integrity of being. The simultaneous subordination and subsumption of the non-universal subject is dangerous if not potentially fatal for such an individual or demographic.

The commodification of medication during the seventeenth and eighteenth centuries by proponents of the Scientific Revolution was accomplished by the establishment of ideas, values, principles, and systems that displaced domestic medicine and its values and systems. What the Scientific Revolution brought, and the medication marketplace that came out of it, has left Western medicine and the global pharmaceutical system with a deeply problematic legacy. Domestic medicine's principles and ethos are not gone, however, and on occasion over the last century, domestic medicine has been used in conjunction with modern science and medicine to very positive effect.

Consider iodized salt. Humans need both sodium and iodine to function. Sodium makes nerves work and helps maintain the right amount of blood plasma, while iodine is necessary for the thyroid to make hormones that regulate metabolism, and therefore affect the growth and functioning of the entire body. Iodine deficiency can make the thyroid gland enlarge and bulge out of the neck, which is called goitre, and causes neurocognitive and neurological damage. Iodine deficiency in utero can lead to stunted growth and weight gain, muteness, deafness, impaired ability to control limbs, impaired motor skills, and even thyroid cancer. As one research team put it, "Fetal development highly relies on thyroid and iodine metabolism and can be compromised if they malfunction."

By far the best delivery method for salt and iodine is eating things with salt and iodine. Salt is pretty easy to find in nature; iodine, not so much. It is only available naturally in edibles that grow in iodine-rich environments, like the ocean or soil near the sea. Take a look at a map of the earth: many people do not have ready access to those foods. At the turn of the twentieth century, in some areas of landlocked Switzerland, 75–80 per cent of schoolchildren had an enlarged goitre. In the "Goiter Belt", a band of territory stretching across the top of the United States from upper New York State to the North-west, 25–75 per cent of schoolchildren had it. Interest in addressing iodine deficiency intensified around 1914, at the outbreak of First World War. In the United States, the number of men disqualified from military service because of goitre was so high that it affected military strength. As Hugh Chamberlen had pointed out more than two centuries earlier, "To preserve Health and save Lives, is always a Public Good, but more especially in time of War."

Domestic medicine provided a solution. At the time, medication and food were sufficiently separate categories that despite knowing about iodine in food, some public health officials proposed administering iodine drops to children. Domestic medicine did not draw such a strong distinction, however, and also held the view that eating and drinking is a form of healthcare. Between 1915 and 1918, Swiss and American physicians began exchanging information and reading each other's research on iodine additives in the school-age population. The results were very promising. Salt was a common household item, a basic ingestible, and iodizing it worked extremely well. Iodized salt is also cheap, easy to produce, extremely effective, and voluntarily consumed by people without thinking too much about it. No "Time to take my iodine", just "What's for dinner?" Once scientists, physicians, public health officials, and the executives of salt companies abandoned that firm distinction between medication and food, they had a solution to widespread iodine deficiency: iodized salt, which everyone could keep on the kitchen table and eat regularly. Is iodized salt food or medication? Yes.

What happened after American and Swiss healthcare providers latched onto iodizing salt, however, is a tale of divergence. Switzerland forged ahead with a national salt iodization programme in 1919 and implemented it in 1922. By the early twenty-first century, iodized salt was in the kitchen of more than 94 per cent of Swiss households. Countries around the world followed suit. Well over 100 now require table and cooking salt to be iodized. In 1990, the World Summit for Children made "Universal access to iodized salt by 1995" one of its goals. At the time, 130 countries grappled with iodine deficiency. By 2016, that number had dropped to nineteen, with thirty-six countries in Asia alone implementing or developing legislation to provide iodized salt for their citizens. On the whole, citizens of countries with iodized table and cooking salt suffer much less iodine deficiency and fewer physiological ills, they bear healthier children, and they have higher IQs than their forebears in the days before iodized salt.

Additionally, continuing to ignore the distinction between food and medication, scientists have continued to find comestibles to iodize. The idea to iodize salt came from observing one culture using naturally iodized salt, but the idea to iodize other items comes from a willingness to continue blurring that boundary. Scientists and physicians accepted the kitchen as the key space in which cures and prevention were to be worked. These elements from domestic medication – the relaxed distinction between food and medication, the community orientation, the kitchen at the centre of health – combined with scientific principles and methods to create an effective solution to a global problem. Governmental commitment to the community, to public health, is vital. The closer that a government gets to mandating that food-grade salt be iodized, the less iodine deficiency there is in the populace.

The United States went about it very differently. There was no national or state legislation. An attempt at the federal level in 1948 to ensure the availability of iodized salt to all consumers failed. Instead, dealing with iodine deficiency through iodized salt began with the corporate sector. Michigan physician and professor of paediatrics Dr David Murray Cowie persuaded the salt corporations to make iodized salt for the Michigan market, and it arrived on grocery store shelves in 1924. "Incredibly," writes Howard Markel, "the salt manufacturers voluntarily produced every box; no laws or regulations were required." The introduction of iodized salt to consumers was so successful that the Morton Salt Company took its product national within months, proving that public health and corporate interest are not inevitably in conflict.

Consistent with findings that greater government investment

in getting iodine into its citizens produces less iodine deficiency in its citizens, however, iodine deficiency is on the rise in the United States. In 2022, the research team of Adrienne Hatch-McChesney and Harris R. Lieberman reported that in 2011–2012, almost 40 per cent of Americans were iodine deficient; a more recent study showed that 23 per cent of pregnant women in Michigan were iodine deficient (ironic considering that Michigan was where iodized salt first became available). In addition, as of 2015, iodine deficiency was on the rise in the American military. Other industrialized countries, particularly in Europe, have the same problem.

Iodine deficiency is most effectively reduced when boundaries between food and medication are relaxed, and its role as a commodity is de-emphasized – when it is treated as a national issue requiring public-sector action. This is not to advocate medicalized food, "wonder foods" that pack a full day's vitamins and minerals into a single processed bar, for instance, or eating a certain fruit or vegetable because it supposedly enhances brain functioning or calorie burning. Treating comestibles as tools for engineering a physiological effect (More energy! Better sleep! Stronger memory!) where there is no actual medical need such as iodine deficiency creates a medical problem where there is none. It also perpetuates the ideas of the body as a mechanism to be manipulated and health as a state to be restored. That does not mean that corporate and public interests cannot coincide. On the contrary, the initial success of iodized salt in the 1920s in the United States or India's recruitment in the 1980s of private salt companies to assist the government's iodization plants show that public health and financial gain can be arranged to work in concert, and not solely to produce citizens fit for war – "food for powder", as Shakespeare's Falstaff says.

Domestic medicine's view of health and treatment as

community concerns has also proved powerfully effective when applied in health crises. The development of treatments for HIV/AIDS in the 1980s and 1990s in the United States illustrates this point. Obeying both Francis Bacon's contention in 1605 that methods of inquiry have to be designed to nullify human biases, and the stricter regulations put in place after thalidomide in 1962, drug trial protocols at agencies around the world became thorough, cautious, and consequently lengthy. In the case of AIDS in the United States, those protocols put the development of treatments on a far slower schedule than the one imposed by the virus on the people it infected. Although researchers at the National Institute of Allergy and Infectious Diseases (NIAID), a division of the NIH, devised a new procedure for testing medications that they considered speedy, it did not seem so when compared with the virus's timetable. To infected people, most of whom were gay and all of whom were dying with appalling speed and in horrific numbers, these protocols were too removed from human concerns and far too slow. "When there were no treatments," Sarah Schulman wrote, "everyone was going to die." The AIDS Coalition To Unleash Power (ACT UP) began publicly and aggressively confronting the scientists (also the public and the federal government) with this charge. The research community initially replied with responses first drafted centuries earlier: only people with special training can understand this stuff, it is too hard for ordinary people, you are too emotionally invested, you are irrational, you cannot do science if you have something at stake in the results, leave it to the experts.

However, "Regulators must find a way to allow access to potentially life-extending therapies," an editorial in the *Lancet* stated in 2021, "while both scientific rigour and the safety of patients are maintained." Everything changed once the researchers and the activists began speaking to each other. Unlike thalidomide, AIDS medications were not approved without thorough testing, but access to experimental treatments expanded. One early, major development in the United States was NIAID's creation of a "parallel track program" that gave AIDS patients access to experimental drugs without having to be in a drug trial. It was a purely voluntary programme, and although there was no guarantee that the drug would work, there was also no chance of receiving a placebo. Unlike aducanumab (Aduhelm), medications for AIDS were approved at the recommendation of the review committees.

Furthermore, although ACT UP was predominantly white and male, its methods and "patient-centered politics, learned from feminism", as Schulman explained, "achieve[d] transformational victories that improve the lives of women, people of color, and poor people". Testing protocols became much more inclusive. HIV-positive people joined research programme supervisory committees. It turned out that the specialists with doctorates were not the only people who could understand retrovirals and science-y stuff. The many voices of those affected by AIDS also convinced officials to expand the definition of AIDS to include symptoms that women but not men experienced, such as acute pelvic inflammatory disease and constant yeast infections, thus recognizing the female body and its difference from the male body. Incorporating affected people into medical research, factoring in human issues such as the rate at which an illness hastens the patient towards death, and working with and within the community have become the norm in many areas of medical and scientific research, including at the FDA and the European Medicines Agency.

The *Lancet*'s editorial made a significant mistake, however, in drawing an analogy between the FDA with aducanumab

(Aduhelm) and the pressure from advocacy groups on Anthony Fauci, then Director of NIAID, to approve untested or under-tested treatments. "At the time," the editorial explains, "he *encouraged changes to the approval process* both to expedite approval and to allow greater patient participation in clinical trial design and approval. For aducanumab and other treatments, regulators must find a way *to allow access*" (added emphasis). Fauci and NIAID did not respond to external pressure by approving an insufficiently studied medication. Rather, Fauci agreed to include more stakeholders in the process, to make the process less opaque and less paternalistic.

A central element of domestic medicine, working with and within the community, has proven vital to other successes. The eradication of smallpox by 1980 would have been impossible without community involvement. The World Health Organization (WHO) launched its global campaign to eradicate smallpox in 1959, but it made almost no headway until 1967, when its approach changed from swooping in with orders and vaccines to partnering with the local community. While the WHO was failing, however, a number of countries and regions established their own, more successful smallpox eradication programmes, forming national, regional, and global webs of people (politicians, tribal leaders, medical professionals, international health officials, local health officials, people in every walk of life, the old, schoolchildren – everyone) working for the same goal.

The WHO has learned a lesson, however. For another scourge, river blindness, the organization now recommends that each country devise its own programme for eradicating it. River blindness, medically known as onchocerciasis, is produced by a parasite that causes skin disease, eye injury, and blindness. A number of countries working to eradicate it formed partnerships with the Carter Center, a non-profit organization founded by Nobel laureate and former US President Jimmy Carter and former first lady Roslyn Carter. Since 1997, one of the Carter Center's goals is the eradication of river blindness. Merck, which makes ivermectin (Mectizan), the medication that kills the parasites, has also joined the partnership: the company donates Mectizan to the Carter Center's programme. These partnerships between national ministries of health, the Carter Center, and Merck are based in the country where the disease is, and the local experts and community leaders take the lead. It is an extremely successful strategy. River blindness has been entirely eliminated in four countries, almost eliminated in two more, and its transmission has been interrupted in swathes of Africa.

"Local" or "community" can refer to national efforts or partnerships, but the term also applies to the very smallest community units. In Malawi, a programme to eradicate sleeping sickness uses theatre performances at community soccer fields and open spaces to teach people about it. The performance was developed collaboratively by parasitologists, epidemiologists, survivors, performing artists, and public health workers from Scotland and Malawi, and involves audience participation as a group. At the end of every performance, the energized, engaged audience has the opportunity to ask questions of the troupe, and very early data indicate that more people took the recommended precautions after the show than before it.

Bangladesh employs an army of women as local health officers (called "shasthya kormi") responsible for treating malaria, another parasitic disease. Everyone in the community knows the woman they can go to if they are sick, and she has the equipment to test for malaria; the training to use it, diagnose, and treat malaria; and the authority to distribute artemisinin, the medication. The programme is a tremendous success, but typical of science's emphasizing technology and medication and erasing women and the domestic, discussions and descriptions of the programme often overlook the significance of the shasthya kormi and emphasize the medication. According to one reporter, "Between 2008 and 2020, malaria cases in Bangladesh plummeted by 93%, thanks largely to this drug." Artemisinin obviously was vital to the precipitous drop in cases, but even miracle drugs cannot walk from the medicine cabinet to the patient on their own. That requires the trained, dedicated women who look after their communities, monitor illness, and possess the medical knowledge and respect to treat it.

Artemisinin is derived from a plant that ought to sound familiar to readers of Part One: wormwood. One species of wormwood, *Artemisia absinthium*, is indigenous to Europe, including Great Britain. That is the wormwood that James Douglas asked the laboratory on "Cheesewell" Street to analyse (see Chapter 6). Another species of wormwood, *Artemisia annua*, is indigenous to China and is the source of quinine. The earliest recorded appearance of wormwood in traditional Chinese materia medica is the fourth century CE, but the search for wormwood's active medicinal compound began in the 1960s in China and concluded with the identification of artemisinin in 1979. Artemisinin and its laboratory-modified versions have been the world's front-line treatment for malaria ever since, with scientists racing to manipulate the original medicinal compound to keep ahead of the development of artemisinin-resistant strains. Laboratory-synthesized versions of artemisinin are vital for another reason: the plant does not grow just anywhere, and a large amount of wormwood is needed to obtain a useful quantity of the compound.

Quinine and its offspring antimalarials constitute one

admittedly compelling example of ethnomedicine, a combination of anthropology and medicine that studies traditional medications in cultures around the world. In the case of quinine, researchers in China scoured their own medical tradition for possible malaria treatments. The term for this is "bioprospecting" and it includes analysing recipes from ancient herbals and materia medica chests in search of medicinal compounds. Scientific analysis and testing have established that traditional treatments such as thyme, saffron, yarrow, sage, and matalafi leaves, used in traditional Samoan medicine for inflammations, really do have the effect that different medicine traditions say they do, which makes these organics potential medicinal bases for pharmaceutical companies. As Seeseei Molimau-Samasoni's research team explained: "Compounds from natural resources are reliable lead templates of new pharmaceuticals, having persisted through evolutionary selection to control fundamental molecular pathways," and because "Medicinal plants in effect have been trialed for activity through centuries of ethnobotanical use [...] traditional medicines [are] an attractive yet challenging source for further investigation." In other words, plants are a great foundation for building curative molecular compounds, and medications used by local healers are a great starting place because they would not be in use if they did not have medicinal properties. Bioprospecting is not about proving that traditional medications work; it starts from that position, then uses scientific methods to identify the (hopefully) replicable or modifiable medicinal compound in the plant.

Bioprospecting is not new, and it goes hand in hand with what intellectual property rights advocates call "biopiracy": taking knowledge from local healers and turning it into a valuable commodity without sharing the profits. The Madagascar or rosy periwinkle, for example, produces two powerful anticancer chemicals, vinblastine and vincristine. Vinblastine's spectacular profitability is not shared with any of the several countries that credibly claim to have provided knowledge of the periwinkle's medicinal properties. It should be more difficult to commit biopiracy since 1992, when the Convention on Biological Diversity (CBD) was signed at the United Nations meeting in Brazil, although the CBD has no enforcement mechanism and is controversial in some quarters. Nevertheless, the global conversation around organic medications has become much more interested in collaboration and consortia to find natural materials and develop medicines from them. Without idealizing anyone or anything, some organizations, governments, and individuals seem to be finding ways to balance the drive for profit that commodified medication with other considerations: partnership, equality, fairness, sharing knowledge, even preserving resources for the future. For example, Molimau-Samasoni's team declared their principles in their published findings:

Working with traditional healers via an ethical, data sovereignty-driven collaboration led by indigenous Samoan researchers, we elucidate the chemical biology of the poorly understood but often-used Samoan traditional medicine "matalafi," the homogenate of *Psychotria insularum* leaves commonly used to treat inflammation-associated illnesses. Our approach unifies genomics, metabolomics, analytical biochemistry, immunology, and traditional knowledge to delineate the mode of action of the traditional medicine rather than by the more common reductionist approach of first purifying the bioactive principles, which can be used to better understand the ethnobotany of traditional medicine.

Developments in bioprospecting suggest that the values of domestic medicine can work effectively with modern science without imperilling anyone's profit or safety. It requires lateral relationships, sharing knowledge and skills, instead of vertical relationships, handing down orders and information.

Acknowledging the herbaceous origin of a medication – or of a huge number of medications – also takes the laboratory and chemistry off their pedestals. Biochemists and botanists are both necessary to pharmacological creation. Admitting partnerships changes the perception of science and medicine, as well as perceptions of the creation of a commodity, and of the roles of humans and of nature. If pharmaceutical companies were willing to admit which and how many of their pharmaceuticals began as a leaf, root, berry, or stem, for instance, their laboratories might have to share centre stage with nature. On the other hand, admitting how much they rely on what is growing out there would call attention to nature, and put a human as well as a financial value on conservation. Think of all the treatments and cures that will never happen if the moss or tree or flower or grass that they come from becomes extinct. Imagine what climate change – what just the Amazon rainforest – would look like if Big Pharma fully and publicly used its muscle to preserve and protect nature.

Put your finger on any nation on the map and the chances are good that some of its population is suffering, perhaps dying, because there is no money to get them the medication that they need. But modern medicine and modern science do not require the commodification of medication. It is a concept that was invented and introduced, and that eventually became the norm not because its invention or acceptance was inevitable, but because of the decisions and actions of people. For the same reason, medication as a commodity and the system that protects (and hides) its commodity status are not immutable. Overhaul, modify, or keep the medication system as is – those actions are all choices. Not doing anything is as much a decision as making change. Of course, whatever you do next, dear reader, is up to you, but whether you act to change or to preserve things as they are, you have made a decision (although not an irreversible one).

The period between 1650 and 1740 in Great Britain saw the replacement by the Scientific Revolution's adherents of an old system of values and treatments with new, "revolutionary" ones. Medication was redefined into a narrower category by its distinction from food, it was re-gendered into a masculine item and a masculine sphere, and it was transformed from a household item and a right into a commercial item and a commodity with limited access. Profit competed with compassion and care, and often triumphed, even when it meant other peoples' injury or death. In the centuries since, there have been some important changes: science's medications have become truly superior to whatever seventeenth-century women or apothecaries were making, and scientists have learned to modify and improve on the original curative elements in a medicinal substance. Moments of crisis have put pressure on the system built by the New Science's revolutionaries and have shown how domestic medicine's irrelevance has been greatly exaggerated. Recovering women in history, and in the history of medicine and science, also recovers values and practices that once upon a time served humanity well.

Bibliography

Of her book *The Restless Republic*, historian Anna Keay wrote that "Nothing would make its author happier than that it inspires the reader to search out other books on this period." The same goes for the author of this book, with the added desideratum that the reader should also be inspired to seek out primary materials from the period. Accordingly, this bibliography is divided into several sections: digital collections available to the general public, framework texts that shaped the entire project, and chapter bibliographies of materials specific to that topic.

DIGITAL COLLECTIONS

There is a wealth of digitized materials on the history of science and the history of medicine. Much of it can be viewed with only an Internet connection. The most famous libraries, such as the British Library and the Library of Congress, have digitized many different collections, as have a number of academic institutions such as the University of Cambridge, the University of Oxford, and Yale University. Specialized libraries, such as the Wellcome Collection, the National Library of Medicine (United States), the New York Academy of Medicine, and the Dibner Library of the History of Science and Technology of the Smithsonian Libraries and Archives have particularly extensive digital collections, as do the libraries at institutions such as the Royal College of Physicians and the Royal Society.

Many libraries also have research databases containing scanned or digitized printed materials, such as Early English Books Online, Eighteenth-Century Collections Online, and the Seventeenth and Eighteenth Century Burney Newspapers Collection. The *Oxford Dictionary of National Biography* is invaluable; I have used it for biographical information throughout my research. However, access to these databases can be restricted to library card holders. Fortunately, there are a number of open-access databases. Of note are Munk's Roll, a list of Fellows of the RCP since its inception, on the RCP website; the Hartlib Papers at the University of Sheffield; the Early Modern Practitioners project at the University of Exeter; and British History Online.

This category includes resources that I used throughout *The Apothecary's Wife*, not only for specific points of information or insight but also to deepen and broaden my understanding of the many aspects of this subject. Accordingly, they will not be listed in chapter bibliographies.

Despite the plenitude of digitized materials, the vast majority of seventeenth-century and eighteenth-century manuscripts and rare books exist only in material form and must be visited in person. In many places, especially county record offices, permission to see rare books and manuscripts comes with membership. The most important sites for *The Apothecary's Wife* have been the British Library, particularly for the Sloane Manuscripts, Brockman Papers, Blenheim Papers, and Miscellaneous Papers relating to the Twysden family; Chawton House Library; the London Metropolitan Archives; the Royal College of Physicians heritage library and archives; the Royal Society; the Society of Antiquaries; Lambeth Palace Library for the Fairhurst Papers, Shrewsbury letters, and Miscellaneous Papers of John Selden and Sir Matthew Hale; the University of Aberdeen's Special Collections; the University of Glasgow's Hunterian Collection; and the Wellcome Collection. I am also indebted to the Devon Record Office, the Sheffield City Archives for the Arundel Castle Manuscripts, the Bedfordshire Record Office, the Warwickshire Record Office, and the Wiltshire and Swindon Record Office for access to their holdings.

It should not surprise anyone to read here that many histories of science and histories of medicine are deficient – to be kind – when it comes to gender, race, ethnicity, class, and imperialism. Fortunately, that situation is changing at the academic level and more slowly for general audiences. (Even books that proclaim their even-handedness manage to disappoint; their index – non-fiction's X-ray – gives them away.) Jack Turner's witty, highly readable *Spice: The History of a Temptation* (2004) is a good starting place. A similar problem attends the history of medical professions in the British Isles. For a long time, histories of apothecaries and physicians were not only all male but also focused on London. These works are useful for getting a sense of chronology, events, and people, and they have informed this book throughout. Penelope Hunting's *A History of the Society of Apothecaries* (1998) is the most recent, concise, and reliable account. I recommend anything by her, actually. Hunting's study was preceded by E. Ashworth Underwood et al., *A History of the Worshipful Society of Apothecaries*, vol. I, 1617–1815 (1963) and W.S.C. Copeman, *The Worshipful Society of Apothecaries of London: A History, 1617-1967* (1967), which are products of their time. Shorter works that focus on the origins of the apothecary include Juanita G.L. Burnby, "The Apothecary as Progenitor", *Medical History* 27, n. S3 (1983), pp. 24–61; John A. Hunt, "The Evolution of Pharmacy in Britain (1428–1913)", *Pharmacy in History* 48, n. 1 (2006), pp. 35–40; Penelope J. Corfield's invaluable "From Poison Peddlers to Civic Worthies: The Reputation of the Apothecaries in Georgian England", *Social History of Medicine* 22, n. 1 (2009), pp. 1–21, and C.J.S. Thompson, "The Apothecary in England from the Thirteenth to the Close of the Sixteenth Century", *The History of Medicine* 8 (1915), pp. 36–44 (old but still useful). The most recent history of London physicians is *500 Years of the Royal College of Physicians*, edited by Linda Luxon and Simon Shorvon (2018). Their work follows the path laid down by George Clark's two-volume *History of the Royal College of Physicians of London* (1964).

For information about practitioners outside London during the seventeenth century and eighteenth century, read almost anything written by Margaret Pelling, such as "Barber-Surgeons' Guilds and Ordinances in Early Modern British Towns – the Story so Far", Working Paper n. 1, *Early Modern Practitioners Working Papers*. Additional informative publications are Alun Withey's "'Persons That Live Remote from London': Apothecaries and the Medical Marketplace in Seventeenth- and Eighteenth-Century Wales", *Bulletin of the History of Medicine* 85, n. 2 (2011); David Harley's "'Bred up in the Study of that Faculty': Licensed

Physicians in North-West England, 1660–1760", *Medical History* 38 (1994), pp. 398–420; Steven King and Alan Weaver, "Lives in many Hands: The Medical Landscape in Lancashire, 1700–1820", *Medical History* 45 (2000), pp. 173–200; and G.H. "Apothecaries in Early Modern Edinburgh", *Pharmacy in History* 37, n. 3 (1995), pp. 135–36.

Fortunately, an efflorescence of research in history, its subfields, and in literature is returning women to the historical record. Early groundbreaking works – *The Mind Has No Sex? Women in the Origins of Modern Science* (1989) and *Nature's Body: Gender in the Making of Modern Science* (1993) by Londa Schiebinger; *Women, Science and Medicine 1500–1700*, edited by Lynette Hunter and Sarah Hutton (1997); and *Men, Women, and the Birthing of Modern Science*, edited by Judith P. Zinsser (2005) – opened the field significantly. Elizabeth Potter's demonstration in *Gender and Boyle's Law of Gases* (2001) that definitions of masculinity were integrated into emerging science laid the foundation for works such as Elinor Cleghorn's *Unwell Women: Misdiagnosis and Myth in a Man-Made World* (2022), Anushay Hossain's *The Pain Gap* (2022), and Caroline Criado Perez's *Invisible Women: Data Bias in a World Designed for Men* (2021). Sheilagh Ogilvie's comprehensive *The European Guilds: An Economic Analysis* (2021) uncovers the reality of women in guilds. In addition to those mentioned in this part of the Bibliography, a few notable books include Lyn Bennet, *Rhetoric, Medicine, and the Woman Writer 1600–1700* (2018); *Inventing Maternity: Politics, Science, and Literature, 1650–1865*, edited by Susan C. Greenfield and Carol Barash (2015); *Women Philosophers from the Renaissance to the Enlightenment: New Studies*, edited by Ruth Habensgruber and Sarah Hutton (2021); *The New Science and Women's Literary Discourse: Prefiguring Frankenstein*, edited by Judy A. Hayden (2011); and my own explanation of how the Scientific Revolution and the invention of the novel fed each other, *Women, the Novel, and Natural Philosophy, 1660–1727* (2014).

The figure of the heroic individual appears frequently in histories, vide biography's popularity. There are stand-alone tomes on any number of science's revolutionaries, such as Hans Sloane (James Delburgo, *Collecting the World: Hans Sloane and the Origins of the British Museum* [2017]), Robert Hooke (Lisa Jardine, *Robert Hooke: The Curious Life of the Man Who Measured London* [2004]), and Nicholas Culpeper (Benjamin Woolley, *Heal Thyself: Nicholas Culpeper and the Seventeenth-Century Struggle to Bring Medicine to the People* [2004]). Readers interested in Vesalius and Paracelsus can find illuminating introductions in Stanley Finger's *Minds Behind the Brain: A History of the Pioneers and Their Discoveries* (2000); Joseph F. Borzelleca, "Paracelsus: Herald of Modern Toxicology", *Toxicological Sciences* 53 (2000), pp. 2–4; and Steven A. Edwards, "Paracelsus, the Man Who Brought Chemistry to Medicine", *American Association for the Advancement of Science* online (2012). The contrast between men and women in this regard is striking. For example, the most recent biography of Lady Mary Wortley Montagu, who brought inoculation to Europe from the Ottoman empire, persuaded the British medical community and the royal family of its efficacy, and consequently saved tens of thousands, probably hundreds of thousands of lives, came out in 2021 (*The Pioneering Life of Lady Mary Wortley Montagu* by Jo Willett); before that, there was Isobel Grundy's biography of her in 2004. In contrast, biographies of Edward Jenner, who created vaccination eighty years later, were published in 2020, 2022, and 2023. On the whole, there have been very few book-length biographies of seventeenth-century and eighteenth-century women involved in the Scientific Revolution between 1998, when Anna Battigelli published *Margaret Cavendish and the Exiles of the Mind*, and 2021, when Michelle DiMeo published her biography of Katherine Jones, Lady Ranelagh.

There are several texts that I recommend for getting a sense of what seventeenth-century and eighteenth-century life was like. To understand the buying power of money during the period, readers can rely on Robert Hume's article, "The Value of Money in Eighteenth-Century England: Incomes, Prices, Buying Power – and Some Problems in Cultural

Economics", *Huntington Library Quarterly* 77 n. 4 (2015), pp. 373–416. *London: Prints and Drawings before 1800* by Bernard Nurse (2017) is dazzling, with beautiful reproductions of some of the best maps of the seventeenth and eighteenth centuries, right down to the garden plots behind houses. David Cressy's *Birth, Marriage, and Death: Ritual, Religion, and the Life-Cycle in Tudor and Stuart England* (1997) is still one of the best accounts of lived life during that time. Sara Read's *Menstruation and the Female Body in Early Modern England* (2013) and Sarah Fox's *Giving Birth in Eighteenth-Century England* (2022) offer valuable insight into women's bodily experiences. *Coffers, Clysters, Comfrey and Coifs: The Lives of Our Seventeenth Century Ancestors* by Janet Few (2012) recounts daily life through the common objects that people used; it is very readable and informative, and not overly scholarly. *The Country House Kitchen, 1650–1900*, edited by Pamela A. Sambrook and Peter Brears (1996) takes the audience on a room-by-room tour of the development of domestic space dedicated to the procurement and processing of medication and foodstuffs. *Family and Business During the Industrial Revolution* by Hannah Barker (2017) provides a different perspective on daily life for women, men, and children. For recipe books, readers might begin with *Reading and Writing Recipe Books, 1550–1800*, edited by Michelle DiMeo and Sara Pennell (2013); *Recipes and Everyday Knowledge: Medicine, Science, and the Household in Early Modern England* by Elaine Leong (2018); and *Recipes for Thought: Knowledge and Taste in the Early Modern English Kitchen* by Wendy Wall (2016). Kristine Kowalchuk's edition *Preserving on Paper: Seventeenth-Century Englishwomen's Receipt Books* (2017) is an excellent place to begin reading the books themselves before tackling the convolutions of seventeenth-century handwriting in digitized manuscripts.

Where a specific item is significant to the chapter, I have identified it in the chapter bibliography. Otherwise, readers should consult the following collections.

I examined recipe books held by the following institutions:
  The British Library
  Chawton House Library
  The Folger Shakespeare Library
  The Harley Foundation
  National Library of Medicine (US)
  New York Academy of Medicine
  The Open Library
  Royal College of Physicians
  Society of Antiquaries, London
  Stanford University
  University of Aberdeen
  University of Glasgow
  University of Pennsylvania
  Warwickshire Record Office
  Wellcome Library

I examined non-recipe book materials at the following institutions:
  Bedfordshire Archives and Records Service
  Bodleian Library, University of Oxford
  Bristol Archives
  Chelsea Physic Garden
  Devon Record Office, Wolborough Feoffees and Widows' Charity
    Papers
  Hammersmith and Fulham Local Archives
  Lambeth Palace Library, including Fairhurst Papers, Miscellaneous
    Papers of John Selden and Sir Matthew Hale
  London Metropolitan Archives, including Sutton's Hospital/
    Charterhouse papers, Diocese of London Papers, St Paul's
    Cathedral, Dean and Chapter papers

Sheffield City Archives, including Duke of Norfolk's Estate, Arundel
  (Arundel Castle Records)
Society of Antiquaries, London
The British Library Western Manuscripts, including the Sloane
  Collection
The Royal College of Physicians
The Royal Society
University of Aberdeen Special Collections
University of Cambridge libraries
University of Glasgow Special Collections, including the Hunterian
  Collection
Wadham College, University of Oxford
Warwickshire County Record Office, including the Waller Family of
  Woodcote Papers, the Warwick Borough Council Papers, Warwick
  Craft Guilds and Mysteries Papers
Wellcome Library
Wiltshire and Swindon Record Office, Yerbury Almshouses Papers

CHAPTER BIBLIOGRAPHIES

Introduction

Secondary Sources

Linda Alcoff and Elizabeth Potter, "Introduction: When Feminisms Intersect Epistemology", in Linda Alcoff and Elizabeth Potter (eds), *Feminist Epistemologies* (Routledge, 1993), pp. 1–14.

Anne Barrett, "Where Are the Women? How Archives Can Reveal Hidden Women in Science", in Claire G. Jones, Alison E. Martin, and Alexis Wolf (eds), *The Palgrave Handbook of Women in Science since 1600* (Palgrave, 2022), pp. 129–47.

Claire G. Jones, Alison E. Martin, and Alexis Wolf, "Women in the History of Science: Frameworks, Themes, and Contested Perspectives", in Claire G. Jones, Alison E. Martin, and Alexis Wolf (eds), *The Palgrave Handbook of Women in Science since 1600* (Palgrave, 2022), pp. 3–24.

Primary Sources

John James Audubon, *The Birds of America* (London, 1827–1838).

Elizabeth Blackwell, *A Curious Herbal Containing Five Hundred Cuts of the Most Useful Plants Which Are Now Used in the Practice of Physick*, vols I and II (London, 1737/1739).

Maria Sibylla Merian, *Metamorphosis Insectorum Surinamensium* (Amsterdam, 1705).

PART ONE
1. Kitchen Physic Is the Best Physic

Secondary Sources

Edward Bever, "Witchcraft, female aggression, and power in the early modern community", *Journal of Social History* 35, n. 4 (2002), pp. 955–88.

Deborah Coltham, *"Ladies in the Laboratory": A Chronological List of Books by, or Relating to Women in Medicine and Science*, Recent Acquisitions Five (Deborah Coltham Rare Books, 2009).

Allen G. Dubus, "Chemists, physicians, and changing perspectives on the scientific revolution", *Isis* 89, n. 1 (1998), pp. 61–81.

Peter Elmer, *Witchcraft, Witch-Hunting, and Politics in Early Modern England* (Oxford University Press, 2016).

Gerry Greenstone, "The history of bloodletting", *British Columbia Medical Journal* 52, n. 1 (2010), pp. 12–14.

Anna Keay, *The Restless Republic: Britain without a Crown* (HarperCollins, 2021).

Molly McClain, "The Duke of Beaufort's Tory Progress through Wales, 1684", *Cylchgrawn Hanes Cymru/Welsh History Review* 18, n. 4 (1997), pp. 593–620.

Steven Shapin and Simon Shaffer, *Leviathan and the Air Pump: Hobbes, Boyle, and the Experimental Life. Including a Translation of Thomas Hobbes, Dialogus Physicus de Natura Aeris, by Simon Shaffer* (Princeton University Press, 1985).

Patrick Wallis, "Plagues, morality and the place of medicine in early modern England", *English Historical Review* 121, n. 490 (2006), pp. 1–24.

A.S. Weber, "Women's early modern medical almanacs in historical context", *English Literary Renaissance* 33, n. 3 (2003), pp. 358–402.

Christopher J.M. Whitty, "British Books and Books Published in English Related to Medicine, 1475–1640: A Handlist of Identified Works", *The Medical World of Early Modern England, Wales and Ireland, 1500–1715*, Working Paper No. 3.

Primary Sources

Anon., *The Accomplish'd Ladies Rich Closet of Rarities* (London, 1687).

Francis Bacon, *Novum Organum (1620)*, Joseph Devey (ed.) (P. F. Collier, 1902).

Francis Bacon, *The Great Instauration in The Advancement of Learning (1605)*, Joseph Devey (ed.) (P. F. Collier, 1910).

[Eleazar] Duncan, *Wholesome Advice Against the Abuse of Hot Liquors* (London, 1706).

John Fothergill, *Lectures on the Materia Medica*, vol. II [only] (Wellcome Library/London, before 1754).

Robert Green, *A Quip Upon the Courtier* (London, 1592).

William Harvey, *Exercitatio Anatomica de Motu Cordis et Sanguinis in Animalibus (On the Motion of the Heart and Blood in Animals)* (London, 1628).

I.M., *A Proper New Booke of Cookery* (London, 1575).

William Lawson, *A New Orchard and Garden with The Country Housewifes Garden (1618)*, a facsimile edition with an introduction by Malcolm Thick (Prospect Books, 2003).

Mary Trye, *Medicatrix, Or The Woman-Physician* (London, 1675).

Andreas Vesalius, *De humani corporis fabrica libri septem* (Basel, 1543).

Christopher Wirtzung, *The General Practise of Physicke* (London, 1605).

2. The Countess of Kent's Recipe Book

Secondary Sources

A.D. Boney, *The Lost Gardens of Glasgow University* (Christopher Helm, 1988).

James Fitzmaurice, "Jane Barker and the tree of knowledge at Cambridge University", *Renaissance Forum* 3, n. 1 (1998), unpaginated.

Antonia Fraser, *The Wives of Henry VIII* (Alfred A. Knopf, 1993).

Patricia Higgins, "Grey, Elizabeth, Countess of Kent (1581–1651)", in Cathy Hartley (ed.), *A Historical Dictionary of British Women* (Routledge, 2003), p. 194.

Lynette Hunter, "Women and Domestic Medicine: Lady Experimenters, 1570–1620", in Lynette Hunter and Sarah Hutton (eds), *Women, Science and Medicine 1500–1700* (Sutton, 1997), pp. 89–107.

Lynette Hunter, "Women and Science in the Sixteenth and Seventeenth Centuries", in Judith P. Zinsser (ed.), *Men, Women, and the Birthing of Modern Science* (Northern Illinois University Press, 2005), pp. 123–40.

Peter Lely, *John Selden (1584–1654)*, *c.* 1644. Oil on canvas, 28 × 24 inches (71.12 × 60.96 cm). Yale University Art Gallery. See also https://

artgallery.yale.edu/collections/objects/47608; accessed 1 Jan. 2021.

Molly McClain, "The Duke of Beaufort's Tory Progress through Wales, 1684", *Cylchgrawn Hanes Cymru/Welsh History Review* 4 (1997), pp. 593–620.

Jennifer Rabe, "Mediating between Art and Nature: The Countess of Arundel at Tart Hall", in Susanna Burghartz, Lucas Burkart, and Christine Gottler (eds), *Sites of Mediation: Connected Histories of Places, Processes, and Objects in Europe and Beyond, 1450–1650* (Brill, 2007), pp. 183–210.

Betty Travitsky and Anne Lake Prescott, *Seventeenth-Century English Recipe Books: Cooking, Physic and Chirurgery in the Works of W.M. and Queen Henrietta Maria, and of Mary Tillinghast* (Routledge, 2008).

Paul Van Somer, *Lady Elizabeth Grey, Countess of Kent. c.* 1619. Oil paint on wood, 1,143 × 819 mm. Tate Gallery.

Wendy Wall, "Literacy and the domestic arts", *Huntington Library Quarterly* 73, n. 3 (2010), pp. 383–412.

Primary Sources

Anon., *The Good Huswife's Handmaide for the Kitchin* (London, 1594).

Anon., *The Widowe's Treasure* (London, 1588).

Anon., *The Ladies Dictionary* (London, 1694).

Thomas Brugis, *The Marrow of Physicke* (London, 1648).

William Bullein, *Bulleins Bulwarke of Defence Against all Sicknesse, Soarenesse, and Woundes that Doe Dayly Assaulte Mankinde* (London, 1562).

Elizabeth Grey, Countess of Kent (attr.), *A Choice Manual of Rare and Select Secrets in Physick and Chryrurgery* (London, 1653).

Henrietta Maria of France (attr.), *The Queen's Closet Opened* (London, 1655).

Alethea Howard, Countess of Arundel and Lennox (attr.), *Natura Exenterata* (London, 1655).

L.M., *Prepositas His Practice* (London, 1588).

Queen Henrietta Maria (attr.), *The Queen's Closet Opened* (London, 1655).

Gervase Markham, *The English Hous-Wife, Containing The inward and outward Vertues which ought to be in a compleat Woman* (London, 1656).

Robert May, *The Accomplish'd Cook* (London, 1660).

Thomas Newton, *Approv'd Medicines and Cordial Receipts* (London, 1580).

Andrewe Plowden, "A Book of Surgerie and Phisick of Mistress Honorie Henslow", Manuscripts, 1601, http://WDAgo.com/s/791cf81b. Wiley Digital Archives: The Royal College of Physicians; accessed 1 Oct. 2021.

Jane Sharp, *The Midwives Book* (London, 1671).

John Smith, *England's Improvement Reviv'd: Digested into Six Books* (London, 1670).

Salvator Winter and Francisco Dickinson, *A Pretious Treasury* (London, 1649).

Hannah Woolley, *The Ladies Directory, in Choice Experiments & Curiosities of Preserving in Jellies, and Candying Both Fruits & Flowers* (London, 1662).

Owen Wood, *An Alphabetical Book of Physicall Secrets* (London, 1639).

3. Chicken Soup and Viper Wine

Secondary Sources

Rotimi Adigun, Hajira Basit, and John Murray, "Cell Liquefactive Necrosis", *StatPearls* (20 Aug. 2021).

Nick Bailey, *The Chelsea Physic Garden* (Chelsea Physic Garden, 2015).

E.W. Bligh, *Sir Kenelm Digby and His Venetia* (S. Low, Marston & Co., 1932).

Rose Bradley, *The English Housewife in the Seventeenth & Eighteenth Centuries* (E. Arnold, 1912).

J. Burnby, "Some early London physic gardens", *Pharmaceutical Historian* 24, n. 4 (1994), pp. 2–8.

Cambridge University Botanic Garden, University of Cambridge Museums and Botanic Garden, *History of the Garden, 1762–Present*. See also www.botanic.cam.ac.uk; accessed 21 Mar. 2020.

Julie Davis, "Botanizing at Badminton House: The Botanical Pursuits of Mary Somerset, First Duchess of Beaufort", in Donald L. Opitz, Staffan Bergwik, and Birgitte Van Tiggelen (eds), *Domesticity in the Making of Modern Science* (Palgrave Macmillan, 2016), pp. 19–40.

Margaret DeLacy, *The Germ of an Idea: Contagionism, Religion, and Society in Britain 1616–1730* (Palgrave Macmillan, 2016).

B.J. Dobbs, "Studies in the natural philosophy of Sir Kenelm Digby", parts I–IV, *Ambix* 20 (1973–1974), pp. 143–63.

Mordechai Feingold, *The Mathematicians' Apprenticeship: Science, Universities and Society in England, 1560-1640* (Cambridge University Press, 1984).

Michael Foster, "Digby, Sir Kenelm (1603–1665)", in *Oxford Dictionary of National Biography Online*, Oxford, 2009, https://doi.org/10.1093/ref:odnb/7629; accessed 21 Dec. 2021.

John F. Fulton, *Sir Kenelm Digby: Writer, Bibliophile and Protagonist of William Harvey* (Peter & Katherine Oliver, 1937).

Eric Griffin, "Copying 'the Anti-Spaniard': Post-Armada Hispanophobia and English Renaissance Drama", in Barbara Fuchs and Emily Weissbourd (eds), *Representing Imperial Rivalry in the Early Modern Mediterranean* (University of Toronto Press, 2015), pp. 191–216.

Lynette Hunter, "Women and Domestic Medicine: Lady Experimenters, 1570–1620", in Lynette Hunter and Sarah Hutton (eds), *Women, Science and Medicine 1500–1700* (Sutton, 1997), pp. 89–107.

Lynette Hunter, "Women and Science in the Sixteenth and Seventeenth Centuries", in Judith P. Zinsser (ed.) *Men, Women, and the Birthing of Modern Science* (Northern Illinois University Press, 2005), pp. 123–40.

Jardí Botànic de la Universitat de València, Botanic Gardens Conservation International, "History". See also https://www.jardibotanic.org/?apid=historia; accessed 21 Mar. 2020.

Molly McClain, *Beaufort: The Duke and his Duchess 1657–1715* (Yale University Press, 2001).

Sam A. Mellick, "Sir Kenelm Digby (1603–1665): diplomat, entrepreneur, privateer, duellist, scientist and philosopher", *ANZ Journal of Surgery* 81 (2011), pp. 911–14.

Wyndham Miles, "Sir Kenelm Digby, Alchemist, Scholar, Courtier, and

Man of Adventure", *Chymia* 2 (1949), pp. 119–28.

Sue Minter, *The Apothecaries' Garden: A History of the Chelsea Physic Garden* (Sutton, 2000).

Joe Moshenska, *A Stain in the Blood: The Remarkable Voyage of Sir Kenelm Digby* (Windmill, 2016).

John Parker, "The development of the Cambridge University botanic garden", *Curtis's Botanical Magazine* 23, n. 1 (2006), pp. 4–19.

Jennifer Rabe, "Mediating between Art and Nature: The Countess of Arundel at Tart Hall", in Susanna Burghartz, Lucas Burkart, and Christine Gottler (eds), *Sites of Mediation: Connected Histories of Places, Processes, and Objects in Europe and Beyond, 1450–1650* (Brill, 2007), pp. 183–210.

Royal College of Physicians of Edinburgh, "The Surgeons' Curriehill House – From Plants to Body-snatchers". See also www.rcpe.ac.uk/heritage/surgeons-curriehill-house-plants-body-snatchers; accessed 21 Mar. 2021.

Rachel Savage, "The herbal tradition and its influence on women's role in garden-making, 1600–1900", *Garden History* 46, n. 1 (2018), pp. 57–73.

Ann Shteir, *Cultivating Women, Cultivating Science: Flora's Daughters and Botany in England* (The Johns Hopkins University Press, 1996).

Anna Simmons, "Medicines, monopolies and mortars: the chemical laboratory and pharmaceutical trade at the Society of Apothecaries in the eighteenth century", *Ambix* 53, n. 3 (2006), pp. 221–36.

Helen Smith, "Eggs, Cheese, and (Francis) Bacon", in Barbara Fuchs and Emily Weissbourd (eds), *Representing Imperial Rivalry in the Early Modern Mediterranean* (University of Toronto Press, 2015), pp. 140–66.

Richard Sugg, *Mummies, Cannibals, and Vampires: The History of Corpse Medicine from the Renaissance to the Victorians* (Routledge, 2011).

Elaine Tierney, "'Dirty rotten sheds': exploring the ephemeral city in early modern London", *Eighteenth-Century Studies* 50, n. 2 (2017), pp. 231–52.

Katherine Tyrrell, "Botanic and Physic Gardens of the Past in London".

Botanical Art & Artists. See also www.botanicalartandartists.com; accessed 20 Mar. 2021.

University of Arizona Health Sciences, "Brain Liquefaction After Stroke is Toxic to Surviving Brain", *ScienceDaily* (20 Feb. 2018).

University of Glasgow, "A Significant Medical History: 18th Century". See also https://www.gla.ac.uk/schools/medicine/mus/ourfacilities/history/; accessed 19 July 2019.

Simon Werrett, *Thrifty Science: Making the Most of Materials in the History of Experiment* (University of Chicago Press, 2019).

Margaret Willes, *The Making of the English Gardener: Plants, Books and Inspiration, 1560–1660* (Yale University Press, 2011).

Margaret Willes, *The Domestic Herbal: Plants for the Home in the Seventeenth Century* (Bodleian Library Publishing, 2020).

Andrea Wulf, *The Brother Gardeners: Botany, Empire and the Birth of an Obsession* (Alfred A. Knopf, 2008).

Primary Sources
By or attributed to Kenelm Digby in chronological order:

A Discourse Concerning the Vegetation of Plants Spoken by Sir Kenelm Digby at Gresham College, on the 23 of January 1660 (London, 1661).

Choice and Experimented Receipts in Physic and Chirurgery, as also Cordial and Distilled Waters and Spirits, Perfumes, and other Curiosities, Collected by the Honourable and truly Learned Sir Kenelm Digby, Kt (London, 1668).

The Closet of Sir Kenelm Digby Kt Opened: Whereby is Discovered Several ways for making of Metheglin, Sider, Cherry-Wine, etc. Together with Excellent Directions for Cookery: As also for Preserving, Conserving, Candying, etc (London, 1669).

Two Treatises, By the Honourable and truly Learned Sir Kenelm Digby Knight. The one, Of Choice and Experimented Receipts in Physic and Chirurgery; as also Cordial and Distilled Waters and Spirits, Perfumes, and other Curiosities. The other, Of Cookery, With several ways for Making of Metheglin, Sider, Cherry-Wine, etc. Together with Excellent Directions for Preserving, Conserving, Candying, etc (London, 1669).

Choice and Experimented Receipts in Physic and Chirurgery... (London, 1675).

A Choice Collections of Rare Secrets and Experiments in Philosophy, as also Rare and unheard-of Medicines, Menstruums, and Alkahests; with the True Secret of Volatilizing the fixt Salt of Tartar. Collected And Experimented by the Honourable and truly Learned Sir Kenelm Digby, Kt (London, 1682).

Chymical Secrets and Rare Experiments in Philosophy (London, 1683).

By others, in alphabetical order:

Anon., *The Ladies Cabinet Opened, Wherein is Found Hidden Several Experiments in Preserving and Conserving, Physick, and Surgery, Cookery, and Huswifery* (London, 1639).

John Aubrey, in Kate Bennett (ed.) *John Aubrey: Brief Lives with An Apparatus for the Lives of our English Mathematical Writers*, vols I (text) and II (commentary) (Oxford, 2016).

Philip Bellon, *The Potable Balsome of Life* (London, 1675).

Elizabeth Blackwell, *A Curious Herbal Containing Five Hundred Cuts of the Most Useful Plants Which Are Now Used in the Practice of Physick*, vols I and II (London, 1737/1739).

Robert Boyle, *Work diaries* (Royal College of Physicians/London).

Henry Bracken, *The Midwife's Companion* (London, 1737).

Richard Bradley, *New Improvements of Planting and Gardening* (London, 1716).

Charles Carter, *The Compleat City and Country Cook: or, Accomplish'd Housewife* (London, 1732).

Nicholas de Bonnefons, *Le Jardinier François* (Paris, 1651).

John Donne, "Sermon X. Preached upon Candlemas Day", in *LXXX sermons preached by that learned and reverend divine, John Donne, Dr in Divinity, late Deane of the cathedrall church of S. Pauls London* (London, 1640).

William Dover, *Useful Miscellanies* (London, 1739).

Charles Evelyn, *The Art of Gardening, Improv'd* (London, 1717).

John Evelyn (trans.), *The French Gardiner* (London, 1658).

F.B., *The Office of the Good House-wife, With Necessary Directions for the Ordering of her Family and Dairy* (London, 1672).

Thomas Fuller, *A Pisgah-sight of Palestine* (London, 1650).

Sarah Harrison, *The House-keeper's Pocket-Book And Compleat Family Cook* (London, 1739).

Alethea Howard, Countess of Arundel and Lennox (attr.), *Natura Extenterata* (London, 1655).

John Jones, *Adrasta: Or, The Womans Spleene, And Loves Conquest* (London, 1635).

Batty Langley, *New Principles of Gardening*, 2nd edn (London, 1739).

Christopher Langton, *An Introduction into Phisycke, with an Universal Dyet* (London, 1545).

William Lawson, *A New Orchard and Garden with The Country Housewifes Garden (1618)*, a facsimile edition with an introduction by Malcolm Thick (Prospect Books, 2003).

Matthew Mackaile, *Macis macerata: or, a Short Treatise, Concerning the use of mace, in meat, or drink, and medicine* (Aberdeen, 1677).

Robert May, *The Accomplish'd Cook* (London, 1660).

John Middleton, *Five Hundred New Receipts in Cookery, Confectionary, Pastry, Preserving, Conserving, Pickling, and The Several Branches of These Arts Necessary To Be Known By All Good Housewives* (London, 1734).

James Millerd, *An Exact Delineation of the Famous Citty of Bristoll and Suburbs* (Bristol, 1673).

Thomas Newton, *Approv'd Medicines and Cordial Receipts* (London, 1580).

Thomas Newton, *The Olde Mans Dietarie* (London, 1586).

John Nott, *The Cook's and Confectioner's Dictionary* (London, 1723).

T.P. (Hannah Woolley attr.), *The Accomplish't-Ladys Delight in Preserving, Physick, Beautifying, and Cookery* (London, 1675).

Dorothy Partridge, *Woman's Almanack for the Year 1694* (London, 1694).

John Partridge, *The Treasurie of Commodious Conceits, & Hidden Secrets* (London, 1573).

John Partridge, *The Widowes Treasure, Plentifully Furnished with Secretes in Phisicke* (London, 1586).

Richard Poulteney, *Historical and Biographical Sketches of the Progress of Botany in England* (London, 1790).

Francis Quarles, "Meditation 10", in *Divine Poems* (London, 1633).

Alexander Read, *The Chirurgicall Lectures of Tumors and Ulcers* (London, 1635).

William Salmon, *Iatrica: Seu Praxis Medendi. The Practice of Curing* (London, 1681).

John Smith, *England's Improvement Reviv'd* (London, 1670).

Henry Stevenson, *The Young Gardener's Director* (London, 1716).

Stephen Switzer, *The Practical Kitchen Gardiner* (London, 1727).

Thomas Tryon, *The Good Housewife made a Doctor* (London, 1692).

Thomas Tryon, *A Pocket-Companion* (London, 1693).

Tobias Whittaker, *The Tree of Humane Life, or, The Bloud of the Grape* (London, 1634).

Thomas Willis, *Pharmaceutice rationalis: or, An Exercitation of the Operations of Medicines in Humane* (London, 1678).

4. Proscriptions, Prescriptions, and Poetry

Secondary Sources

Katherine Allen, "Recipe collections and the realities of fashionable diseases in eighteenth-century elite domestic medicine", *Literature and Medicine* 35, n. 2 (2017), pp. 334–54.

Jonathan Barry, "The 'compleat physician' and experimentation in medicines: Everard Maynwaring (*c.* 1629–1713) and the Restoration Debate on Medical Practice in London", *Medical History* 62, n. 2 (2018), pp. 155–76.

Sarah Birt, "Women, guilds and the tailoring trades: the occupational training of Merchant Taylors' company apprentices in early modern London", *London Journal* (2020), pp. 1–19.

Isabelle Clairhout, "Erring from good huswifry? The author as witness in Margaret Cavendish and Mary Trye", *Renaissance and Reformation/ Renaissance et Réforme* 37, n. 2 (2014), pp. 81–114.

Harold J. Cook, "The Society of Chemical Physicians, the New Philosophy, and the Restoration Court", *Bulletin of the History of Medicine* 61, n. 1 (1987), pp. 61–77.

James Fitzmaurice, "Jane Barker and the tree of knowledge at Cambridge University", *Renaissance Forum* 3, n. 1 (1998), unpaginated.

James Fitzmaurice, "Daring and innocence in the poetry of Elizabeth Rochester and Jane Barker", *In-Between: Essays & Studies in Literary Criticism* 11, n. 1 (2002), pp. 25–43.

Elizabeth Lane Furdell, *The Royal Doctors, 1485–1714: Medical Personnel at the Tudor and Stuart Courts* (Boydell & Brewer, 2001).

Karen Bloom Gevirtz, "Philosophy and/in Verse: Jane Barker's 'Farewell to Poetry' and the Anatomy of Emotion", in Robin Runia (ed.), *The Future of Feminist Eighteenth-Century Scholarship: Beyond Recovery* (Routledge, 2017), pp. 53–70.

Kathryn King, *Jane Barker, Exile: A Literary Career 1675–1725* (Clarendon Press, 2000).

Kathryn R. King, "Of needles and pens and women's work", *Tulsa Studies in Women's Literature* 14, n. 1 (1995), pp. 77–93.

Stanton J. Linden, "Mrs Mary Trye, medicatrix: chemistry and controversy in restoration England", *Women's Writing* 1, n. 3 (1994), pp. 341–53.

Niall MacKenzie, "Jane Barker, Louise Hollandine of the Palatinate and 'Solomons [sic] Wise Daughter'", *Review of English Studies*, New Series 58, n. 233 (2007), pp. 64–72.

Marjorie H. Nicolson, "Ward's 'Pill and Drop' and men of letters", *Journal of the History of Ideas* 29, n. 2 (1968), pp. 177–96.

Sara Read, "'My method and medicines': Mary Trye, Chemical Physician", *Early Modern Women* 11, n. 1 (2016), pp. 137–48.

Philip Walsingham Sergeant, *My Lady Castlemaine: Being a Life of Barbara Villiers, Countess of Castlemaine, Afterwards Duchess of Cleveland* (Hutchinson, 1912).

Deborah Simonton, "Toleration, Liberty and Privileges: Gender and Commerce in Eighteenth-Century European Towns", in Deborah Simonton (ed.), *The Routledge History Handbook of Gender and the Urban Experience* (Routledge, 2017), pp. 33–46.

Richard Sugg, *Mummies, Cannibals, and Vampires: The History of Corpse Medicine from the Renaissance to the Victorians* (Routledge, 2011).

Angela Vanhaelen and Bronwen Wilson (eds), *Making Worlds: Global*

Invention in the Early Modern Period (University of Toronto Press, 2022), pp. 3–21.

Patrick Wallis, "Plagues, morality and the place of medicine in early modern England", *English Historical Review* 121, n. 490 (2006), pp. 1–24.

Primary Sources

Anon. *The Present State of Physick & Surgery in London* (London, 1701).

Jane Barker, *The Galesia Trilogy and Selected Manuscript Poems of Jane Barker*, Carol Shiner Wilson (ed.) (Oxford University Press, 1997).

Jane Barker, *Poems on Several Occasions (1688)*. Magdalen College Library, University of Oxford. *The Perdita Project*, University of Warwick.

Daniel Bellamy, "The Merry Swain" in *Miscellanies in Prose and Verse, Consisting of Dramatick Pieces, Poems, Humorous Tales, Fables, &c. by Daniel Bellamy*. vol 2 (London, 1739).

Robert Boyle, *A Free Inquiry into the Vulgarly Receiv'd Notion of Nature* (London, 1681).

James Bramston, *The Man of Taste. Occasion'd by an Epistle of Mr. Pope's on That Subject* (London, 1733).

Thomas Brugis, *The Marrow of Physicke* (London, 1648).

John Colbatch, *The Generous Physician, or Medicine Made Easy* (London, 1733).

Roger Dixon, *Consultum Sanitatis, A Directory to Health* (London, 1663).

Michael Drayton, *Englands Heroical Epistles* (London, 1689).

Esther Dudley, "Certificate of admission of Esther Dudley to the freedom of the City of London", (1741). Waller Family of Woodcote Papers (Warwickshire Record Office).

Thomas Dyche and William Patton, *A New General English Dictionary* (London, 1740).

John Fothergill, *Lectures on the Materia Medica*, vol II [only] (Wellcome Library, London).

Thomas Fuller, *A Pisgah-sight of Palestine* (London, 1650).

Thomas Fuller, *Pharmacopoeia extemporanea*, 2nd edn (London, 1714).

James Gillray, *The Gout*. 14 May 1799. Hand-coloured etching and aquatint, 260 mm × 355 mm (Metropolitan Museum of Art).

Alexander Gordon, *Lecture notes*. University of Aberdeen Special Collections (University of Aberdeen).

Hermannus Vander Heyden, *Speedy Help for Rich and Poor* (London, 1653).

James Howell, *Paroimiographia Proverbs* (London, 1659).

Nicolas Le Fèvre, *A Discourse Upon Sir Walter Rawleigh's Great Cordial* (London, 1778).

Richard Lower, *Tractatus de Corde: Item de Motu & Colore Sanguinis et Chyli in cum Transit* (London, 1669).

John Marten, *The Attila of the Gout*, 2nd edn (London, 1713).

E. Maynewaring, *A Treatise of Consumptions* (London, 1668).

A Merchant in London, *The Present State of Physick & Surgery in London* (London, 1701).

Roger Pitt, *The Craft and Frauds of Physick Expos'd*, 2nd edn (London, 1703).

John Quincy, *Pharmacopoeia Officinalis & Extemporanea. Or, A Complete English Dispensatory*, 5th edn (London, 1724).

John Quincy, *Lexicon Physico-Medicum: Or, A New Medicinal Dictionary* (London, 1726).

John Ray, *A Collection of English Proverbs* (Cambridge, 1670).

Royal College of Physicians of London, *Pharmacopoeia Londinensis* (London, 1702, 1721, 1724).

William Salmon, *The Family-Dictionary; Or, Houshold [sic] Companion*, 2nd edn (London, 1696).

Sophia, A Person of Quality, *Woman's Superior Excellence Over Man* (London, 1740).

Mary Trye, *Medicatrix, Or The Woman-Physician* (London, 1675).

Hermannus Vander Heyden, *Speedy Help for Rich and Poor* (London, 1653).

Benjamin Welles, *A Treatise of the Gout* (London, 1669).

Thomas Willis, *Cerebri Anatome, Cui Accessit Nervorum Descripto et Usus Studio Thomæ Willis* (London, 1664).

Thomas Willis, *Pathologiæ Cerebri, et Nervosi Generis Specimen in quo Agitur de Morbis Convulsivis, et de Scorbuto* (Oxford, 1667).

5. "Was Once a Science, Now's a Trade"

Secondary Sources

Stuart Anderson, "'A proper person to officiate': apothecaries at Westminster Hospital, London—1716 to 1826", *Pharmacy in History* 49, n. 1 (2007), pp. 3–14.

Attorney General's Office, "Attorney General Bonta Sues Nation's Largest Insulin Makers, Pharmacy Benefit Managers for Illegal Practices, Overcharging Patients", 23 Jan. 2023. See also https://oag.ca.gov/news/press-releases/attorney-general-bonta-sues-nations-largest-insulin-makers-pharmacy-benefit; accessed 4 Apr. 2023.

C. C. Booth, "Sir Samuel Garth, F.R.S.: The Dispensary Poet", *Notes and Records of the Royal Society* 40 (1985–6), pp. 125–45.

Jeremy Boulton, "Going on the Parish: The Parish Pension and its Meaning in the London Suburbs, 1640–1724", in Tim Hitchcock, Peter Searle, and Pamela Sharpe (eds), *Chronicling Poverty* (Macmillan, 1997), pp. 19–46.

Scott Breuninger, "A panacea for the nation: Berkeley's Tar-water and Irish domestic development", *Études irlandaises* 34, n. 2 (2009), pp. 29–41.

Richard I. Cook, *Sir Samuel Garth* (Twayne Publishers, 1980).

Richard Coulton, "'What he hath Gather'd Together Shall not be Lost': Remembering James Petiver", *Notes and Records* 74 (2020), pp. 189–211.

Frank H. Ellis, "The background of the London Dispensary", *Journal of the History of Medicine and Allied Sciences* 20, n. 3 (1965), pp. 197–212.

Karen Bloom Gevirtz, *Life after Death: Widows and the English Novel, Defoe to Austen* (University of Delaware Press, 2005).

David Harley, "'Bred up in the study of that faculty': licensed physicians in north-west England, 1660–1760", *Medical History* 38 (1994), pp. 398–420.

E.E. Harrison, *The History of the Charterhouse and its Buildings.*

Reprinted from the Transactions of the Ancient Monuments Society (1990).

William Hartston, "Medical dispensaries in eighteenth-century London" (abridged), *Proceedings of the Royal Society of Medicine* 56 (1963), pp. 753–58.

Arzu Babayigit Hocaoglu *et al.*, "Glycyrrhizin and long-term histopathologic changes in a murine model of asthma", *Current Therapeutic Research* 72, n. 6 (2011), pp. 250–61.

Muzaffar Iqbal, *The Making of Islamic Science* (The Other Press, 2009).

[Kennedy] Newsroom, "Kennedy, Warnock introduce bipartisan bill to cap insulin prices, lower cost of diabetic care", Office of Senator Kennedy, Senator for Louisiana, 23 Mar. 2023.

William Kerwin, "Where Have You Gone, Margaret Kennix? Seeking the Tradition of Healing Women in English Renaissance Drama", in Liliam R. Furst (ed.), *Women Healers and Physicians: Climbing a Long Hill* (University Press of Kentucky, 1997), pp. 93–113.

Yi Kuang *et al.*, "Antitussive and expectorant activities of licorice and its major compounds", *Organic & Medicinal Chemistry* 26, n. 1 (2018), pp. 278–84.

Joan Lane, "Provincial medical apprentices and masters in early modern England", *Eighteenth-Century Life* 12, n. 3 (1988), pp. 14–27.

Ephraim Philip Lansky *et al.*, "Ficus spp. (fig): Ethnobotany and potential as anticancer and anti-inflammatory agents", *Journal of Ethnopharmacology* 119, n. 2 (2008), pp. 195–213.

Zhongyuan Li *et al.*, "A comprehensive review on phytochemistry, bioactivities, toxicity studies, and clinical studies on Ficus carica Linn. Leaves", *Biomedicine & Pharmacotherapy* 137 (2021) 111393.

Stephen Porter, *The London Charterhouse* (Amberley Publishing, 2009).

Harriet Richardson, "Aberdeen", *Historic Hospitals: An Architectural Gazetteer,* 4 Feb. 2018. See also https://historic-hospitals.com/gazetteer/aberdeen/; accessed 17 July 2019.

Harriet Richardson, "Bristol Royal Infirmary", *Historic Hospitals: An Architectural Gazetteer,* 4 Feb. 2018. See also https://historic-hospitals.com/2018/02/04/bristol-royal-infirmary/; accessed 17 July 2019.

Albert Rosenberg, "The London Dispensary for the sick-poor", *Journal of the History of Medicine and Allied Sciences* 14, n. 1 (1959), pp. 41–56.

Cathy Ross, "'Men of Honour and Power': The Charterhouse's Restoration Governors", *The Great Chamber at the Charterhouse*. See also www.thecharterhouse.org; accessed 23 Feb. 2023.

Royal College of Physicians of Edinburgh, "The College Dispensary", Heritage. See also www.rcpe.ac.uk/heritage/college-history/college-dispensary; accessed 28 May 2023.

Royal College of Physicians of Edinburgh, "The Dispensary Movement", Heritage. See also www.rcpe.ac.uk/heritage/eighteenth-century-dispensary-movement; accessed 28 May 2023.

Bram Sable-Smith, "Insulin's Steep Price Leads To Deadly Rationing", *Kaiser Health News* (7 Sept. 2018).

Bisma A. Sayed *et al.*, "Insulin Affordability and the Inflation Reduction Act: Medicare Beneficiary Savings by State and Demographics" (US Department of Health and Human Services, 24 Jan. 2023).

John F. Sena, "Samuel Garth's The Dispensary", *Texas Studies in Literature and Language* 15, n. 4 (1974), pp. 639–48.

Kevin Siena, "Contagion, Exclusion, and the Unique Medical World of the Eighteenth-Century Workhouse: London Infirmaries in Their Widest Relief", in Jonathan Reinarz and Leonard Schwartz (eds), *Medicine and the Workhouse* (Boydell & Brewer, 2013), pp. 19–39.

Anna Simmons, "Medicines, monopolies and mortars: the chemical laboratory and pharmaceutical trade at the Society of Apothecaries in the eighteenth century", *Ambix* 53, n. 3 (2006), pp. 221–36.

Glenn Sonnedecker, "The Apothecary in a Scottish Infirmary", *Pharmacy in History* 41, n. 3 (1999), pp. 119–20.

Melissa Suran, "All 3 major insulin manufacturers are cutting their prices—Here's what the news means for patients with diabetes", *JAMA Medical News* 329, n. 16 (2023), pp. 1337–39.

G.J. Toomer, *Eastern Wisedome and Learning: The Study of Arabic in Seventeenth-Century England* (Clarendon Press, 2007).

[Warnock] Newsroom, "Senators Reverend Warnock, Kennedy Introduce Bipartisan Legislation to Cap Insulin Costs at $35 a Month for Everyone", Office of Reverend Raphael Warnock, US Senator for

Georgia, 23 Mar. 2023.

J.W. Willcock, *The Laws Relating to the Medical Profession* (J. and W.T. Clarke, 1830).

Matthew Yeo, *The Acquisition of Books in Chetham's Library, 1655–1700* (Brill, 2010).

Primary Sources

Anon., *The Present State of Physick and Surgery in London* (London, 1701).

Anon., *Siris in the Shades: A Dialogue Concerning Tar Water* (London, 1744).

Anon., "The Wandering Beauty", in Janet Todd (ed.), *The Works of Aphra Behn*, vol. 3 "The Fair Jilt and Other Short Stories" (London, 1995), pp. 1–48.

Thomas Brown, *Physick Lies A-Bleeding, or the Apothecary turned Doctor* (London, 1697).

Susannah Centlivre, *The Basset Table*, Jane Milling (ed.) (Broadview Press, 2009).

Hugh Chamberlen, *A Proposal For the better Securing of Health* (London, 1689).

Chymist in the City, *Bellum medicinale, or the present state of doctors and apothecaries in London* (London, 1701).

Anne Clifford, from "Diary, 1616–1617", in Elspeth Graham, Hilary Hinds, Elaine Hobby, and Helen Wilcox (eds), *Her Own Life: Autobiographical Writings by Seventeenth-Century Englishwomen* (London, 1989), pp. 35–53.

Samuel Garth, *The Dispensary. A Poem* (London, 1699).

Thomas Gouge, *The Surest & Safest Way of Thriving* (London, 1673).

Mary Huntington, "Mary Huntington [née Powell] to John Locke: Thursday, 15 January 1699", in Robert McNamee *et al.* (eds), *Electronic Enlightenment Scholarly Edition of Correspondence* (Oxford, 2018).

John Locke, "Second Treatise on Government", in Peter Laslett (ed.), *John Locke: Two Treatises on Government* (Cambridge, 1988), pp. 265–428.

Richard Mead (attr.), *The Triumvirate: Or, The Battel Among Physicians,*

2nd edn (London, 1719).

William Salmon, *A Rebuke to the Authors of the Blew-Book, Call'd The State of Physick in London* (London, 1698).

John Shirley, *The Accomplished Ladies Rich Closet*, 2nd edn (London, 1687).

Henry Stonecastle, *The Universal Spectator, and Weekly Journal: By Henry Stonecastle, of Northumberland, Esq*, n. 332 (20 July 1734).

6. The Laboratory on Cheesewell Street

Secondary Sources

The Aspirin Foundation, "The story of Aspirin – a versatile medicine with a long history". See also www.aspirin-foundation.com/history/the-aspirin-story/; accessed 9 June 2023.

Jonathan Berry, "John Houghton and medical practice in London *c.* 1700", *Bulletin of the History of Medicine* 92, n. 4 (2018), pp. 575–603.

Helen Brock, "James Douglas of the Pouch", *Medical History* 18, n. 2 (1974), pp. 162–72.

Sajed Chowdhury, "Introducing women's alchemical practices", *Early Modern Women: An Interdisciplinary Journal* 15, n. 2 (2021), pp. 89–92.

Deborah Coltham, *"Ladies in the Laboratory": A chronological list of books by, or relating to women in medicine and science*, Recent Acquisitions Five (Deborah Coltham Rare Books, 2009).

Harold J. Cook, "The Society of Chemical Physicians, the New Philosophy, and the Restoration Court", *Bulletin of the History of Medicine* 61, n. 1 (1987), pp. 61–77.

Michelle DiMeo, *Lady Ranelagh: The Incomparable Life of Robert Boyle's Sister* (University of Chicago Press, 2021).

Mordechai Feingold, *The Newtonian Moment: Isaac Newton and the Making of Modern Culture* (New York Public Library and Oxford University Press, 2004).

R.T. Gunther, *Early Science in Oxford*, vol I ,"Chemistry, Mathematics, Physics, and Surveying" (Oxford Historical Society, 1923).

Lynette Hunter, "Sisters of the Royal Society: The Circle of Katherine Jones, Lady Ranelagh", in Lynette Hunter and Sarah Hutton (eds), *Women, Science and Medicine 1500-1700: Mothers* (Sutton, 1997), pp. 178–97.

Lynette Hunter, "Women and Domestic Medicine: Lady Experimenters, 1570–1620", in Lynette Hunter and Sarah Hutton (eds), *Women, Science and Medicine 1500–1700* (Sutton, 1997), pp. 89–107.

Lynette Hunter, "Women and Science in the Sixteenth and Seventeenth Centuries", in Judith P. Zinsser (ed.), *Men, Women, and the Birthing of Modern Science* (Northern Illinois University Press, 2005), pp. 123–40.

Laura Miller, "Masculinity, Space, and Late Seventeenth-Century Alchemical Practices", in Mona Narain and Karen Gevirtz (eds), *Gender and Space in British Literature, 1660–1820* (Routledge, 2014), pp. 165–78.

Jonathan Miner and Adam Hoffhines, "The discovery of aspirin's antithrombotic effects", *Texas Heart Institute Journal* 34 (2007), pp. 179–86.

Mt. Sinai Hospital, "Oxalic Acid Poisoning". See also www.mountsinai. org/health-library/poison/oxalic-acid-poisoning; accessed 29 June 2023.

New Jersey Department of Health, "*Hazardous Substance Fact Sheet: Oxalic Acid*". See also www.nj.gov/health/eoh/rtkweb/documents/fs/1445.pdf; accessed 29 June 2023.

"Nicholas Lémery (1645–1716)", *Nature* 156 (1945), p. 598.

Jennifer M. Rampling, *The Experimental Fire: Inventing English Alchemy, 1300–1700* (University of Chicago Press, 2021).

Hilary Rose, *Foreword*, in Lynette Hunter and Sarah Hutton (eds), *Women, Science and Medicine 1500–1700* (Sutton, 1997), pp. xi–xx.

The Royal Collection Trust, "Charles II and the Royal Observatory Greenwich", Charles II: Art & Power. See also www.rct.uk/collection/themes/exhibitions/charles-ii-art-power/the-queens-gallery-buckingham-palace/charles-ii-and-the-royal-observatory-greenwich; accessed 5 June 2023.

K. Bryn Thomas, "James Douglas of the Pouch, 1675–1742", *British Medical Journal* (1960), pp. 1649–50.

Courtney Weiss Smith, *Empiricist Devotions: Science, Religion, and Poetry in Early Eighteenth-Century England* (University of Virginia Press, 2016).

Primary Sources

Aphra Behn, "The Emperor of the Moon: A Farce", in *The Cambridge Edition of the Works of Aphra Behn*, vol IV, plays 1682–1696, edited by Rachel Adcock *et al.* (Cambridge University Press, 2021), pp. 309–530.

Noah Biggs, *The New Dispensatory* (London, 1651).

Elizabeth Blackwell, *A Curious Herbal Containing Five Hundred Cuts of the Most Useful Plants Which Are Now Used in the Practice of Physick*, vols I and II (London, 1737/1739).

Brockman Papers (British Library/London).

Susanna Centlivre, *The Basset Table*, Jane Milling (ed.) (Broadview Press, 2009).

Daniel Coxe, *"Of the effect of tobacco-oyle"* (Royal Society/London).

Henry Curzon, *The Universal Library: Or, Compleat Summary of Science. Containing above sixty select treatises* (London, 1712).

James Douglas, *Letters*. Sloane Manuscripts (British Library/London).

James Douglas, "The natural history and description of the phoenicopterus or flamingo; with two views of the head, and three of the tongue, of that beautiful and uncommon bird", *Philosophical Transactions* 29, n. 350 (31 Dec. 1716), pp. 523–41.

Sarah Draper, *Recipe book* (Wellcome Library/London).

Richard Fletcher, *A Vindication of Chymistry, and Chymical Medicines* (London, 1676).

John Friend, *Chymical lectures* (London, 1712).

Hunterian Collection. University of Glasgow Special Collections (University of Glasgow Library/Glasgow).

Dr [John] Huxham [?], *English Medical Notebook* (Wellcome Library/London).

George Martine, *Essays medical and philosophical by George Martine, M.D.* (London, 1740).

Dorothea Rousby, *A Cookery Book with Index* [1694] (Stanford

University Library).

Thomas Shadwell, *The Virtuoso*, Marjorie Hope Nicolson and David Stuart Rhodes (eds) (University of Nebraska Press, 1966).

Peter Shaw, *Philosophical Principles* (London, 1730).

Peter Shaw, *Chemical Lectures* (London, 1734).

George Starkey, *A Necessary and Full Apology for Chymical Medicaments* (London, 1656).

Unknown authors, *Medical Accounts* (Wellcome Library/London).

Waller Family of Woodcote Papers (Warwickshire County Records Office).

George Wilson, *A Compleat Course of Chemistry, Containing near Three Hundred Operations; Several of which have not been seen before* (London, 1703).

7. The Doctoress's Cure for the Stone

Secondary Sources

Anon., "Nicolas Lémery (1645–1715)", *Nature* 156 (1945), p. 598.

Juanita G.L. Burnby, "The apothecary as progenitor", *Medical History* 27, n. S3 (1983), pp. 24–61.

Stephen Clucas, "Joanna Stephens's Medicine and the Experimental Philosophy", in Judith P. Zinsser (ed.), *Men, Women, and the Birthing of Modern Science* (Northern Illinois University Press, 2005), pp. 141–58.

John D. Comrie, "English medicine in the eighteenth century", *Proceedings of the Royal Society of Medicine* XXVII, pp. 37–44.

Penelope J. Corfield, "From poison peddlers to civic worthies: the reputation of the apothecaries in Georgian England", *Social History of Medicine* 22, n. 1 (2009), pp. 1–21.

B.J. Dobbs, "Studies in the natural philosophy of Sir Kenelm Digby. Part III. Digby's experimental alchemy–the book of secrets", *Ambix* 21, n. 1 (1974), pp. 1–28.

Christopher Duffin, "Joseph Clutton, c. 1695-1743: A Georgian apothecary", *Pharmaceutical Historian* 48, n. 4 (2018), pp. 85–98.

Sandy Feinstein, "Experience, Authority, and the Alchemy of Language:

Margaret Cavendish and Marie Meurdrac Respond to the Art", *Early Modern Women: An Interdisciplinary Journal* 15, n. 2 (2021), pp. 133–42.

Elizabeth Lane Furdell, *The Royal Doctors, 1485-1714: Medical Personnel at the Tudor and Stuart Courts* (Boydell & Brewer, 2001).

David Harley, "'Bred Up in the Study of that Faculty': Licensed Physicians in North-West England, 1660–1760", *Medical History* 38 (1994), pp. 398–420.

J. Cordy Jeaffreyson, "Doctors out of Practice", *The Leisure Hour* (1884), pp. 346–50.

William Kerwin, "Where Have You Gone, Margaret Kennix? Seeking the Tradition of Healing Women in English Renaissance Drama", in Liliam R. Furst (ed.), *Women Healers and Physicians: Climbing a Long Hill* (University Press of Kentucky, 1997), pp. 99–113.

Edward L. Keys, "The Joanna Stephens Medicines for the Stone: A Faith that Failed", *The Bulletin* (1942), pp. 835–40.

Marjorie H. Nicolson, "Ward's 'Pill and Drop' and men of letters", *Journal of the History of Ideas* 29, n. 2 (1968), pp. 177–96.

Margaret Pelling and Frances White, *Physicians and Irregular Medical Practitioners in London Database* (London, 2004).

Eric Riches, "The history of lithotomy and lithotrity", *Annals of the Royal College of Surgeons of England* 43, n. 4 (1968), pp. 185–99.

Eric Riches, "Samuel Pepys and his stones", *Annals of the Royal College of Surgeons of England* 59 (1977), pp. 11–16.

Romney R. Sedgwick, "Hanbury Williams, Charles (1708–59), of Coldbrook, Mon.", in R. Sedgwick (ed.), *The History of Parliament: the House of Commons 1715-1754*, vol I (Boydell & Brewer, 1970). See https://www.historyofparliamentonline.org/volume/1715-1754/member/hanbury-williams-charles-1708-59; accessed 29 June 2023.

A History of the County of Lancaster: Volume 3, William Farrer and J Brownbill (eds.) (London, 1907).

Arthur J. Viseltear, "Joanna Stephens and the eighteenth century lithontriptics; misplaced chapter in the history of therapeutics", *Journal of the Bulleting of the History of Medicine* 42, n. 3 (1968), pp. 199–220.

Patrick Wallis, "Consumption, retailing, and medicine in early modern England", *Economic History Review* 61, n. 1 (2008), 26–53.

Wayne Wild, *Medicine-by-post: The Changing Voice of Illness in Eighteenth-century British Consultation Letters and Literature* (Brill, 2006).

D. Williams, "Williams, Sir Charles Hanbury (1708–1759), satirical writer and diplomatist", *Dictionary of Welsh Biography Online.*

A. Dickson Wright, "Quacks through the ages", *Journal of the Royal Society of Arts* 105, n. 4995 (1957), pp. 161–78.

Primary Sources
Newspapers
Athenian Gazette
Common Sense or The Englishman's Journal
Country Journal or The Craftsman
Daily Courant
Fog's Weekly Journal
Gentleman's Magazine
Grub Street Journal
London Daily Post
London Evening Post
Post Man and the Historical Account
Universal Spectator
Weekly Oracle or Universal Library

Other sources
"An act for providing a Reward to Joanna Stephens upon a proper Discovery to be made by her for the Use of the Publick, of the Medicines Prepared by her for the cure of the Stone" (Royal College of Physicians/London, 1741).

Anon., *The Country Physician* (Edinburgh, 1701).

Anon., *Siris in the Shades: a Dialogue Concerning Tar Water; Between Benjamin Smith, Lately Deceased, Dr. Hancock, and Dr. Garth, at Their Meeting upon the Banks of the River Styx* (London, 1744).

Anon., *Various Ironic and Serious Discourses on the Subject of Physick* (London, 1739).

Stephen Blankaart, *The Physical Dictionary*, 4th edn (London, 1702).

Blenheim Papers (British Library/London).

Charles Carter, *The Compleat City and Country Cook: or, Accomplish'd Housewife* (London, 1732).

Joseph Clutton, *A True and Candid Relation of the Good and Bad Effects of Joshua Ward's Pill and Drop. Exhibited in Sixty-Eight Cases* (London, 1736).

Corbyn Papers (Wellcome Library/London).

Diocese of London Papers (London Metropolitan Archives).

Alexander Gordon, *Lecture notes*. University of Aberdeen Special Collections (University of Aberdeen Library).

David Hartley, "An Account of the Contribution for Making Mrs Stephens's Medicines Public; with Some Reasons for it, and Answers to the most Remarkable Objections to it", *London Gazette* (26 Mar. 1738).

David Hartley, *Ten Cases of Persons Who Have Taken Mrs Stephens's Medicine for the Stone* (London, 1738).

Richard Lower, *Dr. Lower's, and Several Other Eminent Physicians Receipts*, 2nd edn (London, 1701).

John Moyle, *Chirurgus marinus: or, The Sea-Chirurgion*, 4th edn (London, 1702).

Edward Nourse, *Letter* (Royal Society/London).

Alexander Pope, "The First Epistle of the Second Book of Horace Imitated", in Aubrey Williams (ed.), *Poetry and Prose of Alexander Pope* (New York, 1969), pp. 241–54.

St Paul's Hammersmith Parish Records, 1766–84, in *Church of England Baptisms, Marriages, and Burials, 1538-1812*, accessed through ancestry.com.

David Turner, *The drop and pill of Mr. Ward, consider'd: In an epistle to Dr. James Jurin, Fellow of the College of Physicians. And of the Royal Society* (London, 1735).

Part Two
Ripples and Reflections

ACT UP New York. See also https://actupny.com; accessed 5 July 2023.

Ricardo Alonso-Zaldivar, "Trump Administration Wants to Import Cheaper Prescription Drugs from Abroad", *PBS Newshour* (19 Dec. 2019).

Mariana Alperin *et al.*, "The mysteries of menopause and urogynecologic health: clinical and scientific gaps", *Menopause* 26, n. 1 (2019), pp. 103–11.

Alzheimer Society of Canada, "What should Canadians know about aducanumab (a.k.a Aduhelm)?" See also https://alzheimer.ca/en/about-dementia/how-can-i-treat-dementia/what-aducanumab; accessed 10 Sept. 2023.

Anon. *A Generous Discovery of many Curious and Useful Medicines and Preparations; Both in Physic, Chymistry, Cookery, and Stiffenry* (London, 1725).

Association Canadienne de Thalidomide/Thalidomide Victims of Canada. See also https://thalidomide.ca/en; accessed 6 July 2023.

Fiona C. Baker *et al.*, "Sleep and sleep disorders in the menopausal transition", *Sleep Medicine Clinics* 13, n. 3 (2018), pp. 443–56.

Bayer Global Communications Department, "Bayer starts Phase III clinical development program OASIS with Elinzanetant". See also www.bayer.com/en/ca/bayer-starts-phase-iii-clinical-development-program-oasis-with-elinzanetant; accessed 10 Oct. 2023.

Pam Belluck and Rebecca Robbins, "Three F.D.A. Advisers Resign Over Agency's Approval of Alzheimer's Drug", *New York Times*, 10 June 2021 (updated 2 Sept. 2021).

Sanjoy Bhattacharya and Carlos Eduardo D'Avila Pereira Campani, "Reassessing the foundations: worldwide smallpox eradication, 1957–67", *Medical History* 64, n. 1 (2020), pp. 71–93.

Lorenzo Caputi *et al.*, "Missing enzymes in the biosynthesis of the anticancer drug vinblastine in Madagascar periwinkle", *Science* 360 (2018), pp. 1235–39.

Carter Center, "River Blindness Elimination Program". See also www.cartercenter.org/health/river_blindness/index.html; accessed 17 Aug. 2023.

Hugh Chamberlen, *A Proposal For the better Securing of Health* (London, 1689).

Bill Chappell, "3 Experts Have Resigned From An FDA Committee Over Alzheimer's Drug Approval", *National Public Radio* (11 June 2021).

ChemEurope Encyclopedia, "History of iodised salt". See also www.chemeurope.com/en/encyclopedia/History_of_iodised_salt.html#google_vignette; accessed 2 July 2023.

Jen Christensen and Betsy Klein, "Eli Lilly to cut insulin prices, cap costs at \$35 for many people with diabetes", *CNN* (1 Mar. 2023). See also www.cnn.com/2023/03/01/health/eli-lilly-insulin-prices-diabetes/index.html; accessed 7 July 2023.

Elinor Cleghorn, *Unwell Women: Misdiagnosis and Myth in a Man-Made World* (Dutton, 2021).

Karen Codling *et al.*, "The legislative framework for salt iodization in Asia and the Pacific and its impact on programme implementation", *Public Health Nutrition* 20, n. 16 (2016), pp. 3008–18.

Committee on Oversight and Reform Staff Report, "Drug Pricing Investigation: Celgene and Bristol Myers Squibb, Revlimid", 30 Sept. 2020, United States House of Representatives.

Caroline Criado Perez, *Invisible Women: Data Bias in a World Designed for Men* (Vintage, 2019).

Anna Criddle, "Astellas' VEOZAH (fezolinetant) Approved by U.S. FDA for Treatment of Vasomotor Symptoms Due to Menopause", 13 May 2023. See also www.astellas.com/en/news/27756; accessed 10 Sept. 2023.

Stephanie Cross and Karen Watson, "Medical Hypothyroidism", *Healthline.com*. See also www.healthline.com/health/congenital-hypothyroidism#symptoms; accessed 2 July 2023

Ari Daniel, "Malaria is on the ropes in Bangladesh. But the parasite is punching back", *Goats and Soda: Stories of Life in a Changing World. National Public Radio* (20 Sept. 2023).

Ari Daniel, "A man dressed as a tsetse fly came to a soccer game. And he definitely had a goal", *Goats and Soda: Stories of Life in a Changing World. National Public Radio* (30 July 2023).

Hannah Devlin, "Drug for hot flushes will transform menopause treatment, doctors say", *Guardian* (20 May 2023).

Diabetes UK, "Who Invented Insulin?", *100 Years of Insulin*. See also https://www.diabetes.org.uk/our-research/about-our-research/our-impact/discovery-of-insulin; accessed 6 July 2023.

Selena Simmons Duffin and Carmel Wroth, "Maternal deaths in the U.S. spiked in 2021, CDC reports", *Morning Edition, National Public Radio* (16 Mar. 2023). See also www.npr.org/sections/health-shots/2023/03/16/1163786037/maternal-deaths-in-the-u-s-spiked-in-2021-cdc-reports; accessed 28 Sept. 2023.

Brian G.M. Durie *et al.*, "Bortezomib with lenalidomide and dexamethasone versus lenalidomide and dexamethasone alone in patients with newly diagnosed myeloma without intent for immediate autologous stem-cell transplant (SWOG S0777): a randomised, open-label, phase 3 trial", *Lancet* 389, n. 10068 (2017), pp. 519–27.

Katherine Eban, *Bottle of Lies: The Inside Story of the Generic Drug Boom* (HarperCollins, 2019).

Editorial, "Rapid drug access and scientific rigour: a delicate balance", *Lancet Neurology* 20, n. 1, (2021), P1.

Dean S. Elterman *et al.*, "The quality of life and economic burden of erectile dysfunction", *Research and Reports in Urology* 13 (2021), pp. 79–86.

Ezekiel J. Emanuel, *Which Country Has the Best Health Care?* (PublicAffairs, 2020).

Miriam Erick, "Frances Kathleen Oldham Kelsey", National Women's History Museum. See also www.womenshistory.org/education-resources/biographies/frances-kathleen-oldham-kelsey; accessed 21 Sept. 2023.

James Essinger and Sandra Koutzenko, *Frankie: How One Woman Prevented a Pharmaceutical Disaster* (History Press, 2018).

European Medicines Agency, "Aduhelm: withdrawal of the marketing authorisation application", 22 Apr. 2022. See also www.ema.europa.eu/en/medicines/human/withdrawn-applications/aduhelm; accessed 19 Sept. 2023.

European Medicines Agency, "From Laboratory to Patient: The Journey of a Medicine Assessed by EMA" (EMA, 2019).

European Medicines Agency, "How EMA Evaluates Medicines for Human Use". See also www.ema.europa.eu/en/about-us/what-we-do/authorisation-medicines/how-ema-evaluates-medicines#; accessed 20 Sept. 2023.

Harold Evans, "Foreword", in James Essinger and Sandra Koutzenko (eds), *Frankie: How One Woman Prevented a Pharmaceutical Disaster* (History Press, 2018).

Stephanie S. Faubion *et al.*, "Menopause symptoms on women in the workplace", *Mayo Clinic Proceedings* 98, n. 6 (2023), pp. 833–45.

C. Fauriant, "From bark to weed: the history of artemisinin", *Parasite* 18, n. 3 (2011), pp. 215–18.

Stephen Gandel, "Rep. Katie Porter gives Pharma executive the 'whiteboard' treatment", *MoneyWatch* (1 Oct. 2020).

Karen Geraghty, "Protecting the public: profile of Dr. Frances Oldham Kelsey", *Virtual Mentor: AMA Journal of Ethics* 3, n. 7 (2001), pp. 252–54.

Irwin Goldstein *et al.*, "The association of erectile dysfunction with productivity and absenteeism in eight countries globally", *International Journal of Clinical Practice* 73, n. 11 (2019), p. e13384.

April Grant, "FDA Approves Novel Drug to Treat Moderate to Severe Hot Flashes Caused by Menopause", US Food and Drug Administration (12 May 2023). See also www.fda.gov/news-events/press-announcements/fda-approves-novel-drug-treat-moderate-severe-hot-flashes-caused-menopause; accessed 30 Sept. 2023.

Matthew Harper, "Solving the Drug Patent Problem", *Forbes* (2 May 2002).

Robert Hart, "Roche is Discussing Alzheimer's Drug with FDA Following Regulator's Controversial Approval of Biogen's Aduhelm, CEO Says", *Forbes* (22 July 2021).

Harvard Health Publishing, "Cut salt – it won't affect your iodine intake" (1 June 2011). See also https://www.health.harvard.edu/heart-health/cut-salt-it-wont-affect-your-iodine-intake; accessed 25 Sep. 2023.

Harvard T.H. Chan School of Public Health, "The Nutrition Source: Iodine". See also www.hsph.harvard.edu/nutritionsource/iodine/;

accessed 25 Sept. 2023.

Harvard T.H. Chan School of Public Health, "The Nutrition Source: Salt and Sodium". See also www.hsph.harvard.edu/nutritionsource/salt-and-sodium/; accessed 25 Sept. 2023.

Adrienne Hatch-McChesney and Harris R. Lieberman, "Iodine and iodine deficiency: a comprehensive review of a re-emerging issue", *Nutrients* 14, n. 17 (2022), p. 3474.

Health and Human Services Press Office, "HHS Selects the First Drugs for Medicare Drug Price Negotiation" (29 Aug. 2023). See also https://www.hhs.gov/about/news/2023/08/29/hhs-selects-the-first-drugs-for-medicare-drug-price-negotiation.html; accessed 25 Sept. 2023.

Donna L. Hoyert, "Maternal mortality rates in the United States, 2021", National Center for Health Statistics Health E-Stats (2023); https://dx.doi.org/10.15620/cdc:124678.

John Innes Centre, "Madagascar periwinkle research uncovers pathway to cancer-fighting drugs", *ScienceDaily* (3 May 2018). See also www.sciencedaily.com/releases/2018/05/180503142809.htm; accessed 30 Sept. 2023.

Andrew Joseph, "3 Experts Have Resigned From An FDA Committee Over Alzheimer's Drug Approval", *STAT* (10 June 2021).

Kaiser Family Foundation Health Care Debt Survey, 25 February–20 March 2022.

Carliss Karasov, "Who reaps the benefits of biodiversity?" *Environmental Health Perspectives* 109, n. 12 (2001), pp. A582–87.

James H. Kim and Anthony R. Scialli, "Thalidomide: the tragedy of birth defects and the effective treatment of disease", *Toxicological Sciences* 122, n. 1 (2011), pp. 1–6.

Ashleigh Koss, "Update on Regulatory Submission for Aducanumab in the European Union", Biogen Company Statements (22 Apr. 2022). See also https://investors.biogen.com/news-releases/news-release-details/update-regulatory-submission-aducanumab-european-union-0; accessed 30 Sept. 2023.

Katherine Lang, "Progress and controversy in Alzheimer's research: aducanumab's FDA approval", *Medical News Today* (11 Jan. 2023), www.medicalnewstoday.com.

Linda Lear, "In Memoriam: Frances Oldham Kelsey". See also www. rachelcarson.org/frances-oldham-kelsey; accessed 21 Sept. 2023.

Lauren J. Lee *et al.*, "Increasing access to erectile dysfunction treatment via pharmacies to improve healthcare provider visits and quality of life: results from a prospective real-world observational study in the United Kingdom", *International Journal of Clinical Practice* 75 (2021), p. e13849.

Iliana C. Lega *et al.*, "A pragmatic approach to the management of menopause", *Canadian Medical Association Journal* 195 (2023), pp. e677–72.

Angela M. Leung, Lewis E. Braverman, and Elizabeth N. Pearce, "History of U.S. iodine fortification and supplementation", *Nutrients* 4 (2012), pp. 1740–46.

Gary F. Lewis and Patricia L. Brubaker, "The discovery of insulin revisited: lessons for the modern era", *Journal of Clinical Investigation* 131, n. 1 (2021), p. e142239; doi.org/10.1172/JCI142239.

Hilde Lindemann, "The woman question in medicine: an update", *The Hastings Center Report* 42, n. 3 (2012), pp. 38–45.

Mark S. Litwin, Robert J. Nied, and Nasreen Dhanani, "Health-related quality of life in men with erectile dysfunction", *Journal of General Internal Medicine* 13, n. 3 (1998), pp. 159–66.

Sydney Lupkin, "Drugmakers Blamed for Blocking Generics Have Jacked Up Prices and Cost U.S. Billions", *Kaiser Health News* (23 May 2018).

Soraya Machado de Jesus, Rafael Santos Santana, and Silvana Nair Leite, "Comparative analysis of the use and control of thalidomide in Brazil and different countries: is it possible to say there is safety?", *Expert Opinion on Drug Safety* 21, n. 1 (2022), pp. 67–81.

Howard Markel, "A grain of salt", *The Milbank Quarterly* 92 n. 3 (2014), pp. 407–12.

Alyson J. McGregor, *Sex Matters: How Male-Centric Medicine Endangers Women's Health and What We Can do About It* (Hachette Go, 2020).

Mitzzy F. Medellín-Luna *et al.*, "Medicinal plant extracts and their use as wound closure inducing agents", *Journal of Medicinal Food* 22, n. 5 (2019), pp. 435–43.

Charles Mégier, Grégoire Dumery, and Dominique Luton, "Iodine and thyroid maternal and fetal metabolism during pregnancy", *Metabolites* 13, n. 5 (2023), p. 633.

Giles Milton, *Nathaniel's Nutmeg; or, The True and Incredible Adventures of the Spice Trader Who Changed the Course of History* (Picador, 2015).

Kiho Miyazato, Hideaki Tahara, and Yoshihiro Hayakawa, "Antimetastatic effects of thalidomide by inducing the functional maturation of peripheral natural killer cells", *Cancer Science* 111, n. 8 (2020), pp. 2770–78.

Jennifer Rose V. Moleno, "The aducanumab controversy—how do physicians proceed?", Journal Watch, *New England Journal of Medicine* (29 Sept. 2021). See also www.jwatch.org/na54036/2021/09/29/aducanumab-controversy-how-do-clinicians-proceed; accessed 21 Sept. 2023.

Seeseei Molimau-Samasoni *et al.*, "Functional genomics and metabolomics advance the ethnobotany of the Samoan traditional medicine 'matalafi'", *Proceedings of the National Academy of Sciences* 118, n. 45 (2021), p. e2100880118.

K.M. Muraleedharan and M.A. Avery, "Therapeutic areas II: cancer, infectious diseases, inflammation & immunology and dermatology", in John B. Taylor and David J. Triggle (eds), *Comprehensive Medicinal Chemistry II* (Elsevier, 2007), pp. 765–814.

Edward R. Murrow, "See It Now", *CBS* (12 Apr. 1955).

S.J. Nass, G. Madhavan, and N.R. Augustine (eds), *Making Medicines Affordable: A National Imperative*. The National Academies of Sciences, Engineering, and Medicine – Health and Medicine Division; Board on Health Care Services; Committee on Ensuring Patient Access to Affordable Drug Therapies (Washington, DC, 2017).

National Institute of Child Health and Human Development, "How are Drugs Approved for Use in the United States?" See also www.nichd.nih.gov/health/topics/pharma/conditioninfo/approval; accessed 18 Sept. 2023.

National Library of Medicine, "Dr. Frances Oldham Kelsey" (2015). See also https://cfmedicine.nlm.nih.gov/physicians/biography_182.html; accessed 10 Sept. 2023.

Office of the Inspector General, "Delays in Confirmatory Trials for Drug Applications Granted FDA's Accelerated Approval Raise Concerns", OEI-01-21-00401, 29 Sept. 2022, US Department of Health and Human Services. See also https://oig.hhs.gov/oei/reports/OEI-01-21-00401.asp; accessed 21 Mar. 2024.

J. Orgiazzi and S.W. Spaulding, "Milestones in European Thyroidology: Jean-Francois Coindet (1774–1834)", European Thyroid Association. See also www.eurothyroid.com/about/met/coindet.html; accessed 5 Oct. 2023.

Davide Orsini and Mariano Martini, "Albert Bruce Sabin: the man who made the oral polio vaccine", *Emerging Infectious Diseases* 28, n. 3 (2022), pp. 743–46.

Elizabeth N. Pearce, "Is iodine deficiency reemerging in the United States?" *AACE Clinical Case Reports* 1, n. 1 (2015), p. e81.

Stephen Philips, "The power of no", *Medicine on the Midway* (2011), pp. 24–27.

Anna Poma *et al.*, "Anti-inflammatory properties of drugs from saffron crocus", *Anti-Inflammatory & Anti-Allergy Agents in Medicinal Chemistry* 11 (2012), pp. 37–51.

Seung Won Ra *et al.*, "The safety and efficacy of CKD-497 in patients with acute upper respiratory tract infection and bronchitis symptoms: a multicenter, double-blind, double-dummy, randomized, controlled, phase II clinical trial", *Journal of Thoracic Medicine* 13, no. 1 (2021), pp. 1–9.

Lisa Raffensperger, "How adding iodine to salt boosted Americans' IQ", *Discover Magazine* (23 July 2013).

Melissa Repko, "Walmart unveils low-price insulin as more patients with diabetes struggle to pay for drug", *CNBC* (29 June 2021).

Elizabeth Rosenthal, "KHN On NPR: The Uniquely American Problem of High Prescription Drug Costs: Interview with Elizabeth Rosenthal. By Scott Simon", *National Public Radio* (10 Jan. 2018).

Rita Rubin, "Collaboration and conflict: looking back at the 30-year history of the AIDS Clinical Trials Group", *JAMA* 314, n. 24 (2015), pp. 2604–06.

William Salmon, *A Rebuke to the Authors of the Blew-Book, Call'd The*

State of Physick in London (London, 1698).

Sarah Schulman, *Let the Record Show: A Political History of ACT UP New York, 1987–1993* (Farrar, Straus and Giroux, 2021).

Science Museum, "Thalidomide," Objects and Stories, 11 Dec. 2019. See also www.sciencemuseum.org.uk/objects-and-stories/medicine/thalidomide; accessed 21 Mar. 2021.

S. Singhal and J. Mehta, "Thalidomide in cancer: potential uses and limitations", *BioDrugs* 15, n. 3 (2001), pp. 163–72.

S.A. Skeaf, "Iodine and Cognitive Development", in David Benton (ed.), *Lifetime Nutritional Influences on Cognition, Behaviour and Psychiatric Illness* (Woodhead Publishing, 2011), pp. 109–28.

Peter Staley, "Antony Fauci Quietly Shocked Us All", *New York Times* (22 Dec. 2022).

A. Keith Stewart, "How thalidomide works against cancer", *Science* 343, n. 6168 (2014), pp. 256–57.

Katie Thomas, "The Story of Thalidomide in the U. S., Told Through Documents", *New York Times* (24 Mar. 2020).

Rosa Tikkanen *et al.*, "Maternal Mortality and Maternity Care in the United States Compared to 10 Other Developed Countries", Issue Briefs, The Commonwealth Fund (8 Nov. 2020). See also www.commonwealthfund.org/publications/issue-briefs/2020/nov/maternal-mortality-maternity-care-us-compared-10-countries; accessed 21 Mar. 2022.

Sarah Jane Tribble, "Drug Makers Play the Patent Game to Lock in Prices, Block Competitors", *Kaiser Health News* (2 Oct. 2018).

US Food and Drug Administration, "Drug Approval Process", Development and Approval Process: Drugs. See also www.fda.gov/drugs/development-approval-process-drugs; accessed 5 May 2023.

US Food and Drug Administration Approval Protocols, Code of Federal Regulations Title 21, vol 1, part 56: Institutional Review Boards. See also www.ecfr.gov/current/title-21; accessed 5 May 2023.

US Food and Drug Administration, "Exclusivity and Generic Drugs: What Does It Mean?". See also www.fda.gov/files/drugs/published/Exclusivity-and-Generic-Drugs--What-Does-It-Mean-.pdf; accessed 5 May 2023.

US Food and Drug Administration, "Frequently Asked Questions on Patents and Exclusivity". See also www.fda.gov/drugs/development-approval-process-drugs/frequently-asked-questions-patents-and-exclusivity; accessed 5 May 2023.

US Food and Drug Administration, "FDA Grants Accelerated Approval for Alzheimer's Drug", 7 June 2021. See also www.fda.gov/news-events/press-announcements/fda-grants-accelerated-approval-alzheimers-drug; accessed 5 May 2023.

Wulf H. Utian, "Psychosocial and socioeconomic burden of vasomotor symptoms in menopause: a comprehensive review", *Health and Quality of Life Outcomes* 3 (2005), article 47.

Gail A. Van Norman, "Drugs and devices: comparison of European and U.S. approval processes", *JACC: BTS* 1, n. 5 (2016), pp. 399–412.

Petra Verdonk, Elena Bendien, and Yolanbde Appelman, "Menopause and work: a narrative literature review about menopause and health", *Work* 72, n. 2 (2022), pp. 483–96.

Sheila C. Vir, "National iodine deficiency disorders control programme of India", in *Public Health Nutrition in Developing Countries* (Woodhead Publishing, 2011), pp. 575–605.

Jigang Wang *et al.*, "Artemisinin, the magic drug discovered from traditional Chinese medicine", *Engineering* 5 (2019), pp. 32–39.

Jennifer Whiteley *et al.*, "The impact of menopausal symptoms on quality of life, productivity, and economic outcomes", *Journal of Women's Health* 22, n. 11 (2013), pp. 983–90.

Brett Wilkins, "Katie Porter eviscerates Big Pharma CEO over 'exorbitant' drug prices", *Salon* (4 Oct. 2020).

World Health Organization, "Salt Reduction". See also www.who.int/news-room/fact-sheets/detail/salt-reduction; accessed 29 Sept. 2023.

Michael B. Zimmerman, "Research on iodine deficiency and goiter in the 19th and early 20th centuries", *Journal of Nutrition* 138 (2008), pp. 2060–63.

Acknowledgements

It is a great pleasure to be able to acknowledge and thank the many people and institutions who have made this work possible. The Portland Collection kindly gave permission to reproduce the Digby family portrait. I received funding and time from Seton Hall University and support from my colleagues in the English Department, who generously shouldered unpaid extra work while I was on sabbatical.

Thanks, thanks, and more thanks to my agent, Emma Bal at Madeleine Milburn, who is a book whisperer and a brilliant Virgil. Working with her is a privilege, thrill, and delight. I am deeply grateful to my editor Georgina Blackwell, Iain MacGregor, and the team at Head of Zeus for providing my work its first home, and to Eric Schmidt, my first editor at the University of California Press, Jyoti Arvey, and everyone at UCP for providing a second home on my own shore.

Librarians and archivists are among humanity's very finest exemplars; they have chosen a career of service, preserving human experience and helping people. Everyone at Walsh Library, present and retired, has made possible the last two decades of my research. I also am grateful to and for the librarians and staff at the Smithsonian's Dibner Library, London's Guildhall, the London Metropolitan Archives, the Society of Antiquaries of

London, Lambeth Palace Library, the British Library's Western Manuscripts and Rare Books divisions, the Wellcome Library, the National Archives at Kew, the Wiltshire and Swindon History Centre, the Warwickshire County Record Office, the Sheffield City Archives and Local Studies Library, the Aberdeen City and Aberdeenshire Archives, the Aberdeen Central Library, the Archives and Special Collections at the University of Glasgow, Tim Kirtley of Wadham College Library of Oxford University, Michelle Gait and the staff at the University of Aberdeen's Special Collections, Felix Lancashire and the staff at the Royal College of Physicians, Rupert Baker and the staff at the Royal Society, Darren Bevin and the staff of Chawton House and Chawton House Library, and the docents and staff of the Chelsea Physic Garden.

Although they might be surprised to find themselves here, I also wish to thank everyone at Scotrail who was on duty on 18 July 2023, one of the hottest days on record, when steel rails melted and electrical components burst into flame. I had to travel from Sheffield to Glasgow for research and saw first-hand their resilience and professionalism.

A veritable legion has been vital to this project, notably Lorna Dove, Lauren Kempf, and Marnie Doubek, as well as Marilyn Francus, Al Coppola, Laura Runge, Judith Zinsser, Anne Fernald, Donna Ritter, Laura Atwell, and Debi Rednik. Karen Brown Wheeler is quite simply the best friend ever. Lisa Thaler, development editor, helped me shape a stubbornly academic study into something for "real" people. My writing group (MG) and beta readers have been heroic. The other Visiting Residential Scholars at Chawton House Library – Emily Friedman, Victoria Joule, and Lindsay Seatter –Visiting Independent Scholar Mika Suzuki, and Summer Intern Christine Fulcher helped me articulate and test my ideas at the outset. It is impossible to measure how much I learned from Roger Gaskell and Caroline Duroselle-Melish and my class-mates at the Rare Books School at the University of Virginia; I draw on it constantly. I am incredibly fortunate to work with Ros Ballaster, Jennifer Batt, Line Cottegnies, Leah Orr, Helen Wilcox, Aleksondra Hultquist, Gillian Wright, Claire Bowditch, Mel Evans, Margaret Ferguson, Maureen Bell, Paul Saltzman, and Mary Ann O'Donnell, and to have learned from the late Rob Hume. I also have been graced above my deserts with mentoring from three remarkable women: Jessica Munns, Martine Watson Brownley, and Elaine Hobby.

My family deserves all the gratitude that I can give and then some. Thanks to Amira and Tracy for their encouragement, sympathy, and terrific humour. A daughter-in-law could not possibly have better in-laws than Ed and Marilyn. For my parents, Susan and Steve, Amanda Foreman said it best in her biography of the Duchess of Devonshire: "I owe them much more than I can repay and am more grateful than my demeanor sometimes showed." David and Naama gave me the hearty kick I needed to begin this new journey; I never would have done it without them. To Stephen and our children, thank you. I love you.

Image Credits

Page 1
(Top left) Elizabeth Blackwell, *A Curious Herbal* (1739)
(Top right) Death as an apothecary's assistant making up medicines with a mortar and pestle for the apothecary attending a female patient who sits by the fireside. Watercolour by T. Rowlandson or one of his followers. Wellcome Collection
(Bottom) Lady Elizabeth Grey, Countess of Kent, *c.* 1619, Paul Van Somer *c.* 1577 or 1578 – *c.* 1621 or 22 / Tate Images

Page 2
(Top) Royal Collection of Physicians
(Bottom) The Portland Collection

Page 3
(Top) English Recipe Book, 17th century. Source: Wellcome Collection.
(Bottom left) Images from the History of Medicine (IHM) by Pierre Pomet, 1658–1699 / National Library of Medicine
(Bottom right) Dr [John] Huxham, English Medical Notebook / Wellcome Collection (photograph by Karen Bloom Gevirtz)

Page 4
(Top) Gift of Jill Spalding, 2022 / The Metropolitan Museum of Art
(Bottom) Jesus College, Oxford, Fellows Library

Page 5
(Top) The accomplished ladies rich closet of rarities / [J.S. (John Shirley)].
Wellcome Collection
(Bottom) A man and a woman demonstrating the process of fermentation and distillation in alchemy. Etching, *ca.* 17th century. Wellcome
Collection

Page 6
(Top) A surgeon performing a lithotomy on a patient who is being restrained by three assistants, with five other anatomical illustrations. Engraving by J. Mynde. Wellcome Collection
(Bottom) Gift of Sarah Lazarus, 1891 / The Metropolitan Museum of Art

Page 7
(Top) An apothecary making up a prescription using scales, his wife holds a recipe for him and two assistants are working with the bellows and pestle and mortar. Line engraving by F. Baretta after P. Mainoto.
Wellcome Collection
(Bottom left) Royal Pharmaceutical Society Museum
(Bottom right) © The Board of Trustees of the Science Museum

Page 8
(Top) Interior of a pharmaceutical laboratory with people at work; the shop is visible through a doorway. Engraving, 1747. Wellcome Collection
(Bottom left) Bettmann / Getty Images
(Bottom right) Busy Beaver Button Museum

Index

Gibson, Joan, 47
Gibson, Joanna, 47
Gibson, John, 47
Gibson, Margaret, 221
Gillray, James, 116
Glanvill, Joseph, 93
Glasgow Town Infirmary, 149
goitre, 250
Goodall, Charles, 142–3, 144
Good Hous-Wives Treasurie, The, 82
Good Huswifes Handmaide for the Kitchin, The, 52
Goodyer, John, 90
Gordon, Alexander, 194
Gouge, Thomas, *The Surest & Safest Way of Thriving,* 140
gout, 116–20, 126–7
Grand Specific, 197
Granville, Mary and Anne, 118
Great Fire (1666), 150, 151, 160
Green, Robert, 29
greenhouses, 95
Grey, Elizabeth. *See* Kent, Elizabeth Grey
grocers and Company of Grocers, 21, 27, 198
Grub Street Journal, 206, 213
guilds: training process, 21; women in, 108. *See also* apothecary guilds; Company of Barber-Surgeons; Company of Grocers; Worshipful Society of Apothecaries
Guy's Hospital, 141

H

Hales, Stephen, 227

Hampton Court gardens, 95
handwriting styles, 7–8, 48
Hangmaster, Anne, 85
Hangmaster, George, 85
Harley, David, 220
Harper, Matthew, 237
Harrison, Mary, 41
Hart, Robert, 245
Hartley, David, 222–5, 227; *An Account of the Contributions for Making Mrs. Stephens's Medicines Public,* 224, 225; *Ten Cases,* 222
Hartlib, Samuel, 61, 63, 73, 189, 190
Hartman, George, 74, 77, 78, 79, 85
Harvey, William, 26, 28, 121–2, 157, 160, 161; *Exercitatio anatomica de motu cordis et sanguinis in animalibus,* 26, 122
Hatch-McChesney, Adrienne, 253
Headrich, John, *Arcana Philosophica; or, Chymical Secrets,* 172
Health Canada, 245
Helmont, Jan Baptiste van, 103
Hempson, William, 142
Henrietta Maria of France, Queen of England, 36, 73, 75, 86; *The Queen's Closet Opened* (attributed), 56, 119
Henry VIII, King of England, 27, 133
Henslow, Honore, 40
Herbalist's Charter (1542), 133–4
herbal medicine. *See* domestic

Mason, J., 210
mass-production, 150–51
materia medica, 14–15, 16, 17,
    20, 29, 94, 150, 259,
May, Robert, 54; *The Accomplisht
    Cook*, 73
Mayerne, Théodore de, 36
Mead, Richard, 2, 91, 151, 155,
    210, 217
meath, 75–6
Mectizan (ivermectin), 257
medical chemistry, defined, 169
Medicatrix. See under Trye, Mary
medicinal plants: 21, 89, 94,
    96, combining domestic and
    professional knowledge of,
    123; foraging for, 21, 111;
    herbals as compendiums of,
    1–2, 15; and imperialism,
    89–90, 112–13; modern
    application of, 258–61;
    processing of, in Middle Ages,
    18–19; scientific collection
    and study of, 89–93; and shift
    from organic to chemical
    medication, 177–9. *See also*
    domestic medicine; gardens
    and gardening
medicine: empiric *vs.* theoretical,
    42–3; and public health system,
    163–4; regulation of, 229, 230,
    239, 240–1, 243, 244–5, 254–
    55; standard histories of, 3, 22,
    101–2; terms and definitions,
    9–10. *See also* chemical
    medication; domestic medicine;
    prescriptions and prescription
    system; quack medication

Medicines and Healthcare
    products Regulatory Agency
    (UK), 245
menopause and perimenopause,
    246–7, 248
menstruation, 50, 246
Merck, 257
mercury: metal, 16, 24, 109,
    110–1, 123–4, 178, 179, 187;
    plant, 179
Merian, Maria Sibylla,
    *Metamorphosis Insectorum
    Surinamensium*, 2
Mersenne, Marin, 72
Meurdrac, Marie, *La Chymie
    Charitable et Facile, en Faveur
    des Dames*, 191
Middleton, John, *Five hundred
    new receipts in cookery*, 82–3
midwives, 49, 81, 102, 220
Millman, William, 178
Molimau-Samasoni, Seeseei, 259,
    260
convents and monasteries:
    dissolution of, 133, 139; and
    medical care, 133, 139
Montagu, Mary Wortley, 156
Montagu, William, 56
Moore, John, 220
Morand, S. J., 227
Morgan, Edward, 90
Morris, Benjamin, 204
Morris, Richard, 204
mortality rates, 209–10, 248–9
Morton Salt Company, 252
Moshenska, Joe, 66, 69
Moyle, John, *Chirurgus marinus:
    or, the Sea-Chirurgion*, 195

Munro, Alexander, 194
Murray, F. Joseph, 243

N

National Institutes of Health
(NIH), 243, 254
Newcastle, Margaret Cavendish,
Duchess of, 37
New General Dictionary, A, 115
New Sciences, The and New
Medicine, The. *See* chemical
medication, Scientific
Revolution
Newton, Isaac, 33, 171
Newton, Thomas: *Approv'd
Medicines and Cordial
Receipts*, 52; *The Olde Mans
Dietarie*,
81
NIAID (National Institute
of Allergy and Infectious
Diseases), 254, 255, 256
NIH (National Institutes of
Health), 243, 254
Nott, John, *The Cook's and
Confectioner's Dictionary*, 82
Nourse, Edward, 194, 226–7

O

O'Dowde, Thomas, 101, 102,
105, 106, 179
*Office of the Good House-wife,
The*, 85, 87
Oldenburg, Henry, 189
organic medicine, 80, 85, 92, 93,
111–12, 129, 179, 187, 206,

258–61. *See also* domestic
medicine; medicinal plants
oxalic acid, 185
Oyama, Jiro, 240–1

P

panaceas, 118–19. *See also* quack
medication
Paracelsus, 23–24, 29, 168, 268
Pardoe, Mary, 220
Parkinson, John, 86
Parliament, 65, 225, 228, 229;
acts of 27, 133–4, 222, 229
Partridge, John: *The Treasurie
of Commodious Conceits,
& Hidden Secrets*, 82; *The
Widowes Treasure*, 82
patents, 233–4, 236–7
Pell, John, 36
pepperers and Guild of Pepperers,
15, 21
Pepys, Samuel, 171, 193
perimenopause and menopause,
246–7, 248
periwinkle, 260
Petiver, James, 91, 95, 142–3, 144,
145–6, 151
pharmaceutical corporations,
234–41, 243, 245
Pharmacopoeia Londinensis,
61–2, 110, 116, 195
Philaxa Medicina, 119
Philosophical Transactions
(journal), 91, 92
physic gardens, 93–8, 142, 151
physicians: charity, 139, 141, 142,
143, 144, 149, 152–55; conflict

Q

quack medication: chemical analyses of, 202–3, 210–2, 219–20; claims of, 196–7; criticism of, 200–2, 203–4, 207–13, 215; defence of, 203–4, 205–6; defined, 198; enthusiasm for, 199; markets for, 197–8; vs. professional medicine, 216–20

Quarles, Francis, 62

Quincy, John, 181; *The Complete English Dispensary*, 113; *Lexicon physico-medicum*, 128–9; *Pharmacopoeia Officinalis & Extemporanea*, 112, 113

quinine, 258–9

R

Radcliffe, John, 148, 217

Rand, Isaac, 2, 91, 95, 151

Ranelagh, Katherine Jones, Lady, 73, 189–91, 269

Ray, John, 91

RCP, *See* Royal College of Physicians

Read, Alexander, 61

recipes and recipe books: attributions and signatures, 44–5, 47; treatments for the stone, 52, 183, 195–6; as commodities, 53–4, 57–9; cosmetic recipes in, 40, 71–2; and empiric method, 42–43; food recipes in, 40, 51, 59, 70, 74–5; as genre, 29, 40–2;

184–5; gout treatments, 117–18; handwriting styles in, 8, 48; men's compilation/ use of, 47, 55–6, 58–9, 73–9; and oral tradition, 39–40; vs. "prescriptions", 114–15; in print, 52–5, 56–8, 74, 77–8, 82–3; professionals' recipes in, 45–6, 182–4, 185–7; "secret" label, 55–6, 57, 58; separation of food and medication, 59, 70–71, 78–80, 82–3; women's knowledge shared through, 29–30, 41, 43–4, 46–7, 48–9, 135–7

regulation and regulatory systems, 229, 230, 239, 240–41, 243, 244–5, 254–5

rhubarb, 145, 177

Richardson-Merrell, 240–1, 243

river blindness, 256–57

Roche, 245

rosy periwinkle, 259–60

Rousby, Dorothy, 174

Royal College of Physicians: anatomy theatre, 151, 160; Board of Censors, 221–2; and charity, 138, 142, 152–5; Dispensary, 152–5, 156, 161, 164; establishment of, 27; mentioned, 92, 217; physic gardens, 94, 95–6; revenue sources, 151, 153, 160–1; and Royal Society, 102

Royal College of Physicians, Edinburgh, 149

Royal Navy, 151

Royal Society: botany research,

vinblastine, 260
vincristine, 260
viper wine, 60–3, 70

W

Wallis, Patrick, 111–12, 219
Walmart, 234
Ward, Joshua: background,
198–9; criticism of, 200–2,
203, 207–13, 215, 228–9;
defamation suits, 205, 206,
211; defence of, 203–4, 205–6;
performances of benevolence,
199–200; products and client
base, 199; regulatory exception
for, 229
Wasey, William, 144
Watts, James, 95
Welles, Benjamin, 116
Westminster Infirmary, 140–1,
142, 144
Whitaker, Tobias, *The Tree of
Humane Life*, 80
Widowe's Treasure, The, 52
William III, King of England, 90,
161
Williams, Charles Hanbury, 200
Willis, Thomas, 189, 190; *Cerebri
anatome*, 122; *Pathologiæ
cerebri*, 122; *Pharmaceutice
rationalis*, 61
Wilson, George, *A Compleat
Course of Chymistry*, 180
Winter, Salvator, *A Pretious
Treasury* (with Dickinson), 52
Wirtzung, Christopher, 50
Wise, Henry, 90

Wise, Prudence, 174, 183
witches and witchcraft, 16–17,
22, 62
Wolborough Feoffees and
Widows' Charity, 140
woman of the house, as position,
37
*Woman's Almanack, for the Year
1694*, 87
women: as apothecaries,
204, 220, 221; bodies and
experiences of, considered
in medication discussions,
243–4, 246–7, 248–9, 255;
as bonesetters, 213–15;
domestic roles and household
management, 16, 37–9, 71–2;
exclusion from professional
spaces and practice, 88–9, 107,
116, 125, 127, 172–3, 181–2,
221–7, 229–30; and gout, 116;
in guilds, 108; in histories, 6,
262, 267–9; as physicians, 27,
100, 103–4, 125–6, 220–1,
228, 242–43, 257–8. *See also*
domestic medicine; pregnancy
and childbirth; shasthya
kormi
Wood, Owen: *An Alphabetical
Book of Physicall Secrets*, 52;
*Choice and Profitable Secrets
both Physical and Chirurgical*,
56–7
Woodhouse, Elenor, 221
Woodward, John, 155
Woolley, Hannah, 87; *The
Ladies Directory, in Choice
Experiments & Curiosities*, 55

Wooten, John and Daniel, 209
workhouses, 138, 149
World Health Organization
    (WHO), 256
wormwood, 174–5, 258
Worshipful Society of
    Apothecaries, 94, 95, 102, 138,
    150–1

Y
Yerbury Almshouse, 140

Founded in 1893,
UNIVERSITY OF CALIFORNIA PRESS
publishes bold, progressive books and journals
on topics in the arts, humanities, social sciences,
and natural sciences—with a focus on social
justice issues—that inspire thought and action
among readers worldwide.

The UC PRESS FOUNDATION
raises funds to uphold the press's vital role
as an independent, nonprofit publisher, and
receives philanthropic support from a wide
range of individuals and institutions—and from
committed readers like you. To learn more, visit
ucpress.edu/supportus.